Selection of
Library Materials
in the Humanities,
Social Sciences,
and Sciences

Selection of Library Materials in the Humanities, Social Sciences, and Sciences

Patricia A. McClung
Editor

Section editors

William Hepfer   Marcia Pankake
Stanley Hodge   Beth Shapiro
Patricia McClung   John Whaley

Collection Management and Development Committee
Resources and Technical Services Division
American Library Association

AMERICAN LIBRARY ASSOCIATION · CHICAGO and LONDON · 1985

Designed by Harvey Retzloff

Composed by Impressions, Inc. in
    Sabon on a Penta-driven Autologic
    APS-μ5 Phototypesetting system

Printed on 50-pound Warren's 1854, a
    pH-neutral stock, by the
    University of Chicago Printing Department

Bound in B-grade Holliston linen cloth by
    Zonne Bookbinders

Library of Congress Cataloging-in-Publication Data
Main entry under title:

Selection of library materials in the humanities, social
    sciences, and sciences.

    Includes index.
    1. Book selection. 2. Collection development
(Libraries) 3. Acquisitions (Libraries) I. McClung,
Patricia A.
Z689.S354   1985   025.2'1   85–20084
ISBN 0-8389-3305-X

Printed in the United States of America.

Contents

Preface

This book has a long history and reflects the contributions of many librarians working to advance the practice and theory of the selection of library materials. It is a collection of essays that are focused as much on practical selection techniques as on the sources themselves.

Initial work on the project began in 1974 when the American Library Association (ALA) Joint Committee of the American Association of Publishers and the Resources and Technical Services Division (RTSD) formed several task forces to study the marketing of materials to libraries; one of these groups worked on compiling a list of selection tools. After participants at a 1977 ALA Preconference on Collection Development in Detroit underscored the need for a guide to selection sources, the Collection Management and Development Committee of RTSD assumed responsibility for the project. Many drafts later, this volume finally joins the committee's other collective products geared to improving collection development in American libraries: conference programs, regional institutes, and published guidelines for collection development.

Many people have assisted in the planning and preparation of this volume. The editors particularly thank the past members of the Resources Section Executive Committee and the Collection Management and Development Committee of ALA's Resources and Technical Services Division, especially Jutta Reed-Scott, Paul Mosher, Norene Alldredge, and Connie McCarthy. Thanks to Jean Boyer Hamlin, John Kaiser, Thomas Leonhardt, and librarians in the New York Metropolitan Reference and Research Library Agency who worked on the early stages of this project. The editors also gratefully acknowledge the assistance of John Ryland, Martin Faigel, Michael V. Sullivan, William Bunnell, Joseph Brinley, Bettina MacAyeal, Barbara Walden, and Gerald Bishop. They are also indebted to their home institutions: the libraries of Michigan State University, the University of California at Irvine, the University of California at

Los Angeles, the State University of New York at Buffalo, Texas A&M University, the University of Minnesota, and the Research Libraries Group. Most of all, they are grateful to the writers published here for sharing their trade secrets.

Introduction

A great deal has been written about the information explosion and its impact on libraries. The old myths about "libraries of record," which attempt to collect virtually all of humankind's publications, are of necessity giving way to more practical discussions about collection policies and cooperative collection development. Nevertheless, all libraries face the difficult challenge of having to choose from the voluminous publishing output—both today's and yesterday's—which materials to purchase, catalog, house, circulate, and preserve. Judgments must be made based on current interests and research trends of institutional clientele, as well as in anticipation of future demands, since the majority of the 1983 output will no longer be available in 1986 (much less by the year 2086).

The essays published here join a growing body of literature on the art of selection, including several textbooks that set forth general principles and criteria for selection.[1] In addition, there are a few articles focused on selection in particular subjects, as well as several that discuss the selection process itself. In 1977 Hendrick Edelman delivered a landmark paper at the ALA Detroit Preconference on Collection Development, in which he characterized selection as a decision making process carried out on two levels: decisions for individual items (micro selection) and decisions for groups of materials (macro selection).[2] In 1980 Jean Boyer Hamlin provided an overview of the whole process of selection as a function in a library organization, and briefly described types of selection sources.[3] At

1. Notably, Richard K. Gardner, *Library Collections, Their Origin, Selection and Development* (New York: McGraw-Hill, 1981); Wallace John Bonk and Rose Mary Magrill, *Building Library Collections*, 5th ed. (Metuchen, N.J.: Scarecrow, 1979); William A. Katz, *Collection Development* (New York: Holt, 1980); Robert N. Broadus, *Selecting Materials for Libraries*, 2nd ed. (New York: Wilson, 1981); and G. Edward Evans, *Developing Library Collections* (Littleton, Colo.: Libraries Unlimited, 1979).

2. Hendrick Edelman, "Selection Methodology in Academic Libraries," *Library Resources and Technical Services* 23, no. 1:36 (Winter 1979).

3. Jean Boyer Hamlin, "The Selection Process," in *Collection Development in Libraries: A Treatise*, ed. by Robert D. Stueart and George B. Miller, Jr., 2v. (Greenwich, Conn.: JAI Press, 1980), pp. 185–201.

the first regional institute on collection development in 1981, Martin Faigel addressed the question of how to get on with the task of selection once a collection policy is drafted, and talked of the necessity for each selector or bibliographer to construct an individual profile of selection tools.[4] More recently, Ross Atkinson speculated about the "private, cognitive activity" that occurs as a selector considers a citation and makes a judgment to acquire it or not for the library collection. He also described the various types of information available from selection sources.[5]

Building on this foundation, this volume represents the first guide to specific sources useful for selecting materials in basic disciplines. Two additional volumes are planned—one on interdisciplinary subjects and applied professional literature, and another on foreign area acquisitions. The hope is that these volumes will stimulate further reflection, debate, and publication about professional methods.

The twenty-nine essays in this volume concentrate on sources and techniques for the identification, evaluation, and selection of library materials for research libraries. They are intended to provide practical advice for both beginning selectors and those experienced ones who may need to acquire materials in disciplines where they have little, if any, formal training. Rather than prescribe, the authors discuss sources and strategies they have used successfully, while recognizing that local conditions and personal preferences will influence the choices of each individual involved in the selection of materials.

The arrangement of this volume reflects the editors' intent to examine collection building from three different perspectives: first by discussing general sources and procedures; then by looking at selection techniques specific to particular disciplines in the humanities, the social sciences, and the natural sciences; and finally by analyzing the challenges associated with special formats.

The core academic disciplines generally taught in universities and colleges in the United States define the subjects covered first. Interdisciplinary subjects, the literature serving professional schools, and other more specialized topics, will be covered in another volume. Essays focusing primarily on imprints other than those from the United States, Canada, and Great Britain will appear later; such selection sources are mentioned here only in reference to the role foreign imprints play in a particular discipline, such as Italian books for art history.

The essays in Part 1 describe the basic tools and techniques pertinent to English-language selection, thereby laying the groundwork for the subject and special format essays that follow. The first essay explains dis-

4. Martin Faigel, "The Selection Process," paper delivered at the Stanford Pilot Regional Institute on Collection Development, July 9, 1981.
5. Ross Atkinson, "The Citation as Intertext: Toward a Theory of the Selection Process," *Library Resources and Technical Services* 28, no. 2: 109–19. (Apr./June 1984).

tinctions between current and retrospective selection, and reviews the essentials—ranging from national bibliographies and approval plans to review media, gift acquisitions, and procedures for replacing lost or deteriorated materials. Two additional essays in that section cover the intricacies of selection and acquisition of serial publications and of out-of-print materials.

Essays in the second, third, and fourth parts are grouped within three broad subject areas: humanities, social sciences, and science and technology. To capture a feeling for each subject area and its distinctive literature, as well as its bibliographic and evaluative sources, each discipline is covered separately. The essays in these parts demonstrate the way in which knowledge of the publishing trade and specialized sources on intellectual developments in a particular discipline can assist selectors.

The essays in Part 2 address selection in history, religion, philosophy, art and architectural history, music, and English and American literature. Although these essays are distinctive in the ways in which they approach the literature and analyze selection problems, a common principle unites them: humanities research centers on the use of primary sources, such as texts, musical compositions, or paintings, which are of perpetual artistic importance and research value. Even people who use public libraries for recreational reading or listening (whether it be Jane Austen or Mozart) are interested in the basic document that constitutes a stable element in the humanities collection.

In music, art, and literature—and to a lesser degree in philosophy, religion, and history—a selector makes two categorical judgments. The first concerns the merit of the work of a composer, artist, or writer. Often this judgment will already be well established (perhaps centuries ago); other times a selector must make a difficult judgment on the basis of a first novel or other piece of work. The second concerns the differences in and significance of texts, editions, and variant presentations of such works. Once any work is deemed necessary for the collection, other selection decisions follow about new editions and secondary works of scholarship and criticism.

Part 3 includes essays on selection in five core social science disciplines—anthropology, sociology, economics, political science, and psychology. Interdisciplinary fields such as women's studies, ethnic studies, and criminal justice will be discussed in more detail in a later volume, along with applied fields such as education, journalism, communication, social work, law, business, and urban planning.

Unfortunately for selectors, the literature of the social sciences does not focus as clearly as that of the humanities on a set of identifiable primary sources from which most secondary sources radiate. Understandably, a literature intended to support the study of societies and the interrelationships of its members can encompass a variety of sources in virtually any format. In addition to books, newspapers, and journals, social scientists rely heavily on material published in many of the special formats discussed in Part 5: government publications, machine-readable data files, small press publications, nonprint media, and microforms. Selectors working in the social sciences face the added challenge of differentiating worthwhile secondary resources in a market inundated with marginal publications. Furthermore, they must often make judgments based only on the information included in a bibliographic citation, since most reviews appear too late to be of use for timely acquisition.

Within the broad area called the social sciences, it is difficult—if not impossible—to distinguish the boundaries of each particular discipline. Consider, for example, the problem of defining where anthropology stops and sociology begins. Even if the disciplines could be neatly delineated for collection development purposes, the typical scholar's research patterns tend to flow across fields. All of the essays included here reflect on the ways in which selectors can adapt their selection strategies to accommodate disciplines (not to mention scholars) that defy neat, static characterizations.

An overview chapter and six specialized essays make up the section on science and technology. The overview chapter covers the selection tools and strategies shared by more than one sci-tech discipline, while the subsequent essays focus on pertinent approaches to collecting in the areas of biology, chemistry, computer science, geology, mathematics, physics, and astronomy. Agriculture, engineering, and medicine will be covered in a later volume.

Strategies for sci-tech selection emphasize discovering and obtaining the primary literature, such as journals, technical reports, maps, conference proceedings, monographic series, machine-readable data tapes, and society publications. Because of the way in which journals dominate the typical science acquisitions budget, it is easy—although wrong—to infer that they represent the only essential format in scientific communication. The relative importance of literature in a given format (for example, government documents or commercially published monographs) depends on the specific discipline; generalizations across the natural sciences and technology should be made with care. Furthermore, obsolescence itself does not always mean that older literature necessarily loses its validity. Rather, retrospective standard works become incorporated into the general lore of the sciences, which may well constitute a more cumulative record than the humanities or social sciences.

Selection in the sciences and technology, to a greater extent than in other subject areas, is dependent on specific vehicles of communication that report research results of interest to the library's clientele. For research-level collections, selection in sci-tech subjects requires an immediate, if not anticipatory, response to library users. As research interests tend to follow federal funding trends, selectors may be pressured to pour large portions of acquisitions budgets into the support of specialized research projects with limited life spans. Such pressure, when applied by prize-winning scientists or engineers, may be difficult to resist. In the university setting, such factors must be balanced against long-term curricular needs, and constitute an important part of the challenge facing sci-tech bibliographers.

The final part is entitled "Special Formats and Subjects" and includes essays on government publications, microforms, machine-readable data files, nonprint media, and small press publications. Materials in these categories tend to fall outside the regular book trade sources, often creating difficult problems for the selector. Individuals with responsibility either for these formats or for the humanities, social sciences, and sciences need to be aware of materials in these special categories, since they are not unique to a particular discipline.

Common themes echo throughout the essays. In general, all of the selection sources discussed fall into one of the following categories: library professional sources and tools for bibliographic control, sources related to the publishing trade, and sources related to scholarship in particular disciplines. Selectors exploit, to varying degrees, all three categories in order to identify and evaluate different types of materials.

The professional sources, such as review journals for the library market (*Choice, Library Journal*, etc.) and national bibliographies, are of some use to all, of great use to some, and of little use to others. Related jobber services such as approval plans and notification slips also fall into this category, and their utility depends upon availability and selectors' preferences. Some of the same sources, such as *Library Journal, Weekly Record*, and the *British National Bibliography*, appear in virtually every essay, but the context and relative importance of the tools, as well as the way in which they are used for each discipline, vary.

Selection librarians rely heavily on sources in the publishing trade for general information. The dynamic and ever-changing business of book publishing influences selection decisions. For example, editorial or organizational restructuring may lead to changed marketing and production strategies, ultimately affecting the content and availability of titles. Periodic review of the trade publications keeps librarians apprised of production changes in the industry that may have an impact on libraries.

Trade publications such as *Publishers Weekly*, publishers' advertisements and catalogs, and the book review media, such as the *Times Literary Supplement* and the *New York Times Book Review*, make up another type of source useful for identifying and evaluating materials. Such current media enables librarians to keep up with new authors, as well as shifts in opinion about more established ones. For example, if a selector reads that Raymond Carver's latest book has won an important prize, such an event might result in reconsideration of that writer's importance and lead to additional purchases of his earlier works. Continual change is the bread and butter of a selector's diet.

Publications produced by and for the specialists in a discipline, including scholarly review journals, conference proceedings, festschriften, current bibliographies, and published papers from research institutes, contain information often unavailable elsewhere. Such unique media also collect information about upcoming symposia, research in progress, the formation of new societies, and other current material that suggest changes in the discipline—changes that may produce new publications or subsequently lead a selector to alter collection building policy. These sources usually take the form of scholarly serial publications or annual bibliographies.

While there are many sources of information, the effective bibliographer seeks sources and uses them in a pattern that will provide consistent and systematic coverage. Basic knowledge of a discipline is important; command of the principles and techniques is essential; hard work and discipline are mandatory. A librarian may have little control over what selection sources exist, but he or she can know the sources and can control how they are used.

Part 1

GENERAL
CONSIDERATIONS

Edited by
Patricia A. McClung

SELECTION SOURCES AND STRATEGIES

Patricia A. McClung

Underlying every library's approach to collection development, and ultimately each individual selector's strategy, are a number of complex factors: the history and traditions of the library, the type of institution and community it serves, the expectations of its clientele, and the resources and staff available. Constrained by these constantly changing factors, every library organizes itself to select and acquire books and other materials. While some libraries rely almost entirely on approval plans, standing orders, and/or faculty selection, others assign selection responsibility to full-time bibliographers or other staff members, according to subject, geographical area, or language divisions. Most libraries employ a combination of these approaches.

There is probably no ideal way to address the question of how to allocate selection responsibilities. As a primary goal, however, selectors should seek to minimize duplication of effort. A strict subject approach usually requires that a number of people read the same sources, such as *Weekly Record* or the *British National Bibliography*, and review each approval plan. Less duplication occurs, assuming the collection development policies and goals are well defined, when current selection is divided along the lines of language or geographical area, at least for the social sciences and humanities. Assignments should be discrete enough so that a large number of titles are not identified and contemplated for acquisition by more than one person. Specific subject expertise is still desirable for more elusive or specialized materials, science selection, retrospective purchasing, and various special collections.

A collection development policy might be viewed as a tool designed to clarify and document a library's goals, priorities, and constraints. Whether

The author is deeply indebted to James Campbell for his very helpful recommendations and assistance. She would also like to acknowledge the following people who served as valuable resources for this chapter: William Allen, Eva Chandler, Leslie Hume, James Knox, and Gary Treadway.

or not an institution has a written collection development policy, each individual selector must clearly understand the subject and/or geographical area(s) to be covered, as well as the level, scope, and depth sought for the collection in each area. The available budget, of course, constitutes a crucial factor in developing such a policy.

In addition to understanding the intended parameters of the collection, a selector must be aware of the broader policies that influence individual collection decisions. For example, a library's policy regarding duplication of materials—either within a library or among branches—dramatically affects selection decisions. Ongoing commitments to periodicals and other standing orders take their share of a library's annual book fund allocation, and the selector must be aware that the funds available for commitment to additional standing orders may be limited. The selector should be knowledgeable about areas of potential interlibrary cooperation, and should be informed of any institutional commitments to collecting in certain areas. Memberships in organizations such as the Research Libraries Group (RLG), the Center for Research Libraries (CRL), or regional consortia such as the Triangle Research Libraries Network in North Carolina, affect an institution's collection policies. For example, the Research Libraries Group has devised a system of assigning "primary collecting responsibility" (PCRs), using the RLG Conspectus, to individual institutions in the consortium; this insures that specialized or "endangered" areas are adequately covered by at least one institution, and gives other institutions the option of reducing their collecting in those areas, relying instead on those institutions having PCRs.[1]

A number of models are available to selectors embarking on the preparation of a collection development policy, notably the policies of the University of California, Berkeley, Stanford, and the University of Texas.[2] Moreover, at least twenty-six Association of Research Libraries (ARL) institutions have elected to participate in the Office of Management Studies Collection Analysis Project (CAP), which provides a framework, as well as consulting assistance, for studying and documenting collection policies.[3] Sheila Dowd's enjoyable article "The Formulation of a Collection Development Policy Statement," and the American Library Association's (ALA)

1. Nancy Gwinn and Paul Mosher, "Coordinating Collection Development: The RLG Conspectus," *College and Research Libraries* 44:128–40(Mar. 1983).
2. University of California at Berkeley Library, *Collection Development Policy Statement/ Preliminary Edition* (Berkeley: The Library, 1980); Stanford University Libraries Collection Development Office, *The Libraries of Stanford University Collection Development Policy Statement, 1980*, 1st complete ed. Ed. by Paul H. Mosher (Stanford: The Libraries, 1981); and University of Texas at Austin Libraries, *Collection Development Policy*, 2nd ed. (Austin: The Libraries, 1981).
3. Jeffrey J. Gardner, "A Project for the Analysis of the Collection Development Process in Large Academic Libraries," in *New Horizons for Academic Libraries* (New York: Saur, 1979), pp. 456–59.

"Guidelines for Collection Development Policy Statements" can also provide helpful background for such an undertaking.[4]

As book budgets shrink, book prices increase, and the debate engendered by the Pittsburgh study continues, librarians are under tremendous pressure to anticipate and prepare for their patron's information needs.[5] An awareness of an institution's character and traditions is essential to success. The goals, function, and scope of a research collection differ dramatically from that of a small college library, and so do the appropriate selection techniques. Regardless of how a library sorts out the details of its organizational structure, budget allocation, collection development policy, and institutional goals, responsibility falls to the selector to develop a strategy for acquiring materials within the institutional framework and to decide what tools to employ in the process.

Techniques for selection of research library materials can be as varied and eccentric as the practitioners of the craft or the institutions in which they work.[6] Nevertheless, there are some basic strategies and tools that all selectors have in common. Nowhere is this commonality more apparent than in the selection of materials published or distributed via the North American—and to some extent, the British—book trades. Regardless of the subject, the practicalities of the publishing trade—along with the assorted sources that describe its production—determine the range of options available to the selector.

This paper focuses on the general tools and strategies that are useful for selecting both current and retrospective materials published or distributed in the United States, Great Britain, and Canada. It provides a general framework for the other essays in this volume.

Current Selection

Most of the countries in the Western world produce a national bibliography with the intent to gain bibliographic control over their publishing

4. Sheila Dowd, "The Formulation of a Collection Development Policy Statement," in *Collection Development in Libraries: A Treatise*, ed. by Robert D. Stueart and George B. Miller, Jr. (Greenwich, Conn.: JAI Press, 1980), p. 67; and American Library Assn., Resources and Technical Services Div., Collection Development Committee, "Guidelines for Formulation of Collection Development Policies," in ed. David L. Perkins, *Guidelines for Collection Development* (Chicago: ALA, 1979), pp. 1–8.

5. Allen Kent et al., *Use of Library Materials: The University of Pittsburgh Study* (New York: Dekker, 1979). For information on the controversy it stirred, see also: Neal K. Kaske, "Library Utilization Studies: Time for Comparison," *Library Journal* 104:685–86 (Mar. 15, 1979); Casimir Borkowski and Murdo J. MacLeod, "The Implications of Some Recent Studies of Library Use," *Scholarly Publishing* 11:3–24 (Oct. 1979); and "Pittsburgh University Studies of Collection Usage: A Symposium," *Journal of Academic Librarianship* 5, no. 2:60–70 (May 1979).

6. For a good model of the selection process, see Ross Atkinson, "The Citation as Intertext: Toward a Theory of the Selection Process," *Library Resources and Technical Services* 28, no.2: 109–19 (Apr./June 1984).

British National Bibliography. v.1– . London: Bibliographic Service Div.,
   British Library, 1950– . Weekly.
   National bibliography of UK MARC format bibliographic entries,
      consisting of all new British books received by the British Library's
      Copyright Receipt Office.
   Currency of information varies from prepublication to as much as 6–12
      months late.
   Arranged by Dewey Decimal Classification scheme, making it possible to
      select in specific subject areas without scanning the entire issue.
   Cumulated 3 times per year and in an annual bound volume.
This source also includes advance citations from publishers for works scheduled
for publication, annotated as "CIP entry" and tagged with an asterisk. This
occasionally creates problems when a publication is postponed or canceled, or
when a title changes. However, CIP data allow for very current selection, as
such listings usually appear eight weeks before publication. Citations include
subject tracings, ISBN numbers, and price information.

---

trades. Canada can claim *Canadiana*, Britain the *British National Bibliography*, Germany *Deutsche Bibliographie*, France *Bibliographie de la
France*, and Italy *Bibliografia Nazionale Italiana*. Although they may vary
somewhat in their timeliness, comprehensiveness, and bibliographic reliability, they nevertheless represent invaluable tools to library selectors with
collection development responsibilities for any of these areas of the world.
Without reliable sources for systematically reviewing publishing output,
a selector can have a difficult time identifying all materials of interest to
a particular collection.

   The lack of a national bibliography for new American publications
creates a special challenge for selectors, since there is no one mechanism
for identifying all new publications. *Weekly Record* and Library of Congress CDS Alert Service cards together constitute the best substitutes for
a national bibliography in the United States. Because neither is comprehensive, and there is substantial overlap between them, duplicate review
and searching efforts are required if comprehensive coverage is the goal.

   In addition to problems caused by the overlap among American sources,
there is also a substantial amount of copublishing and codistributing among
publishers in the United States, Canada, the United Kingdom, and even
countries such as the Netherlands and Japan. For example, new titles from
Oxford University Press, which has offices on five continents, may appear
in several different national bibliographies (and at different times), as well
as in *Weekly Record*, thus creating difficulties for selectors trying to avoid
duplicate purchases.

   Such copublishing and codistributing can also prove to be advantageous.
Although there is significant English-language publishing in the Netherlands and Japan, most of these works appear in American and British

Library Journal. v. 1– . New York: Bowker, 1876– . 20/year.

General magazine of librarianship includes reviews of new trade and scholarly books on all subjects.

175–300 reviews per issue (depending on whether it is a month with one or two issues).

Short time lag between book publication and review because the policy is to review from galleys whenever possible. A review can be as early as 1–2 months before publication, or as late as 2–3 months after publication.

Prepublication information in "New Spring Books" (February) and "New Fall Books" (September) issues.

New journals reviewed in a column, "Magazines," by Bill Katz.

A-V materials for public and school libraries, some professional training works in a column, "Audio Visual."

Publishers' announcements and advertisements very useful.

Reference books reviewed annually in April issue.

Short signed reviews by librarians and scholars focus primarily on current English-language monographs, serials, and audiovisual materials. *LJ* includes good current coverage of trade and university press output, as well as complete bibliographic information, price, and appropriate audience recommendation; it often indicates if there are better or related works on the same topic. Advertisements are valuable, especially for publishers that may not be covered in other selection tools.

selection sources, in addition to the national bibliographies of those countries. With respect to the Pacific, many publications will appear in *Weekly Record* due to American distribution arrangements.

If comprehensive coverage is necessary, the *Australian National Bibliography* and the *New Zealand National Bibliography* can be scanned. In addition, many foreign vendors—such as Nijhoff for Dutch and Almquist and Wiksell for other Scandinavian countries—will provide alert service slips for English-language titles. Vendors such as the James Bennett Group and South Pacific Books will also provide slips for publications from Australia, New Guinea, New Zealand, and the smaller Pacific islands. Coverage of English-language publishing in Japan can be achieved by getting on mailing lists for English catalogs from dealers like Orion, Maruzen, and Kinokuniya—all of which have offices in Tokyo and New York.

National bibliographies and sources such as *Weekly Record* are essential for keeping track of new publications; however, they serve no evaluative function. Review sources, such as the *New York Times Book Review* or the *Times Literary Supplement*, are more helpful for evaluating selected materials, while such tools as *Library Journal, Choice, British Book News*, and approval plans can aid both bibliographic control and evaluation of materials before selection. Through combined use of selection tools, it is possible to discover most current publications; but even the well-designed—and labor intensive—strategy will not be foolproof. Inevitably,

Choice. v. 1- . Middleton, Conn.: Assn. of College and Research Libraries, American Library Assn. 1964- . 11/year.
  A monthly selection journal for books and nonprint media, intended to assist library collection development.
  Approximately 300–600 one-paragraph reviews per issue in all subjects.
  Reviews generated from finished books, rather than from galleys. Time lag ranges from a minimum of 4 months to 12 months after date of publication.
  Advertisements for scholarly books.
  "In the Balance" column features bibliographic essays on topics of current interest, e.g., the environment, social welfare issues, the economy.
    Includes a list of works cited that represents a valuable selection source.
  New journals reviewed in column "Periodicals for College Libraries."
Concise reviews of English-language publications that might be appropriate for scholarly collections are grouped by a general subject breakdown in *Choice*. It usually describes work in the context of other sources on the subject, and indicates appropriateness for different types of libraries.

some things will slip through the net. And although the goal is to develop the most efficient method for determining which publications are appropriate for the library's collections, the cost of the selector's time (as well as that of the searching and ordering staff) should be a major consideration in devising any selection strategy. Some libraries choose to live with less thorough bibliographic control, perhaps relying more heavily on approval plans, rather than commit the staff time necessary to chase elusive publications. Other libraries place a high priority on expert selection, tailor-made to the particular institution.

The selector, thus, faces three challenges—gaining bibliographic control over the universe of published materials, judging the value of these materials to the collections, and ensuring that the selected items are acquired rapidly and efficiently. Many tools are available to the selector. For the purposes of discussion those tools used for individual, title-by-title selection are treated separately from approval plans and standing orders. Of course, tools from both these categories can be, and usually are, used in any number of combinations.

APPROVAL PLANS

Approval plans are available in a variety of configurations, and most libraries employ one or more. A 1981 SPEC Kit survey sponsored by the Office of Management Studies indicates that eighty-five percent of the ARL libraries (86 out of 101) responding to the survey had some type of approval plan, from among more than 200 vendors—all listed in the SPEC Kit.[7] These range from comprehensive plans such as those offered by

7. Thomas Leonardt, ed., *Approval Plans in ARL Libraries* (Washington, D.C.: Assn. of Research Libraries, Office of Management Studies, 1982), pp. 11–15.

Blackwell North America (or Blackwell England) and Baker & Taylor, Ballen, and Stevens & Brown, to more focused plans, such as the one for university press publications offered by the Yankee Book Peddlar. One library reported using as many as 190 subject plans.[8]

Choosing which approval plans to employ, if any, represents a crucial element in any collection development strategy. It is often useful to seek out colleagues at comparable institutions, who will usually be pleased to share their experiences and prejudices on the subject. It is also helpful to interview vendors either at the ALA Conference exhibits or at your institution, since most will be willing to send a marketing representative. Practical information on designing or refining approval plans can be found in these three sources: *Approval Plans and Academic Libraries, Practical Approval Plan Management,* and *Shaping Library Collections for the 1980s.*[9]

Libraries use approval plans for a variety of reasons. Most plans can supply current materials quickly, saving the trouble and expense of selecting individual items and producing orders. The opportunity to examine a book before acquiring it provides the best method for evaluation, and the term "approval" implies that any unwanted materials supplied by the plan can be returned. When used effectively, approval plans can eliminate routine bibliographic control efforts, leaving selectors more time to obtain obscure or out-of-print materials.

Approval plans also have disadvantages. Some duplication between regular firm orders and material received on approval is inevitable. The expense of returning duplicates can exceed their cost, and many libraries keep unwanted material to avoid spending staff time and postage to return it. If not carefully monitored, total dependence on approval plans can lead to significant omissions in the collections. By the time gaps are discovered, the missing items may be out-of-print. Approval plans also present budgetary problems, because it is difficult to predict their annual cost. However, if the vendor is given a budget limit, the plan may be "padded" to ensure that all available money is spent.

Despite these constraints, most libraries report that approval plans serve a useful function. Prerequisites for a successful plan include a clearly articulated and flexible profile, as well as an efficient mechanism for monitoring—both for what the plan includes, as well as for what it does not include. The unwanted titles should be returned. Chances are that the vendor will be more motivated to adjust and improve its service given the incentive to reduce the return rate.

8. Ibid., p.2.
9. Kathleen McCullough, Edwin Posey, and Doyle C. Pickett, *Approval Plans and Academic Libraries* (Phoenix: Oryx, 1977); Jennifer S. Cargill and Brian Alley, *Practical Approval Plan Management* (Phoenix: Oryx, 1979); and Peter Spyers-Duran, ed., *Shaping Library Collections for the 1980s* (Phoenix: Oryx, 1980).

Techniques for monitoring approval plans vary, depending on the type of plan and available staff. The best approval plans will supply marked bibliographies (such as *Weekly Record* or *American Book Publishing Record*), from which additional titles may be easily selected. Some vendors, such as Blackwell North America, will supply order forms for books that they do not send on their plan. Such forms can be quickly reviewed and used for firm orders if desired. Most vendors will agree to negotiate some type of arrangement to facilitate monitoring.

STANDING ORDERS

Serving much the same purpose as approval plans, standing orders eliminate the need to individually identify and order each new volume in a series. Standing orders can be placed for monographic series, continuations, and works-in-parts. They operate on the principle that all publications in a series represent similar quality and potential interest to the collection— that is, if it is worth having one volume, it is usually worth having the whole series. Nevertheless, selectors should review subscriptions periodically to ensure that the quality or usefulness to the curriculum has not diminished. Another type of standing order occurs when publishers are instructed to send a library everything it publishes automatically, a common arrangement for acquiring materials from major university presses or scholarly associations.

As for bibliographic control and evaluation of new series, the first volumes are usually reviewed in a number of the standard review media, and should also appear in *Weekly Record* and the *British National Bibliography*, particularly if they are published by a major trade or scholarly press. In addition, approval plan profiles can be drafted to stipulate that volume one of a new series, assuming it is within scope of the plan, will be sent on approval.

JOURNAL AND NEWSPAPER SELECTION

The bibliographic control of new journals can present problems. The length and alphabetical format of *New Serial Titles* makes it an impossible selection tool. Most selectors discover new journals through reviews or ads in scholarly journals or library periodicals, flyers and sample issues received in the mail, and patron requests. *Choice* and *Library Journal* represent timely sources for such information. Of some limited assistance is the quarterly publication *Serials Review* that reviews selected new journals and includes articles relating to collection development, collection evaluation, and preservation of newspapers, monographic series, and journals. In addition, some serials vendors, such as Stevens and Brown, and Swets, periodically produce useful lists of new titles. Sample issues, which most publishers will supply upon request, provide the best opportunity for evaluation, if the selector is aware of the possibility that "volume one, number one" may represent an extraordinary effort for promotional reasons that may not be duplicated in future issues.

Newspaper subscriptions and microform backfiles are so expensive that most research libraries severely curtail their acquisitions in this area. This is an area in which it is essential to have a well-articulated policy to save time dealing with requests for hometown papers (which tend to appear around baseball season). If legitimate needs do arise, however, the *IMS Ayer Directory of Publications* is the most comprehensive source for identifying newspapers published in the United States and Canada. The British have an equivalent called *Benn's Press Directory—United Kingdom*. At the time a current subscription is placed it is essential to make a decision about the backfile because of the serious preservation issues involved with this format. If the judgment is that the backfile is desirable, then a simultaneous microform subscription should be placed, such that the original will be discarded when the microform copy is received.

INDIVIDUAL FIRM ORDER SELECTION

Turning to the specific details of item-by-item current selection of English-language publications, there is no exact formula applicable to all libraries. A selector in a large library—whether public, academic, or special—who is acquiring materials at the research level, should examine at least one of the more comprehensive sources for American bibliographic control, such as *Weekly Record* or the Library of Congress CDS Alert Service cards, as well as the *British National Bibliography*. The choice and timing of their use will depend in large part on the type of approval plans in place, if any. My own preference is to use a specialized approval plan for scholarly university press publications and to supplement it with selections from *Weekly Record* and *British National Bibliography*, if the subject responsibilities are wide ranging, or from targeted call number sections sorted from the CDS Alert Service cards when there is a narrow subject responsibility.

If a more comprehensive approval plan is employed, the *American Book Publishing Record*, which cumulates *Weekly Record* on a monthly basis, can be used to pick up materials not supplied by the plan(s). Although its subject arrangement (by Dewey classification) is preferable to *Weekly Record's* alphabetical organization, its entries are several months old by the time it is published, restricting its usefulness for timely current selection.

Most selection decisions in medium to large research libraries can be made on the basis of a good bibliographic description that includes author, title, publisher, format, imprint, and some subject information, such as

British Book News. v.1- . London; The British Council. Dist. by Basil
Blackwell, 1944- . Monthly.
A journal that reviews current British books.
Features several bibliographic essays and approximately 200 signed reviews
per issue, primarily of scholarly and trade publications.
Reviews are quite current.
Reviews arranged by subject, according to Dewey classification.
Reviews of "New Fiction" most helpful.
This source includes a twenty-page insert listing books planned for publication
during the next month, arranged by subject; this feature is useful for prepub-
lication ordering. There are both author and title indexes.

cataloging subject headings—that is, assuming that clear guidelines exist
defining the intended level and scope of the collections. Such an approach
is less successful for belles lettres, since it is difficult to judge the appropriateness of most novels, poetry, and plays for a collection from just a
bibliographic entry. Evaluative sources—such as the *New York Times Book
Review*, the *Times Literary Supplement, New York Review of Books,
London Review of Books*, the *Literary Review, Poetry, American Poetry
Review*, and *Canadian Literature*—are key sources for reviews of belles
lettres. In large research libraries, just the fact that something is reviewed
by one of these literary sources may qualify an item for selection, even if
the review is less than enthusiastic. It is important to include controversial
materials, along with those that are widely acclaimed.

For smaller college libraries, one or more of the general review sources
such as *Choice, Library Journal*, or *British Book News* can usually provide
both bibliographic control and evaluation. The research library selector
may also wish to examine at least one of these, probably *Library Journal*,
to supplement the bibliographic control source. As a general rule, a selector should care less about the reviewer's judgment that a particular
book is good, bad, or indifferent, than information as to the book's level,
scope, subject matter, and intended audience. A selector must choose with
an eye to the collection goals in the subject areas to be covered, rather
than a single reviewer's verdict on the book's quality. These tools will
provide adequate information for acquiring most current publications.
That is the easy part. In many ways, the smaller the library or its budget,
the more difficult the selection decision.

PUBLISHERS' ANNOUNCEMENTS

The publications that do not make their way into one of these sources
in a timely fashion, or at all, present the biggest problems for selectors.
One important technique for supplementing these sources is through publishers' flyers and catalogs, which often provide the only information about

Associations' Publications in Print. 2v.– . New York: Bowker, 1982– .
   Annually.
   A *Books in Print*-type source for previously hard to find publications of
     organizations, professional associations, scholarly societies, etc.
   Volume 1 consists of extensive subject index to these materials
     (approximately 1500 pages of brief entries).
   Features both print and audiovisual materials.
   Also features an acronymn index that identifies full name of organization.
   The association name index consists of publishers' full address information. This
   list can be used to select institutions for requesting addition to their mailing
   lists. Publisher/Title index in volume 2 makes it possible to locate publications
   by name of association/organization.

small press, scholarly society, or institute publications. The *Encyclopedia of Associations* lists organizations in every conceivable subject area, many of which publish titles of interest to research libraries. The review sections and ads of scholarly journals can also be useful in suggesting institutes and associations with good publishing programs. Once potential associations have been identified, a relatively new annual publication, *Associations' Publications in Print*, is invaluable in determining titles that are still available for purchase.

Most libraries receive catalogs from major trade publishers and university presses automatically. If a library receives a significant proportion of its English-language materials through a general approval plan, these sources may be used more for reference purposes than for selection. The opposite is true if there are no American or British approval plans. In that case, it is possible to select from the spring and fall lists of individual publishers and to read the many review sources—which are much slower to appear and duplicate each other extensively—as back-up sources. A form letter to solicit promotional materials, particularly from publishers whose works are not widely reviewed, can prove very useful. Good lists of publishers and their addresses may be found in *Books in Print, British Books in Print, Publishers Directory*, and Fulton's *Small Press Record of Books in Print* and *International Directory of Little Magazines and Small Presses.*

CURRENT SELECTION STRATEGIES

The English-language Canadian book trade provides a good example of the options available for identifying and acquiring current materials, and the way in which selection strategies may vary, depending on a library's collection policy, budget, and organizational structure. A substantial percentage of English-language Canadian publications can be acquired by using the tools and strategies described for American and British publi-

Canadiana: Canada's National Bibliography. v. 1– . Ottawa: National
Library of Canada, 1950– . 11/year with annual cumulation.
Canada's national bibliography. Lists, by Dewey classification, items
published in and about Canada.
Excludes films, filmstrips, short films and TV films (since 1956 these have
been listed in *Film Canadiana*, published by Canadian Film Institute);
also excludes maps.
Part I, Canadian imprints (200–250 pages with 3 columns of bibliographic
entries, 9–10 per column).
Part II, Foreign imprints of Canadian association (10–20 pages, same
format).
Index covers both parts.
CIP data included.
This source makes for tedious reading, much the same as *British National
Bibliography* and *Weekly Record*. It is nevertheless an important source, en-
hanced by its use of MARC entries with helpful subject tracings.

cations. Copublication and codistribution arrangements among Canadian,
British, and American publishers increase the likelihood that important
Canadian publications appear in sources such as *Choice, Library Journal,
Weekly Record* and CDS Alert Service cards. Approval plan vendors may
also agree to include Canadian materials in their profiles. These methods
will usually prove satisfactory for small- and medium-size libraries.

Large libraries that require more comprehensive coverage have additional options, including specialized approval plans for Canadian publications and several bibliographical tools. In addition, Canada is fortunate
to have a timely national bibliography called *Canadiana*. This monthly
publication lists, by Dewey classification, full bibliographic entries for
current English- and French-language Canadian imprints, as well as foreign
imprints about Canadian subjects. As an alternative to this lengthy bibliography, the vendor John Coutts offers an excellent approval plan for
Canadiana and also produces a monthly bibliography of new Canadian
publications, called *Current Canadian Books (Livres Canadiens Courant)*
that is among the most reliable sources for current selection. Moreover,
the quarterly supplements (called "Forthcoming Books") of the review
publication *Quill and Quire* can be used for the same purpose. Another
source, *Canadian Studies, A Catalog of Publications* (available from the
Canadian Book Publishers Council) provides an annotated listing of current trade publications, many of which are appropriate for research collections. When more information is required, particularly for belles lettres,
valuable reviews are available in *Quill and Quire, Books in Canada*, and
Canadian Literature. Publishers' catalogs provide additional descriptive
information about current publications; for example, Coach House Press
and Talon Books publish some of the best current Canadian fiction, poetry,

Quill and Quire. v. 1– . Toronto: Key Publishers. Monthly with supplements.
>   Canadian book trade magazine, featuring general articles on publishing
>   trade, as well as book reviews and a bibliographic list of current
>   Canadian publications (organized by subject).
>   Features spring and fall announcements.
>   25–35 reviews per issue.
>   Very timely reviews, usually from advance galleys. Rarely later than 6
>   months after publication.
>   Sometimes reviews records in "Sound Advice" column.
>   Subscription includes one copy of each edition of *Canadian Publishers
>   Directory*.
>   Includes quarterly supplements of "Forthcoming Books" that are valuable
>   for selection of items for which reviews are not required.
> This is an important source for thorough Canadian coverage. It promotes the
> Canadian book trade, so most reviews are quite favorable. The spring and fall
> lists and publishers' ads are particularly helpful.

and drama. Addresses for these and other Canadian presses can be found
in *Canadian Books in Print*. And finally, the July issue of the *University
of Toronto Quarterly* includes a comprehensive annual review of Canadian
humanities publications that is useful for both current and retrospective
collection development.

A bibliographer at a research library that emphasizes Canadian studies
would probably want to be familiar with all of these tools; however, since
there is a tremendous amount of overlap, it is not necessary to read and
select from all of them. Most places should find it sufficient to use *Current
Canadian Books* which, thanks to its subject arrangement, is timely and
easy to scan, in combination with several of the sources recommended
for belles lettres.

Retrospective Selection

Retrospective collection development, loosely defined, includes selection
of materials with an original imprint date more than two or three years
old, and might include the following: reprints, out-of-print books or journal backsets, microform editions of newspapers or journals, items from
publishers' backlists, and gift materials. Retrospective collection development is often necessary, needed to fill in gaps in the collections, respond
to curriculum changes, spend available funds, replace materials that have
been lost, stolen or badly deteriorated, or even to establish a new library.

Most bibliographers agree that retrospective selection is among their
most difficult challenges. In addition to requiring a good knowledge of
the book trade and a familiarity with institutional goals and client needs,

retrospective efforts may call for considerable subject expertise. It is not always easy to identify the gaps in the collections, or to obtain desired materials that are out-of-print. And even if located, the expense of out-of-print materials constitutes still another constraint.

The library without serious gaps in its collections is rare indeed, as is one with sufficient staff and money to identify and acquire desiderata. As a result, selectors may only have time to react to patron requests or complaints, even though most would prefer a more systematic approach based on evaluation of the collections and users' needs. Certainly at the research level, responsible collection building requires a good understanding of the scholarly needs of the library's primary clientele, as well as a sensitivity to shifts in the areas of concentration emphasized within academic departments. In *Academic Research and Library Resources*, Charles Osburn advocates increased communication between the research library community and the academic community, based on his findings that in the past twenty-five years libraries have not adequately reflected in their collection policies the shifting research trends in American universities.[10]

A considerable body of literature has grown up around the concept of collection evaluation that is designed to assist the selector in identifying areas of the collection that need attention. Paul Mosher's article "Collection Evaluation in Research Libraries" represents the best explanation of the theory, practice, and benefits of a systematic evaluation program.[11] In addition, the Resources and Technical Services Division of ALA has produced a set of practical guidelines to facilitate the process, while two bibliographical essays, one by George S. Bonn and the other by Thomas Nisonger, pull together additional information on the available techniques.[12] Armed with these sources, it is possible to design or adapt an evaluation strategy suited to individual collections and needs. That is not to say that large-scale collection evaluation is necessary before any retrospective selection can occur. In fact, the selector will discover "holes" in the collection through all kinds of serendipitous methods: browsing the stacks, talking to faculty and graduate students, or reviewing the assorted catalogs and bibliographies that arrive in the mail.

There are a variety of tools and basic techniques available to the selector for retrospective collection development; the extent to which they are used and combined can be tailored to the individual situation. Essentially

10. Charles Osburn, *Academic Research and Library Resources: Changing Patterns in America* (Westport, Conn.: Greenwood, 1979), p. 145.
11. Paul Mosher, "Collection Evaluation in Research Libraries," *Library Resources and Technical Services* 23:16–32 (Winter 1979).
12. American Library Assn., Resources and Technical Services Div., Collection Development Committee, "Guidelines for Evaluation of the Effectiveness of Library Collections," in Perkins, *Guidelines for Collection Development*, pp. 9–19; George S. Bonn, "Evaluation of the Collection," *Library Trends* 22:265–304 (Jan. 1974); and Thomas E. Nisonger, "An Annotated Bibliography of Items Relating to Collection Evaluation in Academic Libraries, 1969–1981," *College and Research Libraries* 43, no.4:300–11 (July 1982).

identifying possible titles. Course reserve lists and supplemental course bibliographies also identify potential candidates for core collections.

MULTIPLE COPIES

The purchase of multiple copies of items in high demand can greatly increase user satisfaction. The question is how to determine the titles to be duplicated. One method is to produce, for selection purposes, a circulation printout of books that have circulated frequently (say, five times or more) during a year, or over a period of several years. To the same end, the circulation department might inform collection development staff of titles that are frequently recalled from patrons due to high demand. Records of actual reserve room use are also good indicators of multiple copy candidates.[15]

GIFTS AND EXCHANGES

Most libraries have assorted exchange agreements with other libraries, and also add gift materials to their collections. The cost of maintaining such arrangements for materials readily available for purchase usually cannot be justified. Regardless of the institution's organization chart and whether or not gifts and exchange and selection activities have a formal relationship, a selector should be familiar with the policies and types of materials acquired through such arrangements, and play an active role in ensuring that they are both efficient and financially defensible. Alfred Lane's *Gifts and Exchange Manual* provides a practical overview of both operations.[16] In the case of gifts, one must weigh the costs of sorting, storing, searching, and processing these materials against the alternative costs of buying the item through regular acquisitions channels. Two general rules of thumb are appropriate here: whatever efforts a library makes to acquire and process gifts should be focused on materials either out-of-print, very expensive, or otherwise unavailable; and the library selector should apply the same criteria when adding gifts to the collection as when selecting materials for purchase. The expense of cataloging, housing, and preserving materials counters any notion that gifts are free.

The best justification of exchange programs occurs when they are used to obtain materials otherwise unavailable, such as publications from Soviet bloc countries. Domestic exchanges in the North American and British libraries should be rare, since the cost of administering them is likely to exceed that of regular paid orders.

For additional sources on this subject, see Robert A. Almony, Jr., "The Concept of Systematic Duplication: A Survey of the Literature," *Collection Management* 2:153–65 (Summer 1978).

Westport, Conn.: Greenwood, 1980.

the tools fall into two categories, those for in-print and those for out-of-print materials. Some selection techniques can be incorporated into regular selection routines; some can best be accomplished by designing special bibliographic projects. Of related interest are those techniques helpful in developing or improving a core collection of materials with anticipated heavy use, such as an undergraduate collection, as well as the collection development issues involved in gifts and exchange and preservation activities.

REPRINT AND MICROFORM SELECTION

A significant amount of retrospective selection can be accomplished as part of the normal routine for current selection. Some reprints and new microform collections will appear in *Weekly Record*, Library of Congress CDS Alert Service cards, and other sources, allowing them to be checked along with the current materials. In addition, a tremendous amount of promotional material will be received from the major reprint and micropublishing companies, such as Greenwood, AMS, Scholarly Reprints, Harvester Press Microform Publications, and Research Publications. Given the frequency and quantities with which such catalogs are supplied to libraries, it is hard to imagine a collection development operation that would not be inundated with them; however, if needed, useful lists of names and addresses can be found in *Guide to Microforms in Print* and *Guide to Reprints*. Many selectors save the best of these catalogs, filed in some retrievable system, in order to determine easily whether or not publishers have issued overlapping, or even identical, catalogs year after year.

Special care is warranted in the selection and bibliographic checking of reprints and microform sets because of the relatively high costs of these publications and the potential for expensive errors. It can be difficult to determine what the sets actually include and how they differ, if at all, from materials already in the collections. A call directly to the marketing division of the publisher may be in order if more detailed information is required. (More detailed information on microform selection appears in Sara Eichhorn's chapter on microforms.)

OUT-OF-PRINT SELECTION

Another valuable source for retrospective material, out-of-print dealers' catalogs, requires special effort and expertise. Because most catalogs advertise only one copy of each item, orders must be placed promptly after a catalog is received. Dealers usually will accept tentative telephone orders or cable orders with the stipulation that confirming orders will follow. Most selectors prefer to work with a limited number of trusted dealers, learning from experience those that are most likely to offer desirable books at fair prices. Section I of the *American Book Trade Directory* lists antiquarian dealers by geographical location; and the excellent handbook *Bookdealers in North America* lists out-of-print dealers geographically, alphabetically, and by subject specialty.

One of the most reliable retrospective selection strategies, assuming there is sufficient support staff, is to check citations in specialized subject bibliographies for materials of potential interest to the collections. After the bibliographies have been searched against the library's holdings, titles not held can then be checked for availability in the in-print sources, such as *Books in Print, Guide to Reprints*, and *British Books in Print*, although in most instances the "hit" rate will be quite low. Those items that are commercially available can be ordered as funds permit, and others that represent high priority desiderata can be pursued on the out-of-print market.

Identifying useful bibliographies to serve as selection guides, once a subject area is targeted for retrospective work, represents a challenge in itself. One good place to begin, when selecting outside a familiar discipline, is with Robert Broadus's *Selecting Materials for Libraries*. Part 5 of that work discusses landmark works and guides to the literature of most scholarly disciplines, emphasizing their possible applications for selection purposes.[13] In addition, sources such as Besterman's *World Bibliography of Bibliographies*, the *New Cambridge Bibliography*, and the *MLA International Bibliography*, can also lead to appropriate specialized bibliographies. These and similar guides to scholarly literature, coupled with consultations with reference colleagues and faculty working in the targeted disciplines, should help produce a reliable list of standard bibliographic sources.

When selecting journals, Bill Katz's *Magazines for Libraries* is useful for identifying and evaluating titles still being published. Sources such as Frank Luther Mott's *A History of American Magazines, 1741–1930* (which is fascinating to read in itself), and Alvin Sullivan's *British Literary Magazines, 1698–1836* provide invaluable assistance for undertaking retrospective projects.

Similar sources abound for newspapers as well. Mott's name appears again because his *American Journalism* gives useful insights into the historical importance of many American newspapers. And, of course, Isaiah Thomas's 1874 *History of Printing in America* and Clarence Brigham's *History and Bibliography of American Newspapers, 1690–1820*, along with the Readex Microprint Corporation's catalogs, are essential for colonial American journalism. At the top of any comparable list for British journalism would inevitably be *The Newspaper Press: Its Origin-Progress-*

and Present Position, as well as *The Metropolitan Weekly Press*, both by James Grant. Depending on the desired rospective activity, there are innumerable other guides state or regional newspapers, as well as those published f groups, such as blacks, Chicanos, or immigrants.

PATRON SUGGESTIONS AND LOST BOOKS

Every selector, regardless of training and experience, be suggestions for specific titles to be purchased and from regarding areas of the collection that need further a should institute simple routines whereby suggestions service points can be relayed promptly and efficiently subject selector, preferably on a standardized form. O is the establishment of a routine to ensure that books circulation desk are also reported to the selectors, wh sider purchasing replacements. Selectors may also wi of outgoing interlibrary loan request forms, in order t patrons were unable to find in the library and to d patron needs. Some selectors gather information fro about their research interests and library needs. One system of faculty representatives from each departme to the library, both to encourage suggestions and fac munication. Faculty and graduate students can also siderata in specialized subjects from out-of-print cat publishers' backlists, and published bibliographies.

DEVELOPING A CORE COLLECTION OR A NEW LIBRAR

As Hendrik Edelman explained in a frequently cit relatively small percentage of books in any given li demand; and those that are usually achieve this period of time.[14] However, there exists for every body of essential works, documenting its history constitutes the "core" of a successful research co

Selection of essential works that have stood tl discipline or subject area in which the library colle by many of the same techniques used for general i checking specialized subject bibliographies and so dent requests. *Books for College Libraries*, preser but about to undergo revision for a third ed

13. Robert Broadus, *Selecting Materials for Libraries*, 2nd ed. (New York: Wilson, 1981), pp. 221–419.

14. "Selection Methodology in Academic Libraries," *Lib Services* 23, no.1:36 (Winter 1979).

PRESERVATION

The collection developer's responsibilities extend beyond selection of new collections to include activities that foster the conservation and availability of materials already in the library. When library materials are lost, stolen, or physically deteriorated, the assignment to find a suitable commercial replacement or to recommend photoreproduction, remote storage, or withdrawal from the collection usually falls to the selector.

When looking for replacements, a bibliographic searcher should begin with commercial sources such as *Books in Print, British Books in Print, Guide to Reprints, Books on Demand,* and *Guide to Microforms in Print.* If those do not yield an appropriate replacement, the next step would be to check the Library of Congress's *National Register of Microfilm Masters,* which gives locations of preservation masters from which service copies can usually be produced for a fraction of the cost of creating another master negative. This searching tends to be tedious because the *Register* has not been cumulated since 1975, and it is necessary to search seven sections including the supplements. The *Register* is also several years behind schedule in publishing updates. Plans are underway to merge the *Register* (beginning in 1984) into the *National Union Catalog—Books* and *New Serial Titles,* which should make this information available in a more timely fashion. A comprehensive search should also include the New York Public Library's *Register of Microform Masters,* as well as the Research Libraries Information Network (RLIN) database, which includes more than 45,000 bibliographic records for preservation masters, as well as titles scheduled for preservation filming. These records are also published periodically on microfiche as the *RLG Preservation Union List.*

Selectors should practice "preventative preservation" whenever possible. In making the original purchase decision, every effort should be made to acquire materials that have the best chance of surviving in the library's environment, taking into account such factors as size, format, type of binding, and potential use. Similarly, when selecting a replacement for a book already in the library that is too brittle to circulate, a selector should consider buying a reprint, microfilm, or microfiche copy, if available, rather than an exact replacement edition, since it is also likely to be on poor paper.

Further preventative measures are possible. As current acquisitions are received, those items that arrive in poor condition should be identified and decisions made at that time as to whether they should be stored in a protective container, microfilmed, photocopied, or even discarded if the costs cannot be justified. In addition, an assistant can check the condition of books already in the collection for possible replacement when reprint editions become available, thus incorporating preservation activities into normal selection routines.

Conclusion

When all is said and done on the art of selection, the fact remains that the decision to buy or not to buy represents the easy part of the job. Developing a policy and adapting it over time—and doing both within the context of a changing university or other parent institution—is at the heart of successful collection development. Furthermore, because disciplines are not so neatly defined and discrete as they once were, it is virtually impossible to allocate the selection responsibility along distinct lines. In such an environment, good communication and cooperation both within the library, as well as with the academic and administrative departments of the institution, become far more important than the selection tools themselves.

Selection Sources

Almquist & Wiksell Bokhandel AB Gamla Brogatan 26, Box 62, S-101, 20 Stockholm, Sweden.

American Book Publishing Record. v. 1- . 1960- . New York: Bowker. Monthly.

American Book Trade Directory. 30th ed. New York: Bowker, 1984.

American Poetry Review. v. 1- . 1972- . Philadelphia: World Poetry. Bimonthly.

Associations' Publications in Print. v. 1- . 1981-. New York: Bowker. Annually.

Australian National Bibliography. v. 1- . 1961- . Canberra: National Library of Australia. Semimonthly with monthly and annual cumulations.

Benn's Press Directory—United Kingdom. 131st ed. Tonbridge Wells, Kent: Benn's Business Information Services, 1983- .

Besterman, Theodore. *A World Bibliography of Bibliographies.* 4th ed. 5v. Lausanne: Societas Bibliographica, 1965–66.

Bibliografia Nazionale Italiana. v. 1- . 1958- . Rome: Biblioteca Nazionale Centrale di Firenze. Monthly.

Bibliographie de la France—Biblio. v. 1- . 1972- . Paris: Cercle de la Libraries. Weekly.

Bookdealers in North America: A Directory of Dealers in Secondhand and Antiquarian Books in Canada and the United States of America, 1983-1985. 9th ed. London: Sheppard, 1983.

Books for College Libraries; A Core Collection of 40,000 Titles. 2nd ed. 6v. Chicago: American Library Assn., 1975. (3rd ed. in progress.)

Books in Canada. v. 1- . 1971- . Toronto: Canadian Review of Books. 10/year.

Books in Print 1983-1984. 3v. New York: Bowker, 1983.

Brigham, Clarence S. *History and Bibliography of American Newspapers, 1690-1820.* 2v. Worcester, Mass.: American Antiquarian Society, 1947.

British Book News. v. 1- . 1944- . London: The British Council. Dist. by Basil Blackwell. Monthly.

British Books in Print 1983; The Reference Catalog of Current Literature. 2v. London: Whitaker, 1983.

British National Bibliography. v. 1- . 1950- . London: Council of the British National Bibliography, British Museum. Weekly with annual cumulations.

Canadian Literature. v. 1– . 1959– . Vancouver: Univ. of British Columbia. Quarterly.

Canadian Studies; A Catalog of Publications. Toronto: Council and Assn. of Canadian Publishers, 1983. (Address: 45 Charles St. East, Toronto, Ontario, Canada M4Y1F2.)

Canadian Books in Print; Author and Title Index. Toronto: Univ. of Toronto Pr., 1975– . Annually.

Canadiana. v. 1– . 1950– . Ottawa: National Library of Canada. Monthly with annual cumulations.

Choice. v. 1– . 1964– . Middleton, Conn.: Assn. of College and Research Libraries. Monthly; bimonthly July/Aug.

Current Canadian Books (Livres Canadiens Courant). v. 1– 1973– . Niagara Falls, Ontario: Coutts Library Services. Monthly.

Deutsche Bibliographie. v. 1– . 1975– . Wochentliches Verzeichnis, Frankfurt: Buchhandler-Vereinigung. Weekly.

Encyclopedia of Associations. v. 1– . 1956– . Detroit: Gale. Biennially.

Forthcoming Books. New York: Bowker, 1966– . Bimonthly.

Fulton, Len, and Ellen Ferber, eds. *International Directory of Little Magazines and Small Presses.* 19th ed. Paradise, Calif.: Dustbooks, 1983.

———, eds. *Small Press Record of Books in Print.* 12th ed. Paradise, Calif.: Dustbooks, 1983. Annually.

Grant, James. *The Metropolitan Weekly and Provincial Press.* London: Routledge, 1872.

———. *The Newspaper Press: Its Origin—Progress—and Present Position.* 2v. London: Tinsley Brothers, 1871.

Guide to Microforms in Print: Author, Title. 2v. Westport, Conn.: Meckler, 1978– . Irregularly.

Guide to Reprints; An International Bibliography of Scholarly Reprints. v. 1– . 1967– . Kent, Conn.: Guide to Reprints. Annually.

The IMS Ayer Directory of Publications. v. 1– . 1975– . Fort Washington, Pa.: IMS Press. Annually.

James Bennett Group, 4 Collaroy St., Collaroy, New South Wales, Australia 2097- T: 989648.

Katz, William A., and Linda Sternberg, eds. *Magazines for Libraries: For the General Reader, and School, Junior College, College, University, and Public Libraries.* 4th ed. New York: Bowker, 1982.

Kinokuniya Co., Ltd., 17-7 Shinjuku 3-chome, Shinjuku-ku, Tokyo, Japan.

Library Journal. v. 1– . 1876– . New York: Bowker. Bimonthly.

Library of Congress. CDS Alert Service cards. Available from: Cataloging Distribution Service, Customer Services Section, Library of Congress, Washington, D.C. 20541.

———, comp. *National Register of Microform Masters.* v. 1– . 1965– . Washington, D.C.: Library of Congress. Irregularly.

Literary Review. no. 8– . 1980– . London: Namora Group. Monthly.

London Review of Books. v.1– . 1979– . London: LRB Ltd. Semimonthly.

Maruzen Co. Ltd., 3-10, Nihonbashi 2-chome, Chuo-ku, POB 505, Tokyo 100-31-T.

Modern Language Assn. of America. *MLA International Bibliography of Books and Articles on the Modern Languages and Literatures.* v. 1– . 1921– . New York: MLA. Annually.

Mott, Frank Luther. *American Journalism.* 3rd ed. New York: Macmillan, 1962.

———. *A History of American Magazines, 1741–1930.* 5v. Cambridge: Harvard Univ. Pr., 1930–68.

National Union Catalog. Books. Washington, D.C.: Library of Congress, 1983– . Monthly. (Microfiche.)

The New Cambridge Bibliography of English Literature. 5v. Cambridge: Cambridge Univ. Pr., 1969–77.

New Serial Titles: A Union List of Serials Held by Libraries in the United States and Canada. v. 1– . 1953– . Washington, D.C.: Library of Congress. Monthly, quarterly, and annual cumulations.

New York Public Library Register of Microform Masters. Monographs. Bellevue, Wash.: Commercial Microfilm Services, 1983. (Microfiche.)

New York Review of Books. v. 1– . 1963– . New York: Ellsworth. Biweekly.

New York Times Book Review. v. 1– . 1896– . New York: New York Times. Weekly.

New Zealand National Bibliography. v. 1– . 1966– . Wellington: National Library of New Zealand. Monthly with annual cumulations.

Nijhoff, Martinus, BV. Postbus 269, Lange Voorhout 9–11, 2501 AX The Hague, The Netherlands.

Nilon, Charles H. *Bibliographies in American Literature.* New York: Bowker, 1970.

Orion Books, 1–58 Kanda, Jimbo-cho, Chiyoda-ku, POB 509, Tokyo International, Tokyo 101–T.

Poetry. v. 1– . 1912– . Chicago: Modern Poetry Assn.

Publishers Directory. 1984–1985. 5th ed. 2v. Detroit: Gale, 1984.

Quill and Quire. v. 1– . 1935– . Toronto: Key Publishers. Monthly.

RLG Preservation Union List. Stanford, Calif.: Research Libraries Group, 1985. Irregularly. (Microfiche.)

Serials Review. v. 1– . 1975– . Ann Arbor, Mich.: Pieran. Quarterly.

South Pacific Books, Box 3433, Auckland, New Zealand.

Subject Guide to Books in Print. 4v. New York: Bowker, 1957– . Annually.

Sullivan, Alvin, ed. *British Literary Magazines, 1698–1836.* Westport, Conn.: Greenwood, 1983.

Times Literary Supplement. v. 1– . 1902– . London: Times Newspapers. Weekly.

Thomas, Isaiah. *History of Printing in America, with a Biography of Printers, and an Account of Newspapers.* 2nd ed. 2v. Albany: Munsell, 1874.

University Microfilms International. *Books on Demand: Author Guide, Title Guide, Subject Guide.* 3v. Ann Arbor, Mich.: University Microfilms, 1977.

University of Toronto Quarterly. v. 1– . 1931– . Toronto: Univ. of Toronto Pr. Quarterly.

Weekly Record. v. 1– . 1974– . New York: Bowker. Weekly.

BUYING OUT-OF-PRINT BOOKS

William Z. Schenck

Acquiring books no longer in print from publishers may seem like a relatively new problem. We have all heard librarians lamenting for the "good old days" when books remained available for years and years. In this light it is interesting to note that the *Oxford English Dictionary* provides this 1674 quote from Robert Boyle in which he refers to his works as "Divers excellent little Tracts, which . . . are already out of print." An 1895 prospectus for the Early English Tract Society stated that "Half the Publications of 1866 are already out of print, but will be gradually reprinted."

Hala Piekarski stated that a title goes out of print when plates for it are destroyed, the type is redistributed, and the publisher's supply of copies is exhausted.[1] While this definition is archaic in terms of new methods of printing (for example, would you discard the computer tape that generated the print instead of the old printing plate?), it does provide a general idea of the concept. The last part of Piekarski's definition is probably the most important; when the publisher no longer has the book and has declared the title out-of-print, the librarian must then acquire the book through channels outside the normal in-print book trade.

Having defined what out-of-print (O. P.) means, we need to consider the out-of-print book trade. This may seem to be elementary since, as librarians, we know at least something about buying books, especially those no longer in print. Yet it is very important to remember that while the library profession is basically built on order and control, the used book world often appears random, almost to the point of anarchy.

The out-of-print market is one of the last bastions of individuality; no conglomerates are involved in the O. P. market, and for good reason. As

---

This article has been substantially revised since it was first published as "The Acquisition of Out-of-Print Books" in *AB Bookman's Weekly* (Dec. 7, 1981).

1. Hala Piekarski, "Acquisition of Out-of-Print Books for a University Library," *Canadian Library Journal* 26:34–52 (Sept. 1969).

many out-of-print booksellers would agree, very few people have ever gotten rich selling used books. It is important for librarians to understand that, while there is no particular order or neatness in the O. P. world, it is a composite of many interesting people who operate in their own individual ways. While there are some developments involving the introduction of personal and small business computers into the out-of-print world, it remains, and will continue to be, an unorganized yet fascinating business.

While having books go out-of-print is not a new phenomenon, in recent years the length of time in which a book is available has decreased. More books are going out-of-print sooner. This is true for a current bestseller as well as a university press treatise.

There are three reasons for this trend toward rapid disappearance. First is economic. Publishers are trying to judge markets better, printing only the number of titles they hope to sell in a set period of time. It is expensive to inventory books. No doubt the Internal Revenue Service regulation on how inventoried books are taxed exacerbated this situation. Nevertheless, even without the Thor Power Tool decision, publishers would be keeping books in-print for shorter time periods. The number of special sale catalogs issued by university and scholarly presses in recent years attests to the expense of keeping these titles in inventory for years after the sales chart has flattened out.

Second, short-run printing has become more economical. While this is especially true for reprinters, it also means that the university press or other scholarly publishers can print 2000 to 2500 titles (or less) at a reasonable price.

Third, publishers know that declaring a book out-of-print no longer necessarily relegates it to obscurity. Not only is the out-of-print market larger now, but there are alternative sources where libraries (and others) can get the book after the publisher declares it out-of-print. These ways include reprints, microforms, and even photocopying. Also, improved resource sharing among libraries, especially through the Research Libraries Information Network (RLIN) and OCLC Interlibrary Loan Systems, ensures that researchers can have access to a copy of a needed volume. Previously, university presses often felt that they owed it to scholarship to keep a title in print. Now they know that it may still be available, even if not from them.

There is a recent trend that will help keep some titles in-print. Edmund Fuller, the book review editor of the *Wall Street Journal*, described the phenomenon in the June 27, 1983, issue.

> Today, for writers of books, staying in print is distressfully more difficult than getting into print—which also is bad for readers and for publishing. There are some signs of a counter-trend. A few major houses, certain university

presses and an increasing number of small publishers throughout the country are beginning to bring back works both old and relatively recent that deserve to be in print. More should be done.

The request for an out-of-print book will come to you from a variety of sources, and the number of items you need to hunt for on the O. P. market will depend to some extent on the size of your library's collection, your book budget and, of most importance, the strengths of your collections.

Surprisingly, considering the size of their book budgets, major research libraries such as Harvard and Yale spend little on basic O. P. items, since they already have most of the items. (They do, of course, a great deal of specialized purchasing for their special collections, as well as replacement copies.) A small college or university library trying to build its collections or to make up for past lapses in book funds may purchase heavily on the O. P. market. Public libraries need to replace titles in demand that have worn out through heavy use. The point is that no matter what the size of your collection or type of library, you will need to do some buying on the O. P. market, and out-of-print dealers will be happy to work with you. The average O. P. dealer would go broke if he or she relied on purchases from Yale or Harvard.

The first step in working with an O. P. request is to see if it really is not in-print. If the item has been selected by a faculty member or his or her research assistant, you cannot be sure that the book is out-of-print just because it was not listed in *Books in Print* (*BIP*). It may be listed under title or editor, or a variant spelling of the author's name. Therefore, it may be necessary to recheck *BIP*. Also, the book may be from a nontrade publisher that does not list its publications in *BIP*. The R. R. Bowker publication, *Associations' Publications in Print*, can be very useful in checking the availability of this type of publication. If the publisher does not list in either of these helpful publications, you will have to assume that the material is available and order it either directly from a dealer or the publisher.

It is possible that you will not know that the book is out-of-print until you order it and the order returns from the dealer marked "Out-of-Print." Book jobbers have a vested interest in supplying accurate reports back to libraries, as they get paid only for books delivered, even though they incur costs for ordering a book from a publisher only to find out it is out-of-print. Therefore, unless there is a special reason to question a jobber's out-of-print report, it should be accepted. If time and staff permit, you should first redirect the order to the publisher, perhaps with a form saying that while you received a note indicating that the book was out-of-print, you need this for your collection and you hope that the publisher can supply at least one copy. This often works, and not because the publisher was devious or did not know its stock, although that certainly happens. Some publishers with computerized inventory will automatically declare a book out-of-print (or at least out of stock) when supply drops to a certain level, say twenty-five copies. Thus, the stock clerk responding to your order is technically correct in reporting the book out-of-print even though some copies are available.

The ideal way to get around this is to know someone in the shipping department of the publisher, but this is, unfortunately, not always feasible. A somewhat more direct method once proved rather successful for me: the library needed four copies of a work from a major Midwest publisher for reserve, and the order came back marked "no longer available—out of print." Temporarily stymied, I then discovered that the president of the firm was an alumnus of the university. A personal letter to him followed, and within a week I not only had the four copies, but they came gratis. I certainly realize that this system cannot work all the time, and even if you have a contact, you should use him or her selectively. But every school has some graduates in publishing, and perhaps your alumni or development office can give you a current directory of these people.

If the book is not available from the original publisher, check other sources. Check *Guide to Reprints* to see if the book has been reprinted. Be careful, however, of those reprinters who list a title but do not publish it until they have a sufficient number of orders. Fortunately, this does not often occur, but with a decrease in library book budgets and the high cost of borrowing money, this practice is again on the increase. If in doubt, call the publisher or find the bibliographic record on OCLC or other networks and see if there are holding statements, or some indication that the reprint has been published. If you have reason to believe that the book has been reprinted, you might examine some reprint dealer catalogs separately, as not all reprinters list all titles in *Guide to Reprints*.

Another alternative, if this format is acceptable, is to check *Guide to Microforms in Print*. Along those same lines, you can search the *National Register of Microform Masters* to see if another library has the book on film and might be willing to make a photocopy or a film copy for you. You are more likely to find older and more esoteric items in the *National Register*, and copyright can be a problem. As more libraries microfilm older parts of their collections in order to preserve the information, this method will become easier.

Many publishers will remainder copies of material they no longer wish to stock. It is often difficult to find out to whom a publisher has remaindered copies. This is not because publishers are secretive, but the order department usually does not have access to this information. If you happen to live in a large metropolitan area, you can keep up with remainders by visiting large bookshops.

It is also valuable to look in *British Books in Print* to determine if the book is in-print in England. This is becoming increasingly important, as many British books are being published or distributed here. You can use either the printed *British Books in Print* or the edition available on microfiche, with a monthly cumulation. While this service costs somewhat more, it is worth the cost to have current information on what is in-print and the cost.

A final source to use as an alternative to the original is University Microfilm's Books on Demand project. University Microfilms offers almost 100,000 titles in this program. The books are expensive; the cost depends on the number of pages of the original. There are some titles, especially some Slavic ones, that are very difficult, if not impossible, to acquire on the O. P. market, and even if a copy could be located, it would be in poor condition. Nevertheless, the majority of titles in the Books on Demand program really should be considered for purchase only after a search on the O. P. market.

Once you have decided that a book is actually out-of-print, you then have to decide how to get it. There are basically two ways: The first is to advertise and the second is to work with dealers. Many librarians think that while they would like to advertise, they cannot afford the time and money. I disagree with this view; with a little planning and little staff time you can handle advertising.

There are two ways to advertise. The first is to compile a list of desired titles and send the list to dealers. This is basically what many booksellers do when looking for books for clients. This method is not recommended, as you can only reach a limited number of dealers. In addition, unless you make it perfectly clear that this is a list circulating to other dealers, you may mislead a dealer into thinking that it is a unique list. And if you clearly state that the list has been sent to many dealers, the individual dealer may well ignore it, believing that since other dealers are also working on the list, the number of titles the dealer will be able to sell to that library will be too small to be worthwhile.

The second way to advertise is to use one of the two major trade journals, *AB* or *Library Bookseller*. *AB* is the better-known of the two, and certainly has the wider circulation. In addition, the articles are always of a high quality and provide an excellent source of information about the O. P. trade.

Although libraries can run small ads in *AB*, full-page ads are suggested. A page ad will take about sixty-five titles; the actual number will depend on the compactness of the bibliographical citation. Do not try to provide complete bibliographical citations; just list the basic information. Give the author, last name and first initial, unless the last name is so common that more identification is necessary, and the first three or four words of the

---

AB Bookman's Weekly. Clifton, N.J.: AB Bookman's Weekly, 1948– .
Weekly.
Trade periodical.
Articles on the out-of-print book trade and ads for books.
Valuable for articles on various aspects of the out-of- print book trade, this journal features special issues that highlight specific categories of books—photography, childrens, music, etc. The majority of each issue contains ads from booksellers of books wanted or for sale. Libraries may also advertise.

---

title. List other information only if necessary to identify the books. For example, put simple listings for: "Kahn, L., ed. *Domebook One*," and "Price, S. D. *Take Me Home*," but more complex for: "Dubois, W. E. B. *Souls of Black Folk*, with a new intro. by Herbert Aptheker," to make sure that it is clear that the reprint edition is wanted. List your return address, and if possible put a code or person's initials so that the mail opener will be sure where to direct the mail. Since many out-of-print dealers expect and need cash with orders, and since this is often difficult for libraries to do, state "no CWOs please" in the ad.

In a study done at the University of North Carolina at Chapel Hill (UNC-CH) advertising in *AB* proved to be a quick and inexpensive way to acquire O. P. titles.[2] From July 1979 to June 1980, UNC-CH advertised for 1711 books, and obtained 740 of them for a forty-three percent success rate. And for the first three months of fiscal year 1980/81, it listed 400 titles and purchased 147, or thirty-seven percent. The books were acquired at a lower price in this manner than if the library tried to obtain them through O. P. dealers. The average price paid for the 147 books purchased through *AB* in these three months was $13.14; if the cost for ads is prorated on these titles, the cost for ads per title is only $1.32. During the same time it cost $15.54 for the average book purchased from a dealer on a quote. In 1979/80, the average price for a book purchased for the UNC-CH library through *AB* was $13.04, while the library acquired 351 books from dealers through quotes at $23.00.

There was some preselection done before ads were compiled and sent to *AB*. Books that a librarian felt were not available in the U. S. out-of-print book trade were not listed, nor were very specialized and older (pre-1900) titles.

The other journal in which to advertise is *The Library Bookseller* (formerly *TAAB*). This journal is free to libraries; the journal makes its money from the subscription charges to dealers. *The Library Bookseller* has a more limited circulation than *AB*. Unlike *AB*, where the vast majority of ads are from dealers, in *The Library Bookseller* most are from libraries.

2. William Z. Schenck, "Acquisition of Out-of-Print Books," *AB Bookman's Weekly* 68:4015–32 (Dec. 7, 1981).

The Library Bookseller. West Orange, N. J.: Albert Saifer, 1945– . Bimonthly.
   Trade periodical.
   Contains only ads from libraries for books needed.
   This journal, often referred to by its previous title, *TAAB*, has, along with the
   ads, a "Titles Wanted Index." This is a single list, by author, of titles not supplied
   by out-of-print dealers and still desired.

Those libraries that use *The Library Bookseller* report a response rate
similar to the UNC-CH study with *AB*.

Whether you advertise in either journal, you will need to decide if you
want to respond to all quotes received. This is, as anyone knows who
regularly reads the pages of *AB*, a hotly debated topic. Since most O. P.
dealers are holding the book while you decide, it is fairer to let them
know if you are not interested. However, this might become too expensive,
and it is certainly time consuming. A way to solve this, at least partially,
is to state in the ad:

   Firm orders sent for accepted quotes within 3 weeks of receipt. Other quotes
   should be considered declined after that time. Thank you.

While this certainly is not as good as a personal response, it is probably
a fair compromise. Most quotes arrive within a three-week period from
the date of the ad. Usually quotes come in three major groups after an
ad runs. The first group comes from those dealers who get *AB* sent first
class mail. These will often arrive on your desk before the magazine gets
there, which can be somewhat disconcerting. The second group comes
from regular subscribers, and the third from English dealers. There will
not be too many of the latter, but you can expect some.

I mentioned earlier that the out-of-print book trade defies categoriza-
tion. After you place your ad, be it in *AB* or *The Library Bookseller*, be
prepared to receive a lot of handwritten postcards, ranging from pictures
of the Golden Gate Bridge to index cards turned into postcards. And
typewriters are practically nonexistent, apparently; you will get a large
number of hard-to-read cards. I would suggest that you tell your mail
room to send all undecipherable 3x5 cards to you; they will probably
contain quotes.

The second way to get O. P. books is to send a list to one dealer. I
stress one dealer, because a dealer should have an exclusive search on an
item for a reasonable period of time. Unless the material is very hard to
get, six months is a reasonable time. At the end of that time, you can
send the item to another dealer. Since many dealers specialize in certain
subjects, it is a good idea to keep a list of dealers and their subject expertise.
There are some good guides available. The best one is the *Directory of*

Specialized American Bookdealers.[3] In addition, you can get a lot of information from just reading the ads in *AB* each week. Also from ads in *AB* or *The Library Bookseller* responses, you will develop contacts. If you send a dealer a request for an item, make sure that you indicate that you want a quote. When the dealer responds with that quote, get back with your response as quickly as possible. After working with a dealer for awhile, you might want to develop some guidelines so that the dealer can automatically ship any item under a certain price. This will help cut some of the dealer's time and expenses (and yours) and also get the book to you faster. Many libraries use $35.00 as a cutoff under which dealers can automatically ship the book.

There are five types of dealers who sell books to libraries. The first is the basic out-of-print dealer who has a stock of books. In many cases this dealer operates a store open to the public. The dealer may be a specialist or have a general stock. Even if the dealer cannot fill the order from stock, he or she may know where there is a copy. Another category of dealer operates the large search service. These dealers, such as International Bookfinders in California, often run multipage ads in *AB*. They have little or no stock themselves, but simply act as an intermediary between a dealer and a library.

Several library jobbers will search for books not in-print. They do this as part of their service to libraries, but their search methods are similar to methods used by out-of-print dealers. For a description of the search used by Blackwell North America, see the article by Bob Langhorst and Jack Walsdorf in *Technicalities* called "Building a Better Book Trap: Tracking Down the Elusive Out-of-Print Book."[4]

The fourth type of dealer, and there are not many of this breed, visits libraries and checks the library's holdings against the titles he or she has in stock. While time consuming, it does provide the selector with a list of titles probably not held. In most cases, these dealers initiate contact with libraries. They are difficult to locate as they often deal with a small number of libraries. An interesting extension of this could occur as more libraries convert their holdings into an online database. The technology will make it possible for a dealer to check stock against a library's holdings without leaving the store.

The dealer who issues catalogs is the type most familiar to librarians. This method of acquiring O. P. books is perhaps the most interesting. More dealers are compiling and mailing catalogs, and many of these contain titles you may want. It is a good idea to buy at least one or two books from a dealer each year, just to be sure that the catalogs keep

3. *Directory of Specialized American Bookdealers* (New York: Arco, 1981).
4. Bob Langhorst and Jack Walsdorf, "Building a Better Book Trap: Tracking Down the Elusive Out-of-Print Book," *Technicalities* 3, no. 7:7–8 (July 1983).

coming in. With increased postal costs, dealers cannot afford to send catalogs to nonproductive customers. You can examine the catalogs to see if there are items listed, and then act with all deliberate speed. Call the American and British dealers, and if you or your staff have the language ability, call the European dealers. At least cable. However, be selective in the catalogs you examine on a regular basis. Fun as it is to read these, it is time consuming, and the occasional book purchased may not make up for the time spent.

Whether you send lists to dealers or you advertise in trade journals, keep one thing in mind. Once you have accepted a quote from a dealer and received the book, pay the invoice quickly. Out-of-print dealers operate on a small margin, and they cannot afford to have outstanding accounts. Taking thirty days to pay is too long. The faster a library pays, the more likely the dealer is to offer books to that library in the future. I remember vividly the words on the bottom of an invoice from one dealer: "Slow payers will be shot."

This paper has described ways to acquire out-of-print U. S. imprints. Foreign titles represent an entirely different challenge. Because there are many British titles available in the United States, it is possible to either advertise or work with a dealer who specializes in that subject area. Fortunately, most English and European dealers have expertise in their respective O. P. markets and can search for your needed titles. Firms such as B. H. Blackwell's, Harrossowitz, and Nijhoff all have good and long-established antiquarian departments. Unless a library has very specialized needs and selectors with extensive knowledge of the European book trade, a library should rely on established English and Continental booksellers.

Records need to be kept for those books being searched, be it with an ad or on a quote to a dealer. The type of record kept depends on the order files kept in your library. At a minimum, there should be a record of the book wanted included in the regular order file, and there should be a way to review these orders on a regular cycle. Unlike orders for inprint titles, however, nothing should be encumbered until an actual quote comes from the dealer.

It is possible for librarians to get books on the O. P. market, as long as they keep in mind some of the unique aspects of the out-of-print book trade. It can be both enjoyable and rewarding.

SERIALS

Marcia Tuttle

Librarians responsible for collection building work with an integrated body of information. Serial literature is a significant part of this body, used and collected together with printed monographs and nonprint formats. At the same time, serials differ from monographs. Serials continue: a subscription or standing order is invoiced and arrives until someone acts to end the commitment. Serials change: they change title, price, frequency, format, and content. Serials encroach: they consume funds needed for other materials; they spread into space reserved for acquisitions of five years hence; they get fatter and require more than their share of binding funds. Most of all, serials keep coming; when they do not, the real problems begin. These qualities of serials require that they be managed separately even while they are part of an integrated collection.

The significance of serials is increasing in library collections. As a traditionally fast means of publication, serials have always been essential to science and technology. In the last twenty years scholars writing in other disciplines have turned to serial, and particularly periodical, publication, thereby creating a demand for more titles. In April 1982, an article in the *Chronicle of Higher Education* featured some of the problems created by the "enormous proliferation of journals": increasing academic specialization, pressure on faculty members and researchers to publish, and few serious obstacles to starting a new journal. Libraries cannot afford to purchase all the journals they need, and scholars cannot keep up with the contents of journals in their field. Both librarians and faculty members are calling for a limit to the number of journals and for a means of evaluating serials.[1]

1. Karen J. Winkler, "When It Comes to Journals, Is More Really Better?" *Chronicle of Higher Education* 24: 21–22 (Apr. 14, 1982).

Identifying Serials

This discussion is limited to currently published American serials, although many of the sources mentioned are broader in scope, both geographically and chronologically. Often, more than one tool is required to ensure that the serial is identified and that the bibliographical data are current and correct. With the high incidence of change in serials, the date of the information itself (not necessarily the date of publication) is significant. The time lag between collection of data for printed directories and the appearance of the published work means that, to a certain extent, guides are obsolete by the time they reach the library.

This situation can be overcome by subscribing to online databases available from the publisher or through BRS and DIALOG, but the expense of online identification is considerably greater than the cost of printed counterparts. For example, *Ulrich's International Periodicals Directory* and *Irregular Serials and Annuals* are standard, reasonably priced sources for the identification by subject of periodicals and nonperiodical serials. Data used for these directories are available online in the Bowker Serials Database at a cost of up to $75.00 an hour, with extra charges for printed citations. Similarly, *Standard Periodical Directory (SPD)* is a good printed source for subject access to American and Canadian small-circulation, ephemeral, and processed serials, as well as to more general titles. It is available online as part of a database named Select Periodical Data, available from Oxbridge at a cost comparable to the Bowker database. Libraries where speed is a high priority may find the online services worth the extra cost; many will be best served by the traditional directories.

Printed sources exist for the identification of special types of serials. *IMS Ayer Directory of Publications* has been a standard guide to American and Canadian newspapers for more than a century, and its coverage has expanded to magazines, although *Ulrich's* and *SPD* are better sources for those. *International Directory of Little Magazines and Small Presses* is the standard work for identification of literary and political serials. For American federal document serials, *Monthly Catalog of United States Government Publications* is available in print, or online through the Government Printing Office database.

Subject access to serial titles is of more value to selectors than alphabetical arrangement. Bibliographies, periodical indexes, and abstract journals usually provide a list of serials consulted. For example, the *MLA International Bibliography* list of titles has evolved into a separate directory of serials, giving not only bibliographic information but also facts useful to scholars wishing to publish in the journals. *L'Annee Philologique* also lists titles, although these serials are not as well identified as *MLA*'s.

Ulrich's International Periodicals Directory. v.1– . 1932– . New York:
  Bowker. Annually.
  Identification source for current journals.
  Subject arrangement.
  List of new journals.
  List of cessations.
  12–18-month lag time between collection of information and publication.
Ulrich's is a standard source for identifying current journals and is arranged by
subject with a title index and liberal cross-references. It provides subscription
information, ISSN, indication of where a title is indexed, a list of cessations
since the last edition, and a list of new periodicals. *Ulrich's International Periodicals Directory* is updated by *Ulrich's Quarterly.*

Irregular Serials and Annuals. v.1– . 1967– . New York: Bowker. Annually.
  Identification source for current nonperiodical serials. Subject arrangement.
  List of international documents.
  ISSN finding list.
  12–18-month lag between collection of data and publication.
This is a companion volume to *Ulrich's International Periodicals Directory* and
is also arranged by subject. *Irregular Serials and Annuals* gives the same bibliographic and subscription information about nonperiodical serials that *Ulrich's*
gives about journals. This work includes a list of international documents and
an index to ISSN for all types of serials. It is updated by *Ulrich's Quarterly.*

Standard Periodical Directory. v.1– . 1963– . New York: Oxbridge.
  Biennially.
  Covers current North American periodicals and annuals.
  Subject arrangement.
  Valuable for ephemeral publications.
SPD features a subject arrangement with a title index. It covers United States
and Canadian serials that are published at least once every two years, and it
includes some newspapers. This source is particularly valuable for small-circu-
lation, ephemeral, and processed publications. Data are more business-oriented
than *Ulrich's.*

Virtually all periodical indexes and abstract journals describe the titles
included. The best give publication data, making it easy to check the serials
against the library's holdings. A selection of indexes and abstract journals
for examination can be made from the listing in *Ulrich's.*

Librarian selectors need to identify new serial titles more often than
established titles. *Ulrich's* and *Irregular Serials and Annuals* are standard
sources for older titles; *Ulrich's Quarterly*, readily available and easy to
use, updates both publications. It is also part of the online Bowker Serials
Bibliography database. *SPD* once had updates, but these have been discontinued.

New Serial Titles (*NST*) is a standard source for identifying serials,
although its usefulness diminished considerably when the Classed Subject

IMS Ayer Directory of Publications. v.1- . 1869- . Fort Washington, Pa.: IMS Press. Annually.
Best source for identifying current North American newspapers.
Geographic arrangement.
Classified lists of newspapers.
Particularly good for information about newspapers, *IMS Ayer* also lists magazines published at least quarterly. Its scope is United States and territories, Canada, and a few other places. The work is arranged geographically, with information about each state or province and city. Among details included are circulation and editorial slant of publication. Contents include a title index and several classified lists of newspapers and magazines.

International Directory of Little Magazines and Small Presses. v.1- . 1965- . Paradise, Calif.: L. V. Fulton. Annually.
Standard source for current little magazines and small presses.
Editorial and subscription information.
Feedback from editors.
This useful work contains in one alphabetical list detailed information about both little magazines and small presses. Subject and regional indexes increases its value. The guide includes editorial and subscription information, as well as editor and/or publisher comments.

MLA Directory of Periodicals: A Guide to Journals and Series in Languages and Literatures. 1st- ed. 1978/79- . New York: Modern Language Assn. of America. Biennially
Authoritative source for international language and literature serials.
Subscription and editorial data.
Alphabetical arrangement.
A companion volume to *MLA International Bibliography*, this source contains subscription and editorial data on all titles in MLA's "Master List." It is arranged alphabetically by title. The selector knows that all titles included are considered worthy of being indexed by MLA.

Ulrich's Quarterly. v.1- . Spring 1977- . New York: Bowker. Quarterly.
Subject arrangement.
Cumulating title index.
Lists periodicals and nonperiodical serials.
Useful for subject selector.
This service updates both *Ulrich's International Periodicals Directory* and *Irregular Serials and Annuals* with new and additional serials. It is arranged by subject, with a title index that cumulates throughout the volume. *Ulrich's Quarterly* is a manageable printed tool for the selector working by subject.

Arrangement edition was discontinued after 1980. *NST* now reproduces in alphabetical order complete bibliographic records for both current and retrospective serials entered into the OCLC database by CONSER (CONversion of SERials to machine readable form) participants.[2]

PRICE INFORMATION

Most new periodical titles come to the attention of selectors through unsolicited samples and announcements from the publishers. There is nothing systematic or balanced about identification of new titles by this means, but the practice supplements the use of the sources noted above. Additionally, subscription agents and standing order vendors issue updating periodicals that list and often describe new serials. *Nijhoff Serials, EBSCO Bulletin of Serials Changes*, and *Swets Info* are examples. B. H. Blackwell sends customers an annotated list of new serials with its monthly report. Most agents will attempt to obtain free sample copies requested by the library, although some of them downplay the service.

Double-digit inflation has been the rule for American periodicals for some time. For this reason, wherever one has identified a title, it is well to check the annual catalog issued by one of the large subscription agencies to verify the price. Faxon sends its customers the *Faxon Librarians' Guide*, and EBSCO distributes its *Librarians' Handbook*. The two catalogs are published at different times during the year, so first one and then the other is likely to be more nearly current regarding price. With the changeable nature of serials and the difficulty of maintaining a file of over 150,000 titles, the accuracy of the data varies. It has been the author's experience that the Faxon guide is more likely to be correct and is easier to use, but that often the EBSCO catalog will contain exactly that piece of infor-

---

Swets Info. Lisse, The Netherlands: Swets Subscription Service. Quarterly
  with annual cumulation.
  Includes new titles, with subscription information.
  Changes in serials noted.
  European emphasis.
  Subject index to new titles.
This vendor publication lists new journals, annuals, and series available through Swets. Cessations, changes, and delays are also included. Its scope is international, with a European emphasis, reflecting the vendor's specialization. Bibliographic details of new titles are given, including publisher, price, frequency, date of first issue, and ISSN. Occasionally, one-sentence descriptions appear. A useful feature for selectors is the subject index to new titles. The 1983 cumulation lists 900 new publications.

---

2. For more about the CONSER Project, see Marcia Tuttle, *Introduction to Serials Management* (Greenwich, Conn.: JAI Press, 1983), pp. 177–83.

Faxon Librarians' Guide to Serials. Westwood, Mass.: Faxon, 1931- .
   Annually.
   Authoritative source for current price of journals.
   Arranged alphabetically by title/main entry.
   Accompanied by comprehensive microfiche, listing all titles handled by
      company.
Issued by a leading subsription agent, this catalog is arranged alphabetically,
according to library cataloging rules. It is a good printed source for the current
price of journals and for an indication of cessations, ISSN, and where a title is
indexed. The catalog is not useful for selection, except as verification or identification of details about titles. Data contained in this source may be accepted
as accurate at time of publication because of the authority of the company's
database. The printed catalog contains only titles for which Faxon has three or
more orders, but accompanying microfiche contain "low-use" titles as well.

Librarians' Handbook. v.1- . 1970/71- . Birmingham, Ala.: EBSCO
   Subscription Services. Annually.
   Alphabetical arrangement by serial's cover title.
   Does not follow library cataloging rules for entry.
   May contain subscription information not found elsewhere.
Arranged alphabetically by cover title of serial, this catalog contains a wealth
of information drawn from the vendor's database. It lists more titles than Faxon's
printed catalog, and has more information about nonperiodical serials, some of
it very old. Use for selectors is in confirming or identifying details about specific
serials.

mation that permits one to unravel a problem. The Faxon guide is easy
to use because it is arranged according to cataloging entry, although it
has not yet been converted to AACR2, while the EBSCO handbook seems
to be arranged for nonlibrarians. These catalogs cannot replace other
sources for identifying serials, because they do not give publication information and they are arranged alphabetically; however, they provide the
best approximation of cost.

The Faxon and EBSCO bibliographic and publication files are available
through the Linx and EBSCONET automated serials systems. Both give
notice of new titles online, and Faxon has activated a component named
"InfoServe" that reproduces contents pages and other data for journals
of certain publishers. Libraries can subscribe to one of these systems directly from the subscription agent and can also participate in the online
serials check-in feature of the system selected. Again, the cost is high and
will not be attractive to all libraries.

Most of the sources mentioned can supply the International Standard
Serial Number (ISSN). Once a selector has the ISSN, the title can be
accessed in virtually any database and is uniquely identified for transactions
with vendors, publishers, and patrons. The subscription agents are adding

this number to their files; however, *Ulrich's* and *Irregular Serials and Annuals* have the most complete listing, because Bowker was responsible for the initial assignment of ISSN.

Evaluating Serials

The selector has any number of sources for the intelligent selection of monographs: review periodicals, scholarly journals, professional literature. Unfortunately, few scholarly or professional journals review serials. Notice of subscription information and a summary of contents is the rule. One must rely on publishers' ads, recommendations of colleagues, and sample copies. As budgets shrink, the examination of a sample journal issue by both librarian and potential user becomes mandatory so that a purchase can be defended. The factors that push subscription prices up often force publishers to charge libraries for a sample issue, in contrast to earlier times when samples were free. This is money well spent, however, for it can keep the library from committing its continuing serial funding to the wrong titles.

Librarians need reviews and other qualitative, authoritative serial review devices similar to those available for books. They need evaluations of new titles done by subject specialists and included in the standard monograph review tools. Yet, reviewing a serial involves a risk that does not exist when reviewing a monograph. The reviewer can assess only what is in hand, and one never has in hand all of an active serial. Reviews of serials can be equated with reviews of monographs only after publication has ceased, and selectors need the review during the title's early years. The reviewer cannot predict from the first issue or even the first few volumes of a serial what future content will be. This uncertainty may be a factor in the exclusion of journals from book review media.

Serials Review, the first library-oriented journal devoted to reviews of serials, contains both evaluative reviews and articles in the field of serials management, with the editor aiming for half reviews and half articles. *New Magazine Review* is another source of serial reviews, one directed primarily toward the public library. Among the evaluative sources for serials are annotated guides based on *Ulrich's* and *Irregular Serials and Annuals*, respectively: Bill Katz's *Magazines for Libraries* and Joan Marshall's *Serials for Libraries*.

Choice contains a monthly column, "Periodicals for College Libraries," compiled by Richard Centing. Titles included are all recommended and must have been published for several years; newer journals are mentioned briefly and designated "worth consideration." Each issue of *Library Journal* contains a column edited and often written by Bill Katz, reviewing

Serials Review. v.1– . 1975– . Ann Arbor, Mich.: Pierian. Quarterly.
Best source for evaluative reviews of serials, new and old.
Subject review articles.
In-depth reviews of a single or a few related titles.
Signed reviews, most written by librarians.
The best source thus far for reviews of serials, this journal contains both subject review articles and in-depth reviews of one or a few related titles. A recent issue held over 150 reviews, plus evaluations of several cumulative indexes. All reviews are signed, and most are written by librarians. Serials reviewed are both established titles and new ones; little magazines and local interest periodicals are covered especially well. An index to titles reviewed appears in each issue. With vol. 10 (1984), the journal resumed publication of "Serials Review Index," listing reviews of serial publications from approximately 175 journals.

Katz, William A., and Linda Sternberg, eds. *Magazines for Libraries: For the General Reader, and School, Junior College, College, University, and Public Libraries.* 4th ed. New York: Bowker, 1982.
Classified arrangement.
Includes annotations for 6500 titles from *Ulrich's.*
Covers all types of journals, popular to research.
Magazines for Libraries, using a classified arrangement, annotates 6500 recommended titles from *Ulrich's.* Coverage ranges from popular to research journals, with appropriate audience noted. In addition to information found in *Ulrich's,* this source includes a journal's policy on refereeing, the extent of book review coverage, and advertising availability. It is revised every few years.

Marshall, Joan K., comp. *Serials for Libraries: An Annotated Guide to Continuations, Annuals, Yearbooks, Almanacs, Transactions, Proceedings, Directories, Services.* New York: Neal Schuman; Santa Barbara, Calif.: ABC-Clio, 1979.
Includes 2000 titles from *Irregular Serials and Annuals.*
Excludes monographic series.
List of special issues.
A companion volume to Katz, this work needs to be revised as often. Titles, all recommended and all annotated, are drawn from *Irregular Serials and Annuals* and presented in a subject arrangement. Monographic series are not included . A unique feature is a list of special issues published by journals. Another useful list is "When to Buy What." The guide gives appropriate audience for each entry.

new and fairly new periodicals. It is an excellent source for evaluating little magazines, but coverage of all types of new periodicals of interest to librarians is representative.

Most publishers and vendors issuing regular bulletins of serials information list only title and some bibliographic details. An exception to this practice is the British subscription agent, Stevens & Brown. The company's *Quarterly Serial Bulletin* lists several pages of new serials with descriptive annotations that often include the contents of the first issue. The reviews

Stevens & Brown Quarterly Serial Bulletin. Godalming, Surrey: Stevens & Brown. Quarterly.

Complete bibliographic data and description of new journals and series.

Notations of serials' changes and delays.

Compiled from publishers' information.

This free-of-charge vendor publication contains the usual information about serials changes and delays, but in addition it has a large section devoted to new journals and several pages describing new series. These features give complete bibliographic information, usually a listing of contents or topics to be covered in the first issue, and often some description of the journal's scope and purpose, as provided by the publisher. The most useful to the selector of this type of bulletin, because of its descriptions of many new serials. A title index cumulating annually would increase its value.

---

are not usually evaluative, but they give adequate information for ordering and several paragraphs of description. Data provided by the publisher are acknowledged.

Persons evaluating serial titles for library purchase can supplement any reviews located with other measures of worth. For example, coverage of a title in periodical indexes and abstract journals is an indication of both quality and ease of access. These reference works almost always contain a list of the titles consulted. It has been said, but not documented, that publishers of periodical indexes give misleading information about the titles included in an effort to enhance the appeal of the indexes. *Ulrich's* is another source of indexing information, but a recent study casts serious doubt upon the accuracy of this aspect of the guide's coverage.[3] Subscription agents' catalogs include indexing information in the listings, and the author suspects that this source may be more nearly accurate than *Ulrich's.*

Most criteria for serials selection are the same as for monograph selection, but they assume added importance because of the long-term commitment of an increasing amount of money. As with monographs, the needs of the library's users are a prime consideration. Also, the quality of the serial must be determined: is it well written, well produced, supported by a recognized editorial board? The reputation of the publisher is less significant than for a monograph, because many serials are self-published. Still, enough are produced by established companies (and this is an apparent trend in serials publishing) that one should consider the record of the publisher: are journals issued on schedule, have price increases been especially high, do issues fall apart with minimal use?

The library's environment is a strong factor in selecting serials. What resources are available elsewhere on campus, in town, or in the region?

3. Cynthia Swenck and Wendy Robinson, "A Comparison of the Guides to Abstracting and Indexing Services Provided by Katz, Chicorel, and Ulrich," *RQ* 17: 317–19 (1978); Diana Wyndham, "An Evaluation of References to Indexes and Abstracts in *Ulrich's* 17th Edition," *RQ* 20: 155–59 (1980).

Does the library belong to the Center for Research Libraries? Is there a local consortium that could be a source of titles marginally related to the collection? Is there a similar type of library nearby, and is that library willing to lend or photocopy? The number of libraries holding a serial, as determined from union lists and the bibliographic utilities, is an indication of the popularity or perceived value of a title. The discovery that a title is held by a nearby library, perhaps a resource-sharing partner, may be reason to refrain from placing a subscription or standing order.

Some criteria are more crucial to serial than to monograph selection; for example, the cost of the journal or series. If the title is unique and meets other selection criteria, it is probably worth the cost. One must consider for serials more than for monographs whether a title fits into the collection. A monograph that is not appropriate can often be discarded and chalked up to experience; cancellation of a continuing order can create havoc within the serial acquisitions unit if the timing is bad: a letter must be written, confirmation obtained, and possibly a refund requested; encumbered funds must be liquidated and reassigned; a record of the decision must be kept so that when an unexpected issue arrives or someone else requests the title, the whole story can be explained. Conversely, an inappropriate serial order not canceled is expensive in terms of payment, processing, and space.

A serial backfile purchase is a one-time transaction, similar to the acquisition of a monograph. Because of cost, selection criteria must be applied even more stringently to the selection of backfiles than to continuing orders. Serial volumes increase in price after publication, and the cost of as little as three prior years of a scientific journal often exceeds $1000. The selector needs to assess the lasting value of the serial's contents, in the context of resource sharing agreements, before placing a continuing order. If the information is ephemeral or will be generally available later, purchase of a backfile or retention of the title is not necessary. If the decision to retain or discard is not made at the time of subscription, the marginal title is likely to be routinely bound or the significant backfile never purchased.

PROJECTING AND MEASURING PATRON USE

For nearly all libraries, use or potential use of the collection determines its value. Three approaches to evaluating patron use of a serials collection are use studies, citation analysis, and core lists of serials. Many articles have described serials use studies by such means as circulation counts, colored dots, and questionnaires.[4] The key to a meaningful survey is a

4. For example, see Robert Goehlert, "Periodical Use in an Academic Library: A Study of Economists and Political Scientists," *Special Libraries* 69:51–60 (1978); W. M. Shaw, Jr., "A Practical Journal Usage Technique," *College and Research Libraries* 39: 479–84 (1978).

clear understanding of what constitutes use of a serial, but it is difficult to measure patrons' use of library serials even with a satisfactory definition of "use" and even when each item is delivered over a desk from a closed collection.

Serial citation analysis is a ranking based on the frequency with which journal articles are referred to in a specific group of titles. This technique gives the library direction in evaluating the collection, but it must be used with care, because several variables, most notably availability and access, must be accounted for. Two excellent survey essays about citation analysis appear in Stueart and Miller's *Collection Development in Libraries.*[5]

An RTSD committee, the Serials Section's ad hoc Committee to Study the Feasibility of Creating Dynamic Core Lists of Serials, has been at work since 1978. Lists already exist in several subjects, but the committee is charged with developing general criteria for the use of subject specialists in determining basic serials for undergraduate use in each major subject. Members have been wrestling with several questions concerning scope and criteria, and the committee still has not determined whether developing the lists is feasible. The concept of core lists is a good one; ideally they would be based on multiple criteria including use, citation analysis, cost, and number of subscriptions; keyed to different types of libraries according to mission and budget; compiled by librarian subject specialists; and updated often.

Acquiring Serials

Once the decision has been made to receive a serial on a continuing basis, a different set of considerations comes into play, with different problems and the need for additional sources of information. While this may be the point at which responsibility for the title passes from the selector, an understanding of the intricacies of serials acquisition facilitates communication and, therefore, receipt of the publication.

SEARCH AND VERIFICATION

The first phase of the acquisition process is searching the title against library records to ensure that a duplicate order is not being placed inadvertently. Even a subscription intended to be a duplicate is searched, because this search supplies ordering information such as source of existing order, latest price, and bibliographic information useful in cataloging.

5. Shirley A. Fitzgibbons, "Citation Analysis in the Social Sciences," in *Collection Development in Libraries*, ed. by Robert D. Stueart and George B. Miller, Jr. (Greenwich, Conn.: JAI Press, 1980), pp. 291–344; Kris Subramanyam, "Citation Studies in Science and Technology," in *Collection Development in Libraries*, pp. 345–72.

After searching, titles new to the library are verified in databases or printed sources accepted as standard: OCLC, RLIN, *New Serial Titles, Ulrich's,* and other, more specialized tools.

Much of the verification procedure for serial orders takes place today at the computer terminal. The CONSER database, online through OCLC, gives serials catalogers increasingly useful records. These records are the best place for most libraries to check the accuracy of bibliographic and publication data on serial orders, provided they understand that CONSER participants have put more effort into building the database than updating it. The number of catalogers able to change the database is limited; most libraries are not able to improve these records except on their own tapes and catalog cards, a source of great frustration to serials catalogers. Not all OCLC serial records are CONSER records, because any library that catalogs a title unique to the database enters that record. Local records are subject to the same obsolescence as CONSER contributions, but if the CONSER and non-CONSER records are used with care, and if questionable data are checked elsewhere (as in a subscription agent's catalog), OCLC, or one of the other bibliographic networks, is the best place to verify a new serial order.

Should the title requested not be in the database, or should the details not be sufficient for verification, some searchers can go to other online sources. If the library has access to DataLinx or EBSCONET, details can be checked against these databases. In some respects, these sources are better than the bibliographic utilities, because the subscription agent is more likely to list the latest price and publisher address than an OCLC record that may be several years old. However, vendors' databases do not carry the authority of files constructed by library catalogers. The Bowker Serials Bibliography database is probably midway between the bibliographic utilities and the subscription agents in authority. The printed sources derived from this file are respected, and the data are more nearly current online than in printed form.

For libraries without access to the above databases, very good manual sources remain—the pre-1981 *National Union Catalog* for Library of Congress cataloging or cataloging from a cooperating library; *New Serial Titles* or the *Union List of Serials; Ulrich's* or *Irregular Serials and Annuals*; and other lists of serials. Periodicals and other serials that have begun publication very recently will not have had time to appear in printed sources, so the procedure for verifying new titles may be abbreviated. Before abandoning the search, one may check the vendor publications discussed earlier.

Often the use of several verification sources turns up a conflict, such as two publisher addresses or two forms of the title. In this case, it is advisable to pursue the search to see if one address or title appears significantly

LINX. Westwood, Mass.: Faxon. Available online directly from the
publisher.
Contains Faxon's publisher and title information files.
InfoServe module displays new journals from several international
publishers.
Budgeting data available for three-year period.
This online serials system consists of several components. Those most useful
for selectors are DataLinx, Faxon's publisher and title information files, and
InfoServe, listings of all new titles and a forum for publishers to display their
journals to LINX users. Since LC call number is an access point, selectors can
access titles by subject. Financial data, by LC class, publisher, etc., is available
for a three-year period. The system includes an electronic mail function for
ordering, claiming, and communication with Faxon and other LINX users.

more often than the other and to use that one. If there are nearly equal
occurrences of each, consider the authority of the sources and choose.
Be sure to note the conflict and the sources, and use the alternative form
later if necessary.

At times during the verification process, one finds information that
changes the name under which the title is to be ordered. Whenever this
happens, it is necessary to research library records under the new entry.

SERIAL VENDORS

The decision to use a subscription agent or standing order vendor as an
intermediary in the purchase of serials, or to deal directly with the publisher, is one each library must make based on its own needs and priorities.
This decision may be a blanket policy governing all serial orders, or it
may be made for specified types of orders or for each order individually.
Size and scope of the serial collection are major factors in the decision.
The policy that the library follows needs to be continually evaluated as
computer technology and library budgets change and as vendors and their
promised services change.

Until recently, many American journal publishers gave subscription agents
discounts that were not available to libraries. The agents were able to pass
on savings to the library customer. Rising costs and serial publishing practices have reduced or eliminated agency discounts, and the vendor now
must add a service charge to the cost of publishers' prices in order to
cover expenses and make a profit. The service charge is usually a percentage
of the total list price of the periodicals, although some companies make
other arrangements for the highest priced titles. Agents compete not only
on the annual cost of subscriptions, but also on the service they give. The
largest agents are extensively automated and can give almost any infor-

mation or special handling the customer wants. How much of this service an agent will provide and how much will be done without additional cost depend largely on the company's willingness to please the customer.

The automated periodical fulfillment center is a relatively recent by-product of the computer age, selling a service to publishers of mass circulation magazines. The fulfillment center contracts with a number of publishers to perform a group of related processes—receiving, entering, and filling subscriptions. By means of the economies of scale, it can do the work at lower cost than the individual publishers. Titles falling into this category can be identified from the address on the contents page to which address changes are sent. Major fulfillment centers are located in Boulder, Colorado; Des Moines, Iowa; and Marion, Ohio. A subscription address in one of these cities, especially if it is a post office box, provides the clue.

Libraries are not important to fulfillment centers, because the companies deal with mass circulation titles. *Steinbeck Quarterly* does not come from a fulfillment center, but *US News* does. Even though nearly every library in the country receives at least one copy of *US News*, those subscriptions are a small percentage of the total. Thus, library claims and complaints have very little clout.

Library problems with fulfillment center titles concern duplicate or overlapping subscriptions, gaps in receipt, and unsatisfactory claim response. In the fulfillment center everything is keyed to the coded data appearing on the mailing label. Individuals can easily renew personal subscriptions, because a copy of the label accompanies the check. Unless libraries follow the same practice, they have problems. Subscription agencies are working hard to resolve the problems, but at the present time a library has more success by placing fulfillment center orders direct. For best results, monitor the mailing labels and use the computer-produced renewal notices several weeks before the expiration date shown on the label.

Finally, the subscription or standing order request sent to the vendor should identify clearly what title the library wants to receive, when the order is to begin, the shipping and invoicing address(es), the library's order number, and (as inconspicuously as possible) essential data for internal use, such as funding, routing, and searching history. This internal information can confuse the vendor, so separate it as clearly as possible from the bibliographic data and instructions to the agent or publisher. The best location for local use data is on the back of an order form or on a copy of the order that remains in the library.

This chapter is meant to guide, not to restrict. New sources of information will appear and will lead to new ways of selecting. As serials change, so do effective techniques.

Selection Sources

EBSCO Bulletin of Serials Changes. v.1– . Birmingham, Ala.: EBSCO Industries, 1975– . Bimonthly.

IMS Ayer Directory of Publications. v.1– . 1869– . Fort Washington, Pa.: IMS Press. Annually.

International Directory of Little Magazines and Small Presses. v.1– . 1965– . Paradise, Calif.: L. V. Fulton. Annually.

Irregular Serials and Annuals. v.1– . 1967– . New York: Bowker. Annually.

Katz, William A., and Linda Sternberg, eds. *Magazines for Libraries: For the General Reader, and School, Junior College, College, University, and Public Libraries.* 4th ed. New York: Bowker, 1982.

L'Annee Philologique. v.1– . 1924– . Paris: International Society of Classical Bibliography. Annually.

Marshall, Joan K., comp. *Serials for Libraries: An Annotated Guide to Continuations, Annuals, Yearbooks, Almanacs, Transactions, Proceedings, Directories, Services.* New York: Neal-Schuman; Santa Barbara, Calif.: ABC-Clio, 1979.

MLA Directory of Periodicals: A Guide to Journals and Series in Languages and Literatures. 1st– ed. 1978/79– . New York: Modern Language Assn. of America. Every 2 years.

MLA International Bibliography of Books and Articles on the Modern Languages and Literatures. 1st– ed. 1921– . New York: Modern Language Assn. of America, Annual.

Monthly Catalog of United States Government Publications. Washington, D. C.: Government Printing Office, 1895– . Monthly.

New Magazine Review. v.1– . Nov./Dec. 1978– . North Las Vegas, Nev.: New Magazine Review. Bimonthly.

New Serial Titles: A Union List of Serials Held by Libraries in the United States and Canada. Washington, D. C.: Library of Congress, 1953– . Monthly with quarterly and longer cumulations.

Nijhoff Serials. v.1– . 1979– . The Hague, The Netherlands: Martinus Nijhoff. Quarterly.

Serials Review. v.1– . 1975– . Ann Arbor, Mich.: Pierian. Quarterly.

Standard Periodical Directory. v.1– . 1963– . New York: Oxbridge. Biennially.

Stevens & Brown Quarterly Serial Bulletin. Godalming, Surrey: Stevens & Brown. Quarterly.

Swets Info. Lisse, The Netherlands: Swets Subscription Service. Quarterly.

Ulrich's International Periodicals Directory. v.1– . 1932– . New York: Bowker. Annually.

Ulrich's Quarterly. v.1– . Spring 1977– . New York: Bowker. Quarterly.

Union List of Serials in Libraries of the United States and Canada. 3rd ed. 5v. New York: Wilson, 1965.

Part 2

THE
HUMANITIES

Edited by
Marcia Pankake

ENGLISH AND AMERICAN LITERATURE, WITH NOTES ON SOME COMMONWEALTH LITERATURES

Susan J. Steinberg and Marcia Pankake

In selecting library materials in English and American literature, there is a mass of publishing first to identify, and then to winnow. Literature, literary studies, and fiction form a large component of American and English publishing. Preliminary figures for 1983 reveal 5433 new hardcover and trade paperback titles in language, literature, poetry, drama, and fiction published in America and 3721 new titles and reprints in those subjects published in Britain.[1] While their books are not recorded consistently in official tallies, small presses produce books and serials in quantity, too. Estimates place the number of small literary magazines in the United States at about 700 to 1100, and about 14,000 small publishers produce books.

Librarians in many large academic and public libraries succumb to the blandishments of ardent book dealers eager to supply the core of these materials on some version of an approval plan. They will be wise to succumb as promptly as possible, for the highly developed book trades of the United States, Great Britain, Canada, Australia, and New Zealand are well equipped to save library staff a great deal of largely mechanical effort. (See "Selection Sources and Strategies," pp. 1–24.) However, supplying current fiction and poetry calls for greater caution on the dealer's part than does almost any other subject, and evaluating it requires greater judgment by the selection officer.

Librarians in most large libraries will wish to acquire a substantial core of literary history and criticism, reference works, biographies, new editions of classics, and significant contemporary fiction, poetry, and drama. Although opinions will differ over definitions of these categories and the

The authors gratefully acknowledge the assistance of Robert Baley, Richard J. Kelly, Stephen Lehmann, Susanne Roberts, and Nancy Tufford.

1. The most commonly cited figures for currently published books are those prepared annually for *Publishers Weekly* and subsequently published in the *Bowker Annual*. See Chandler B. Grannis, "Book Title Output and Average Prices: 1983 Preliminary Figures," *Bowker Annual* 411–18 (1983).

works that fall within them, even sharper differences arise between libraries' policies on publications that fall outside them. Does the library intend to supply the recreational reading needs of its community? If so, should it include Harlequin Romances or should it stop short at what one librarian calls "light frothy fiction to take to the seashore"? Does the library intend to document current cultural history by buying bad novels of surpassing popularity? Does it regard such popular books as detective stories and science fiction as respectable genres, and how great a commitment to these does it wish to make? Does the library wish to maintain a comprehensive collection of poetry, and how hard is it willing to work to do so? How much current drama is needed?

The selector whose job it is to decide, book by book, what will be added to the library's collections must have firmly in mind his or her library's answers to these questions. He or she must also have a broad knowledge of English and/or American literature and a lively working knowledge of what is going on now, both in the subject and its intellectual background and in the publishing world that produces the books and periodicals.

Current Selection: Books

GENERAL SOURCES

A large number of sources exist to aid selection officers in English and American literature in evaluating what the approval plan supplies, in finding, evaluating, and acquiring what is beyond the plan's scope, or in identifying and evaluating titles for ordering in the absence of an approval plan.

The complete beginner may want to turn to the chapters "Literature" and "Prose Fiction" in Broadus's text, *Selecting Materials for Libraries*, to review general principles and broad statements about the functions of literature collections. James Thompson's *English Studies* contains a very short chapter on selection, and serves usefully in its listings of basic bibliographies, histories, and reference works to introduce the basic reference literature of the discipline.

Many of the most useful selection tools for English and American literature are sources that selectors in many fields employ. These general sources are valuable in literature as in other disciplines because of their currency, comprehensiveness, or reliability. Because most large libraries value promptness of receipt and cannot afford the luxury of waiting for reviews, one of the most useful sources is the publisher's flyer, which often arrives in advance of publication, and usually supplies full bibliographic detail and information about content. Only the passage of time and the accumulation of experience can enable selectors to judge the reliability of a particular publisher's information, and to develop that very valuable skill, the ability to see what has been left out. Publishers' catalogs, seasonal and annual, provide much the same information, although less punctually, but often are useful in giving a sense of a publisher's overall quality and output, or to monitor receipts on an approval plan.

Very small publishers often use the flyer or catalog as their only method to announce a book to the world. Some of the books publicized in this way may be vanity publications, ephemeral or superficial, but others may be valuable, if esoteric, scholarly contributions. Aspiring poets and novelists, more than writers in nonliterary disciplines, seem to promote their books by letters to libraries. The experienced selector readily can separate the chaff from the grain while reviewing the "junk" mail to find the specialized bibliography, the small collection of letters, or a local ethnic writer.

One may want to save flyers describing costly microform sets, because often they provide information that is to be found nowhere else.

The *Weekly Record (WR)*, the closest thing we have in this country to a national bibliography, is a timely, inclusive, and largely accurate listing of current English-language publishing in the United States. Its alphabetical arrangement makes it no joy to use for just one or two subjects, but it has extensive listings of current American fiction, literary scholarship, and criticism with occasional listings of some small press titles. It can be a useful tool for checking on an approval dealer's performance, especially if the dealer can be persuaded to supply a marked copy with selections indicated. Some librarians trade the speed of the *Weekly Record* for the ease of using the classified monthly cumulation, *American Book Publishing Record*.

The *Weekly Record* now lists numerous British imprints distributed by American publishers or booksellers, such as Augustine Martin's *W. B. Yeats*, published in Dublin by Gill and Macmillan in 1983 and distributed in the United States in 1984 by the Irish Book Center in New York. This expanded coverage may aid librarians who do not use British sources, and it may complicate use of *WR* for those who do. One must pay attention to dual imprints and distribution arrangements (and unfortunately not all are identified in the *WR* entries) and avoid selecting such titles if one also uses the *British National Bibliography*. This often is easier said than done, however; as a publisher like Oxford University Press issues books both in New York and London, and as other firms more and more publish or distribute books they do not originate, determining what is or is not an American book becomes an arcane and perhaps immaterial point.

Like the *Weekly Record*, the *British National Bibliography* (*BNB*) is fundamental for identifying new publications in all disciplines. For literature, its arrangement by Dewey classes is an advantage and requires less dogged determination to read than does *WR*. Its listings, full and accurate, include nontrade poetry, fiction, and serials in fair quantity. Its detailed subject classification eases the identification and selection of works in the English literatures of Canada, Australia, New Zealand, and some other countries as well. Although *BNB* does a good job of annotating works originally published in the United States, nearly simultaneous copublication is not so clearly noted and because of the numerous connections between U.S. and U.K. publishing houses, this can cause considerable duplicated searching effort if not duplicate purchases.

A selection librarian's best tool is an infallible memory, which very few have. Lacking that, a librarian needs system and discipline in using selection tools in order to avoid selecting the same title repeatedly. Unless one has unlimited clerical assistance and/or unlimited time on the computer terminal one must resist the impulse to select a good title every time the title appears. A few "rules" for operating help achieve efficiency, and the rule of national imprints according to national sources is a primary one. Select only American imprints from *WR* and only British from *BNB*. If patrons, such as a library committee or faculty members, select or recommend titles, instruct them to avoid a University of California imprint in the *BNB* or from other British sources.

Publishers Weekly (*PW*) and *Library Journal* (*LJ*) are each useful in different ways for American and English literature selection, as they are for many other disciplines, for both supply invaluable library and trade background as well as current reviews. Because it is the house organ of the American publishing trade, *PW*'s reviews are none too rigorous. Its main value lies instead in its information on particular publishers and editors, and publishing trends and problems. It annually publishes statistics on book production and prices and it frequently runs articles about specific publishers. Its "reviews" of new books, generally appearing in the "Forecasts" section about six weeks before the official publication date, more frequently run to descriptions or enthusiastic promotions rather than evaluations of books. The contents notes, however, make these reviews informative, with remarks like "virtually complete collection of newspaper pieces" or "poems she didn't want published during her lifetime," or a note that an excerpt will appear in a popular magazine. If selecting a title at this point, keep in mind that it will be listed again within two months in the *Weekly Record*.

The features in *Publishers Weekly* most useful for the literature selector are prompt news reports about literary awards and prizes and frequent interviews with writers. Both allow a librarian a second chance to pick up notable books that might have been overlooked or were omitted in accord with collecting policy. The writers' interviews provide persuasive introductions to some of the more popular contemporary writers. Quotations from the writer may give some flavor of his or her language, and the writer may speak explicitly about intentions and purposes. Usually the writer's important works are mentioned and so the interview can offer the occasion for a quick-and-dirty check of holdings.

Library Journal's reviews are also timely and are much more critical. It has recently introduced symbols indicating which of the books reviewed are of "outstanding quality, significance, or popular appeal," but these are for the most part books that larger libraries would acquire as a matter of course. *LJ*'s band of sharp-witted and sharp-tongued reviewers serve literature selectors well, particularly in each issue's dozen or so reviews of current fiction and poetry, although most of these are from mainstream publishers. Most distinctive is the survey of first novels, previously published once a year and now published twice yearly; some of the works reviewed the library may want to purchase to fulfill an obligation to encourage the production of new literature or to keep its collection vital, containing the newest writers.

Choice carries a relatively large number and percentage of reviews for the selector of English and American literature. In 1983/84 *Choice* published 638 reviews in "Language and Literature—General" (books on the novel or the theory of criticism, necessary to a collection serving scholars) and "Language and Literature—American and English." These amounted to twenty-five percent of their reviews in humanities, or ten percent of the 6296 books reviewed in total. Secure in its good reputation as a selection tool for academic libraries and for scholarly books, *Choice* has been the object of at least four published studies.[2]

A selector in a smaller collection or in one with patrons who do not demand their books before or as soon as they are published could do very well using *Choice* as a major selection tool, supplemented with *Library Journal* and/or the *New York Times Book Review* for fiction (*Choice* reviews poetry but not fiction.) Selectors would read also the sections in *Choice* for "Communication Arts" and "Reference" to find other pertinent reviews.

Choice aims to publish a review within six months of a book's publication, but because it does not review from galley proofs, some reviews appear relatively late compared to other sources. Selectors in large col-

2. Daniel Ream, "An Evaluation of Four Book Review Journals," *RQ* 19: 149–53 (Winter 1979); Beth Macleod, "*Library Journal* and *Choice*: A Review of Reviews," *Journal of Academic Librarianship* 7: 23–28 (Mar. 1981); Richard Hume Werking and Charles M. Getchell, Jr., "Using *Choice* as a Mechanism for Allocating Book Funds in an Academic Library," *College and Research Libraries* 42: 134–38 (Mar. 1981); John P. Schmitt and Stewart Saunders, "An Assessment of *Choice* as a Tool for Selection," *College and Research Libraries* 44: 375–80 (Sept. 1983).

lections who use many other sources may find *Choice* less important than selectors in smaller libraries. A large library will already have purchased many books by the time their reviews appear in *Choice*, as they will have come on the approval plan or the selector will have chosen them from the *Weekly Record* and/or the *BNB*. Such selectors may use *Choice* for imprints less likely to have been identified by other sources, such as publications of research institutions, or European English-language imprints with American distributors, or for works like poetry, for which reviews are more necessary. Librarians who delegate selection to faculty members may prefer to subscribe to *Choice* reviews on cards.

the *New York Times Book Review*, appearing weekly, reviews several dozen books of all sorts and subjects. The reviews are short essays, often by some of the country's best writers and most astute critics. A fiction or poetry review in the *Times Book Review*, even an unfavorable one, creates a presumption in favor of purchase by many large libraries. It would be possible, however, to spend $100 to $200 a week just buying titles reviewed in the *NYTBR*, and so even here a librarian needs to be selective. The *New York Times Book Review* can also serve as a useful spot check of an approval plan's efficiency.

The *New York Review of Books* is almost useless as a selection tool. Its long essay reviews often relate only tenuously to the books under review, and commonly appear long after a book's initial release. Often the critics seem to regard the books reviewed as a sadly necessary springboard for the essays they intended all along to write. On the other hand, the *New York Review of Books* is widely read and influential in literary and cultural circles, and can be a superb source of background information on intellectual trends for those with the fortitude to read those great long articles.

The basic source for the reviews that *BNB* cannot supply is the grand old lady of the English literary scene, the *Times Literary Supplement*. The *TLS* publishes weekly some of the most intelligent criticism to be found anywhere, and does so in timely fashion and graceful prose. Though the books reviewed run the gamut of subjects, each issue includes some two dozen reviews of current fiction, poetry, and literary scholarship, including notices of some small press publications. Most of the fiction and poetry and nearly all of the literary scholarship reviewed in *TLS* would be wanted in most large literature collections. *TLS* is the fastest source for reviews of current English fiction, and probably the most authoritative for thoughtful criticism of major new editions, such as the Cambridge Shakespeare.

The Bookseller: The Organ of the Book Trade, published weekly, is a British equivalent of *Publishers Weekly*. Although it lacks reviews it does supply useful information on British publishing and book selling, and its giant spring and fall issues give early notice of forthcoming books that

Times Literary Supplement. v.1– . 1902– . London: Times Newspapers Ltd.
  Weekly.
  Literate newspaper supplement.
  About 50 reviews per issue. Books on all subjects. Usually 10 to 12 or
    more reviews pertinent to English and American literature.
  Current.
  Can quickly locate reviews grouped together on pages headed "Fiction,"
    "Poetry," "Literature and Criticism," "Biography," and "Drama." Index
    by author or editor of book reviewed on second-to-last page.
  Read the letters for current literary disagreements and controversy.
  TLS is the best source for reviews of current British literature and for current
  scholarly criticism.

can be a useful check on an approval plan's efficiency. The *London Review
of Books* resembles its New York namesake in format, intent, and use,
although perhaps not yet in influence. The monthly *British Book News*,
culling from the large mass, is excellent for the smaller selective general
collection or for the library where one or two people do most of the
selection.

Using Library of Congress cards (the former "LC proof slips," now
called the "LC CDS Alert Service cards") is a profitable investment of time
for selectors in large collections or those building collections comprehensively for some figures or topics. Such selectors probably will ignore
cards for American trade imprints, especially those with CIP (Cataloging-
in-Publication) copy that appear here one to fourteen or more months in
advance of publication. Selectors who do use LC cards for selection look
for foreign imprints, and there are considerable from France, Germany,
Italy, Russia, China, and other countries; for obscure private publishers,
especially for works of a regional interest; and for publications from academic departments of universities, libraries, and other institutions. LC
cards are a somewhat haphazard way to identify titles, for they reflect
works that happen to have been added to the largest library in America.
Sometimes the information provided by the LC cataloging staff aids in a
selection decision, however; for example, the reliable series notations. Or,
as another example, a volume by Gwendolyn Brooks called *Hymn to
Chicago* might be sought as an acquisition until one sees the LC card,
which notes it is only seven pages, with alternate pages blank. The accurate
description of this volume then may lower its priority for purchase in
many libraries.

Although not strictly a source for current selection, sale catalogs from
publishers and dealers float between current and retrospective selection.
They are less useful for retrospective work than for current selection
because they are transitory. They arrive like a current source, and they

must be handled quickly. Flooded with sale catalogs, librarians learn by experience which bear valuables and which are flotsam. New selectors may want to dip cautiously into sale catalogs, for the catalog an individual purchaser may endorse might not be one an institution can use profitably. Select, verify, and order a few titles to discover whether the stock is so small that orders cannot be filled, or whether the stock duplicates the remainder table at the local bookstore. Before working the catalog notice if it displays an expiration date. The librarian will prefer a catalog listing books in literature in one discrete section, with publisher and date of publication identified. Librarians with online processing systems are freed from the necessity of an alphabetical listing, which few sale catalogs employ.

Since the Thor Power Tool decision encouraged faster reduction of publishers' inventories, scholarly publishers have begun to use sale catalogs frequently. These offer good bargains, and in many cases merit checking almost as current selection sources because they list scholarly books two to three years after publication, just about the time they receive good notices in scholarly journals or are cited in best books lists or in cumulative "round-up" reviews. It is about this time also that the books begin to receive more sustained use in the library collection and the librarian can determine the need for added copies. Individual university presses publish sale catalogs, and at present two good catalogs that combine titles from many university presses are *Daedalus Books* and *The Scholar's Bookshelf.*

Librarians in small collections will want to check the monthly list of new titles analyzed in *Essay and General Literature Index,* sent to subscribers by the publisher, H. W. Wilson. (In larger collections most or all of these titles will have been selected from other sources.)

Finally, the selector benefits, of course, from patronizing or at least visiting bookstores of many kinds. It may be expedient to pick up replacement copies of standard editions of old works cheaply, but more importantly, the selector can see new editions—to judge the physical characteristics of that first volume in the Library of America series before it is widely reviewed, or to judge the suitability for recreational reading of the new one-volume Chatham River Press editions of classic works.

SPECIALIZED SOURCES

The sources discussed so far serve selectors in many disciplines, and these sources alone may be sufficient for smaller collections. Specialized book dealers and journals of the separate scholarly disciplines supplement the more general tools and are necessary adjuncts for selectors in larger collections or in collections with specialized emphases. If an approval plan and some or all of the selection and review media already mentioned are used, more specialized sources can be employed to identify and evaluate lesser known titles. If the approval plan and more general selection mechanisms are functioning properly, only a small percentage of desired materials need be sought through specialized media.

First and foremost, selection officers should regularly read, or at least sample, the literary journals the library currently receives. It is the best way to know who the featured writers are and what kind of work they do, what critical schools are ascendant and who their leading exponents are, and to get some feeling for "what is in the air." No one has time to look at all or most of the hundreds of scholarly and literary journals published in English and American literature. The following are a few distinctively useful for librarians.

The *American Poetry Review* features poems and interviews with poets. Although it is not a selection source, it is the sort of reading bibliographers need to do on a regular, if selective, basis. The interviews, selections from works in progress, advertisements for special issues of literary magazines and for small presses contribute to educating the bibliographer. *American Literature*, published with the participation of the American literature section of the premier scholarly association, the Modern Language Association, illustrates another type of source. A specialized scholarly journal, it includes book reviews, most published too late to serve in selection, a more useful section of brief mentions, and current bibliography. Its utility for bibliographers lies in its scholarly articles; scanning their titles and skimming some, once or twice a year, will keep one up-to-date on academic considerations and allow, for example, the academic librarian who dismissed Richard Brautigan in the 1970s as a mere scribbler to reconsider purchasing his works upon seeing a scholarly article on *Trout Fishing in America*.

Specialized publications focusing on particular regions of the country exist as well as those on country, period, or genre, ranging from a *New York Review of Books*-style of newsprint formats for a number of cities and areas, to other scholarly journals like the *Mississippi Quarterly* and *Western American Literature*. *Mississippi Quarterly* publishes, in addition to articles and reviews, an annual checklist of scholarship on southern writing that, though lacking reviews and heavily dominated by periodical citations, is valuable as a test of a library's collections in this important aspect of American literature. *Western American Literature* is a quarterly with useful review articles that include discussions of some small press publications, although standard trade and academic presses predominate. It also publishes the "Annual Bibliography of Studies in Western American Literature." Libraries with strong regional literary interests and collections need to pay particular attention to such specialized journals, which no general discussion such as this can begin to cover in detail.

To give some special attention to Afro-American, American Indian, and other minority American literatures, look at the quarterly *MELUS News-notes*. Published by the Society for the Study of Multi-Ethnic Literature as a supplement to *MELUS*, it provides notices about forthcoming publications, especially anthologies of creative writing and materials helpful to the classroom teacher.

If the selector's responsibility for literature extends to language and writing, it will be worthwhile to receive *Simply Stated*, a free monthly newsletter dedicated to the cause of clear writing. It carries news of events (lawsuits, college courses) and notices of unusual publications about specialized kinds of writing.

The *Literary Research Newsletter* publishes information about research and publications in progress (for both English and American literature), and is especially useful on the occasions that it deals with topics that are hard to get at, like computerized or computer-assisted works. Its reviews, like those in other scholarly journals, are too late (the winter 1983 issue reviewed thirteen titles with publication dates ranging from 1978 to 1982) to serve for primary identification, but are informative because they group together related resources for research, like bibliographies on one writer. These critical and comparative reviews are especially helpful to the librarian who does reference or bibliographic instruction in literature.

For selecting current English fiction, the *Year's Work in English Studies* provides in the summer issue an annual review with critical comments on important editions and works of English literature and fiction of the previous year. Likewise, the last two issues of each year's *English Studies* review new writing (the novel, the short story, drama, and poetry), both English and American, and secondary works. The treatment of new editions can be especially informative. This may serve as a selection source to substitute for *TLS* for librarians in smaller institutions buying for the collection rather than for immediate demand.

Also, do not overlook the possibilities offered by general periodicals. One can use almost any publication as a back-up, and the *New Republic* is one of the best examples of a general periodical useful in selection. Although it is not principally a book review magazine, it is perhaps the third or fourth largest general magazine in the United States in numbers of reviews published. It publishes about 500 reviews a year, including reviews of two or three works of fiction weekly and many first novels. Its reviewers are good established writers and critics, people like Anne Tyler, Irving Howe, and Paul Fussell, who often persuade the librarian that a title passed over recently in the *Weekly Record* really merits purchase.

Finally, selectors seeking comprehensively for specialized or esoteric topics may consider using selectively portions of the annual *MLA International Bibliography*. A source of last resort, it has a time lag of at least fifteen months, is literally voluminous, and the format changes in 1981 and 1982 made it difficult to work with for selection. Its location in reference collections in libraries also may impede the selector. However, by choosing sections carefully, especially from the "General Literature and Related Topics" volume, one can deepen one's selection from the works identified here. Most citations can be quickly skipped over as they are for periodical articles or for books one would have identified from the ordinary selection sources of the year. The valuable distinctive titles found here are festschriften, conference proceedings, foreign imprints, publications emanating from academic departments of universities, and collections whose titles would have classed them in other sources in some other discipline or sphere of responsibility such as history, psychology, classics, or other fields.

SMALL PRESSES

Publications of small presses (also known as independent or alternative presses or publishers) are a particular challenge both to identify and to evaluate. (See "Small Presses," pages 335–48, for a broader discussion.) Most of these publications are not listed in the general sources, and few make it into the specialized sources, so the librarian who wants to know of their existence or wants to add some to the collection of creative writing must use extraordinary sources and means. Some of the sources discussed below cover both books and serials.

The most affluent periods of government support for the arts in the 1960s and 1970s produced a flood of little magazines and small press literature, but even in today's more straitened circumstance the quantity is huge. Because of the elusiveness of this type of publication and the short life expectancy of little magazines, tools for rapid identification and evaluation are especially important. Fortunately, a number of very useful reference works and periodicals exist to help selection officers get some grip on this mass. Dustbooks of California publishes several of these—the *International Directory of Little Magazines and Small Presses*, the *Small Press Record of Books in Print*, and the *Small Press Review*. The *International Directory* seems intended more for writers than librarians, but the information provided—including types of writing sought, authors recently published, and any special ideological slant—can be useful to both. Although American listings predominate, there is substantial coverage of British, Canadian, Australian, and New Zealand small presses as well. The reviews the *International Directory* lacks are supplied monthly by the *Small Press Review*, which publishes some fifteen to twenty reviews in each issue, along with brief listings of from 75 to 100 books and little magazines. Its reviews are crucial for any library trying to build a collection of experimental fiction and poetry.

Small Press Review. v.1– . 1966– . Paradise, Calif.: Dustbooks. Monthly.
Eclectic independent magazine of and for small press publishing.
15 to 20 reviews in each issue, usually more serials than books. Brief
listings of scores more.
Brings attention to currently available materials, some of which are long-
established serials.
Indispensable source of information on new and continuing little
magazines.
News of events, competitions.
Questions and answers about independent publishing.
Editorials, letters, advertisements.
Although not directed principally to librarians, they are almost professionally
obligated to read this review for the healthy contrast it offers to the institutional
point of view libraries engender.

The *Review of Contemporary Fiction* offers twice a year, among critical
and other articles, reviews of new fiction, some of which is from small
presses. A librarian seeking only a small sampling of new fiction might
rely upon this source.

Reviewing "current books of literary interest," mostly fiction and poetry,
the demanding *American Book Review* covers more trade and university
than small press titles, but those it includes are valuable. Its reviewers are
often writers themselves, like Diane Wakoski, or academics, and it is not
to be consumed hastily.

An additional or substitute source is the handy dealer's catalog for new
small press poetry and fiction, *Writers and Books.* This nonprofit endeavor,
which began in 1973 as the Bookbus Project and is supported by the
National Endowment for the Arts and the New York State Council on
the Arts, distributes books from American and foreign independent publishers. The 1983 annual catalog listed books of 290 publishers, and the
list of publishers in the back engenders the confidence that selections from
here need not be duplicated from individual publishers' catalogs. The
important facts of date of publication and publisher noted for each title
make this catalog more useful than many. Arranged by genre, including
a section of the newer "image" books of collages, photographs, photocopies, and other media, a brief annotation and a note on the number of
pages, important especially for poetry, accompanies each title.

Current Selection: Serials

Selecting periodicals in any subject is risky because increases in serial costs
have been so dramatic in recent years and they can easily and unobtrusively
come to dominate the acquisitions budget, as Marcia Tuttle suggests (pp.

34-48). Selecting serials in English and American literature is demanding because the serial literature is both old and voluminous, yet it is important because it plays a central role in literary scholarship. Another reason serials selection in literature is a demanding task is because there is a great variety and quantity of publication, especially of "little" magazines and of literary journals produced by and for a particular college's students or faculty but with some national pretensions. Of literary magazines alone, Brownson estimates 4000 have been published since 1900 and about 700 currently exist.[3] Yet these complications cannot cause a librarian responsible for the literature collection to shy away from serials. Scholars of literature depend more heavily on books than do scholars in other disciplines, but their use of serial literature is important and distinctive. Heinzkill found that twenty percent of literary scholars' citations were to serials, and this twenty percent of their research literature is comprised of a larger number and variety of journals than is the serial literature used by scholars in other disciplines.[4] Literature has a less well-defined core of serials; this breadth can require considerable work from the librarian to keep the scope and contents of the serial collection suitable to the patrons' needs.

However good the announcing and reviewing media are for serials, there is no substitute for seeing an actual sample issue to answer the crowd of questions necessary before subscribing. Are the editors prominent in the field? Who are the contributors? Are they well-known, up-and-coming, deservedly unknown? Does the journal publish poetry and fiction only, or essays, reviews, experimental art? Is there heavy reliance on that weak reed of the struggling literary magazine, the interview with a famous writer? And, a basic but important consideration, is the writing of lasting significance? Without a copy in hand, a selector's answers to these questions can only be partial and secondhand.

For identifying literary periodicals to seek as samples, *New Serials Titles* functions rather as a serial equivalent of *PW*, although its listings are a great deal less timely. *NST* is published monthly by the Library of Congress and, as might be expected, its bibliographic information is superb, and its indication of holdings in LC and other North American libraries very useful. It has no review information, however, and—as happens all too frequently—its more convenient version, arranged by Dewey decimal subject classifications, has been discontinued.

Serials Review is a useful and pleasantly apposite adjunct to *NST*, for it presents informative reviews of periodicals of all sorts. Of particular interest for American literature selectors is the regular feature "Reviews and Recommendations: Little Magazines," with long but sharply focused

---

3. Charles W. Brownson, "Access to Little Magazines," *RQ* 22: 375-87 (Summer 1983).
4. Richard Heinzkill, "Characteristics of References in Selected Scholarly English Literary Journals," *Library Quarterly* 50: 352-65 (July 1980).

Serials Review. v.1–. 1975– . Ann Arbor, Mich.: Perian. Quarterly.
Professional journal.
4 to 6 review articles on types or groups of serials in each issue. Helpfully
covers many serials in one subject.
Index by title of serials reviewed and by author of books on serials
reviewed on the last page of each issue. Unfortunately, excludes titles of
serials covered in comprehensive survey reviews.
Articles for librarians on serials and serials management.
"Little Magazines" feature by Cristine C. Rom reviews 6 or more literary
magazines in each issue.
"Serials Review Index" indexes reviews of serials in 175 journals.
It is worth looking at every issue of this review as it arrives, both for articles
on serials management and for reviews or studies of individual serial titles. One
seldom can anticipate exactly what will appear here, but it is always useful
information.

---

articles on both new and long-established serials. The article on "Michigan
Little Magazines" in the summer 1983 issue is a good example, with listings
for twenty Michigan titles, eight of them reviewed at length, the rest more
briefly—all of them relatively unusual serials and otherwise difficult to
identify. You cannot go far wrong with a review journal whose assessment
of one "little mag" was: "Here is an utterly unpredictable magazine. One
can never be certain when or if it will appear, what will be in it, and
whether or not it will be legible." Another very helpful feature in *Serials
Review* is the "Serials Review Index" to reviews of serials in other journals,
useful in finding opinions in considering retaining or beginning a new
subscription to an established periodical.

Robert Peters' judgments of twenty-seven established American literary
magazines (in his *Black and Blue Guide to Current Literary Journals*) may
help librarians evaluate or add to their holdings of this genre. Katz's *Magazines for Libraries*, although much broader, likewise provides annotations of established journals. Basic directory information is in the *MLA
Directory of Periodicals*.

The specialist will want to read the regular "Journal Notes" column in
the scholarly *PMLA* for announcements of new journals preceding their
inaugural issues, and also for notices of special issues of journals, particularly those with bibliographic surveys that can be useful as selection
sources or as collection evaluation aids.

One interesting but problematic genre is that of author newsletters and
journals. Margaret Patterson's *Author Newsletters and Journals: An International Annotated Bibliography of Serial Publications Concerned with
the Life and Works of Individual Authors*, updated twice in *Serials Review*, is a fine source of information. Although English and French writers
have prompted most of these author-specific journals, a healthy number

deal with American authors. The listings give bibliographic and ordering information and brief descriptions of content—for example, whether reviews, bibliographies, abstracts, or notices of upcoming meetings and events are emphasized. Although a special collecting emphasis might require a library to subscribe, for instance, to all of the twenty-eight periodicals devoted to Arthur Conan Doyle/Sherlock Holmes, many libraries will wish to distinguish between those publishing substantial reports of research and those specializing in upcoming lunches and conference schedules.

In addition to the several sources mentioned earlier that identify little magazines and small press publishing, several indexes to English-language little magazines may also be of use, although not primarily intended as selection tools. Marion Sader's *Comprehensive Index to English-Language Little Magazines, 1890–1970* (series 1 in eight volumes; a second series said to be in preparation) is useful in identifying core titles. Stephen Goode's *Index to Commonwealth Little Magazines* is especially useful because most of the titles indexed, originating in England, Ireland, Scotland, Australia, and other Commonwealth nations (excepting Canada), are indexed nowhere else.

Librarians with smaller or very selective serials collections may be content using the monthly serials review columns in *Choice* and *Library Journal*. Both are very selective, with *Choice* listing or reviewing about ten percent of what it receives. Because of its academic orientation, the columns in *Choice* will be more productive for the literature selector than those in *LJ*, but both regularly review literary magazines and scholarly journals in literature.

Irish, Scots, and Welsh literatures in English and Commonwealth literatures are published in books and serials in America and England, and so of course can be identified and evaluated by many of the sources specified above. For the large or specialized collection, however, a selector may want to seek national imprints and more works. Books and serials are treated together in this section, as there are fewer of them and no sources are specialized by format.

The *BNB* and *TLS* cover Welsh publications and Welsh literature in Welsh and in English. They both also cover some Scots and some Irish publications. The *Irish Literary Supplement*, a new biennial review, presents Irish imprints but for the librarian these are diluted with American publications also. *Irish University Review*, a scholarly interdisciplinary journal, has numerous reviews, mostly on literature. *Books Ireland* is more general, covering all subjects with reviews in English and Irish. Its "Books Received" column includes imprints from Ireland, England, and America. The column "Periodicals Received" may be its most useful feature, for it notices both new journals of Irish creative writing and special issues of established journals. *Etudes Irlandaises* provides an annual review in "The Year's Work in Anglo-Irish Literature," and the *Year's Work in Modern Language Studies* offers an annual survey of publications on language. The *Annual Bibliography of Scottish Literature* lists secondary literature only.

Commonwealth Literatures

In some libraries the librarian responsible for English and American literature also selects Commonwealth literature. In other libraries the literature in English outside of Britain and the United States may be selected by those with broad responsibilities for Africa, India, the South Pacific, the West Indies, or Canada. In the former case, when libraries do not give great emphasis to publications of these countries, librarians may not feel the need to give any special attention to Commonwealth literature per se, for works by and about the best known writers, such as V. S. Naipal or Derek Walcott of the West Indies, Chinua Achebe or Wole Soyinka of Africa, R. K. Narayan (India), Katherine Mansfield (New Zealand), Patrick White (Australia), or Margaret Atwood (Canada), are published by English and/or American publishers, and thus the selector finds their works through the ordinary bibliographic means of the national and trade bibliographies and reviews.

CANADIAN LITERATURE IN ENGLISH

The most careful selector will not rest complacent about the coverage *BNB* and *WR* provide, however. Relying exclusively on the *BNB* for a half dozen years will cause the collection of Australian and New Zealand authors to increase at twice the pace of the collection of Canadian authors. Careful selectors may take one of two alternate courses. They may regularly and continuously use supplementary current sources, or they may perodically review a number of specialized sources to select works in batches.

Librarians who give Canada special attention can do so either by an approval plan for Canadian literature with John Coutts, the vendor specializing in Canadian imprints, or by using the national bibliography, book trade bibliography, and reviewing sources.

In Part 1 Patti McClung describes general comprehensive sources for Canadian imprints. A selector for literature may use *Canadiana*, which offers the advantage of Dewey classification and the inclusion of sound recordings, should the selector be responsible also for recordings of literature. It gives good coverage to the remarkably active small press sector in Canada. Its main fault is the long gap between publication and listing in *Canadiana*, this time lag reduces its value as a current selection source if timeliness is important. Because different libraries have different values and standards, timeliness is a relative and subjective value, and currency within a year in *Canadiana* may be perfectly acceptable.

The selector may use instead, depending upon the scope of the library collection and the necessity for faster acquisitions, either *Quill and Quire* or *Books in Canada*. Published monthly, *Quill and Quire* reviews books in all subjects but every issue has (usually several long) reviews in literature. A separate insert, *Forthcoming Books*, identifies, alphabetically within broad Dewey classes, newly published books of the month from information provided by the National Library. Read *Quill and Quire* rather than *Canadiana* if you enjoy seeing the ads and the book trade news, but remember that you will see few if any nontrade publications there.

Books in Canada, published ten times a year, is both useful and a pleasure to read. It provides thought-provoking articles on publishing in Canada, but is mainly concerned with authors and the books they write. Each issue has essay reviews of several dozen current books, in all subjects but usually including literary scholarship and current literature. An especially valuable department is the "First Novels" feature. Libraries building strong Canadian literature collections would probably wish to acquire all the books reviewed in *Books in Canada*, with the possible exception of the popular culture series books occasionally included.

An additional specialized source exists, however, that is valuable both for the librarian building a comprehensive collection or the librarian seeking only a small representation of Canadian imprints. The Association of Canadian Publishers annually issues the *Literary Press Group Catalogue*. The 1983 volume lists 1000 titles from thirty-two literary publishers. A description of each publisher augments the annotations of individual books (some annotations leave something to be desired, but others quote from serious reviews) that give enough information to allow a selection decision. Because the catalog lists books available, rather than just one year's imprints, it is especially useful for librarians who want work in batches to build up the contemporary drama or poetry collection or to spend some extra money on fiction. The list of bookstores who will supply by mail is an extra bonus.

Finally, the *Journal of Commonwealth Literature* offers for Canada, as it does for other countries, an annual bibliography useful to selectors in both large and small collections. The librarian in the latter may wait to select once each year from the *Literary Press Group Catalogue* and the *JCL* annual bibliography, choosing a few works from the bibliographies and criticism identified in the latter to augment the selections made from the American and English book trades.

Literary Press Group Catalogue. v.1- . 1975- . Toronto: Assn. of Canadian
   Publishers. Annually.
   Combined publishers' catalog.
   1983 volume lists 1000 books from 32 publishers of literature and works
      about literature.
   Both books of the current year and older titles still in print.
   Arranged by genre.
   Indexed by authors and titles.
   Descriptions of publishers.
   Annotations or quotes from reviews for every title.
   Addresses of bookstores selling by mail.
One can use this as a primary source in Canadian literature or as a back-up,
looking for publishers one does not ordinarily see.

Journal of Commonwealth Literature. v.1- . 1965- . Oxford: Hans Zell.
   Semiannually.
   Scholarly journal.
   6 to 12 articles including surveys of national literatures and genres,
      checklists, and bibliographies.
   Roughly two years behind, like any scholarly journal.
   Only an occasional review.
   Annual bibliography of Commonwealth literature published as the second
      issue of each year. Divided by country—General Commonwealth; Africa:
      East and Central; Africa: Western; Australia and Papua New Guinea;
      Canada; India; Malaysia and Singapore; New Zealand and South Pacific
      Islands; Sri Lanka; Pakistan; South Africa. Coverage changes slightly
      from time to time. Bibliographies are prefaced by review articles on the
      notable accomplishments or changes of the year (1982, South Africa:
      "But what marks the year most sharply is the closing of ranks by black
      writers to their white colleagues . . ." p. 153).
   Bibliographies separate drama, poetry, anthologies, criticism. Includes both
      books and articles. Includes many national imprints.
If one wants to limit supplementary sources in Commonwealth literature to one
source, let it be this one.

AUSTRALIAN LITERATURE

Relatively easy additional coverage for Australia for the collection of
modest aims can be attained by the *BNB* supplemented by the slips sent
out biweekly by the Australian book dealer James Bennett. One can request Bennett's "New Publications Information" slips, printed six to a
page on perforated sheets, by topic: Australian literature, poetry, literary
criticism, omitting other disciplines. In addition to finding out about new
books, the selector may be amused, for the terse descriptions sometimes
are unintentionally very funny. Another cautionary note: dual imprints are
seldom identified. Alternatively, depending on how comprehensive one
aims to be, one may use the semimonthly or the monthly subject cumulation of the *Australian National Bibliography*. This source lists a high

percentage of books few American libraries would want, such as text-books, dual imprints, and joke anthologies. Sticking with discipline to the special classification number A820 gives a better return on one's investment of time.

James Bennett also will send the annual *Australian Book Scene*, promoting the current book trade, full of advertisements for new books, seasoned with descriptions of the Literature Board, the Australian Society of Authors, descriptions of publishing houses, and a singularly helpful list of currently published literary journals. The latter is the best aid for the Australian literature serials collection.

Australian Literary Studies publishes in each May issue an annual review bibliography of primary and secondary works, and the *Journal of Commonwealth Literature* gives attention to creative writing.

AFRICAN

Internationally known established African writers, like other Commonwealth writers, are published in New York and London, and so the librarian selecting from the *Weekly Record* and the *British National Bibliography*, or from an approval plan based on or tied to those sources, will routinely discover their works. For more extensive selection, use the convenient *African Book Publishing Record*, a quarterly compilation of bibliographic citations, book reviews, publishing trade news, and articles. New books (and serials) in English, French, and African languages are listed both by subject and by country. The reviews, thirty to forty in each issue, are helpful for fiction by less well-known writers.

Both *Research in African Literatures (RAL)* and *WLWE: World Literature Written in English* also offer reviews of African literature, in the latter grouped by country. Like other scholarly journals, the reviews published are late; the fall 1984 issue of *RAL* reviewed 1981 and 1982 imprints. *RAL* offers more reviews, eight to two dozen per issue, and seems deliberately to seek out African imprints along with Canadian, German, and other imprints. Because *WLWE* appears only twice a year, it may be sufficient to look at it only once every twelve or eighteen months as a supplementary source. Both *WLWE* and *RAL* publish occasional bibliographical articles and useful surveys. *Africana Journal*, sometimes considered as supplementing Zell's guide to African literature, does not serve particularly well in selection because its scope is far broader than literature, but it does have occasional useful articles and bibliographies. The *Journal of Commonwealth Literature* is the most helpful of all for its annual bibliographic surveys and the occasional articles surveying the literature produced by one country.

Finally, although concerned mostly with social sciences, the *Africana Libraries Newsletter* carries notes about bibliographical works in progress and news about publications and library acquisitions of African publications. Librarians greatly interested in these more general topics or in social sciences can get on the mailing list, at this writing still free, from the University of Illinois.

If India, the West Indies, New Zealand, Malaysia, and other areas of the Commonwealth are important enough to require national imprints, the library's needs probably are sufficiently sophisticated to have one or more area specialists familiar with the national book trades, the national bibliographies, and suppliers. One may want to be cautious about blanket orders, which can be established through the Caribbean Imprint Library Services and the African Imprint Library Sources, because of the wide variation in the quality of fiction published in some of these countries.

For selection less deep in all of Commonwealth literature, one can do nicely with the handy *Journal of Commonwealth Literature*, for if buying only for a well-rounded collection rather than for demand, the time lag in identifying works by this journal should not inconvenience readers.[5]

Warwick's *Commonwealth Literature Periodicals*, a union list, cites serials by country, helpful in identifying titles.

Retrospective Selection

ENGLISH AND AMERICAN

If the nature of retrospective selection in literature varies considerably from that in other disciplines, it is because most libraries already possess established deep and broad literature collections. Publishing in literature is as old as publishing itself, and reading, collecting, and studying literature have occupied people's attention for centuries. Yet library collections, especially older ones, must be maintained and renewed, and old books sought for and newer ones deliberately passed over added later. Literary scholars use old books—they use them more, perhaps, than scholars in any other discipline. Stern's study of the characteristics of literary scholarship revealed that eighty-three percent of the citations in research about writers were to books, and that older books were a substantial part of these research materials. Scholarship on Milton leaned heavily on pre-1900 materials—forty-four percent; on Henry James, fifty-five percent of

5. A fuller discussion of British and Commonwealth sources, along with extended consideration of many topics referred to here, probably will appear in the lengthier treatment afforded in the volume tentatively titled "Selection Tools and Procedures for English and American Literature Bibliographers" in preparation under the auspices of the ACRL English and American Literature discussion group, directed by Scott Stebelman and William McPheron.

the works cited were twenty years old or more.[6] The use of older books distinguishes scholarship in literature.

Such data may lead librarians to think "If you've got it, keep it," but what if you don't have it, or even know what it is?

To write briefly of retrospective collection development may be misleading or deceptive. Every retrospective project varies and any retrospective work may require the librarian to use a tremendous range of general and specialized reference works, books, and articles to identify, evaluate, and acquire a particular book or serial or a group of materials. (See Schenck's essay, pages 25–33, for a discussion of the acquisition of out-of-print books and the use of dealers' catalogs.) Selectors in English and American literature will always use basic general tools like the *British Library Catalogue* and the *National Union Catalog Pre-56 Imprints* to ascertain the existence of specific books, but they also will use two orders of aids more specific to literature: the standard comprehensive literary reference works and the specialized guides and bibliographies in literature. The most commonly useful of the latter category are suggested below; many others exist and will be needed in particular projects.

A librarian may often seek out-of-print books, reprints, and older titles still in-print to replace works in the collection, and such work with discrete individual titles differs from larger retrospective projects. In both this limited collection management work and in larger project buying, librarians working in literature may use a great array of reference works to identify authors, to ascertain their original significance and current importance, to identify their works, to distinguish editions, and to identify secondary literature.

The two sister disciplines of English and American literature are better equipped than many with bibliographies of great distinction and currency covering all genres, periods, and authors. The *New Cambridge Bibliography of English Literature*, for instance, is superb. Watters' *Checklist of Canadian Literature and Background Materials*, although now a decade old, is comprehensive. Excellent introductory works like Altick and Wright's very concise *Selective Bibliography for the Study of English and American Literature*, Bateson and Meserole's *A Guide to English and American Literature*, and *Australian Literature: A Reference Guide* by Fred Lock and Alan Lawson, abound. For most large libraries, which presumably have well-established literature collections of considerable size, these splendid works seldom serve a selection function, for much of the core they describe should already be in place. They can, however, aid in collection evaluation projects. The *New Cambridge Bibliography*, for instance, served as the basis for a very useful English literature evaluation

6. Madeleine Stein, "Characteristics of the Literature of Literary Scholarship," *College and Research Libraries* 44: 199–209 (July 1983).

project carried out in 1982 by a number of libraries in the Research Libraries Group.

A way to find out more about these and other standard bibliographies is to begin with the basic histories and a specialized guide such as Patterson's *Literary Research Guide* or Schweik and Riesner's *Reference Sources for English and American Literature.* These cite specialized bibliographies for authors, genres, topics, and periods too numerous and varied to specify here.

One type of retrospective work occurs when the librarian reevaluates holdings in a genre, sometimes sparked or aided by the publication of new studies and bibliographies. For example, the "iffy" category of detective/thriller fiction, always great in quantity, has recently experienced some increase also in critical esteem, in part due to the high quality writing of such authors as Ross Macdonald and P. D. James and in part to such thoughtful and witty reevaluations as Robin Winks' *Modus Operandi.* A number of recent bibliographies exist to aid in assembling a core collection. Among the most useful of these is *Twentieth Century Crime and Mystery Writers,* edited by John M. Reilly. This bulky work includes brief descriptive and evaluative essays, lists of works and bibliographies of hundreds of mystery writers, primarily British and American, and is an invaluable aid to anyone creating a mystery collection. *The Armchair Detective,* published quarterly, is a useful continuing source of background, book listings, and reviews and, for a treat, the perceptive and amusing reviews of the aforementioned Professor Robin Winks (in the Boston Globe Syndicate) are a pleasant way to keep abreast of current output.

A common and demanding retrospective project deals with younger living writers or with writers and literatures of countries other than America and the British Isles. Libraries are less likely in these cases to have comprehensive collections and the bibliographic apparatus is less complete and less concentrated. The process is the same, but one must search harder to compile a working list of titles to add to the collection.

Literature in English of Ireland, Scotland, and Wales is covered to some extent in English sources, such as the *Cambridge History of English Literature* and the *New Cambridge Bibliography of English Literature.* Sources of a more specialized scope are necessary, however, to consider the possibility of these literatures as independent national traditions. A few of these sources are listed below. Margaret Patterson, as usual, identifies additional sources, some of which may be useful in particular projects.

Still regarded as the authoritative source, Douglas Hyde's *Literary History of Ireland* provides extensive background. Robert Hogan's *Dictionary of Irish Literature* is the most comprehensive biographical and bibliographical collection, listing selectively primary and secondary works for about 500 writers. Brian Cleeve's *Dictionary of Irish Writers*, while very, very concise, identifies obscure and neglected writers. Brian McKenna's *Irish Literature, 1800-1875* is large, but limited to the nineteenth century, citing primary and secondary works for 100 writers.

A recent ambitious guide by W. R. Aitken, *Scottish Literature in English and Scots*, identifies the two basic histories and other sources, and cites primary and secondary works for slightly over 100 writers.

Thomas Parry's *History of Welsh Literature* is still the standard literary history and survey. Jarman and Hughes' *Guide to Welsh Literature*, with the first two volumes covering to the sixteenth century, is a comprehensive history with bibliographies.

COMMONWEALTH

Canadian. For retrospective work in Canadian literature one should begin with the *Annotated Bibliography of Canada's Major Authors* by Lecker and David for works by and about the most important writers. Still in publication, the first six volumes cover only 29 writers. Watters' *Checklist of Canadian Literature and Background Materials, 1628-1960* offers the opposite alternative, primary and secondary works of 7000 authors, but helpfully arranged by genre. Klinck's *Literary History of Canada* provides perspective on writers and movements. The thorough bibliographer may want to update any list compiled from these sources by using the annual bibliographies in *Essays on Canadian Writing* and *Journal of Commonwealth Literature* and the annual review articles in *University of Toronto Quarterly* ("Letters in Canada"), covering both English and French-Canadian literature.

Australian. To identify writers and their works one should begin with Miller and Macartney's basic list in *Australian Literature . . .* and with the *Oxford History of Australian Literature*, supplemented by Lock and Lawson's *Australian Literature: A Reference Guide*. Three recent Gale bibliographies, Andrews and Wilde's *Australian Literature to 1900*; Jaffa's *Modern Australian Poetry, 1920-1970*; and Day's *Modern Australian Prose* cover both more recent writers and more recent secondary works.

African. Bernth Lindfors, although discussing all African literatures, and Margaret Patterson point to Zell's *A New Reader's Guide to African Literature* and Jahn and Dressler's *Bibliography of Creative African Writing* as places to begin. Zell lists fewer writers, but gives annotations. Jahn and Dressler list more than 2000 books in English, European, and African languages. These volumes, along with other works they and Patterson cite, identify and evaluate books in African literatures.

Conclusion

Much more can be said about the sources for selection in English and American, British and Commonwealth literatures, and as more scholarly guides and aids are published, more will be said. A brief survey such as this can only generally recommend the helpful sources, with little assurance that such recommendations will not be soon outmoded. The sources currently published change from time to time; older works are supplanted or augmented by newer works published.

The breadth and depth of a library's literature collections determine which selection aids will be of most use. Many tools will be valuable to both comprehensive and highly selective collection efforts. Librarians in comprehensive collections will use current tools in all the branches of literature in English and do so aggressively. Librarians in other libraries will wish to rely on those, like the reviews in *Choice* and *Library Journal*, that identify materials for a basic collection. Regardless of the sources used, the selection officer's accumulated knowledge of books and serials, of literature, of the collection, and of the patrons' needs are crucial. Few disciplines are as richly endowed with valuable tools to facilitate the selection of library materials, and this wealth of tools and sources contributes to the challenge and satisfaction of the rewarding work of developing literature collections.

Selection Sources

Africana Journal. v.5– . 1975– . New York: Holmes & Meier. Quarterly. (From 1970–74: *Africana Library Journal.*)

Africana Libraries Newsletter. no. 1– . 1975– . Urbana: Univ. of Illinois. Irregularly (Address: Yvette Scheven, *Africana Libraries Newsletter*, 328 Library, Univ. of Illinois, 1408 W. Gregory Dr., Urbana, Il 61801.)

African Book Publishing Record. v.1– . 1975– . Oxford: Hans Zell. Quarterly.

Aitken, William Russell. *Scottish Literature in English and Scots: A Guide to Information Sources.* Detroit: Gale, 1982.

Altick, Richard D., and Andrew Wright. *Selective Bibliography for the Study of English and American Literature.* 6th ed. New York: Macmillan, 1979.

American Book Publishing Record. v.1– . 1960– . New York: Bowker. Monthly.

American Book Review. v.1– . 1979– . New York: Writers Review. Bimonthly.

American Literature. v.1– . 1929– . Durham, N.C.: Duke Univ. Pr. Quarterly.

American Poetry Review. v.1– . 1972– . Philadelpha: World Poetry. Bimonthly.

Andrews, Barry G., and William H. Wilde, eds. *Australian Literature to 1900: A Guide to Information Sources.* Detroit: Gale, 1979.

Annual Bibliography of Scottish Literature. v.1– . 1969– . Stirling: The Bibliothek. Annually.

The Armchair Detective. v.1– . 1967– . New York: Mysterious Pr. Quarterly.

Australian Book Scene. v.1– . 1977/78– . Annually. (Special export supplement of *Australian Bookseller and Publisher*; supplied at no cost by James Bennett.)

Australian Literary Studies. v.1– . 1963– . St. Lucia, Queensland: Univ. of Queensland. Semiannually.

Australian National Bibliography. v.1– . 1961– . Canberra: National Library of Australia. Monthly.

Bateson, F. W., and Harrison T. Meserole. *A Guide to English and American Literature.* 3rd ed. New York: Gordian, 1976.

Books in Canada: A National Review of Books. v.1– . 1971– . Toronto: Canadian Review of Books, Ltd., 10/year. (Address: 366 Adelaide Street East, Suite 432, Toronto, Ontario, M5A 3X9.)

Books Ireland. no.1– . 1976– . Goslingstown, Kilkenny, Ireland: Jeremy Addis. 10/year.

The Bookseller: The Organ of the Book Trade. v.1– . 1858– . London: Whitaker. Weekly.

British Book News: A Guide to Book Selection. v.1– . 1940– . London: British Council. Monthly.

British National Bibliography. v.1– . 1950– . London: British Library. Weekly.

Broadus, Robert N. *Selecting Materials for Libraries.* 2nd ed. New York: Wilson, 1981.

Canadiana. v.1– . 1950– . Ottawa: National Library of Canada. Monthly.

Choice. v.1– . 1963– . Middletown, Conn.: Assn. of College and Research Libraries. 11/year.

Cleeve, Brian T. *Dictionary of Irish Writers.* 3v. Cork, Ireland: Mercier, 1967–71.

Commonwealth Literature. Intro. by William Walsh. London: Macmillan, 1979.

Daedalus Books. 2260 25th Place, N.E., Washington, D.C. 20018. (202)526-0558.

Day, Arthur Grove, ed. *Modern Australian Prose, 1901–1975: A Guide to Information Sources.* Detroit: Gale, 1980.

English Studies: A Journal of English Language and Literature. v.1– . 1919– . Lisse: Swets & Zeitlinger. Bimonthly.

Essay and General Literature Index. New Titles Elected for Essay and General Literature Index. New York: Wilson, 19-- . Monthly.

Essays on Canadian Writing. no. 1– . 1974– . Toronto: Essays on Canadian Writing. Quarterly.

Etudes Irlandaises. v.1– . 1972– . Lille: Centre d' Etudes et de Recherches Irlandaises. Annually.

Goode, Stephen H. *Index to Commonwealth Little Magazines.* v.1– . 1964– . New York: Johnson Reprint Corp. Biennially.

Hogan, Robert, ed.-in-chief. *Dictionary of Irish Literature.* Westport, Conn.: Greenwood, 1979.

Hyde. Douglas. *Literary History of Ireland.* New ed., with intro. by Brian Ó Cuív. London: Benn; New York: St. Martins, 1980.

International Directory of Little Magazines and Small Presses. v.9– . 1973– . Paradise, Calif.: Dustbooks. Annually.

Irish Literary Supplement. v.1– . 1982– . Selden, N.Y.: Irish Literary Society. Semiannually.

Irish University Review. v.1– . 1970– . Dublin: Wolfhound Pr., University College. Semiannually.

Jaffa, Herbert C., ed. *Modern Australian Poetry, 1920–1970: A Guide to Information Sources.* Detroit: Gale, 1979.

James Bennett Pty. Ltd., 4 Collaroy St., Collaroy, N.S.W. 2097, Australia.

Jarman, A. O. H., and Gwilym Rees Hughes. *Guide to Welsh Literature.* Swansea: C. Davies, 1976.

Journal of Commonwealth Literature. v.1– . 1965– . Oxford: Hans Zell. Semiannually.

Katz, William, and Linda Sternberg Katz. *Magazines for Libraries.* 4th ed. New York: Bowker, 1982.

Klinck, Carl F., ed. *Literary History of Canada: Canadian Literature in English.* 2nd ed. 3v. Toronto: Univ. of Toronto Pr., 1976, c 1965.

Lecker, Robert, and Jack David, eds. *The Annotated Bibliography of Canada's Major Authors.* 6v. Downsview, Ont.: ECW Press; Boston: Hall, 1979–85. (To be complete in 10 v.)

Library Journal. v.1– . 1876– . New York: Bowker. Bimonthly.

Library of Congress. CDS Alert Service cards. Washington, D.C.: Library of Congress, 1981– . Weekly.

Lindfors, Bernth. "Researching African Literatures." *Literary Research Newsletter* 4: 171–80 (Fall 1979).

Literary Magazine Review. v.1– . 1982– . Manhattan: Kansas State Univ. Quarterly.

Literary Press Group Catalogue. v.1– . 1975– . Toronto: Assn. of Canadian Publishers. Annually. (Address: 70 The Esplanade, 3rd floor, Toronto, Ont. M5E IR2.)

Literary Research Newsletter. v.1– . 1976– . Bronx, N.Y.: Dept of English and World Literature, Manhattan College. Quarterly.

Lock, Fred, and Alan Lawson, eds. *Australian Literature: A Reference Guide.* 2nd ed. New York: Oxford Univ. Pr., 1980.

London Review of Books. v.1– . 1979– . London: LRB Ltd. Bimonthly.

MELUS Newsnotes. no.1– . 198?– . Cincinnati, Ohio: Society for the Study of the Multi-Ethnic Literature of the United States, Dept. of English, Univ. of Cincinnati. Comes with subscription to MELUS (v.1– , 1973–).

MLA Directory of Periodicals: A Guide to Journals and Series in Languages and Literatures. New York: Modern Language Assn., 1979– . Biennially.

MLA International Bibliography of Books and Articles on the Modern Languages and Literatures. v.1– . 1922–. New York: Modern Language Assn. Annually.

McKenna, Brian. *Irish Literature, 1800–1875: A Guide to Information Sources.* Detroit: Gale, 1978.

Miller, E. Morris. *Australian Literature: A Bibliography to 1938, Extended to 1950 . . .* Ed. by Frederick T. Macartney. Sydney: Angus & Robertson, 1956.

Mississippi Quarterly. v.1– . 1947– . Mississippi State: Mississippi State Univ. Quarterly.

New Cambridge Bibliography of English Literature. Ed. by George Watson. 5v. Cambridge: Cambridge Univ. Pr., 1969–77.

New Republic. v.1– . 1914– . Washington, D.C.: New Republic. Weekly.

New Serial Titles. v.1– . 1953– . Washington, D.C.: Library of Congress. Monthly.

New York Review of Books. v.1– . 1963– . New York: New York Review of Books. 22/year.

New York Times Book Review. v.1– .1896– . New York: New York Times Co. Weekly.

Oxford History of Australian Literature. Ed. by Leonie Kramer. New York: Oxford Univ. Pr. 1981.

PMLA. Publications of the Modern Language Association of America. v.1– . 1884– . New York: Modern Language Assn. Bimonthly.

Parry, Thomas. *A History of Welsh Literature.* Trans. by H. Idris Bell. Oxford: Clarendon Pr., 1955.

Patterson, Margaret C. *Author Newsletters and Journals: An International Annotated Bibliography of Serial Publications Concerned with the Life and Works of Individual Authors.* Detroit: Gale, 1979. Updated in *Serials Review* 8:4 (Winter 1982) and 10:1 (Spring 1984).

————. *Literary Research Guide.* 2nd ed. New York: Modern Language Assn. 1983.

Peters, Robert. *The Peters Black and Blue Guide to Current Literary Journals.* Silver Springs, Md.: Cherry Valley Editions, 1983. Dist. by Writers and Books, 892 S. Clinton Ave., Rochester, NY 14620.

Publishers Weekly. v.1- . 1872- . New York: Bowker. Weekly.

Quill and Quire. v.1- . 1935- . Toronto: Key Publishers. Monthly.

Reilly, John M., ed. *Twentieth Century Crime and Mystery Writers.* New York: St. Martin's, 1980.

Research in African Literatures. v.1- . 1970- . Austin: Univ. of Texas. Quarterly.

Review of Contemporary Fiction. v.1- . 1981- . Elmwood Park, Ill.: Review of Contemporary Fiction. 3/year.

Sader, Marion. *Comprehensive Index to English-Language Little Magazines, 1890–1970.* Series 1. 8v. Millwood, N.Y.: Kraus-Thomson, 1976.

The Scholar's Bookshelf. 51 Everett Drive, Princeton, NJ 08550.

Schweik, Robert C., and Dieter Riesner. *Reference Sources in English and American Literature: An Annotated Bibliography.* New York: Norton, 1977.

Serials Review. v.1- . 1975- . Ann Arbor Mich.: Pierian. Quarterly.

Simply Stated. no.1- . 19-- . Washington, D.C.: Document Design Center, American Institutes for Research. Monthly. (Address: 1055 Thomas Jefferson Street, N.W., Washington, D.C. 20007. (202)342-5000.)

Small Press Record of Books in Print. 1- . 1966- . Paradise, Calif.: Dustbooks. Annually.

Small Press Review. v.1- . 1966- . Paradise, Calif.: Dustbooks. Monthly.

Thompson, James. *English Studies: A Guide for Librarians to the Sources and Their Organization.* 2nd ed. London: Clive Bingley, 1971.

Times Literary Supplement. v.1- . 1902- . London: Times Newspapers. Weekly.

University of Toronto Quarterly. v.1- . 1931- . Toronto: Univ. of Toronto Pr. Quarterly.

WLWE: World Literature Written in English. v.1- . 1961- . Arlington, Tex.: Univ. of Texas. Biennially.

Warwick, Ronald, comp. *Commonwealth Literature Periodicals: A Bibliography, Including Periodicals of Former Commonwealth Countries, with Locations in the United Kingdom.* London: Mansell, 1979.

Watters, Reginald E., ed. *Checklist of Canadian Literature and Background Materials, 1628-1960.* 2nd ed. Toronto: Univ. of Toronto Pr., 1972.

Weekly Record. v.1- . 1974- . New York: Bowker. Weekly.

Western American Literature. v.1- . 1966- . Logan: Univ. of Utah. Quarterly.

Winks, Robin W. *Modus Operandi: An Excursion into Detective Fiction.* Boston: Godine, 1982.

Wortman, William A. *A Guide to Serial Bibliographies for Modern Literatures.* New York: Modern Language Assn, 1982.

Writers and Books Catalogue. Rochester, N.Y.: Writers and Books. Annually; quarterly supplement will begin late 1984. (Address: 892 So. Clinton Ave., Rochester, N.Y. 14620. (716)473-2590.)

Year's Work in English Studies. v.1- . 1921- . London: English Assn. Annually.

Year's Work in Modern Language Studies. v.1- . 1931- . London: Modern Humanities Research Assn. Annually.

Zell, Hans M.; Carol Bundy; and Virginia Coulon. *A New Reader's Guide to African Literature.* 2nd ed. New York: Africana, 1983.

HISTORY

Nancy C. Cridland

History is a very broad rubric that covers a wide range of time periods, geographical areas, subjects, methodologies, and formats; "historical re-search" is a flexible term that encompasses many specialized and changing interests. Traditional political history comes to mind first, and is probably the easiest for the selector to identify, but it constitutes a very small part of today's historical research. Economic, legal, religious, scientific, de-mographic, and intellectual history, and the infinite varieties of social his-tory, open ever wider horizons.

Historians distinguish between primary source material, which includes records constituted at the time of the event and the reports of firsthand participants, and secondary sources, comprising all the interpretative lit-erature based on primary source material or on other secondary material. (Of course, what is secondary material for one purpose may become a primary source for another, as the literature itself is studied.) Most of what the library collects will be secondary material, but primary sources such as parliamentary proceedings, filmed archives, collections of docu-ments, and autobiographies are part of the collection also, in printed, microform, or computerized form. Special collections may include man-uscripts or original archives.

The key mode of communication in the historical fields is the scholarly monograph. To be sure, there is a specialized journal for nearly every specialized field, and there are landmark articles in the periodical literature. Many a topic too narrow to warrant book-length treatment has been developed only in journal articles. But typically, serials will take a much smaller bite of the history budget than of the science and social science budgets.

Historians are usually heavy and appreciative users of the library col-lection, and even in very large libraries they are among the principal users of interlibrary loan. They are major users of government publications, and many make extensive use of newspaper files. They use all kinds of archives, and appreciate local copies of archival guides to aid in planning their research. Increasingly they also use computerized databases, a trend that will surely grow as files of statistical and other data grow to cover longer time periods.

No library can really collect in depth for all the fields of history. Most American libraries try to maintain a strong collection in U.S. and perhaps in English history, with particular regional or topical strengths, and collect at varying levels for other areas, with some very strong areas and other areas less so according to local interests, existing specialties, and funding available.

Larger collections usually have area bibliographers who select at least the vernacular material for the nontraditional fields such as Latin America, Africa, Asia, and the Cyrillic-alphabet countries, where knowledge of local sources and languages is vital. This essay will not deal with those fields, except for English-language materials.

Defining the Scope of the Collection

The broad decisions about the shape of a collection are usually already made, shaped by the nature and interests of the clientele and the size of the budget. Building on existing strengths is usually preferable to attempting to give even-handed treatment to all areas. This is especially true in history, for which retrospective collections are so important and so difficult to build in any real depth. It doesn't make sense to take needed maintenance funds from a rich collection of long standing in order to make random additions in an area that will probably never be strong enough to support much research because key material (or funding) is simply unavailable. Sometimes, of course, a new area must be built up anyway to meet institutional needs.

Of course the selector needs to begin by touching base with selectors for economics, political science, religion, classics, and other disciplines, perhaps even music and fine arts, and with area studies bibliographers if there are any, to be sure who is covering what and where the lines are drawn. This will be easier if a carefully drawn collection policy is in place, but there will always be some overlap. However, in large libraries history seems to be a catchall class, filling in many gaps and assuming responsibility for many interdisciplinary materials. This seems quite appropriate, since in future years much of the material will be of primarily historical interest. Indeed, one of the most satisfying aspects of building a history collection is the knowledge that, unlike many fields in which researchers use primarily contemporary materials, history is a discipline in which "retrospective" material is of the essence. Many materials chosen today will be increasingly useful for generations to come.

A prime responsibility of any bibliographer is to be alert for new trends in research and to anticipate need by collecting materials as they appear. Public history, psychohistory, quantitative history, and demography are examples of growth from a novelty to an established part of the curriculum.

As current events develop, the bibliographer needs to make prompt decisions about whether to collect exhaustively on a topic or to settle for broad general coverage. In a smaller library, every topic may be adequately dealt with by the general periodicals and eventually a few well-chosen monographs. But for a larger collection, policy decisions must be almost daily: will this library collect all the Watergate memoirs? All the Iranian hostages' narratives? All the campaign pamphlets on the proposed (and doomed) Anglican-Methodist union? All the student movement publications for some given organization or crisis? ("All" means all that can actually be obtained, for ephemeral materials.) Budgetary factors, clientele interests, collection strengths, and the interests, abilities, and time constraints of the bibliographer enter into each decision. But ephemeral and highly specialized material is of little use unless it has been collected comprehensively enough to form a critical mass that will support local research.

A well-defined collection policy, written in cooperation with user groups, and a well thought out program of resource sharing for local needs that exceed local resources are central to collection planning. Limiting the collection to fields of history taught locally is a standard and reasonable way to stay within the budget, but is easier said than done, and has very limited application to English-language material. And as every selector learns even in three or four years, tailoring the collection to fit the clientele is shooting at a moving target. Continuing consultation with the academic departments is essential, but probably won't eliminate all surprises. Of course, most libraries of any size need a basic collection in English in nearly every field.

Basic Current Selection Tools

There are two major considerations in collection-building strategy for a large and active research library, and it takes a combination of tools to satisfy both. The first is timeliness—having the book quickly for the researcher who needs it. The second is complete coverage—picking up all the important materials within the defined scope of the collection. No single tool answers both requirements. Each bibliographer eventually works out the combination of selection aids that best suits his or her own working habits and the needs of the collection at hand.

ADVANCE NOTICE SELECTION AIDS

Timeliness is more important for some collections than for others. But most selectors want to have at least heard of an important book by the time someone asks for it. Defensive reading of reviews in the general periodicals prevalent in academia is recommended: the *New York Times Book Review*, the *New York Review*, *Atlantic*, *Time*, *Newsweek* and so on. No one can read them all, but whatever the selector can manage to cover will help in spotting important new titles quickly. *Publishers' Weekly*, the London *Times Literary Supplement*, and *Library Journal* are also good "early warning" systems. The advertisements (not the reviews) in the major historical journals and in the annual meeting programs of historical organizations such as the American Historical Association, the Organization of American Historians, and the Association for Asian Studies are also helpful.

Publishers' blurbs and catalogs are worth going through for announcements early in the season. Most feature new titles up front and also include a backlist, so that it is easy to give careful attention to new titles. But unless a list is from an unfamiliar publisher, it is usually not worthwhile to read a publisher's catalog that doesn't clearly distinguish the new titles from the backlist. It is a waste of time to follow up on titles that were duly acquired three years before and then forgotten.

The selector for a large history collection doesn't usually need to see reviews of most titles before ordering them. Most research material within the scope of the collection is readily identifiable and will be purchased. If in doubt, wait. But it is false economy to devote much time to the consideration of an inexpensive item; it's cheaper to make occasional mistakes.

Library Journal and *Choice* are both good sources of prompt, reliable reviews. There is so much overlap that not many selectors use both. *Library Journal* is a little faster, and Choice is a little more geared toward academic collections. Neither attempts to review everything or even nearly everything of merit, and neither reviews many of the scholarly works that are not suitable for undergraduates.

Publishers' Weekly is another early notice tool that reviews some history, but not very much and not very critically. It is worthwhile for general information about publishing trends, copyright, and so forth, but anyone who uses other general tools that carry prepublication announcements may find it redundant for selection purposes. However, redundancy is largely in the eye of the beholder. With a little practice, each selector soon learns which tools add something to the coverage and which do not.

There is really nothing like the London *Times Literary Supplement* in this country, and it is tempting to say that any educated person needs it; certainly anyone selecting historical materials for a large collection will want to see it. The reviews are usually very current and cover a surprising amount of serious historical literature. They are apt to be idiosyncratic and often give more space to the reviewer's thoughts on the topic than to the actual book at hand. The selection of books reviewed is wide-ranging and sometimes capricious, often calling to the reader's attention worthwhile but offbeat things that wouldn't have been considered otherwise. Recent issues have included, for example, Teresa McLean's *The English at Play in the Middle Ages*, which lacks scholarly apparatus but is nevertheless a serious work containing a great deal of information about the sports, songs, drama, and other recreation of medieval England, and Eva Crane's *The Archaeology of Beekeeping*, a solid account of all aspects of beekeeping from the earliest times to the nineteenth century.[1]

COMPREHENSIVE COVERAGE

For full coverage, Bowker's *Weekly Record* (for U.S. books) and the *British National Bibliography*'s (*BNB*) weekly edition are good "fail-safe" tools for trade publications. The *Weekly Record* is relatively slow, except for its Cataloging-in-Publication (CIP) listings, which may appear in advance of publication. *BNB* used to be slow, too, but now includes many CIP listings. Both these tools will overlap greatly with other aids, but are comprehensive enough to offer reasonably good insurance against missing needed trade publications, and may be the only notice of some useful items. The lack of evaluative information is partially offset by the inclusion of subject headings. It is easy to identify pamphlets and, usually, textbooks, but one must move cautiously with unfamiliar publishers. *Weekly Record* is strictly alphabetical by main entry, and too time consuming to be used for much less than comprehensive collecting. *BNB*'s classified arrangement is much easier to use, but the selector of history materials needs to cover the social science and religion classifications as well as the history section. Indeed, any classified tool is a mixed blessing for the history selector; it is nearly always necessary to select from many additional sections and not just from the one formally labeled as history.

The Library of Congress CDS Alert Service cards (formerly known as proof slips) used to offer late-but-thorough coverage, too, but CIP has transformed the service, at least for many trade publications. The cards are now early, often excessively early. The advance information may be useful, but often the number of pages and the price are not included, and

1. Teresa McLean, *The English at Play in the Middle Ages* (Windsor, England: Kensal, 1983); Eva Crane, *The Archaeology of Beekeeping* (London: Duckworth, 1984).

even the title may change before publication. In some cases, publication will be abandoned. It is well to ignore cards with a publication date a year or more in advance. Another caution in using the cards is that the official Library of Congress format sometimes seems to lend a spurious respectability to the dubious, and may lead the unwary selector to order items previously rejected.

The Alert Service is a prime source of publication information about nontrade publication of conference proceedings, which can be hard to track down, and of academic, institute, and other nontrade publications. It may be more useful otherwise for European than for American trade publications.

USE OF HISTORICAL JOURNALS FOR SELECTION

There are several specifically history-oriented review publications, geared more to teaching faculty than to libraries. *History: Reviews of New Books* comes out about ten times a year and is very broad in coverage, with reliable reviews, but the reviews are now running about six months after publication. It could be very useful for a smaller collection, or where selectivity is more important than speed. *Reviews in American History*, a quarterly publication on American history only, runs longer review articles, often covering groups of books on a given topic, with a time lag of six months to two years after publication. It doesn't cover enough titles to be very useful for selection.

Reviews in the regular historical journals tend to be too late to be of much use for selection purposes. (Sometimes the book is out-of-print by the time the review appears.) It is important to look over the journals, though, to keep in touch with research trends and with critical reaction to the books. The reviews are important also for areas or languages in which collection is limited and selective. They are also useful for calling the selector's attention to titles that were overlooked or mistakenly rejected. Many journals also carry an announcements section of some sort that may provide order information for elusive publications, conference proceedings, or new journals.

History: Reviews of New Books. v.1- . 1972- . Washington D.C.: Heldref, 10/year.
Review journal.
35–40 reviews an issue.
Reviews books in English only, covering many fields in history.
6-month time lag between publication and review.
Signed reviews by scholars, 250–400 words in length.

The American Historical Review. v.1- . 1895- . Washington, D.C.: American
    Historical Assn. Quarterly.
    Scholarly journal.
    About 200 reviews an issue.
    Reviews cover many subjects and languages in all fields of history.
    6–18-month time lag between publication and review.
    Signed reviews by scholars, ranging in length from 500 to 1200 words.
    Books received listed.
    New journals announced.
    Documents and bibliographies received listed.
    Contents of collected volumes listed.
    Publishers' announcements.
    List of books received is unselective but includes some useful titles not
        listed elsewhere.

The *American Historical Review* and the *Journal of American History*,
both quarterly, are key U.S. journals both for articles and reviews. In
England there's the *English Historical Review*. Those selecting in French,
German, and Italian will want also to look at the *Revue Historique*, *Historische Zeitschrift*, and *Rivista Storica Italiana*. With the exception of
the *Journal of American History*, defined by its title, all these journals
publish reviews of books in several languages and in various fields of
history.

Many more countries have their own major journals, and there are
additional general journals, some very good. Most, though not all, publish
book reviews. *Annales: Economies, Sociétés, Civilisations* reviews only a
few books, sometimes none, but its highly useful blue sheet, "La Choix
des Annales," lists a selection of outstanding new books, not necessarily
straight "history," and may be the first notice of an outstanding and perhaps unusual new European title.

The Journal of American History. v.1- . 1914- . Bloomington, Ind.:
    Organization of American Historians. Quarterly.
    Scholarly journal.
    About 100 reviews an issue.
    Reviews books in many areas of American history; lists some local history
        items that might otherwise escape notice. Reviews some government
        publications.
    Time lag from publication to review 6–18 months.
    Signed reviews by scholars, about 400 words in length.
    List of books received.
    Lists of articles, bibliographies, and dissertations.
    Publishers' announcements.

Most journals, however, specialize in a particular region (e.g., the *Journal of Southern History, French Historical Studies*); a time period (*Eighteenth Century Life*); a topic (*Diplomatic History*); or an approach (*Journal of Psychohistory*). It is worthwhile to look at as many in the library's collecting areas as time allows. The *William and Mary Quarterly* (colonial America), *Speculum* (medieval period), and the *Renaissance Quarterly* are outstanding examples of useful specialized quarterlies.

Ancient History

Ancient history overlaps so greatly with classical studies, archaeology, and even fine arts that it may be well covered with little attention from the history bibliographer; or, conversely, the history bibliographer may have responsibilities in these areas. Considerable literature appears in English, or at least in English translation, and some in other European languages.

Many English-language publications come from the university presses or even from regular trade publishers, and can be identified in the general tools. But much important material appears in the publications of the various institutes and academies, such as the British School at Rome, the Deutsches Archaeologisches Institut, the Ecole Francaise d'Athènes, the Accademia Nazionale dei Linceii, and others, for which large libraries usually have standing orders.

Surprisingly few of the major journals in ancient history publish reviews of books. One German journal, *Gnomon: Kritische Zeitschrift für die Gesamte Klassiche Altertumswissenschaft*, is devoted chiefly to reviews of the literature in all areas of classical studies, and *Historische Zeitschrift* also publishes many reviews in this area. The *Journal of Roman Studies* and the *Journal of Hellenic Studies* also publish some reviews.

A great deal of monographic literature on the ancient Near East is published by Brill in Leiden, the Netherlands. Brill also operates as a vendor, and issues lists that sometimes include titles from other publishers. Other literature in this area comes from university presses, from small specialty publishers such as Undena in Malibu, California, and from such institutions as the Oriental Institute of the University of Chicago and the Deutsches Archaeologisches Institut, among others. The *Journal of Near Eastern Studies* is a useful source of reviews. Another review journal in this area is *Bibliotheca Orientalis*, published by the Nederlands Instituut voor het Nabije Oosten; it is relatively slow and runs heavily to linguistic materials. Other journals publish reviews in this area; history usually accounts for only a small part of the material covered.

The standard guide to ancient history is Hermann Bengtson's *Introduction to Ancient History*. Bengtson includes many short bibliographies

Gnomon: Kritische Zeitschrift für die Gesamte Klassiche Altertumswissenschaft. v.1– . 1924– . Munich, West Germany: C. H. Becksche Verlagsbuchhandlung. 8/year.
Review journal.
25–35 reviews an issue.
Covers all fields of classical antiquity, in many languages.
Time lag for reviews 1–3 years.
Signed reviews by scholars, ranging in length from 750 to 1800 words.
Announces new journals.
Lists of books, articles, and dissertations.

Historische Zeitschrift. v.1– . 1829– . Munich, West Germany: Oldenbourg Verlag. Bimonthly.
Scholarly journal.
75–125 reviews an issue.
Covers many fields of history and includes books in many languages.
Especially strong on ancient, medieval, and German history.
Time lag 6–18 months.
Signed reviews by scholars, ranging in length from 125 to 800 words.
Topical review articles.
List of books received.
Publishers' announcements.

that can be useful for retrospective collecting, and also discusses the important academies, journals, manuals, and so forth.

Medieval History

For the medieval and Renaissance periods, particular care needs to be taken to coordinate efforts with other selectors to avoid gaps. Materials relating to this period do not fall into subject categories as neatly as for later periods. Publications appear in many languages and from many publishers. Useful series are published by the Pontifical Institute in Toronto, the Mediaeval Academy of America in Cambridge, Massachusetts, the Istituto Storico Italiano per il Medio Evo in Rome, and others.

Many reviews appear in *Speculum: A Journal of Mediaeval Studies*, published by the Mediaeval Academy of America, and also in the general journals such as the *American Historical Review, English Historical Review,* and *Historische Zeitschrift.* For the later period the *Renaissance Quarterly* lists of books received are especially useful.

Louis Paetow's standard *Guide to the Study of Mediaeval History* and its five-volume successor, Gray C. Boyce's *Literature of Medieval History 1930–1975* are useful for retrospective collecting.

Asian History

Much Asian history is published in English. Materials of high quality include Harvard University Press's *Harvard East Asian Series* and *Harvard East Asian Monographs*, the publications of the University of Michigan's Center for Chinese Studies and Center for Japanese Studies, and the publications of the Center for Chinese Studies and Center for Japanese and Korean Studies of the University of California. English-language material is also published in Taiwan, Hong Kong, and mainland China. The Chinese Materials Center in San Francisco distributes useful lists.

The *Journal of Asian Studies* is a source of reviews; many journals carry some reviews relating to Asia.

Bibliographies useful for retrospective collecting include Charles Hucker, *China: A Critical Bibliography* and Bernard S. Silberman, *Japan and Korea: A Critical Bibliography*, both covering works in English only; Peter Berton, *Contemporary China: A Research Guide*, which covers many languages and subjects but refers only to 1949–63; and the history sections of Maureen Patterson's massive *South Asian Civilizations: A Bibliographic Synthesis*.

European History

Much European history, of course, is published in English, in the United States or in Great Britain. Most libraries buy less intensively in European languages than in English. Many European publications appear later in English translation, but unfortunately it is rarely possible to know in advance which will be translated. The most important works should usually be bought both in the original and in the English translation.

There is little point in buying translations *from* English to European languages, but even the wary selector does it inadvertently on occasion. Learn the word and the abbreviation for "translated" in each language you select in; "Trad." in French and "Ubers." in German are examples. Also be wary of familiar-sounding titles or of suspiciously American names.

Translations from one foreign language to another are usually not necessary acquisitions. However, sometimes it is worthwhile to get a work in a language more accessible to more patrons, e.g., in German translated from Russian.

Depth of collection in foreign languages will depend on the academic programs, the language competencies of user groups, and the budget. A good rule of thumb is that the more scholarly and more specialized foreign language works are the more likely to be needed, because they are unique and no comparable English work can be substituted. A general survey may be an important purchase if it is by a noted scholar or is of exceptional quality. But, other things being equal, most American library patrons prefer English-language materials for general information. A research collection for advanced research will need materials in all relevant languages and will, if possible, acquire scholarly materials without regard to language, but for other collections supporting less intensive research, the library will purchase more selectively.

For fields in which there are currently no academic programs, there may be little collecting beyond English-language materials. The best approach in such cases is to buy key materials of permanent value, such as reference materials and perhaps the memoirs of key figures and the works of top scholars. Then there will be a nucleus if the area is developed later, and money is not lost on ephemeral material that passes into obsolescence untouched.

Most European countries publish a national bibliography that can be used for selection purposes, as can the Library of Congress CDS Alert Service. The major historical journals are a good back-up.

An excellent basic bibliography for a start in retrospective collecting is John Roach, *A Bibliography of Modern History*. The standard histories of the various countries usually include good bibliographies.

A few notes on individual countries follow:

GERMANY

In addition to the national bibliographies, East and West, the Otto Harrassowitz firm in Wiesbaden publishes bimonthly lists of publications in history that are sent to its customers. *Historische Zeitschrift*'s reviews and lists are also an important resource. Much local history is reported by the LC CDS Alert Service. An important series is *Deutsche Geschichtsquellen des 19. und 20. Jahrhunderts*, published by Boldt Verlag.

FRANCE

Livres Hebdo, the French equivalent of *Publishers' Weekly*, carries a classified list of current publications. PUF (Presses Universitaires de France) and other university presses, and CNRS (Editions du Centre National de la Recherche Scientifique) are important publishers to watch.

The reviews in *Revue Historique* are helpful. *French Historical Studies* lists but does not review publications.

SPAIN

Spanish history is published in French as well as in Spanish. Vendors such as Puvill Libros in Barcelona publish regular lists of Spanish historical publications, and the *Indice Histórico Español* is a good continuing bibliography. The reviews in *Hispania*, the major journal, are helpful. The LC CDS Alert Service is also useful.

ITALY

Italian Books and Periodicals reports on many Italian publications, with annotations that are informative but totally uncritical. The LC CDS Alert Service and the reviews in *Rivista Storica Italiana* and the general journals are probably the most useful adjuncts to the national bibliography.

SCANDINAVIA

Very little Scandinavian history is published in English. Though the Scandinavian countries have a thriving historical literature, translations into English are rare. The national bibliographies and the major journals will guide those who collect in this area. The journals are similarly titled: *Historisk Tidskrift* (Sweden); *Historisk Tidsskrift* (Denmark); *Historisk Tidskrift: Utgitt Av Den Norske Historiske Forening* (Norway); *Historisk Tidskrift för Finland.*

Selecting Journals and Other Continuations

New journals usually send out brochures lavishly to libraries, or to teaching faculty who will pass on any they are seriously interested in. New journals are sometimes reviewed in *Library Journal,* and often reported or advertised in ongoing journals. The first announcement is often simply a call for articles, with no subscription information, but a query at that time will usually put the library on a mailing list. Most journals, old and new, respond promptly to requests for sample copies.

Inclusion in a standard index is usually an important criterion for selection, but the brand-new journals won't be included, and sometimes the first few issues are the best ones. Sometimes the caliber of the editorial board is a clue to potential quality. Other things being equal, when the budget is tight, give priority to continuing a journal you have a long run of, rather than substituting a new one not urgently needed. In fields such as business, where only current literature is heavily used, a steady turnover in titles makes sense, but in history, with its emphasis on the retrospective, it will help the scholar in the long run (not to mention interlibrary loan personnel) if he or she can learn which journals the library has and which not, without having to remember an assortment of dates as well. If needs change later, it is usually easier to get a whole run than to fill in odd gaps.

It's a rare series that is of uniform quality, but many are consistently good enough that the library will want all titles. It saves time and trouble to enter a standing order for such standbys as the *Chicago History of American Civilization*, the *Rise of Modern Europe*, the *New American Nation*. The disadvantage of a standing order, of course, is that once it is on the books, it tends to stay there, eating up money indefinitely regardless of decline in quality, unless the list is reviewed periodically.

It often doesn't work to enter a standing order for the conference proceedings or other publications of a small scholarly organization, because the place of publication will change with every change of officers, and there is no staff to process and maintain standing orders. Even though it is a nuisance, the only sure way to get such works is to watch for announcements of each one.

Special Problems

MICROFORMS

Microforms of individual titles are not a problem, of course; they can be selected on the same basis as any other material. Large heterogenous collections are another matter. Some are essential and contain extraordinarily useful research material; some are redundant, in that a large library already has most of the material (which isn't always easy to determine from the glossy brochures); some contain useful material that will never be used because there is no satisfactory access through finding aids. Some are unsatisfactory in technical quality. *Microform Review* is the best tool and for many sets the only tool for this kind of information. Occasionally the reviewers seem to lack experience in determining the usefulness of the material itself, but the basic information is there. If the set is useful but expensive, consider alternatives to local ownership. The Center for Research Libraries may buy the set, and other libraries that buy will also often lend.

BIOGRAPHY

Biography is a tricky area. There are many scholarly biographies, but there is also a lot of very good serious biographical writing for a general audience. The totally frivolous can be skipped, but it's hard to know where to draw the line. Second-rate biographies often get most of their use when there is no copy of the "best" one on the shelf; it would seem logical to buy fewer second-raters and more copies of the best ones. But any serious scholar working on a historical figure will want to see every serious study.

Even a very poor book about a contemporary figure can be worth getting sometimes, because it captures information that will be hard to come by later. But it is usually safe to skip a poor book about Abraham Lincoln, or even about a contemporary figure on whom much has been written.

MILITARY HISTORY

Military history needs special attention because sometimes serious and useful studies come from presses, such as Presidio, that also publish more popular material. A great deal of military material is hobbyist in nature, and should be bought only if your intent is to supply the military buff— or if your collection is by intent very comprehensive in this area. The hobby material, though usually not very expensive, seems unfortunately to be highly vulnerable to theft.

LOCAL HISTORY

Local history is another gray area. It covers a vast spectrum from the deadly serious (in which the locality is often selected simply as a case study) to the home-brewed, which endeavors to include the names of as many prospective purchasers as possible. It is easy to include the former and exclude the latter, but not so easy to draw the line. Most libraries collect more comprehensively for their own region or locality than for others.

The state historical societies publish journals, which vary widely in quality, and many have a publications series also. Very large collections will routinely acquire nearly all offered. In a smaller library, cater to local interests, if any, and buy selectively from the societies of other states.

Local history is often sold privately rather than through the regular book trade, but many amateur hopefuls send brochures or letters to libraries. Much of this material is of little value, but some is useful. State historical journals very often announce or even review such material, and can be very useful in collecting intensively for a locality. In particular, private publications may merit consideration when they deal with areas for which little else is available.

Much British local history is published by the many record societies, some of which have been collecting and publishing source materials for many years. Many of these are excellent; some may seem too specialized for a collection that does not support intensive research in this field. The largest collections will subscribe to most or all. To expand a collection, look at the lists in *Titles in Series* to get an idea of what kinds of material each society publishes. (Backfiles of many are now available in microform.) It makes sense in many libraries to continue the ones you've got a full set of, to buy separately the odd volume in other series that seems useful, and to rely on interlibrary loan for the rest if needed.

SMALL AND OFFBEAT PUBLISHERS

The problem with small, private, and offbeat publishers is in identifying the useful and worthwhile. The CDS Alert Service often includes such items, but with no evaluation and all too often with no adequate address and no price. Historical journals do sometimes pick up on such publications and review them, and so do some general review journals. Even the vanity presses occasionally publish valuable materials, such as Timothy White's *A People for His Name.*[2] Reliable reviewers will identify some titles for you; *Church History* noted White's book, now standard for its topic. A trained eye for gaps in the literature and a willingness to take occasional mild risks will bring in others.

RETROSPECTIVE COLLECTING

Retrospective collecting is not done as extensively as it used to be, in these days of stringent budgets, and the strategy varies with the topic. For anyone who is in the library-school-exercise position of building a collection from scratch, or whose collection is badly in need of basic upgrading, the *Harvard Guide to American History* revised edition, edited by Frank Freidel, is certainly the basic tool for American history, and the *Bibliography of British History* series, a joint effort of the American Historical Association and the Royal Historical Society, for British. Suggestions for other areas have in some cases been included in those sections. The *American Historical Association's Guide to Historical Literature* is still useful, though now badly out of date.

A SMALL CAVEAT

One additional problem is worth calling attention to: we in large research collections are truly the captive customers of eminent historians. Not every work of even top-flight scholars is of research quality. They also produce, from time to time, potboilers and popularized works; they also edit collections of reprinted readings to which they contribute two-page introductions. Grit your teeth, if necessary, but *buy them.* When the work is cited, in a padded bibliography or a careless footnote (and it will be) as a work on that topic by that historian, the scholar of the future will certainly feel he or she needs to see it, and will not consult a reference librarian about the nature of the work before ordering it on interlibrary loan. Perhaps one glance will be enough to dismiss the book, but this

2. Timothy White, *A People for His Name* (New York: Vantage, 1968).

happens far too often, with the truly illustrious names, for interlibrary loan to be a cost-effective way to handle the problem.

This is by no means a general rule, of course; fortunately, few names are illustrious enough to warrant this treatment. Most collections of readings can be bypassed when they contain little or no new material. This is a judgment call, depending on the material and the usefulness of an anthology on a given topic.

Office Tools

Even if the history bibliographer is not a reference librarian (and most are), a few office tools are very helpful in selection. Foreign-language dictionaries are essential, for as many languages as one selects in. Beyond that, the size of the collection depends on available funding and also on the convenience of the general reference collection.

Next to foreign-language dictionaries, perhaps the most useful volumes are biographical dictionaries, such as *Webster's Biographical Dictionary* and *Chambers's Biographical Dictionary*. *Webster's* is stronger on American figures, *Chambers's* on most others. The *Chambers's* entries are apt to be longer and often include bibliographical references, which *Webster's* lacks. The dictionaries can be used to determine whether an unfamiliar name is actually an artist, poet, or otherwise out-of-scope for the history selector; if a name does not appear in either, it is usually safe to wait for further information or reviews.

The history volume of the current *Directory of American Scholars* is very useful. Though certainly it would be out of the question to get every edition of *Ulrich's Periodical Directory* and the *World of Learning* for personal use, it is worthwhile to requisition slightly older editions or even to buy the new one very occasionally, if the general reference collection is at a distance.

Well-indexed general histories of the individual countries are very useful for reference purposes. (Textbooks will serve and may be available gratis from one source or another.) A historical atlas or two will help in moments of perplexity about places. Standard bibliographies such as the *Harvard Guide to American History*, Monroe Work's *Bibliography of the Negro in Africa and America*, and John Roach's *Bibliography of Modern History* are useful for retrospective collecting and also helpful in evaluating reprints. If student assistants are available to search such office copies of bibliographies, adding call numbers and holdings, the searched copies are invaluable not only for reference work, but for selection and for a perspective on the strength and shape of the collection.

Wider Responsibilities

In addition to his or her own collection responsibility (as if that were not enough), the history bibliographer needs to be as active, knowledgeable, and visible as possible in the more general areas of collection policy in the library. Historians have a very big stake in the selection of reference tools, general periodicals, atlases, directories, books on statistics and computer applications; they have perhaps the biggest stake of all in the development of the permanent newspaper collection. In addition, historical volumes appear in such general series as Princeton's *Bollingen Series* and the *Transactions* of the American Philosophical Society, so that the history bibliographer needs to keep an eye on these subscriptions and any decisions relating to them. Because historians have such voracious appetites for a wide range of materials, they also have an exceptionally big stake in all our cooperative collection development and resource sharing efforts.

Collecting for the Future

Perhaps the most challenging task of the history bibliographer is the assembling of the research materials of the future—an effort that often elicits little enthusiasm from contemporary patrons, who may see little scholarly value in "yellow journalism" or in publications of new and radical political or religious groups, let alone in agricultural and aviation manuals, cookbooks, child rearing manuals, autobiographies of popular evangelists, comic books, popular magazines, popular self-help manuals, and so on through an endless list of future primary sources. Many an orator or movement, hitherto regarded with contempt, achieves scholarly respectability by the simple act of dying. None of us can collect all of this material, or even guess at the usefulness of all of it, but those of us in larger institutions can choose thoughtfully which areas we will collect in and follow through systematically and zealously. More importantly, we have a collective responsibility to be aware of each other's efforts and to be sure that someone is collecting in each significant area. We can't afford excessive duplication of effort, because such specialized collecting is time consuming and costly. But we do need to be sure that enough copies are secured to assure preservation, to allow for inevitable losses, and to offer reasonable access to scholars.

As anyone realizes who collects in more than a narrowly defined historical field, it is scarcely possible to know enough history to be a history bibliographer. Fortunately, it is often possible to make what one does know stretch a long way, since recognition on sight is sufficient for most selection purposes. The collection will benefit from each bibliographer's growing and changing areas of special expertise.

But history will never be a field that anyone can "work up" with a few months' practice. To collect in any field requires broad knowledge both of scholarly output and of key figures and developments in many areas, or useful items will be missed. To expand to other countries, languages, and time periods increases geometrically the expanse of knowledge required. Most libraries collect a little more selectively (or a lot more selectively) in foreign languages, increasing still further the need for specialized knowledge to make the right choices. And since no one can know it all, in most libraries collecting means tapping local resources also, by getting to know the historians, talking to them, and encouraging their input.

There are many possible approaches to various fields other than those suggested here. Some bibliographers will find that other tools work better for them depending on their collection, local interests, and arrangements, and on the bibliographer's own skills, interests, and preferences. The tools suggested are at least a starting point, and will lead to others that may be more appropriate to the task at hand. Covering many fields of history for a large collection is a lifelong learning process for all of us, with new discoveries, new tools, and new fields of research appearing regularly to create new challenges.

Selection Sources

American Historical Association's Guide to Historical Literature. New York: Macmillan, 1961.

American Historical Review. v.1– . 1895– . Washington, D.C.: American Historical Assn. 5/year.

Annales: Economies, Sociétés, Civilisations. v.1– . 1929– . Paris: Colin. Bimonthly.

Bengtson, Hermann. *Introduction to Ancient History.* Trans. from 6th ed. by R. I. Frank and Frank D. Gilliard. Berkeley, Calif.: Univ. of California Pr., 1970.

Berton, Peter. *Contemporary China: A Research Guide.* Stanford, Calif.: Hoover Institution on War, Revolution and Peace, 1967.

Bibliography of British History Series:

    Graves, Edgar B. *A Bibliography of English History to 1485.* Oxford: Clarendon Pr. of Oxford Univ. Pr., 1975.

    Read, Conyers. *A Bibliography of British History: Tudor Period, 1485–1603.* 2nd ed. Oxford: Clarendon Pr. of Oxford Univ. Pr., 1959.

    Davies, Godfrey. *A Bibliography of British History: Stuart Period, 1603–1714.* 2nd ed. Oxford: Clarendon Pr. of Oxford Univ. Pr., 1970.

    Pargellis, Stanley, and D. J. Medley. *A Bibliography of British History: The Eighteenth Century, 1714–1789.* Oxford: Clarendon Pr. of Oxford Univ. Pr., 1970.

Hanham, H. J. *A Bibliography of British History, 1851–1914.* Oxford: Clarendon Pr. of Oxford Univ. Pr., 1976.

Bibliotheca Orientalis: International Bibliographic and Reviewing Monthly for Near East and Mediterranean Studies. v.1– . 1943– . Leiden: Nederlands Instituut voor het Nabije Oosten. Bimonthly.

Boyce, Gray C. *Literature of Medieval History 1930–1975.* 5v. New York: Kraus, 1981.

Church History. v.1– . 1932– . Wallingford, Pa.: American Society of Church History. Quarterly.

Diplomatic History. v.1– . 1977– . Wilmington, Del.: Scholarly Resources for the Society for the History of American Foreign Relations. Quarterly.

Eighteenth Century Life. v.1– . 1977– . Williamsburg, Va.: College of William and Mary. 3/year.

English Historical Review. v.1– . 1866– . London: Longmans. Quarterly.

French Historical Studies. v.1– . 1958– . Columbus, Ohio: Society for French Historical Studies. Semiannually.

Gnomon: Kritische Zeitschrift für die Gesamte Klassíche Altertumswissenschaft. v.1– . 1924– . Munich: Beck'sche Verlagsbuchhandlung. 8/year.

Harvard Guide to American History. Rev. ed. 2v. Ed. by Frank Freidel. Cambridge, Mass.: Belknap Pr. of Harvard Univ. Pr., 1974.

Hispania; Revista Espanola de historia. v.1– . 1859– . Munich: Oldenbourg Verlag. Bimonthly.

Historische Zeitschrift. v.1– . 1859– . Munich: Oldenbourg Verlag. Bimonthly.

Historisk Tidskrift. v.1– . 1916– . Stockholm: Svenska Historiska Foereningen. Quarterly.

Historisk Tidskrift för Finland. v.1– . 1916– . Helsinki: Historiska Foereningen. Quarterly.

Historisk Tidskrift: Utgitt Av Den Norske Historiske Forening. v.1– . 1870– . Oslo: Universitetsforlaget for Norske Historiske Forening. Quarterly.

Historisk Tidsskrift. v.1– . 1840– . Copenhagen: Den Danske Historiske Forehing. Biennially.

History: Review of New Books. v.1– . 1972– . Washington, D.C.: Heldref. 10/year.

Hucker, Charles. *China: A Critical Bibliography.* Tucson: Univ. of Arizona Pr., 1962.

Indice Historico Espanol. v.1– . 1953– . Barcelona: Centre de Estudios Historico Internationales, Universidad de Barcelona. 3/year.

Italian Books and Periodicals. v.1– . 1958– . Rome: Istituto Poligraficodello Stato. Monthly.

Journal of American History. v.1– . 1914– . Bloomington, Ind.: Organization of American Historians. Quarterly.

Journal of Asian Studies. v.1– . 1941– . Ann Arbor, Mich.: Assn. for Asian Studies. Quarterly.

Journal of Hellenic Studies. v.1– . 1880– . London: Society for the Promotion of Hellenic Studies. Annually.

Journal of Near Eastern Studies. v.1– . 1884– . Chicago: Univ. of Chicago Pr. Quarterly.

Journal of Psychohistory. v.1– . 1973– . New York: Assn. for Psychohistory. Quarterly.

Journal of Roman Studies. v.1– . 1911– . London: Society for the Promotion of Roman Studies. Annually.

Journal of Southern History. v.1- . 1935- . New Orleans: Southern History Assn. Quarterly.

Microform Review. v.1- . 1972- . Westport, Conn.: Microform Review. Quarterly.

Paetow, Louis. *A Guide to the Study of Mediaeval History.* Rev. ed. New York: Crofts, 1931.

Patterson, Maureen. *South Asian Civilization: A Bibliographic Synthesis.* Chicago: Univ. of Chicago Pr., 1981.

Renaissance Quarterly. v.1- . 1948- . New York: Renaissance Society of America. Quarterly.

Reviews in American History. v.1- . 1973- . Baltimore: Johns Hopkins Univ. Pr. Quarterly.

Revue Historique. v.1- . 1867- . Paris: Presses Universitaires de France. Quarterly.

Rivista Storica Italiana. v.1- . 1884- . Naples: Edizioni Scientifiche Italiane. Quarterly.

Roach, John. *A Bibliography of Modern History.* Supplementary vol. to the *New Cambridge Modern History.* Cambridge and New York: Cambridge Univ. Pr., 1981.

Silberman, Bernard S. *Japan & Korea: A Critical Bibliography.* Tucson: Univ. of Arizona Pr., 1962.

Speculum: A Journal of Mediaeval Studies. v.1- . 1936- . Cambridge, Mass.: Mediaeval Academy of America. Quarterly.

William and Mary Quarterly. v.1- . 1892- . Williamsburg, Va.: Institute of Early American History and Culture. Quarterly.

Work, Monroe N. *A Bibliography of the Negro in Africa and America.* New York: Wilson, 1928.

INSTITUTES AND ACADEMIES

(A representative list only; there are many others.)

Accademia Nazionale dei Linceii: Palazzo Crosina, Via Della Lungara 10, 00165 Rome, Italy.

American Historical Association: 400 A St. S.E., Washington, DC 20003.

British School at Rome: Via Gramsci 61, 00197 Rome, Italy.

Deutsches Archaeologisches Institut: 100 Berlin 33, Podbielskialleer 69–71, GDR.

Ecole Francaise d'Athènes: Odos Didotou 6, Athens, Greece.

Ecole Francaise de Rome: Piazza Farnese 67, Rome, Italy.

Istituto Storico Italiano per il Medio Evo: Piazza dell' Orologio 4, 00186 Rome, Italy.

Mediaeval Academy of America: 1430 Massachusetts Ave., Cambridge, MA 02138.

Nederlands Instituut voor het Nabije Oosten: P.O.B. 9515, 2300 RA, Leiden, Nederlands.

Oriental Institute of the University of Chicago: 1155 E. 58th St., Chicago, IL 60637.

University of California, Berkeley, Center for Chinese Studies: University of California, Berkeley, CA 94720.

University of California, Berkeley, Center for Japanese and Korean Studies: University of California, Berkeley, CA 94720.

University of Michigan Center for Chinese Studies: University of Michigan, Ann Arbor, MI 48109.

University of Michigan Center for Japanese Studies: University of Michigan, Ann Arbor MI 48109.

PHILOSOPHY AND RELIGION

Andrew D. Scrimgeour

Religion and philosophy are venerable cousins in the intellectual history of the Christian West. This essay explores the richness of their publications and presents tools and strategies for their purchase, which are connected to a variety of collecting needs in academic libraries. The literature of religion is the more difficult to profile and monitor because of its complex publication patterns outside the strict academic study of religion.

Religion

Religious studies, or the study of religion, is not a discipline. It is rather a *field of study* more akin to "American studies" or "ethnic studies" than to psychology, philosophy, or anthropology. Subject fields are conglomerates, embracing a variety of disciplines and a welter of phenomena.[1] Participating in the study of religion are sociology, anthropology, psychology, philosophy, history, philology, literary criticism, phenomenology, theology (including biblical studies, ecclesiastical and dogmatic history, and ethics), and the history of religions.

The critiques of this essay, at several stages of development, by Milton J Coalter, Jr. (Louisville Presbyterian Seminary), Maria Grossmann (Harvard University), Dikran Y. Hadidian (Pittsburgh Theological Seminary), David S. Herrstrom (AT&T Information Systems), and Channing Jeschke (Emory University) are gratefully acknowledged.

1. Schubert M. Ogden, "Theology and Religious Studies: Their Difference and the Difference It Makes," *Journal of the American Academy of Religion* 46 no. 1:3–15 (1978); John F. Wilson, "Introduction: The Background and Present Context of the Study of Religion in Colleges and Universities," *The Study of Religion in Colleges and Universities*, ed. by Paul Ramsey and John F. Wilson (Princeton: Princeton Univ. Pr., 1970), pp. 3–22; Claude Welch, *Graduate Education in Religion: A Critical Appraisal* (Missoula: Univ. of Montana Pr., 1971), pp. 3–63; and Walter H. Capps, "On Religious Studies, in Lieu of an Overview," *Journal of the American Academy of Religion* 42 no. 4: 727 (1974).

For a bibliographic review of this topic see William A. Clebsch and Rosemary Rader's "Religious Studies in American Colleges and Universities: A Preliminary Bibliography," *Religious Studies Review* 1 no. 1: 50–60 (1975).

The critical study of religion is largely a Western phenomenon and takes place in two principal contexts: the academy and the church. The scholar working in a department of religion is primarily concerned with description and analysis. Methodologically, he or she is an agnostic. The theologian, on the other hand, whether working in a university or seminary, is a self-conscious representative of a particular religious tradition. While often critical and revisionary of that inheritance, the theologian's primary task is to interpret that legacy to society at large, the academy, and the churches.[2] The theologian in the seminary and divinity school environment is actively involved in the education of persons for ministry.

But what is religion? Each discipline that participates in the study of religion brings its own answer to this inquiry. While definitional debates abound, reminiscent of what Freud called "the narcissism of small differences," the essence of religion is found in its concern with transcendence, the numinous, the Other, the sacred. Through prayers, rituals, institutions, scriptures, beliefs, and doctrines, people seek, affirm, celebrate, remember, and study the holy. The religious world view provides a symbol system that enables persons, individually and corporately, to answer questions of ultimate meaning.

To speak of "religion" is, of course, an academic abstraction. There is no entity called religion. There are only religions. A taxonomy of religions must include prehistoric religions and the faiths of ancient peoples. It would also embrace Hinduism and other religions of India, Buddhism, indigenous religions of East Asia, African religions, Amerindian religions, Judaism, Christianity, and Islam. A host of other religions and religious movements in the modern world could not be neglected, either.

Leadership in religious scholarship in the United States has historically been lodged in the seminaries. But since World War II the center of gravity has shifted to the universities and their departments of religion.[3] While the traditional curricula of the Christian seminaries still loom large in these departments, the methodologies of the social sciences are increasing in importance. The history of religions is the major new emphasis in the university and is a corrective to the academic hegemony of the Judeo-Christian tradition.[4] The entire seminary curriculum, however, has not migrated to the university; the arts of ministry, including liturgics, hymnology, homiletics, pastoral care and counseling, religious education, mis-

2. David Tracy, *The Analogical Imagination: Christian Theology and the Culture of Pluralism* (New York: Crossroads, 1981), p. 20.
3. Krister Stendahl, "Biblical Studies in the University," *The Study of Religion*, ed. by Ramsey and Wilson, p. 23; P. Joseph Cahill, *Mended Speech: The Crisis of Religious Studies and Theology* (New York: Crossroads, 1982), pp. 1–15; and George Lindbeck et al., *University Divinity Schools: A Report on Ecclesiastically Independent Theological Education* (New York: Rockefeller Foundation, 1976), pp. 35–41.
4. H. P. Sullivan, "The History of Religions: Some Problems and Prospects," *The Study of Religion*, ed. by Ramsey and Wilson, pp. 246–80; and Cahill, *Mended Speech*, pp. 79–100.

siology, and church administration remain as the fairly exclusive province of the seminaries.[5]

Religious studies have not yet produced a common curriculum nor a clear consensus on methodology. It is no surprise, then, that a single text has not emerged as the standard introduction to this field. A helpful survey, however, may be found in T. William Hall's anthology, *Introduction to the Study of Religion*.[6] A concise introduction to the study of religion and its subfields is John F. Wilson's "The Study of Religion" in *Research Guide to Religious Studies*.[7] Though dated, the two volumes on religion in the Princeton University series, *Humanistic Scholarship in America*, offer authoritative and extensive overviews.[8] The essays on scholarship trends in *A Theological Book List, 1971* are also valuable summaries.[9]

The North American learned society that encompasses the broadest array of religious interests is the American Academy of Religion. Other major scholarly societies include the Society of Biblical Literature, the American Society of Christian Ethics, the American Society of Church History, the American Society of Missiology, the Catholic Biblical Association, the Catholic Theological Society of America, and the Society for the Scientific Study of Religion. These professional societies publish a host of journals and are linked through a federation of learned societies of religion, the Council on the Study of Religion (CSR). The CSR *Bulletin* is an invaluable source of articles and news pertaining to the teaching of religion, the work of the several societies, developing publication projects, and computer research for religious studies.[10] An international roster of professional societies in religion may be found in the *World Christian Encyclopedia*.[11]

The American Academy of Religion and the Society of Biblical Literature stage their annual meetings together. It is the largest gathering of North American religionists each year. The program book is a unique

5. Edward Farley, *Theologia: The Fragmentation and Unity of Theological Education* (Philadelphia: Fortress, 1983), pp. 73–124. Farley traces the historical development of the seminary curriculum. Don S. Browning, ed., *Practical Theology: The Emerging Field in Theology, Church, and World* (San Francisco: Harper, 1983). These essays provide a current review of practical theology but neglect to include liturgics.
6. T. William Hall, ed., *Introduction to the Study of Religion* (San Francisco: Harper, 1978).
7. John F. Wilson, "The Study of Religion," *Research Guide to Religious Studies*, by John F. Wilson and Thomas P. Slavens (Chicago: American Library Assn., 1982), pp. 3–15.
8. Clyde A. Holbrook, *Religion, A Humanistic Field*, Humanistic Scholarship in America (Englewood Cliffs, N.J.: Prentice-Hall, 1963); and Paul Ramsey et al., *Religion*, Humanistic Scholarship in America (Englewood Cliffs, N.J.: Prentice-Hall, 1965).
9. A. Ward, *A Theological Book List, 1971* (London: Theological Education Fund, 1971), pp. 1–32.
10. *The Council on the Study of Religion Bulletin*. v.1–16. 1970–85. A new periodical, *Religious Studies Newsletter*, will succeed the *Bulletin* on a trial basis.
11. *World Christian Encyclopedia: A Comparative Study of Churches and Religions in the Modern World, AD 1900–2000*, ed. by David B. Barrett (Nairobi: Oxford Univ. Pr., 1982).

barometer on the study of religion on this continent, its leading scholars, key issues, current research interests, and pivotal publications.[12]

The major publishers of scholarly works on religion in America include the university presses, certain denominational presses, Harper & Row, Doubleday, Scribners, Greenwood, Crossroads, Beacon, Winston-Seabury, Edwin Mellen, Pickwick Publications, Orbis, Academic Press of America, and Scholars Press. Scholars Press is one of the leading publishers of scholarly monographs and journals in this country and serves as the publishing arm for several learned societies. Academic Press of America is quickly expanding its inventory of scholarly monographs and moving beyond its vanity press base of doctoral dissertations. Denominational publishers that cannot be ignored include Fortress, Westminster, Abingdon, and John Knox.[13] Representative publishers outside North America include E. J. Brill and Martinus Nijhoff (Netherlands), SCM (England), T & T Clark (Scotland), Brepols Publishers (Belgium), J. C. B. Mohr; Paul Siebeck; and Herder (Germany). A helpful list of publishers in the field of religion is *Book Publishers Directory in the Field of Religion.*[14]

Several recent studies document the congruence of religious publication patterns with those that generally obtain in the humanities. Julie Hurd of the University of Chicago has completed one of the first citation analysis studies on religious bibliography. Her 1983 study of current periodical articles in religion documents the prominence of book citations over periodical citations at a ratio of two to one. Nevertheless, periodical citations represent twenty-five percent of the total citations in current journal articles. The greatest density of non-English language material was German, followed by French. The importance of current publications (defined as within the last ten years) was relative to the subspecialties of the various disciplines within religious studies. Disciplines working heavily with social science publications (sociology of religion, pastoral counseling) showed heavier reliance on current publications than did theological or historical studies where numerous references were made to literature published before 1900. Authors working in the area of pastoral arts tend to work fairly exclusively in English materials, while scholars in the biblical, historical, and theology fields work with a diversity of language publications. Less than half the citations of the Hurd study were to "current" literature, sending a warning to library bibliographers that retrospective acquisitions

12. *1984 Annual Meeting*, American Academy of Religion and the Society of Biblical Literature and ASOR (Chico, Calif.: Scholars Pr., 1984); *Abstracts*, American Academy of Religion, Society of Biblical Literature, 1983 (Chico. Calif.: Scholars Pr., 1983).

13. It is regrettable that Judith S. Duke's study, *Religious Publishing and Communications* (White Plains, N.Y.: Knowledge Industry, 1981), while providing useful profiles of some religious publishers, is idiosyncratic in its choices and omits most of the major religious publishers.

14. *Book Publishers Directory in the Field of Religion*, RIC Supplement 50–52 (Strasbourg Cedex, France: CERDIC Publications, 1980).

cannot be ignored.[15] Chronological and linguistic chauvinism undermines research.

THE STRUCTURE OF RELIGIOUS LITERATURE

Acquisition responsibility for the area of religion seems fairly straightforward at first blush. But when the selector confronts the diverse citations that sprawl under the 200s in the *British National Bibliography* alone, the complexity begins to dawn. Even a cursory reading of the books reviewed in *Library Journal* and *Choice* reveals that religion spawns a literature that encompasses more than the scholarly works from university and academic presses.

This complexity has been simplified by Stephen Peterson of Yale University. Advocating that "library materials should be assessed in light of their function in scholarship and that library acquisition programs should be based on this functional analysis," he divides religious literature into three categories—source literature, critical literature, and historical literature.[16]

Source literature is published by and for the religious communities. It is of two types. First, there are the official documents of these groups—the minutes, proceedings, official reports, and policy statements that record and govern the life of the churches and their institutions. This literature is self-consciously documentary.[17] The extensive bibliographic footnotes of the *Encyclopedia of American Religions* provide helpful introductions to these publications.[18]

Religious life naturally evokes a second type of literature, however, that is not written or published from documentary motives, though collected by libraries for this purpose. Because it grows out of personal faith and experience, this is religious literature in the most profound sense. Often its purpose is to evoke, nurture, or protect faith. And, as the literature closest to the religious life and thought of people, it has a sense of immediacy.[19] Written by persons within the communities of faith, it may be popular, academic, or ephemeral. But once the currency of these publi-

15. Julie M. Hurd, "A Citation Study of Periodical Articles in Religion," *Summary of Proceedings*, Thirty-seventh Annual Conference of the American Theological Library Association 37: 159–71 (1983).

16. Stephen Lee Peterson, "Documenting Christianity: Towards a Cooperative Library Collection Development Program," *Summary of Proceedings*, Thirty-second Annual Conference, American Theological Library Assn., 37:83–103 (1978); cf. his "Collection Development in Theological Libraries: A New Model—A New Hope," *Essays on Theological Librarianship Presented to Calvin Henry Schmitt*, ed. by Peter De Klerk and Earle Hilgert (Philadelphia: American Theological Library Assn., 1980), pp. 143–62, and "Theological Libraries for the Twenty-First Century: Project 2000 Final Report," *Theological Education* 20: 23–53 (Supplement).

17. Peterson, "Documenting Christianity," pp. 83–84.

18. J. Gordon Melton, *The Encyclopedia of American Religions*, 2v. (Wilmington, N.C.: McGrath, 1978).

19. Peterson, "Documenting Christianity," p. 84.

cations wanes, this material is almost always studied historically. Some texts endure the weathering of decades and even centuries, such as scriptures, creeds, liturgies, and classical writings, and enjoy canonical or authoritative status in the community. Other genres include prayers, hymns, sermons, devotional literature, evangelistic writings, tracts, popular and semipopular treatments of all aspects of religion, and curricula for religious education.

Critical literature is scholarly reflection on source literature and religious phenomena that advances the academic discussion of a stated problem or textual tradition. It is governed by the prevailing methodologies of scientific scholarship. This is the literature of biblical studies, historical studies, theology, ethics, philosophy of religion, psychology of religion, sociology of religion, and the history of religions. Critical literature is by definition contemporary, for once its currency has been rendered obsolete by new scholarship, it ceases to be critical literature.[20] This evolution establishes the third category of Peterson's bibliographic trinity, historical literature.

Historical literature is displaced critical literature. These are the works that once advanced scholarship but are now bibliographic artifacts in the history of the discipline. Thus, this group differs from source literature by virtue of its original intent, yet it differs from critical scholarship in that it no longer enjoys currency in its discipline or tradition. Such works document the history of a problem or a scholarly tradition. Research with a wide chronological scope must always have recourse to this literature.[21]

A collection development policy for religion must be keyed to these categories of literature. Critical literature is the presumed core of most college and university collections and is closely integrated with a school's curriculum and the research needs of its faculty. Historical literature is largely the domain of research collections, where the full chronicle of a discipline or tradition is essential for advanced research. However, as microform technology matures, formerly unobtainable historical resources are increasingly attractive and available. Source literature is needed in every library that is serious about its religious holdings. Many college and university libraries are skimpy, if not anorexic, when it comes to the primary texts of religious communities.[22] Without the scriptures, liturgies, hymnals, and leading publications of a given religious tradition, the voices of that community have been muted in favor of interpreters.

20. Ibid.
21. Ibid.
22. I suspect that the influence of Lester Asheim's *The Humanities and the Library* (Chicago: American Library Assn., 1957), especially pp. 32–40, in the education of librarians is telling in this regard. See Susan Avallone's "Receptivity to Religion," *Library Journal* 109: 1891–93 (1984) for vestiges of an Asheim-like aversion to any religious literature that is not scientific and embracing of all other traditions.

The bibliographic net for religion must be carefully woven, for "religion is not a subject that waits to be appropriated by a single academic discipline, however imperial the intellectual ambitions of that discipline may be. Nor, if the truth be told, does religion accommodate easily to the interests of a single profession, even where the interests of that profession are acknowledged to be substantial."[23]

CURRENT ACQUISITIONS

Bibliographers in religion can avoid setting out like Stephen Leacock's mounted policeman, in all directions at once, if they first develop a collection development policy. Informed by an understanding of the bibliographic structure of religious publications, the curricular and research needs of the faculty, the maturity of the collection, special collections, and budget, such a policy will inform, though never govern, daily decision making. But a caution is in order. Purchasing decisions can never be unduly tied to the curriculum, even in the small college setting. Balanced ordering, attentive to the range of disciplines focusing on religion, is necessary to balance an ever-changing faculty, course offerings, and independent study options, as well as to accommodate students following footnotes and syllabi recommendations, and faculty conversing more than ever before across disciplines. Rationalized ordering will take the library closer to the profession's "Holy Grail," a balanced collection offering a degree of predictability in its holdings.

National Bibliographies and Approval Plans. It is essential to develop a monitoring scheme that insures comprehensive and timely coverage for the countries or geographic areas in which one is most interested. Certainly the publications of English-language nations are essential to the needs of this readership. Thus *Weekly Record*, *British National Bibliography*, and the Library of Congress CDS Alert Service are fundamental tools. The European publications are essential to libraries serving advanced degrees. Here the *Deutsche Bibliographie*, *Das Schweizer Buch*, *Les Livres du Mois*, *Bibliografia Nazionale Italiana*, *El Libro Español*, and the Scandinavian bibliographies are fundamental. The national bibliographies of the African, Central American, and South American countries, when available, are vital to balancing religious research that tends to hold conversation with Continental scholarship only, excluding the Third World. Given the vagaries of biblographic control in Central and South America, *Bibliografia Teológica Comentada* must be consulted for Spanish and Portuguese publications.

The substantive discussion of many of these sources in the following chapter by Christie Stephenson need not be repeated here. A few com-

23. Stephen R. Graubard, "Religion," *Daedalus: Journal of the American Academy of Arts and Sciences* 111, no. 1: v (1982).

ments may be of supplemental value. While many of these bibliographies are in a classed arrangement, they are bibliographically abstract. That is, beyond the citation and perhaps subject tracings, they are bereft of evaluative comment. These bibliographies thus tend to serve those libraries that have large budgets and can afford to comprehensively purchase the critical as well as the source literature of these countries. The value of national bibliographies for libraries that have more modest budgets is still significant, but recognizing key scholars and the reputation of individual presses becomes more critical.

Since the *Weekly Record* should be a valuable tool for most of this readership, let me offer a few very practical tips. Do not let these issues pile up. Working through a pile of *Weekly Records* invites carelessness, headaches, and insanity; it also compromises timely ordering. I have found it useful to work through each issue twice. The first review scans authors and titles. A second pass notes Dewey numbers—the 200s, of course, but also those numerical interstices that interlock religion with ethics (170–179), sociology (306), architecture (726), art (704), and music (783), to name a few. The second review scans subject headings. I also use a distinctive marking for titles I have considered but will not order (I underline the Dewey number). Such a notation, combined with those marked for ordering, enables one to return to the issue at a later date with a critical eye for entries that were within the subject scope but missed.

Approval plans have proven beneficial in many settings where significant purchasing, especially in foreign languages, is substantial. In honing a liaison with a foreign firm it is essential that the selection profile be regularly reviewed and studied. Some firms will mark the national bibliography for items to be sent and forward the bibliography for library review. The firm of Otto Harrassowitz enjoys a favored status in many theological libraries for the bibliographic and bookkeeping care demonstrated for several decades in the German market.[24] The approval plan approach is almost mandatory when the library does not have the requisite language skills and must make timely purchases. Most firms will encumber accounts as the selection progresses through the fiscal year and suspend further selection when a specified cap is reached. By the same token, they are always cooperative in issuing pro forma invoices for specified amounts when a library knows that it will not fully expend its budget and does not want to loose those funds to the diastolic movement of the budget at the end of the fiscal year.

Review Publications and Subject Bibliographies. The journals and subject bibliographies of religion enable the bibliographer to select publications with greater confidence than with national and trade bibliogra-

24. Otto Harrassowitz, POB 2929–6200 Wiesbaden, Germany. North American address: P.O. Box 340, Cassville, MO 65625.

phies.[25] The single, most important review publication for the area of religion is *Religious Studies Review* (*RSR*). Begun in 1975 by the Council on the Study of Religion, it is, as its subtitle promises, "a quarterly review of publications in the field of religion and related disciplines." If a religion bibliographer were restricted to a single review publication, this is that tool. Each issue provides succinct reviews of about 250 books organized under 30 subject categories. These reviews tend to feature books published within the past two years, but ones three years old are not infrequent. International publications are reviewed in substantial numbers, but English titles dominate. Brevity being a corollary to extensiveness of coverage the annotations do not exceed 100 words. The reviews are fashioned by religious scholars in North American colleges, universities, and seminaries and are signed.

RSR also specializes in "review essays" as well as "bibliographic essays." In this regard it has become the North American incarnation of the venerable *Theologische Rundschau*. Review essays discuss recent landmark studies, the corpus of leading scholars, and clusters of related titles in depth. Frequently, companion essays by scholars from separate fields or divergent points of view will critique the volumes. These essays, with their extensive footnotes, are a must to the religious bibliographer, since the works reviewed are generally essential to most academic libraries purchasing in the field of religion. Moreover, *RSR* regularly lists reprintings, recent North American dissertations in religion, and dissertations in progress. It is less successful in reviewing reference works, but is pledged to filling this lacuna. New journals and audiovisual resources are not monitored.

Two European publications balance the North American cast of *Religious Studies Review*. *Theologische Literaturzeitung* (*TL*) is a monthly review journal dating from 1876 that ranges through general religion, philosophy of religion, biblical studies, church history, systematic theology, creeds and confessions, ethics, religious education, missions, sociology of religion, psychology, art, and literature. Each issue carries some forty reviews by German scholars. British, German, and other European publications are reviewed and the evaluative essays are in German. There is a definite Protestant slant to the choice of publications and the evaluative perspective offered. World religions are not included.

Complementing *TL* is *Theologische Revue*. It is the Catholic counterpart to *TL* and is a virtual clone in appearance. The subjects covered resemble *TL* with several major and predictable exceptions. Canon law is included and liturgics is given greater attention. However, history of religions, sociology, and psychology are not included. Between thirty and forty critical

25. Peterson, "Documenting Christianity," p. 92.

Religious Studies Review: A Quarterly Review of Publications in the Field of Religion and Related Disciplines. v.1– . 1975– . Hanover, Pa.: Council on the Study of Religion. Quarterly.

   Scholarly review journal.

   About 200 reviews per issue.

   1–2-year lag between book publication and review; 3–4-year time lags not uncommon.

   5–7 extensive "review essays" per issue.

   Bibliographic essays appear regularly.

   Dissertations in progress listed.

   Completed dissertations listed.

   Annual index in October issue.

The single most important review publication for the academic study of religion, this work provides signed book reviews by scholars that average 100 words; these are descriptive and evaluative with recommendations to appropriate curricular or library collecting level. Reviews appear in "Notes on Recent Publications" section and are classified under some thirty subject categories. These include the social-scientific study of religion; ritual, cult, worship; philosophy of religion; theology; ethics; arts, literature, and religion; ancient Near East; Christian origins; history of Christianity; history of Judaism; Islam; the Americas; and Asian religions. Bibliographic information is complete. The "Review Essays" are vital to establishing the most influential works in religion. Reference works are slighted and new journals and media are not reviewed; consult the *ADRIS Newsletter* for information on new reference works and journals.

---

reviews appear in each issue. Distinctive to *Theologische Revue* is a bibliography section that lists books, journal articles, and dissertations. Essay collections are also analyzed in this section.

   With the exception of history of religions scholarship, the use of these two monthlies will provide solid, critical coverage of the major European scholarship in religion. For libraries using national bibliographies for German and English publications, these journals offer access to essential French, Italian, and Scandinavian publications.

   Several other publications may serve the library well that wants to purchase very selectively in foreign-language publications. An international panel of scholars nominates works for an annual roster of outstanding scholarly publications. This is *Scholar's Choice.* Another helpful service is the *German Book Digest* issued quarterly by Otto Harrassowitz. The philosophy and religion edition is a selective listing of recent European publications from Germany, Austria, and Switzerland. Other sources for guidance in collection development are the acquisition lists of leading theological libraries. One of the most important is the *Mitteilungen und Neuerwerbungen,* issued by the theological library of the University of Tübingen.

   The library supporting a variety of advanced degrees in religion must employ a variety of sources to review current publications and to monitor, at all comprehensively, international publications beyond national bibliographies. With the demise of the *International Bibliography of the History of Religions*,[26] the most comprehensive subject bibliography for religion is the Belgian work "Elenchus Bibliographicus" in *Ephemerides Theologicae Lovanienses (ETL)*. While not as well known as its Italian counterpart in biblical studies, *Elenchus Bibliographicus Biblicus*, it has no rival for international publications. European, Third World, and North American publications are included. Books, pamphlets, festschriften, conference proceedings, and ecclesiastical documents are listed. There are no annotations, so *ETL* does not displace review journals. But its comprehensive listings insure the bibliographer of seeing much literature, both published and ephemeral, that would otherwise escape.

The traditional areas of theology are well served, and the history of religions monitoring is solid. The cognate areas of the social sciences are not included. The Latin subject headings are easily deciphered and should not deter the non-Latinist. It is annoying at times to sort through the hundreds of journal articles that are also included, but one's eye quickly learns to winnow book entries from journal entries. The 1983 issue listed largely 1982 publications, so its value as a timely yet comprehensive listing is clear. The other issues of this learned journal offer listings of international conferences and congresses, publication announcements, and faculty appointments of interest to a global academic audience.

ETL defers ecclesiastical history to its sister journal, *Revue d'Histoire Ecclésiastique (RHE)*, which is the standard church history bibliography. Over 800 pages each year are dedicated to a classified bibliography for international books, articles, and reviews that appear in three installments, one in each trimester issue. The full classification outline and author index appear with the final issue of the year. While somewhat awkward to use because of its sequential publication and inclusion of journal articles, it offers the bibliographer a panoramic sweep of international publications. As one becomes familiar with the classification scheme, one can scan the sections of particular interest, whether history of religious art, socioeconomic themes, or the history of a particular country or region. The bibliography sections should not be missed for leads on very specialized reference works, as well as bibliographies useful for collection evaluation and retrospective collection development.

The "Chronicle" section, separate from the bibliography proper, is a splendid source of information on museum catalogs, congresses, important reference publications, new journals, and the careers of leading historians of religion. While the classified citations do not carry any evaluative com-

26. Announced in *Numen: International Review for the History of Religions* 27: 194–95 (1980). The journal *Science of Religion* (Amsterdam: Institut voor Godsdienstwetinschap) will continue *IBHR*'s listings of journal articles, but no provision for the monitoring of books and other genres has yet been announced.

"Elenchus Bibliographicus." In *Ephemerides Theologicae Lovanienses.* v.1- .
1924- . Louvain: Ephemerides Theologicae Lovanienses, Bibliotheque de
l'Universite. Quarterly.
The bibliography appears as the combined second and third issues.
Classified bibliography of international books and journal articles.
One year time lag between publications and their listing.
Author index.
Modest subject index for personal names.
Cumulative index for 1947–81 available (F. Neirynck and F. Van Sebroeek,
  Ephemerides Theologicae Lovanienses 1924–1981. Tables generales.
  Bibliotheca Ephemeridum Theologicarum Lovaniensium 1947–1981.
  Louvain: Ephemerides Theologicae Lovanienses, 1982).
Most comprehensive annual bibliography for religion, *ETL* is a classified listing
of international books, articles, pamphlets, festschriften, conference proceed-
ings, and ecclesiastical documents. It is the most comprehensive annual bibliography of religious publications for both scholarly and confessional writings.
Subjects include bibliography, history of theology, history of religions, biblical
studies, theology, canon law, liturgics, and religious education. These areas are
further subdivided. Church history and social scientific treatments of religion
are not included. A particularly rich listing of biographies on recently deceased
scholars and clerics may be found in "In Memoriam" in the Generalia (1) section.
The "Chronicle" that appears in the first and fourth issues is a good source for
reports on international congresses, activities of renowned scholars, and major
publication announcements. Consult *Revue d'Histoire Ecclésiastique* for coverage of church history and *Religious Studies Review* for history of religions.

ment, a separate section offers an index to current book reviews ("Comptes
Rendus D'Ouvrages Precedemment Annoncés"). Because articles are seg-
regated from the monographs, *RHE* is less awkward to use than *ETL*.
The bibliography focuses the previous year's publications, but items missed
in a given year are added the following year. While there are many bibliographies and journals dedicated to specific historic periods, such as the
Patristic and Reformation, *RHE* is the most comprehensive service for
the entire historic spectrum.

Source literature makes only modest appearances in most of the national
and trade bibliographies. Given the flood of this material, most libraries
must choose representative publications and insure the selection of material central to the religious denominations and organizations in which
they have interest. The subject headings "Devotional writing" and "Popular writing" are often helpful in spotting source literature. The deft bibliographer will also learn the denominational or confessional alliance of
the religious presses.[27] But a caution is in order. While many publishing
houses are known for their popular or devotional titles (Word Press,
Moody Press, Zondervan), they will also publish important reference works

27. Consult the *Book Publishers Directory*

and the classics of their tradition. Some university bibliographers eschew all denominational publishing houses. Such practice insures the loss of core scholarship, for several of the major denominational houses are also leaders in the distribution of critical literature. Westminster, Fortress, John Knox, Mercer Press, and KTAV are representative.

Some genres of source literature are particularly difficult to monitor. Bibles, prayer books, rites, and liturgies are central examples. Locating current publication information for these genres is now aided by the Bowker annual, *Religious Books and Serials in Print*.[28] When a particular religious tradition is chosen for special development in a collection, it is essential to follow the publication announcements and reviews in the journals, magazines, and newsletters of that community. Sources of information for the publications and addresses of religious organizations can be found in the "Directory" of the *World Christian Encyclopedia* (non-Christian groups are also included), the *Directory of Religious Organizations in the United States and Canada*, *A Directory of Religious Bodies in the United States*, and the *Yearbook of American and Canadian Churches*.[29] The diversity of religious life in North America, let alone the world, is not comprehensively documented in the libraries of the United States and Canada.[30] Thus the opportunities are rich for libraries looking to develop unique areas of specialization.

There is a spate of specialized bibliographies and review journals for the disciplines comprising the field of religious studies. A critical introduction to most of these will be found in Michael Walsh's splendid volume, *Religious Bibliographies in Serial Literature: A Guide*.[31]

Books published in series constitute a large portion of the critical studies in religion. An excellent source for monitoring series is the annual index, *Religion Index Two: Multi-Author Works*.

The review journals in religion offer only spotty coverage of multimedia publications. The *Media Review Digest* should thus be consulted. Two significant library catalogs of religious media are those of Union Theological Seminary in Virginia and Princeton Theological Seminary.

The best source for information on computer databases for religious studies is the *CSR Bulletin*. "Offline: Computer Research for Religious Studies" is a new section of the *Bulletin* that was inaugurated in the June 1984 issue.[32]

28. *Religious Books and Serials in Print, 1982–83: An Index to Religious Literature Including Philosophy* (New York: Bowker, 1982).

29. *World Christian Encyclopedia*, pp. 893–977; *Directory of Religious Bodies in the United States* (New York: Garland, 1977); *Directory of Religious Organizations in the United States and Canada* (Wilmington, N.C.: Consortium Books, 1977); and *Yearbook of American and Canadian Churches 1916–* (Nashville: Abingdon), annually.

30. Peterson, "Theological Libraries for the Twenty-First Century," pp. 37–42.

31. Michael J. Walsh et al., *Religious Bibliographies in Serial Literature: A Guide* (Westport, Conn.: Greenwood, 1981).

32. "*Offline* will deal with such matters as bibliography and the availability of computer data, relevant technological developments with special (but not exclusive) reference to microcomputers, and printing and publication capabilities," *CSR Bulletin* 15, no. 3: 89 (1984).

STARTING A CORE COLLECTION

Assistance in developing a core collection in religion may be gained from Wilson and Slavens' *Research Guide to Religious Studies*. The most comprehensive bibliographic tool that directly addresses such a task is the work of Raymond Morris of Yale University and some ninety international scholars and librarians. Their effort, *A Theological Book List*, lists over 5400 volumes in a classified arrangement with occasional notes and indispensable essays.[33] Three subsequent volumes (edited by A. Ward) extend the value of the original volume and enlarge its international coverage.[34] The volumes are ecumenical in breadth and attentive to global religious traditions.

The selection of key reference works is facilitated by Robert Kepple's *Reference Works for Theological Research* (2nd edition, 1981). Kepple supplants John Bollier's less extensive volume, *The Literature of Theology*.[35] Kepple, however, should be supplemented by James McCabe's *Critical Guide to Catholic Reference Books* (2nd edition, 1980) and for world religions, Leszek Karpinski's *The Religious Life of Man: Guide to Basic Literature* (1978) for world religions. Charles Adams's much cited *A Reader's Guide to the Great Religions* can also be helpful, but the idiosyncratic style of each chapter essay tends to bury the reference works.[36] Gerhard Schwinge's *Bibliographische Nachschlagewerke zur Theologie und ihren Grenzegbieten* (1975) is indispensable in its listings of international reference works.

Religious Studies Review and the *ADRIS Newsletter* will update all of these volumes. The projected four-volume project of G. E. Gorman and Lyn Gorman may well eclipse Kepple, McCabe, and Karpinski. They have just published *Theological and Religious Reference Materials: General Resources and Biblical Studies*.[37]

In choosing journals, it is vital to link subscriptions to periodical indexes. Two essential indexes for religion are *Religion Index One: Periodicals (RIO)* (formerly *Index to Religious Periodical Literature*)[38] and the *Cath-*

33. Raymond P. Morris, *A Theological Book List* (Middleton, Conn.: Greeno, Hadden, 1971).
34. A. Marcus Ward, *A Theological Book List*, English Supplement no. 1 (Naperville, Ill.: Allenson's, 1963); idem, *A Theological Book List*, English Supplement no. 2 (London: Theological Education Fund, 1968): idem, *A Theological Book List*, English Supplement no. 3 (London: Theological Education Fund, 1971).
35. John A. Bollier, *The Literature of Theology: A Guide for Students and Pastors* (Philadelphia: Westminster, 1979).
36. Charles J. Adams, ed., *A Reader's Guide to the Great Religions*, 2nd ed. (New York: Free Pr., 1977).
37. G. E. Gorman and Lyn Gorman, *Theological and Religious Reference Materials: General Resources and Biblical Studies*, Bibliographies and Indexes in Religious Studies, no. 1 (Westport, Conn.: Greenwood, 1984).
38. *Religion Index One: Periodicals* (Chicago: American Theological Library Assn., 1977–).

olic Periodical Literature Index (CPLI).[39] Under a long-standing informal agreement between the editors of these two publications, neither service will add titles covered by the other. One refinement on this recommendation would be to determine the overlap of coverage for particular journals by comparing the journal lists of *RIO, CPLI, Readers's Guide to Periodical Literature, Humanities Index,* and *Arts & Humanities Citation Index.*

RETROSPECTIVE COLLECTION DEVELOPMENT

Retrospective purchasing in religion is difficult, time consuming, and expensive. Rare are those miraculous quantum jumps that enable a library to surge in research strength with a single purchase. Such was the case in 1975 when Emory University purchased the renowned Hartford Seminary Foundation collection. Such a bibliographic coup rarely presents itself. But a development of even greater magnitude should be studied closely.

The American Theological Library Association has announced a major microfilming project that has begun to systematically film religious monographs published internationally between 1860 and 1929.[40] The principle source of volumes for the initial years of filming is the library of Union Theological Seminary in New York City. The thoughtful will at once realize that a revolution is in the making—one that democratizes traditional centers of research while saving a fragile and disappearing record of religious life and thought.

Microforms in Print and the *National Register of Microform Masters* will direct the bibliographer to much material that is available on film and fiche. The American Theological Library Association has been filming religious serials for a quarter of a century, and its regularly updated catalog is indispensable.[41] The filming of University Microfilms International extends to religion. However, many of its listings for older runs of religious periodicals serve as advertisements to trigger actual filming when sufficient inquiries have been received. Other major sources of microform collections include Lost Cause Press and Inter Documentation Company.[42]

There is a host of secondhand book dealers specializing in religious bibliography. Many of them regularly issue subject classified lists and offer search services. An excellent list of international dealers may be found in Brevard Childs' *Old Testament Books for Pastor and Teacher*; a com-

39. *Catholic Periodical and Literature Index* (Haverford, Pa.: Catholic Library Assn., 1967–).
40. For information write: The ATLA Preservation Board, P.O. Box 111, Princeton, NJ 08542.
41. Ibid.
42. Lost Cause Press (750–56 Starks Building, Louisville, KY 40202), and Inter Documentation Company (Poststrasse 14, 6300 Zug, Switzerland).

panion volume by Ralph Martin, *New Testament Books for Pastor and Teacher*, offers a valuable supplement to Childs' roster.[43]

For those libraries working on retrospective holdings for North American publications, the newly published *Religious Books 1876-1982* is indispensable. It is "the most comprehensive bibliography of books on religion for North American usage."[44]

The shrewd bibliographer aggressively seeks specialty collections that are tailored to the curricular and research needs of the institution. Specialty collections may also add distinction to a library and are often attractive to a donor, when establishing endowed book funds is not. Seeking such collections directly, rather than working through a dealer, is often the most successful approach. For example, if a library needed to strengthen its holdings in the Hebrew scriptures, it would do well to scan the field of biblical scholars to find a professor approaching retirement whose scholarship and personal library were well known. Frequently such scholars need to radically trim their libraries when they leave the academic setting and move from houses to apartments. Often they are at a loss as to how to responsibly divest.[45]

Another tack is nurturing a relationship with the seminaries and divinity schools in one's geographic area. The libraries of these schools regularly receive the libraries of retired and deceased faculty and clergy as gifts. The basements of many of these libraries are crammed with boxes of unprocessed donations. Some of these libraries have become very sophisticated in processing, adding, and selling such titles. They can be a Mecca for the impecunious and aggressive library.

A further refinement on this strategy is to write a seminary of a particular denominational heritage when needing histories of that tradition. The confessional lineage of a particular school can be determined by consulting the *Yearbook of American and Canadian Churches*. News of seminary closings and mergers that potentially place libraries on the market is often found in the *Christian Century*.

The American Theological Library Association (ATLA) has a periodical exchange service for members that is very active.[46] Many libraries have made significant gains in periodical holdings through this informal, though well-regulated, system. Some of the circulated lists of available journal runs are very substantial.

43. Brevard Childs, *Old Testament Books for Pastor and Teacher* (Philadelphia: Westminster, 1977), p. 116; and Ralph P. Martin, *New Testament Books for Pastor and Teacher* (Philadelphia: Westminster, 1984), pp. 145–46. To these lists I would add Amphisbaena Rare Books (320 North Fourth Street, Stillwater, MN 55082).

44. *Religious Books 1876–1982*, 4 v. (New York: Bowker, 1983), p. vii.

45. For a case study in a shrewd purchase of a scholar's library see "A Literary Treasure for UTS," and "Calvin Scholar Applauds Acquisition," in *UTS Focus* (Richmond, Va.: Union Theological Seminary, Mar. 1984), pp. 2–5.

46. For information write Executive Secretary, ATLA, 5600 S. Woodlawn Avenue, Chicago, IL 60637.

The range and vintage of religious publications challenge the most seasoned bibliographer. Northrup Frye recently asked of that quintessential religious volume, the Bible, "Why does this huge sprawling, tactless book sit there inscrutably in the middle of our cultural heritage, frustrating all our efforts to walk around it?"[47] Perhaps this discussion of selection tools and strategies will enable bibliographers to circumambulate this massive body of literature with less frustration.

Philosophy

Philosophy is a discipline at the heart of the humanities. Until this century it was dominated by metaphysics, speculative reflections on the nature of the universe and being.[48] Philosophy has experienced an international flowering in the university since 1945, and some commentators view post–World War II philosophy with rhapsodic chauvinism.[49] It is clear to most observers that the number of philosophers and philosophical societies and their publications have grown enormously in the last four decades.[50]

The traditional divisions of philosophy are metaphysics (the nature of reality), epistemology (the theory of knowledge), logic, ethics, and aesthetics (the analysis of beauty and the arts). Within the contemporary period, roughly 1945 to the present, philosophy has been organized into at least sixteen major areas, and each part of the history of philosophy has become a specialty in its own right. These include, exclusive of the five classical areas: philosophy of language and linguistic philosophy, philosophy of mind, philosophy of action, axiology (values), philosophy of science, philosophy of history, social-political philosophy of psychology, philosophy of law, philosophy of religion, philosophy of psychology and psychoanalysis, and philosophy of education.[51]

The interdisciplinary nature of contemporary philosophy is readily apparent. Herein resides the principal challenge for the bibliographer-selector. While the surveying of current publications in the major areas of philosophy is relatively easy, managing the interdisciplinary discussion in print is difficult. Increasingly, the selector realizes that there is no longer a stigmata by which a philosophical publication can be readily recognized.

47. Northrup Frye, *The Great Code: The Bible and Literature* (New York: Harcourt, 1982), p. xviii.
48. Charles Harvey Arnold, "Philosophy and Religion," *Library Trends* 459–77 (Jan. 1967).
49. John R. Burr, *Handbook of World Philosophy: Contemporary Developments since 1945* (Westport, Conn.: Greenwood, 1980), pp. ix–xxii; and Terrence N. Tice, *Research Guide to Philosophy*, by Terrence N. Tice and Thomas P. Slavens (Chicago: American Library Assn, 1983), p. ix.
50. Arnold, "Philosophy and Religion," p. 461.
51. Tice, *Research Guide*, pp. 306–10.

Philosophy may be studied as the lengthened shadows of the great philosophers—Plato, Aristotle, Thomas Aquinas, Kant, Hegel, Locke, Whitehead, Wittgenstein, and Derrida; it may also be viewed as a congeries of movements. Some of the major movements include idealism, Thomism, existentialism, phenomenology, pragmatism, Marxism, and deconstructionism. Or, philosophy can be approached through a series of classical questions or problems—theodicy (the nature of good and evil), God, freedom, immortality, mind, and nature. Finally, of course, this field can be studied historically, century by century, and geographically, country by country. Most of the bibliographies and review publications that this essay will introduce will reflect these structures in whole or in part.

A brief introduction to philosophy may be found in the *Encyclopedia of Philosophy*.[52] A dependable historical overview is Frank Thilly's brief survey, *A History of Philosophy*.[53] A current volume that outlines the principle changes in philosophy and the history of philosophy is Tice and Slavens' *Research Guide to Philosophy*. The philosophy volume in the Princeton series, "Humanistic Scholarship in America," edited by Roderick M. Chisholm, is helpful for the 1930 to 1960 period.[54] A valuable supplement to both Thilly and Chisholm is John R. Burr's compendium, *Handbook of World Philosophy: Contemporary Developments since 1945*.[55]

The principal genres in philosophical publishing are the monograph, monographic series, journal article, and transactions of the philosophical societies. Richard T. De George's bibliographic guide is often cited as a key source for determining essential reference tools for philosophy.[56] But it is also a marvelous presentation of the publication profile for this field. The introductions that head each major chapter are valuable orientations. Extensive treatment of the history of the development of the bibliography of philosophy is offered in Michael Jasenas's Columbia University doctoral dissertation.[57] Other bibliographic essays of aid to the selector include Charles Arnold's article "Philosophy and Religion" (*Library Trends*, 1967), and the three articles by William Gerber in *The Encyclopedia of Philosophy* ("Philosophical Bibliographies," "Philosophical Dictionaries and En-

---

52. John Passmore, "Philosophy," *Encyclopedia of Philosophy*, vol. 6 (New York: Macmillan, 1967), pp. 216–26.

53. Frank Thilly, *A History of Philosophy*, 3rd. ed., rev. by Ledger Wood (New York: Holt, 1957).

54. Roderick M. Chisholm et al., *Philosophy*, Humanistic Scholarship in America (Englewood Cliffs, N.J.: Prentice-Hall, 1964).

55. Burr, *Handbook*.

56. Richard T. De George, *The Philosopher's Guide to Sources, Research Tools, Professional Life, and Related Fields* (Lawrence: Regents Pr. of Kansas, 1980).

57. Michael Jasenas, "History of the Development of the Bibliography of Philosophy," D.L.S. thesis, Columbia Univ., 1967.

cyclopedias," and "Philosophical Journals").[58] The chapter on philosophy in A. Robert Rogers' *The Humanities* is also useful.[59]

Learned societies in philosophy have proliferated in recent decades. Several of the major societies include the American Philosophical Association, the American Catholic Philosophical Association, and the International Society for the History of Ideas. Two essential directories for determining the full roster of philosophical associations and societies are the *Directory of American Philosophers* (12th edition)[60] and the *International Directory of Philosophy and Philosophers, 1982–85*.[61] These two directories will orient the selector to the proceedings, journals, monographic series, and occasional publications of these organizations.

As a library hones its collection, it will undoubtedly choose areas for special concentration. Such choices naturally evoke the search for related ephemeral documents. Following the international meetings of philosophical organizations and special congresses is fundamental in such collection development. Tracking these meetings is now eased by *The Philosophical Calendar*, published by the Conference of Philosophical Societies.[62] The "Chroniques" section of *Revue philosophique de Louvain* may also be consulted in this regard, as can Burr's *Handbook*.[63]

The scholarly journal has had a venerable history in philosophy. Several of the journals that were founded in the seventeenth century survive to this day. A valuable introduction to philosophical journals and their history is found in the Gerber essay.[64] A descriptive overview of current periodicals may be found in De George's *Philosopher's Guide*,[65] and a comprehensive listing in *Répertoire Bibliographique de la Philosophie*.[66] While dated, the 1967 publication, *Liste Mondiale des Périodiques Spécialisés*, is helpful.[67] It provides a short analysis of each periodical as well as title listings by subject. The list of journals indexed by *Philosopher's Index*, *Humanities Index*, *Arts & Humanities Citation*, and *Bulletin signalétique: sciences humaines, philosophie* should also be consulted when determining or evaluating journal subscriptions so as to insure full access to their contents.

58. William Gerber, "Philosophical Bibliographies," *Encyclopedia of Philosophy*, vol. 6, pp. 166–69; "Philosophical Dictionaries and Encyclopedias," ibid., pp. 170–99; and "Philosophical Journals," ibid., pp. 199–216.

59. A. Robert Rogers, "Accessing Information in Philosophy,"*The Humanities: A Selective Guide to Information Sources*, 2nd ed. (Littleton, Colo.: Libraries Unlimited, 1979), pp. 14–30.

60. *Directory of American Philosophers 1984–85*, 12th ed., ed. by Archie J. Bahm (Bowling Green, Ohio: Philosophy Documentation Center, 1984).

61. *International Directory of Philosophy and Philosophers, 1982–85*, 5th ed., ed. by Ramona Carmier et al. (Bowling Green, Ohio: Philosophy Documentation Center, 1982).

62. *Philosophical Calendar* (Lawrence, Kans.: Conference of Philosophical Societies, 1978–). Monthly.

63. Burr, "Appendix II: Congresses and Meetings," *Handbook*, pp. 583–604.

64. Gerber, "Philosophical Journals."

65. See pp. 118–48.

66. See "Periodiques Depouilles" in each volume.

67. *Liste Mondiale des Périodiques Spécialisés*, Publications Serie C, Catalogues et Inventaires I (Paris: Mouton, 1967).

University presses as well as learned societies play a major role in the publishing of philosophical research. Profiles on presses and scholarly guild publications may be garnered from the *Directory of American Philosophers* and the *International Directory of Philosophy and Philosophers.*[68] When selectors wish to monitor particular presses around the world and be free of undue dependence upon the mailings of these presses, they may consult *Bibliographie de la Philosophie* which, in its "Table des Editeurs," provides an annual international roster of publications by publisher.

There are several renowned lecture series in philosophy that should be followed, particularly those that have become well established in the field. These include the Paul Carus Lectures, Ernst Cassirer Lectures (Yale University), Gifford Lectures (Aberdeen University), William James Lectures on Philosophy (Harvard University), and the Woodbridge Lectures (Columbia University).[69]

Several monographic series should also be considered for acquisition. A selective list may be found in De George's *Guide.*[70] De George is also a sound source for determining the critical core of reference works.

CURRENT ACQUISITIONS

The comments on national bibliographies and approval plans for religion obtain for philosophy as well, and will not be repeated here. Many of the tools discussed in that section overlap with philosophy and should be reviewed when determining a key list of selection tools for philosophy. This will be most obvious in the areas of philosophy of religion and ethics.

Given the preeminence of university presses in the field of philosophy, access to timely reviews of their releases is a primary concern of the selector. The *University Publishing New Books Supplement*, which is in its first year, promises comprehensive and timely reviews of all university press publications. If this new quarterly proves to have editorial independence of the presses and can offer critical appraisals and not mere content overviews, it will serve the bibliographer of philosophy well.

The most valuable monitoring service for the field of philosophy is *Bibliographie de la Philosophie (BP)*. This quarterly offers international coverage of philosophical books. All new publications receive objective and dependable abstracts that sometimes run to 300 words, written by an international cast of philosophers. *BP* is also a valuable source for information on reprints, new translations, and editions. If the selector has a range of subject responsibilities beyond philosophy and must rely on a single tool for selection, the *Bibliographie de la Philosophie* should be that tool.

68. See note #61.
69. De George, *Philosopher's Guide*, provides a helpful listing (pp. 145–46).
70. Ibid., pp. 146–48.

Bibliographie de la Philosophie/Bibliography of Philosophy. v.1– . 1937– .
  Paris: International Institue of Philosophy, Libraraire Philosophique.
  Quarterly.
  Scholarly abstracting service for books.
  About 250 abstracts per issue.
  New books receive abstracts, reprints do not.
  Classification by subject.
  Annual indexes in final issue of each volume.
  Aim of publication is international completeness.

The bibliography offers international coverage of books published in philosophy. This is achieved by a monitoring system built around thirty-three national centers. Abstracts are in a variety of languages and include the traditional areas of religious thought as well as interdisciplinary discussion. The major subject headings are: philosophy in general; logic and philosophy of science; philosophical psychology; aesthetics; ethics and values; social philosophy; culture and education; religion; history of philsophy; and reference books and miscellanea. There are indexes for authors, titles, subjects, quoted names, and publishers. Journal literature is not included, but reprints, new editions, paperbacks, and translations are. The bibliographic citations are full and accurate. A valuable tool for monitoring particular countries and presses, as well as the individual subspecialties of philosophy.

Répertorie Bibliographique de la Philosophie. v.1– . 1949– . Louvain-la-
  Neuve, Belgium: Éditions de l'Institut Supérieur de Philosophie,
  L'Université Catholique de Louvain. Quarterly.
  Bibliography of international books and articles.
  Strict interpretation of the scope of philosophy.
  Classification by subject.
  Annual indexes in fourth issue of each volume.
  List of books is considered exhaustive.

Philosophical literature, both book and journal articles, is listed if published in English, Dutch, French, German, Italian, Latin, Portuguese, Spanish, or Catalan. The definition of philosophy is rather strict and excludes some of the auxiliary sciences of philosophy and the history of philosophy. Thus the scope of books included in the *Bibliographie de la Philosophie* is somewhat larger than the *Répertoire*. The reading of the introduction is essential to understanding the placement of entries. A list of book reviews (Repertorie des comptes rendus) appears in the November issue and is helpful in locating critical reviews. The general index of names (Table onomastique) enables one to find, under an author's name, all the publications that he or she has written, translated, or edited (including book reviews), as well as titles that cite his or her name. Writers of the ancient and patristic periods are classified under the Latin form of the name by which they are commonly known. An asterisk precedes the entry for books; thus books are easily distinguished from the journal articles.

Complementing *BP* is *Répertoire Bibliographique de la Philosophie.* While more restrictive in both its definition of philosophical literature and languages than *BP*, it includes journal literature and offers the means to monitoring new journals and publications of special congresses and learned societies. It also augments *Philosopher's Index* as an avenue to locating review literature.

Between *BP* and *Répertoire* the selector can be confident of close to exhaustive international coverage of the major areas of philosophical discourse. The review articles in journals of interdisciplinary discussion should be followed as well. Representative of these journals are *Philosophy & Social Criticism*, *Philosophy & Public Affairs*, and *Philosophy & Phenomenological Research*. Following the reviews in specialized journals that reflect the focused interests of a given library as well as the footnotes and bibliographies of their articles remains a valuable step in locating unpublished and other ephemeral writings.

STARTING A CORE COLLECTION

Three volumes that will prove helpful in establishing a core collection in philosophy are Tice and Slavens' *Research Guide*, De George's *Philosopher's Guide*, and Matczak's *Philosophy*.[71] The English-language bias limits Tice and Slavens as well as Matczak. Friedrich Ueberweg's history of philosophy has been known for its full bibliographies since its initial publication in the 1860s. Now in its fourteenth edition, *Grundriss der Geschichte der Philosophie* is a helpful source for determining a core research collection of international publications.[72] A new edition promises to update the bibliographies. Michael Jasenas provides a unique tool for the selector constructing a core collection. His "Short Title List of Major Philosophical Works Discussed in Standard Histories of Philosophy, Arranged by Centuries" is a desideratum list for any library offering advanced degrees in philosophy.[73]

RETROSPECTIVE COLLECTION DEVELOPMENT

Many of the volumes introduced above will also be useful in retrospective work. Access to specialized lists, tailored to historical periods, individual philosophers, movements, and problems, is facilitated by Herbert Guerry's compilation of philosophical bibliographies.[74] Mining the volumes of *Philosopher's Index* and *Bibliographic Index* will also yield valuable bibliographies. Another tack is to consult the published catalogs of libraries

71. Sebastian A. Matczak, *Philosophy: A Select, Classified Bibliography of Ethics, Economics, Law, Politics, Sociology*, Philosophical Questions Series no. 3 (New York: Humanities Pr., 1970).
72. Friedrich Ueberweg, *Grundriss der Geschichte der Philosophie*, 14th ed., 3 v. (Basel/Stuttgart: Schwabe: 1958–1960). English translation: *History of Philosophy, from Thales to the Present Time, 1887* is from the 4th edition and does not carry the bibliographic information of the German original. A new German edition has been announced by Schwabe Verlag of Basel.
73. Jasenas, "History of the Development," pp. 269–305 (appendix II).
74. Herbert Guerry, ed., *A Bibliography of Philosophical Bibliographies* (Westport, Conn.: Greenwood, 1977).

holding collections of international repute. Such an example is the 1973 catalog of Harvard University.[75] Philosophy of religion can be approached in a similar manner through the catalog of Union Theological Seminary (New York City).[76]

Gabriel Marcel, in his 1949 Gifford Lectures, spoke of philosophy as "aid to discovery rather than a matter of strict demonstration."[77] It is hoped that this essay will help the selector in philosophy to discover dependable tools for monitoring a discipline that has experienced a renaissance of publishing in the last forty years.

Selection Sources

ADRIS Newsletter. v.1– . 1971– . Bronx: Department of Theology, Fordham Univ. Quarterly.
Bibliografia Teologica Comentada. v.1– . 1973– . Buenos Aires, Argentina: Instituto Superior Evangelico de Estudios Teologicos. Annually.
Bibliographie de la Philosophie; Bibliography of Philosophy. v.1– . 1937– . Paris: International Institute of Philosophy, Libraraire Philosophique. Quarterly.
Council on the Study of Religion. Bulletin. v.1– 16. 1970–85. Waterloo, Ontario: Council on the Study of Religion. 5/year.
De George, Richard T. *The Philosopher's Guide to Sources, Research Tools, Professional Life, and Related Fields.* Lawrence: Regents Pr. of Kansas, 1980.
"Elenchus Bibliographicus," *Ephemerides Theologicae Lovanienses.* v.1– . 1924– . Louvain, Belgium: Ephemerides Theologicae Louvanienses, Bibliothèque de l'Université. Quarterly.
Elenchus Bibliographicus Biblicus. v.49– . 1968– . Rome: Pontifical Inst., Biblical Pr. Semiannually.
German Book Digest, a Selective Listing of Recent European Publications Primarily from Germany, Austria and Switzerland. v.1– . 1977– . Weisbaden, Germany: Harrassowitz.
Karpinski, Leszek M. *The Religious Life of Man: Guide to Basic Literature.* Metuchen, N.J.: Scarecrow, 1978.
Kepple, Robert J. *Reference Works for Theological Research: An Annotated Selective Bibliographical Guide.* 2nd ed. Washington, D.C.: Univ. Pr. of America, 1981.
The Listening Library, Speech Studios Catalog of Recordings. Princeton, N.J.: Princeton Theological Seminary, 1979.
McCabe, James Patrick. *A Critical Guide to Catholic Reference Books.* 2nd ed. Littleton, Colo.: Libraries Unlimited, 1980.
Media Review Digest. v.1– . 1980– . Ann Arbor, Mich.: Pierian. (Formerly *Multi Media Reviews Index.*) Annually.

75. *Philosophy and Psychology, Harvard University Library,* 2v. (Cambridge: Harvard Univ. Library. Dist. by Harvard Univ. Pr., 1973).
76. Union Theological Seminary, *The Shelf List of the Union Theological Seminary in New York City in Classification Order,* 10v. (Boston: Hall, 1960).
77. Gabriel Marcel, *Mystery of Being, I, Reflection & Mystery* (Chicago: Regnery, 1960), p. 2.

Neuerwerbungen Theologie und Allgemeine Religionswissenschaft. v.1- . 1982- .
Tübingen: Universitats-bibliothek, Theologische Abteilung. Monthly.
Reigner Recording Library Catalog, 1981. Richmond, Va.: Union Theological
Seminary in Virgina, 1981.
Religion Index Two: Multi-Author Works. v.1- . 1976- . Chicago: American The-
ological Library Assn. Annually.
Religious Books 1876-1982. 4v. New York: Bowker, 1983.
*Religious Studies Review: A Quarterly Review of Publications in the Field of
Religion and Related Disciplines.* v.1- . 1975- . Hanover, Pa.: Council on the
Study of Religion. Quarterly.
Répertoire Bibliographique de la Philosophie. v.1- . 1949- . Louvain-la-Neuve,
Belgium: Éditions de l' Institut Súperieur de Philosophie, L'Université Catholique
de Louvain. Quarterly.
Revue d'Histoire Ecclésiastique. v.1- . 1900- . Louvain, Belgium: Bibliothèque de
l'Université, Université Catholique. 3/year.
Scholars' Choice. no. 1- . 1960- . Richmond, Va.: Library, Union Theological
Seminary. Annually.
Schwinge, Gerhard. *Bibliographische Nachschlagewerke zur Theologie und ihren
Grenzgebieten.* Munchen, Germany: Verlag Dokumentation, 1975.
Theologische Literaturzeitung. v.1- . 1876- . *Monatsschrift fur das Gesamte Ge-
biet der Theologie und Religionswissenschaft.* Berlin, German Democratic Re-
public: Evangelische Verlagsanstalt. Monthly.
Theologische Revue. v.1- . 1902- . Munster, Westfalen, Federal Republic of Ger-
many: Aschendorffsche Verlag. Bimonthly.
Theologische Rundschau. v.1- . 1897- . Tübingen: J. C. B. Mohr. Quarterly.
Tice, Terrence N., and Thomas P. Slavens. *Research Guide to Philosophy.* Chicago:
American Library Assn., 1983.
The University Publishing New Books Supplement. Berkeley: Univ. of California
Pr., 1984- . Quarterly.

ART AND ARCHITECTURAL HISTORY

Christie D. Stephenson

Modern art historical inquiry employs methods and materials common to other disciplines as well as those unique to it. The librarian seeking to select materials to support current research and teaching in art and architectural history must first possess a knowledge of the development of the discipline and the range of its current methods, from connoisseurship through iconology to social history and psychological studies. Several basic guides provide excellent background, including W. Eugene Kleinbauer's *Modern Prespectives in Western Art History* and his more recent *Research Guide to the History of Western Art*, written with Thomas P. Slavens. In addition, David Watkin's *The Rise of Architectural History* provides a fascinating survey of the evolution of modern architectural history from its roots in antiquarianism.

The broad range of scholarship outlined in these works has equally far-reaching implications for the development of library collections. An effective collection must include, first and foremost, adequate documentation of the primary data of art history—the works themselves—through both reproductions in books and photographic archives.[1] Published primary sources, such as documents, drawing collections, and other archival materials, must be acquired. The vast output of secondary source materials, ranging from the "coffee table" book to the scholarly oeuvre catalog, must be reviewed and evaluated for its potential usefulness to the collection. And, finally, access to relevant titles from allied disciplines, from aesthetics to Marxian history, must be insured.

---

1. Slide collections also play an important role in supporting teaching in art and architectural history. Although a discussion of slide acquisition is beyond the scope of this article, a useful guide exists: *Slide Buyers Guide*, 4th ed. (Kansas City: Mid America College Art Assn., Visual Resources Group, 1980). A new edition is in preparation; meanwhile an update appears regularly in the "Slide Market News" column of the *International Bulletin for Photographic Documentation of the Visual Arts* (v.1– . 1974– . Ann Arbor, Mich.: Visual Resources Assn. Quarterly.).

Certain categories of subject-specific material play particularly important roles in supporting research in art and architectural history. These include:

1. Photographic archives—compilations of photographs, usually without accompanying texts, often in microfiche. Examples are the hardcopy *Courtauld Institute of Art Illustration Archives* and the microfiche *Marburger Index* and *Historic American Buildings Survey.*

2. Topographic surveys—building-by-building inventories of monuments in a particular country, region, or city, heavily illustrated, including basic documentation but little or no interpretation. Important examples are George Dehio's *Handbuch der deutschen Kunstdenkmäler* and the *Survey of London.*

3. Exhibition catalogs—usually organized around the work of a particular artist, theme, or medium, often including extensive catalog entries and important essays.

4. Museum catalogs—provide basic documentary evidence and other important data relating to the works in the permanent collections of the world's museums.

5. Oeuvre catalogs and *catalogues raisonnés*—usually comprehensive lists of the works of a particular artist or school, including physical description, provenance, documentary evidence, attributions, and bibliography; may also include include interpretive analysis. Recent examples include the *Corpus Rubenianum Ludwig Burchard* and *A Corpus of Rembrandt Paintings.*

6. Typological corpora—compilations of photographs and documentation of a particular type of object or building. Examples include the monumental *Corpus Vasorum Antiquorum* and the *Corpus Vitrearum Medii Aevi.*

These categories serve to emphasize the broad variety of literature that must be acquired to support research and teaching in art and architectural history. With the exception of the essays in Philip Pacey's *Art Library Manual,* there is little published information available to serve as a handbook to train or guide the selector in identifying and acquiring this literature. While the present essay is not intended to be the definitive statement on the topic, it does attempt to give specific and practical guidance based primarily on my own experience as a bibliographer.

A collection of articles appearing in a recent issue of *Library Acquisitions: Practice and Theory* addressed the pros and cons of various methods of acquisition for the art library.[2] Each of the authors acknowledged that a combination of standing orders, approval plans, and firm orders was most effective. Although I concur with this viewpoint, my comments

2. These articles, based on papers presented at the Tenth Annual ARLIS/NA Conference, February 1982, were published under the collective title "Art Libraries: Collection Development in the 1980's," *Library Acquisitions: Practice and Theory* 7: 3–20 (Jan. 1983).

focus primarily on item-by-item selection. Tools and techniques for current and retrospective collection development are discussed, including specific advice concerning selection sources for art and architecture materials, jobbers, and specialist dealers (in- and out-of-print). The identification, selection, and acquisition of artists' books is excluded,[3] as is any detailed discussion of microforms.[4]

Current Selection Tools and Techniques

The sources of information about new art and architecture publications are many and varied, including national bibliographies, dealers' catalogs, publishers' catalogs and announcements, specialized published bibliographies, and book reviews. No one of these can be relied upon entirely to identify current materials for acquisition. Each selector must devise a plan for coverage that balances the need for comprehensive review against the demands on one's own time and on that of support staff.

NATIONAL BIBLIOGRAPHIES

The most reliable sources of bibliographic data are the various national bibliographies, which insure relatively systematic coverage of the art and architectural history materials published in the United States and Western Europe. These include the *Weekly Record* or *American Book Publishing Record*, the *British National Bibliography*, *Deutsche Bibliographie*, *Bibliographie de la France*, *Bibliografia Nazionale Italiana*, *Das Schweizer Buch*, and *El Libro Español*. In addition to providing broad coverage and detailed bibliographic information on current imprints, they appear on a weekly, biweekly, or monthly basis and therefore lend themselves to routine accomodation into the workflow. With the exception of the *Weekly Record*, all of these tools have a classified arrangement, making it possible to review systematically only the relevant art and architecture sections of each issue.

The *British National Bibliography* appears weekly and is arranged by Dewey decimal classification, with full bibliographic information, including ISBN and price, given for each entry except CIP entries. As with a number of the classed lists, some titles of interest are listed outside the

3. A practical introduction to the selection and acquisition of artists' books was recently provided in a collection of articles edited by Clive Phillpot, "An ABC of Artists' Book Collections," *Art Documentation* 1: 169–81 (Dec. 1982).

4. Criteria for the selection of microforms are well documented in Virginia Carlson Smith's essay, "Microforms," in *Art Library Manual*, ed. by Philip Pacey (London and New York: Bowker, 1977), pp. 236–44; and in an article by Evelyn K. Samual, "Microforms and Art Libraries," *Microform Review* 10: 141–47. (Summer 1981).

700s. For instance, books on architectural preservation may be listed in the technology section and those on classical archaeology in history. To avoid reading the entire issue, it is helpful to alert other selectors in the library to your collecting interests and ask that they refer pertinent items to you.

The *Deutsche Bibliographie* aims to be comprehensive in its coverage of both West German imprints and German-language publications from elsewhere. Also appearing weekly, most art and architecture publications are listed in the sections *"Architektur"* and *"Bildende Kunst,"* with those listed elsewhere fully cross-referenced. Two parts of each issue warrant regular checking—*"Reihe* N," which includes abbreviated CIP entries, and *"Reihe* A," which includes full catalog entries for trade books. Inclusion of German imprints is very prompt, but German-language titles from other countries are somewhat slow in appearing.

Both the French and Italian national bibliographies are compiled as books received on copyright deposit are cataloged by their respective national libraries. As a result, they are slow to include new titles and serve better as back-up selection sources for those countries. The *"Livres"* section of the *Bibliographie de la France* appears in twenty-five yearly issues, organized by Universal Decimal Classification, with art and architecture titles appearing primarily in Section 7, *"Arts, Jeux et Sports."* Here, too, exceptions occur; books on illuminated manuscripts, for example, appear in Section O, *"Generalités."* Because coverage is not timely, the classed listings in the weekly book trade journal, *Livres Hebdo,* or their monthly cumulation in *Les Livres du Mois,* serve as more effective primary selection sources for French imprints. However, the more comprehensive coverage, particularly of exhibition catalogs, makes back-up checking of the *Bibliographie de la France* worthwhile if time permits. This is also true of the *Bibliografia Nazionale Italiana,* which appears monthly and is organized by Dewey Decimal Classification. In this case, we use the *BNI* as a back-up to bibliographic information on new Italian imprints provided by our Italian jobber.

Das Schweizer Buch and *El Libro Español* are two other classed national bibliographies that are useful as current selection tools for art and architectural history. Those from other countries must be evaluated on the basis of frequency, arrangement, timeliness, and coverage elsewhere to determine their potential usefulness. If your library does not subscribe to these national bibliographies for use by selectors, vendors will often supply marked copies as a part of their approval plan service. Whether used for item-by-item selection or to monitor and supplement an approval plan, they remain the single most important category of bibliographic tool available to the selector of current imprints in any subject area.

DEALERS' CATALOGS

There are a large number of in-print dealers specializing in art and architecture materials, both in the United States and abroad. Many publish catalogs on a routine basis, and these catalogs can serve as alternative selection sources. Dealers of this sort are eager to attract business and often blanket both the library and faculty with their catalogs. In addition, dealers may advertise in relevant professional journals. There is also an extensive list of art booksellers and their addresses included in the *International Directory of Arts*. A form letter will usually suffice for procuring current and future catalogs.

Through their lists, specialist dealers such as Wittenborn or Michael Shamansky provide a kind of preselection service for the librarian who does not have the time to review all the national bibliographies. In addition, they sometimes provide information on publications before they appear in primary selection sources. Dealers' catalogs can also be useful sources of information about books from countries whose publishing output is not reviewed routinely and systematically by a selector.

When using dealers' catalogs as a primary selection tool, one must acknowledge the resulting lack of comprehensive coverage. It is an individual decision, based primarily on the concern for expediency. Another source of concern may be the fact that bibliographic information in dealers' catalogs is often less complete than in other selection sources. Publishers' names, translation information, or series notes are sometimes omitted. The result may be an unintentional duplication or some other unjustifiable purchase.

In addition to the catalogs published by book dealers specializing in art and architecture materials, one must consider the bibliographic information provided by library jobbers, domestic and foreign, as a potential selection source. Jobbers often provide a range of services, from catalogs or notification slips to full approval plans. Although jobbers are usually selected by the library's acquisition department on the basis of discounts, response time, reporting, and shipping and billing procedures, the availability of bibliographic services such as these are often considered as well. In certain countries where bibliographic information is slow to appear in the national bibliography, the jobber's list can serve as the primary selection tool. For instance, the computer-produced cards received monthly from Casalini Libri in Fiesole serve as our main source of information on new Italian art and architecture materials. Like dealers' catalogs, the lists of library jobbers can provide bibliographic coverage for those countries whose national bibliographies are not routinely examined. Nijhoff, for example, provides excellent lists of art and architecture materials published in the Netherlands.

PUBLISHERS' CATALOGS AND ANNOUNCEMENTS

Although reliance on national bibliographies and jobbers' lists as primary selection sources will insure relatively thorough coverage, a number of other sources can provide valuable back-up information. First among these are publishers' catalogs and announcements. The key to dealing with this mass of information is to learn to judge what is worth just a cursory glance and what mandates thorough checking as a selection source. One must balance the need for timely and comprehensive coverage of the output of specific publishers against the likelihood of wasting staff time checking the same item two or three times. For instance, because our faculty and students are keenly interested in having rapid access to Rizzoli's architectural books, I select and we order from each new season's catalog as soon as it is received. This insures that the books will be on order no matter how long it takes for them to be listed in the *Weekly Record*. Duplicate searching and the inevitable flow of "NYP" (not yet published) reports must be accepted as trade-offs in this method of selection.

As with dealers' catalogs, most libraries find themselves included on the mailing lists of most of the major art book publishers, such as Abrams, Alpine, Thames & Hudson, Phaidon, Mann, Electa, and Picard. If, however, you find you are not receiving current catalogs or you come across a new or unknown publisher and are curious about its list, a form letter can be sent to acquire the necessary information. Addresses can usually be located in the *International Directory of Arts*, the *Publishers International Directory*, or the appropriate books-in-print volume.

Except in cases like the one previously described, most announcements and catalogs from major art and architectural publishers need not be marked and searched for ordering because of the timely inclusion of their titles in primary selection sources. They can, however, serve as an important source of knowledge for the selector. Much about the nature of a particular publisher can be learned from simply examining the design and content of its promotional literature.

Announcements from nontrade publishers, such as galleries, historical and learned societies, and associations should receive more careful attention as selection sources. Although publications of some major art historical associations and institutes, such as the College Art Association and the Kunsthistorisches Institut in Florence, are published or distributed by trade publishers, many are not and are slow to appear in standard selection sources. It is a worthwhile project to undertake a systematic mailing to the various art historical learned societies listed in the *International Directory of Arts* and *World of Learning* to acquire their publications lists. A similar undertaking for museums, using directories such as *Museums of the World*, can provide valuable information on both current and retrospective museum publications.

OTHER SECONDARY SELECTION SOURCES

Given the rapidity with which most art and architecture books go out-of-print, it is seldom feasible to wait for reviews to appear in the major scholarly journals in order to make selection decisions. In the past few years, however, two new reviewing journals have appeared that are devoted entirely to recent publications in art and architecture. Both *Art Book Review* and *Design Book Review* provide relatively timely reviews of English-language books.[5] In addition, the "Books Received" lists of several major scholarly journals can serve as valuable back-up selection sources. Among the journals providing fruitful lists of this type are the *Art Bulletin*, *American Journal of Archaeology*, and the Society of Architectural Historians' *Newsletter*. In reviewing these lists, it is most efficient to skip trade publications likely to have been identified in the primary selection sources and to concentrate, instead, on nontrade publications from learned societies, museums, and the like.

Another group of lists serving a similar purpose are the accession lists from various special libraries. We currently receive and review those from the British Architectural Library, the American Institute of Architects Library, and the Library of the National Trust for Historic Preservation. The National Trust list is particularly helpful in identifying the elusive publications of local historical societies and other architectural preservation groups.

Several of the major art historical indexing services, while concentrating on periodical literature, do include bibliographic information on certain types of books as well. Most notable among these are *RILA, International Repertory of the Literature of Art* and the *Répertoire d'art et archéologie*. *RILA* includes entries for many of the most important exhibition catalogs, but is perhaps most useful for its "Collected Works" section, which includes bibliographic information on festschriften and conference proceedings as well as collections of essays. These works are thoroughly indexed in the same issue, insuring that, if acquired, patrons will have adequate access to their contents. A similar list has been included in the *Répertoire* since 1980. It can be found under the title "*Liste des recueils collectifs depouillés au cours de l'année*" in the annual index issue.

For those countries in Western Europe where review of the national bibliography is not practical, annual bibliographies published in the major art historical journals can provide a valuable cross-check on other selection sources. In general, however, these cannot be considered "current" selection sources, as they often run about three years behind. Examples of this type of list are the "Bibliographical Survey of Publications in the Field

5. Another similar journal, the *Art International Book Supplement* (v.1– . 1983– . Lugano: James Fitzsimmons) has been announced, but I have been unable to verify whether or not publication has begun.

Art Book Review; An International Review of Art Literature. v.1- . 1982- .
  London: Art Book Review Co. Quarterly.
  Review journal.
  Primarily British trade and U.S. and British university press books included.
  Only English-language works reviewed, with emphasis on art history, but
    including architecture, decorative arts, and photography.
  20–50 signed reviews an issue.
  Most books reviewed within year of publication.
  Prompt coverage.
  Publishers' announcements.
  Advertisements for U.S. and British art bookdealers.
  Regular column, "Meet the Publisher," features interviews with major art
    book publishers.
Art Book Review offers lengthy signed book reviews, many by major scholars,
as well as numerous unsigned short notices. The citations' failure to include
publication date is, however, a major drawback. The "Meet the Publisher"
column provides valuable and elusive information on art book publishing history
and trends.

Design Book Review. v.1- . 1983- . Berkeley, Calif.: Design Book Review.
  Quarterly.
  Review journal.
  Architectural history, design, decorative arts, and landscape architecture
    books.
  Emphasis on English-language titles.
  60–90 reviews an issue.
  Most books reviewed within year of publication.
  Publishers' announcements.
  Advertisements for journals and architectural bookdealers.
This journal provides substantial and informative signed book reviews by schol-
ars and practitioners. It includes some lengthy collective reviews of related titles,
and good coverage of architectural exhibition catalogs, scholarly, popular, and
technical books. It is a more timely source of reviews than most scholarly
journals. Full bibliographic information, except ISBN, is provided.

of Art History and Several Related Areas Published in the Netherlands,"
appearing annually in *Simiolus*, and the "Bibliografia" in *Archivo español
de arte*. Similar bibliographies devoted to other countries and more specialized topics are listed in the "Bibliography" section of Etta Arntzen and
Robert Rainwater's *Guide to the Literature of Art History* under "Current
Serials" and individual country headings.

Two trade bibliographies, published by art book dealers, are sometimes
mentioned as selection sources, but are very limited in scope and usefulness. *Art Kunst; International Bibliography of Art Books* is based primarily on publisher-contributed information and appears annually. Coverage is spotty and too slow and incomplete to be relied upon as a selection
tool. *The Literature of Art* was a monthly listing, now ceased. It cumulated

the art, architecture, photography, and cinema sections of the *British National Bibliography*, *American Book Publishing Record*, *Whitaker's*, and *Livres de France*. Since it appeared about three months after the materials had been listed in each of the national bibliographies, it would be useful only to those librarians without access to the original listings.

Selection Criteria for Current Materials

While the sources of selection information on art and architectural history materials can be enumerated in a rather straightforward manner, the actual selection process is more elusive. Unless every potential title is received on approval and can be returned without penalty, a librarian will be required to decide, with some degree of certainty, whether or not particular books should be purchased for the collection. If there is an "art" to book selection, surely it lies in the ability to predict the nature of a book from the often scant bibliographic information available. The development of this ability is particularly important in selecting art and architecture books. Small print runs make it difficult to wait for published reviews to aid in the selection process. If a "mistake" is made, the price is often quite high. In addition, a book's value is often determined by its format, the quality of its reproductions, or other physical characteristics. The selector must attempt, therefore, to "see" what a book will look like on the basis of cataloging information in a national bibliography, a dealer's description, or a publisher's blurb.

Every piece of information presented about a specific title, plus the accumulated knowledge of the selector about the book trade, the output of particular publishers, and the nature of particular series, becomes part of the decision making process. Assuming that, based on author/title/subject information, a work is judged to be in scope for your collection, what other questions must you ask yourself in order to "see" the book and make a decision whether or not to acquire it? Among them are:

1. What do I know about the publisher? Can I draw any conclusions about the audience for this work from the nature of its backlist? Are its books well produced, with high-quality reproductions?

2. Have I seen titles in this series before? If so, do they represent important contributions to the literature? Are they simply old information, repackaged as a marketing technique?

3. From the collation statement, can I determine if a work is primarily plates, with little text? If so, do we have a need for more illustrative material on this subject?

4. Is there any indication of the presence of critical apparatus, implying that the book is intended for a scholarly audience?

5. Do the price and format indicate an intended audience? Is it a $4.95 mass-market paperback? An expensive "edition de luxe" with a signed lithograph?

6. Is the work a revised edition? If we own the original, is the revision significant enough to merit purchase?

7. Is the work a translation? If we own it in the original language, do we need it in English as well? Conversely, is the work likely to be translated into English promptly?[6]

Although some of these questions can be answered from the information at hand, most depend on the selector's accumulated knowledge of art and architecture publishers and publishing trends. This base of knowledge is built from a variety of sources. As previously noted, publishers' announcements and catalogs can, from both their content and appearance, indicate something of the quality and intended audience for their titles. If I am suspect about a particular publisher, I often send off a form letter requesting a catalog before making a decision to purchase a specific work. Talking with publishers' representatives at conferences and browsing through trade publications like *Publishers Weekly* can also provide valuable insights.[7]

However, the most vital source of information about publishers, series, and the like is looking at the books themselves. If you are fortunate enough to live in the vicinity of a specialist dealer, your may be able to examine some titles before ordering them. Otherwise, you must content yourself with a careful examination of new books as they are received by the library. This process is a kind of "reality testing" for the selector. New acquisitions can be examined for quality of production and readership level. The verso of the title page or front matter can provide information concerning the succession of editions, revisions, translations, and copublishing agreements. In addition, jackets or back matter can include series lists or lists of related publications valuable for retrospective checking.

Serial Selection

The methods of identification and selection of new periodicals and serials in art and architecture differ little from those in other disciplines. Many publishers announce new titles using direct mail promotion, in an effort to attract library subscriptions. Titles can also be identified through ad-

6. This question is difficult to answer in most cases. Except for the long-established translation agreements, like the one between Skira and Rizzoli, it is difficult to predict when one can expect prompt English translation of foreign-language titles.

7. An example is the three-part series on American art books published by Barbara Braun appearing last year in *Publishers Weekly*; "Art Books—A World of Change," *PW* 22–37 (Aug. 19, 1983); "Art Books—Reaching for an Audience," *PW* 24–33 (Oct. 21, 1983); and "Art Books—Leftovers and New Directions," *PW* 24–30 (Oct. 28, 1983).

Art Documentation. v.1– . 1982– . Tucson, Ariz.: Art Libraries Society/North
America. 5/year. (Supersedes *ARLIS/NA Newsletter.* v.1–9. 1972–81.
Glendale, Calif.: ARLIS/NA. Bimonthly.)
Professional journal for art librarians: official organ of Art Libraries
    Society/North America.
10–25 books reviewed an issue.
Emphasis on English-language publications.
6–24-month lag between book publication and review.
Books received listed.
New periodicals noted in "Periodical Update" column.
Publisher and dealer advertisements.
Sometimes features annotated bibliographies devoted to particular topics,
    such as "Women Artists: A Resource and Research Guide," 1: A3–A20.
    (Oct. 1982).
Reference works in progress noted.
Librarians write the signed, medium-length reviews. Comparative reviews of new
and older reference works often are included. Much valuable information on
microform publications, government documents, serials, periodicals, and reference works is included in regular columns, as well as in the book review
section.

vertisements in other journals and listings in national bibliographies. Another extremely useful source of new title information is the "Periodical
Update" column in *Art Documentation*, which also includes detailed information on title and frequency changes, cessations, and the like. There
remains, however, no single, comprehensive, and timely source for the
identification of new serial titles.

The criteria for selection must be carefully delineated to avoid an investment in marginal titles but to insure rapid subscription to key ones.
Since reviews are rare, the safest way to evaluate a serial is to order a
sample issue from the publisher. Factors to consider in evaluation include
the intended audience, editorial policy, composition of the editorial board,
presence of scholarly apparatus, and quality of production. Each of these
must be considered in light of the single most important determinant—
the "fit" of the title into the research and curricular needs of your institution.

For the art and architecture selector, perhaps the most difficult type of
serial to evaluate is the "school" publication, emanating from an art history
department or an architecture school. They range from irregular, mediocre
presentations of student work to very slick and scholarly productions often
cited elsewhere. The quality of any given title can vary greatly, depending
on the editorial input in a particular year. Examples of solid publications
of this genre are the *Rutgers Art Review* and the numerous architecture
school journals distributed by Rizzoli and the MIT Press.

For the identification of continuing core serial titles that might have been missed at their outset, the selector can rely on both general lists, such as those in *Ulrich's* and *Magazines for Libraries*, and subject-specific lists. These include periodical lists in bibliographies such as Arntzen and Rainwater and, more importantly, the lists of journals indexed in *Art Index*, *Répertoire*, *RILA*, the *Architectural Periodicals Index*, and the *Avery Index to Architectural Periodicals*.

Acquisition of Current Materials

As I stated at the outset, some combination of firm ordering, approval plans, and standing orders will provide the most efficient and cost-effective means of acquiring art and architectural history materials. Determination of the proper mix of these methods of acquisition depends largely on local circumstances. Size of the materials budget, available staff time, and the need for control and rapid delivery are among the factors to be considered.

In addition to standing orders for serials, periodicals, and auction catalogs, this form of acquisition is most appropriate to provide control over complex multivolume titles, published over a long period of time. Among the categories of monographic materials best handled by this method are multivolume permanent collection catalogs from major museums, some oeuvre catalogs, multivolume reference works appearing over time, city surveys, and topographic inventories. Some libraries may also want to consider standing orders for all the publications of a specific museum, including permanent collection and exhibition catalogs, all the books published by specific presses, or all the titles in a particular series, such as Princeton Monographs in Art and Archaeology or Zwemmer's Studies in Architecture.

An examination of the issues in the debate between approval plans and firm ordering is beyond the scope of this article.[8] My own opinion is that approval plans function most efficiently when a subject profile is applied to the output of specific publishers (e.g., all U.S. university presses) or the library is supplied with a marked copy of the national bibliography, indicating what titles will be sent on approval. This eliminates some of the frustrations involved in monitoring the plan's effectiveness. Expectations of what will and will not be supplied are clear, and a selector's time is freed for the more challenging aspects of collection development.

Vendor selections can be extremely important in an art and architecture library. Again, convenience and available staff time must be balanced against

8. The issue receives considerable attention in "Art Libraries: Collection Development in the 1980's," *LAPT* 7: 3–20 (Jan. 1983).

the need for stretching the budget to acquire materials economically. Specialist dealers can be a convenient and prompt ordering source, if they have the required items in stock. It is important to note, however, that they are relatively small-volume businesses, often catering to a diverse audience. One cannot expect to receive the standard library discount for domestic publications that would be available from a publisher or jobber. Similarly, the prices of foreign publications are marked up to cover the dealer's costs and insure at least a marginal profit.

Purchasing through library jobbers in the country of origin is generally the most economical and efficient means of acquisition. In addition to paying lower prices for materials than one does through a specialist dealer, the support mechanisms of invoicing, claiming, and reporting are well developed to meet the specific needs of libraries.

The problems inherent in identifying and acquiring current exhibition catalogs has been given considerable attention in the literature.[9] A similar combination of firm order, approval plan, and standing order can be devised to handle the acquisition of these materials. Bibliographic control over exhibition catalogs appears to have improved a great deal recently.[10] It is now possible to select and acquire catalogs effectively on a title-by-title basis to supplement "gathering" plans like the one offered by Worldwide Books and the museum standing order plan. Again, each library must determine whether its staffing levels and budget can support this more controlled, but more labor-intensive, form of acquisition.

Retrospective Collection Development

The importance of older materials to research in art and architectural history is well documented. No matter how extensive a library's collection, there will always be lacunae to be filled as programs grow and users' interests change. The consequent need for retrospective collection development must be balanced against the cost and burgeoning number of current imprints, a shrinking materials budget, and the ever-escalating price of antiquarian books. These competing demands mandate careful adherence to established collection development goals and a thorough and timely knowledge of the book trade and the research needs of users. Only then can wise choices be made in filling gaps in a library's holdings.

The identification of lacunae can be achieved through a number of techniques. One of the most common is the checking of holdings against

9. See especially the articles by Brian Gold, "Acquisition Approaches to Exhibition Catalogues," *Library Acquisitions: Practice and Theory* 7: 13–16 (Jan. 1983); and by Anthony Burton, "Exhibition Catalogues," in *Art Library Manual* (Pacey, ed., 1977), pp. 71–78.

10. This statement is based only on empirical evidence. The question of the bibliographic coverage of exhibition catalogs in national bibliographies and other selection sources would be an excellent topic for more systematic study.

standard art and architecture bibliographies. These include Arntzen and Rainwater's *Guide to the Literature of Art History* and three bibliographies compiled by Donald L. Ehresmann—*Fine Arts: A Bibliographic Guide to Basic Reference Works, Histories and Handbooks*; *Applied and Decorative Arts*; and *Architecture*. In addition, the checking of carefully selected, more specialized bibliographies, both separately published and in books and articles, can generate desiderata in specific areas of the collection earmarked for evaluation and/or expansion.

An equally valuable technique for the identification of significant gaps in the library's collection is to review outgoing interlibrary loan requests. This permits you to keep in touch with active areas of research interest and is particularly helpful in setting priorities for serial backfile acquisitions. Monographic requests must be viewed more critically, as the patron usually has only scanty information on the ultimate usefulness of any given item. Akin to this method for identification of lacunae is the "we ought to have" (*get!*) conversation with a faculty member, which usually yields a number of incomplete citations scribbled on a piece of scrap paper, challenging your verification skills to the limit.

Establishing good working relationships with specialized antiquarian bookdealers is an important facet of any retrospective collecting activity. A first step is to get on the mailing lists of as many dealers as possible. Lists of specialists in art and architecture can be found in a number of directories including the series published by the Sheppard Press, London— *European Bookdealers*; *Bookdealers in North America*; and *A Directory of Dealers in Secondhand and Antiquarian Books in the British Isles*. New and established dealers often advertise in *Art Documentation* and other journals. As catalogs are received, reviewed, and ordered from, it is helpful to annotate your address file with information concerning dealer performance, accuracy, and completeness of bibliographic description, specialities, the availability of hard-to-find items such as single periodical issues and the like for future reference. The catalogs of dealers such as Ben Weinreb or Charles Wood, devoted to limited topics and with extensive annotations, will become part of your permanent reference collection, while others can be discarded without a second glance.

The acquisition of materials from dealers' catalogs is often not the wisest technique of retrospective collection development; one is tempted to buy simply because an item is available, not because it is high on the library's list of desiderata. The purchase of out-of-print materials from dealers' catalogs should be balanced by active searching, through dealers or direct advertisement in journals such as *AB Bookman's Weekly*, for specific high-priority desiderata. Though one may have to pay more for an item to cover the dealer's searching costs, there is more control and less frustration involved in this method of out-of-print buying.

It is important to remember that for many art historical publications, "old" does not necessarily mean out-of-print. In direct contradiction to my earlier statement about the speed with which many trade publications go out-of-print, it is also true that many scholarly books, particularly those of European learned societies, stay in-print and available from the publisher for years (and often at the original prices!). These same books, since they look like they *must* be out-of-print, often appear in antiquarian catalogs at greatly inflated prices. Here is a striking example from my recent experience. In the course of a publisher's catalog checking project, we just acquired A. P. Frutaz's monumental study of Roman city maps, *Le Piante di Roma*, through our Italian jobber for approximately $200. The same three-volume work was listed recently in the catalog of a reputable U.S. antiquarian dealer for $1,250!

The availability of publications like this makes the publisher's catalog one of the most powerful retrospective collection development tools available to the art and architecture librarian. In addition, many European publishers will list all backlist titles, both in- and out-of-print, providing a simple means of establishing and filling in titles in series, serials, and the like. Although it may seem time consuming and expensive, an aggressive campaign to acquire and thoroughly check publishers' catalogs from European scholarly publishers and learned societies can save time in future bibliographic research and precious book funds as well.

Reprints and microforms deserve special mention as two alternatives to acquiring retrospective materials in original editions. Both formats have their place in the art and architectural history collection, but careful evaluation of their characteristics in relation to the needs of the collection must be made on a title-by-title basis. Some of the factors to consider are the artifactual role of a title within a specific collection, the scarcity of the original edition, the probable (or actual) physical condition of the original, the nature of the illustrations in the original, the presence of additional critical apparatus or finding aids in the reprint or microform edition, and the physical format, quality, and cost of the reprint or microform.

In this essay, I have discussed a variety of bibliographic sources and practical hints for the selector of library materials in art and architectural history. There are, no doubt, other useful sources, as well as differing and equally valid approaches to the selection and acquisition process, developed to suit the circumstances of specific libraries. Whatever tools and techniques are used, the selector is involved in a continual learning process, perpetually building on a knowledge of the discipline itself and the published materials that spring from and support it.

Selection Sources

American Journal of Archaeology. ser. 1, v.1–11, 1885–96; ser. 2, v.1– , 1897– . Boston: Archaeological Institute of America. Quarterly.

Architectural Periodicals Index. v.1– . 1972– . London: RIBA Publications. Quarterly.

Archivo español de arte. t.14– . 1940– . Madrid: CSIC, Instituto Diego Velázquez. Quarterly.

Arntzen, Etta, and Robert Rainwater. *Guide to the Literature of Art History.* Chicago: American Library Assn.; London: Art Book Co., 1980.

Art Book Review; An International Review of Art Literature. v.1– . 1982– . London: Art Book Review Co. Quarterly.

Art Bulletin. v.1– . 1913– . New York: College Art Assn. Quarterly.

Art Documentation. v.1– . 1982– . Tucson, Ariz.: Art Libraries Society of North America. 5/year.

Art Index. v.1– . 1929– . New York: Wilson. Quarterly.

Art Kunst; International Bibliography of Art Books. no. 1– . 1972– . Basel: W. Jaggi. Annually.

Avery Index to Architectural Periodicals. 2nd ed. and supplements. Boston: Hall, 1973, 1975, 1977, 1979.

Bookdealers in North America. 9th ed. London: Sheppard, 1983.

Design Book Review. v.1– . 1983– . Berkeley, Calif.: Design Book Review. Quarterly.

Directory of Dealers in Secondhand and Antiquarian Books in the British Isles. 10th ed. London: Sheppard, 1981.

Ehresmann, Donald L. *Applied and Decorative Arts.* Littleton, Colo.: Libraries Unlimited, 1977.

———. *Architecture.* Littleton, Colo.: Libraries Unlimited, 1984.

———. *Fine Arts: A Bibliographic Guide to Basic Reference Works, Histories, and Handbooks.* 2nd ed. Littleton, Colo.: Libraries Unlimited, 1979.

European Bookdealers. 5th ed. London: Sheppard, 1982.

International Directory of Arts. v.1– . 1952/53– . Frankfurt am Main: Art Address Verlag Müller. Annually.

Kleinbauer, W. Eugene. *Modern Perspectives in Western Art History.* New York: Holt, 1971.

———, and Thomas P. Slavens. *Research Guide to the History of Western Art.* Chicago: American Library Assn., 1982.

Literature of Art. no.1–?. 1979–82?. Art Book Co. Monthly.

Museums of the World. v.1– . 1973– . Munich: Säur. Irregularly.

Pacey, Philip, ed. *Art Library Manual.* London and New York: Bowker, 1977.

Publishers International Directory. v.1– . 1964– . Munich: Säur. Annually.

Répertoire d'art et archéologie. 1st ser., v.1–68, 1910–64. n.s., v.1– , 1965– . Paris: Centre National de la Recherche Scientifique. Quarterly.

RILA; International Repertory of the Literature of Art. v.1– . 1975– . Williamstown, Mass.: RILA. Semiannually.

Simiolus. v.1– . 1966/67– . Maarssen, Netherlands: Gary Schwartz. Quarterly.

Society of Architectural Historians. *Newsletter.* v.1– . 1957– . Philadelphia: Society of Architectural Historians. Bimonthly.

Watkin, David. *The Rise of Architectural History*. London: Architectural Pr.; Westfield, N.J.: Eastview, 1980.
World of Learning. v.1– . 1947– . London: Europa. Annually.

Other Works Cited

A Corpus of Rembrandt Paintings. The Hague and Boston: M. Nijoff, 1982– .
Corpus Rubenianum Ludwig Burchard. London and New York: Phaidon, 1968.
Corpus Vasorum Antiquorum. Paris: E. Champion, etc., 1922– . (Imprint varies.)
Corpus Vitrearum Medii Aevi. Comité International d'Histoire de l'Art, 1956– . (Imprint varies.)
Courtauld Institute of Art Illustration Archives. London: Harvey Miller, 1976– .
Dehio, George. *Handbuch der Deutschen Kunstdenkmäler*. 5v. Berlin: E. Wasmuth, 1905–12.
Frutaz, A. P. *Le Piante di Roma*. 3v. Rome: Istituto di Studi Romani, 1962.
Historic American Buildings Survey. Cambridge: Chadwick-Healey; Teaneck, N.J.: Somerset House, 1980.
Marburger Index. Munich: Säur, 1976– .
Rutgers Art Review. v.1– . 1980– . New Brunswick, N.J.: Dept. of Art History, Rutgers Univ. Annually.
Survey of London. London: London County Council, London Survey Committee, 1900– .

MUSIC

Michael A. Keller

The selector of materials for a research music library must have a comprehensive understanding of music as a performing art, a creative endeavor, a subject for scholarly study, and as a theoretical construct. Most frequently this comprehensive understanding is attained by years of experience in several facets of this art form. The study of music, the art form, is, of course, a humanistic discipline, one that arose from German philology in the mid-nineteenth century. That discipline, musicology, is usually understood to incorporate historical subjects as well as systematic subjects, such as acoustics, pedagogy, theory, aesthetics, psychology, and sociology. Musicology is both informed by and informs the performance and composition of music.

Most institutions in North America that support research in music do so in coordination with curricular programs. Selectors for most research music libraries must also be prepared to provide materials for these programs, which generally treat music in the broad categories of music history and literature, performance, music theory, ethnomusicology, and composition. The composition of music is, in a sense, a forward-looking endeavor. The study of music from a cultural, historical, or theoretical perspective is retrospective or perhaps synoptic. The performance of music, of course, is entirely oriented to the moment, even when recorded. These characteristics and other factors of the music publishing and distribution industry should force most music research collection selectors to be forward-looking and even prophetic, rather than merely responsive. We must conserve today what scholars and other patrons may come to regard tomorrow as suitable and interesting objects or ideas for their contemplation.

Copyright ©1985 by Michael A. Keller
  The author gratefully acknowledges the assistance of Katherine Holum, Eileen Hunt, and Keith Stetson.

139

Bibliothecal issues typical of other library specialties are also typical of music libraries. In most research settings, music libraries are separate services because of the specialized nature and use of the materials. Most music curricular programs require the use of the broadest range of media, printed *and* recorded music as well as monographs, primary sources (usually in microform), an elaborate, unsystematic, and developing bibliographic apparatus, the usual plethora of serial articles, maps, and atlases, and the full range of visual media, including the newer video forms. Because most undergraduate curricular programs focus on various repertoires, multiple copies of scores and recordings are required. Most students and libraries cannot afford enough copies of these fundamental works, so complex circulation procedures and relatively short loan periods are devised to spread equitably the music under close examination among the community of scholars and students.

Printed and recorded music are produced by and obtained from publishing and distributing firms with distinctly different characteristics from those of the word publishing industry. Marketing music to research institutions as well as to individuals is a most specialized service industry, or rather constellation of service industries. A selector of music will want to build a fairly well-developed sense of these marketplaces, and also of the economic and creative forces driving them. The exigencies of supply and delivery in music publishing, which routinely and traditionally has small press runs and which is fundamentally an international marketplace, affect directly the selections and specifications made by selectors. This point will be made clear in the following examinations of each facet of the general topic.

Finally, the music selector works in a web of personal or personalized relationships. Music selectors must maintain effective and constant contacts with their faculty colleagues, with the patrons of the music library, with other specialist librarians, and with the host of paraprofessional colleagues who provide the unremitting labor for item-level activities and without whom most libraries would simply collapse. The most successful selectors maintain close contacts with the dealers, publishers, and creators of the materials they purchase for their libraries. Business relationships are of particular importance due, in general, to the global nature of the marketplace in combination with the lack of systematic bibliographic/discographic information/control for printed and recorded music as commodities. The patchwork quilt of dealers and publishers lists, catalogs, announcements, of "recently received" lists in professional, scholarly, and popular periodicals, and of the very few national or cooperative bibliographic control agencies' "publications" serves best when close working relationships with producers and vendors flourish.

This essay is founded principally upon traditional foci of collection building programs and, of course, curricular programs in larger research libraries in this country. "Applied" disciplines such as music education and pedagogy, music psychology, music therapy, and commercial music are not discussed directly. The special characteristics of selection for ethnomusicology and the study of popular music are mentioned incidentally, but are clearly deserving of another whole essay.

Printed Music

The selection and acquisition of printed music has long been one of the most intriguing and satisfying experiences for music librarians.

The process is intriguing because the variety of forms, formats, versions, editions, and issues of musical scores forces one to weigh quantities of information about the music, its published forms, and intended use. Under the rubric of information about the composition in question comes composer, title, date, place, and circumstances of composition and later revision, style period, original instrumentation, possibly tessitura, other musical characteristics, and relation to other art works and/or historical events. Under the rubric of published forms comes proximity to the composer (and presumably his or her intentions), reduction, arrangement, key, version, edition, size, publisher, and supplier. And under the rubric of intended use comes the library's and/or patrons' needs; will the score be for study use only, or as an aide-memoire at a concert, that might allow one to select a miniature score of the original version in a reputable edition? Or, will the score be for reference purposes, requiring large size for easy consultation in the best scientifically prepared and published edition? Or, perhaps the score is intended for rehearsal purposes and could be a piano reduction of the original. The list of variables is very long and the permutations possibly even longer.

A most salient characteristic of printed music is an enormous variety of editions and versions of a moderate-sized body of literature. Most research music libraries hold less than 100,000 titles of printed music, though they might have a considerable number of editions of a given title. The largest research collection in the world, that of the Library of Congress, has cataloged only about 470,000 items and holds about 10,500,000 printed items, mostly scores.[1]

Information on the availability of printed music (scores) comes to music selectors in patchwork quilt fashion, as has been mentioned above. Se-

1. See the microfiche edition of the Library of Congress Music Shelflist (Ann Arbor, Mich.: University Microfilms, 1979) and an analysis of it: Michael A. Keller with Holly Rowe, "An Analysis of the LC Shelflist for Music" in *Cum Notis Variorum*, the newsletter of the Music Library of the Univ. of California at Berkeley, no. 78 (Dec. 1983).

lectors, once on the mailing lists, frequently get more than one announcement of a newly published score from domestic and foreign dealers. In addition, some music publishers advertise directly. If one is familiar with the publisher's general selection and editing policies, with the reputation of the composer if the music is contemporary or with the reputation of the editor if one is named, then one could make the decision to purchase without further consideration, presumably placing the order with one's favorite vendor for that publisher's products.

Getting on the publishers' and dealers' mailing lists is accomplished by writing to them directly on the basis of their advertisements in the professional and scholarly journals. A two- or three-sentence letter usually suffices. Another good way to get on these lists *and* to get to know the people publishing and marketing music is to visit the booths in the exhibitor's hall of the annual meetings of the Music Library Association, American Musicological Society, Society for Ethnomusicology, College Music Society, and Music Educators National Conference. Joining these associations is another way of getting on the mailing lists, since most of the major marketing organizations purchase mailing lists annually to direct their efforts to the most likely customers. I maintain an online file of music dealers and send out requests every third year or so. The annual directory issue of *Musical America* has a list of publishers and distributors one might use as the basis for one's own list. George Hill's irregular column, "Music Publishers' Catalogues," in *Notes* provides the best information on corporate addresses for music publishers; his information is international in scope, so one can direct inquiries to or near to origin of the score.[2]

Alternatively, one could wait for the appearance of announcements and reviews of the score in question. Reviews begin appearing within a few months of publication and continue even two or three years after the date of publication, especially if the edition is of scholarly significance worthy of close examination in one of the leading journals. A fairly small portion, perhaps fifteen percent, of published music ever gets reviewed, however, so reliance upon reviews is neither a timely nor comprehensive strategy.

The Library of Congress CDS Alert Services cards (formerly known as "proof slips") and final copy of its catalog cards have been valuable adjuncts to music selectors. For the period through the 1970s, it was possible to depend in large part on Library of Congress cards to keep one abreast of what was available. Library of Congress' own selection process for materials worthy of cataloging, winnowed from the copyright deposits and their immense collecting efforts, made these cards most valuable. One

2. The latest of these columns is in *Notes* 40: 576–83 (1983/84).

needed only to flip through them as they came, albeit a year or so after publication, to select the solid core of "what every research music library should have." One then referred to the other sources for very up-to-date selections and to fill in the cracks the Library of Congress somehow left unfilled.

As the Library of Congress began, in the early 1980s, to cope with the onslaught of AACR2 and to prepare for the implementation of online cataloging of printed and recorded music, the quantity of catalog copy has dropped off. Library of Congress' most recent prediction is that it will provide new cataloging for about 4500 musical items, books, scores, and sound recordings each year. This number will not provide the music selector with broad enough coverage of the annual published output in any of these media, so decreased reliance on Library of Congress cards as a "hard core" selection tool is likely. The use of Library of Congress copy as a selection tool should speed up processing of orders and cataloging on receipt, however. With the distribution of MARC copy for printed and recorded music, selectors may be able to use Library of Congress' cataloging in a more timely fashion if the utilities of the in-house systems allow browsing by classification and date of loading (the so-called update factor). We selectors will then have to clamor for terminal time *and* make use of local storage devices or high-speed printers.

As Library of Congress' quantity of output has decreased, many music selectors have grown more and more dependent upon the *European Music Catalog* of the firm Otto Harrassowitz,[3] and similar services of Blackwell's Music Shop,[4] and May and May among other European dealers.[5] Of the

3. *European Music Catalog (EMC)* is issued nine times a year with an index and covers the European and Eastern European Music publishing scene rather broadly. The major publishers' products are listed with prepublication and publication citations. There are special purchase prices regularly advertised that are often better than any other offerings, and these special prices are held in force even in the face of occasional difficulty arising from changes in publishers' plans. *EMC* coverage of France, Spain, and Portugal is not as comprehensive as coverage for the rest of Europe, but is good enough for most purposes. The *Harrassowitz Book Digest*, formerly the *German Book Digest*, issued several times a year is very good for staying current with German and other monographic publications; there is a music section. Harrassowitz also offers slip-form announcements of European books in a number of subjects, including music. The standard-setting services of this firm in providing printed materials in music is well described in promotional literature available from: Otto Harrassowitz, POB 2929, D–6200 Wiesbaden, Germany, *or* their American representative, Jane Maddox, Box 340, Cassville, MO 65625.

4. Blackwell's Music Shop provides excellent coverage of British publications but also distributes music of most European publishers; they claim special coverage of France. Among the literature Blackwell's provides are genre lists (piano music, organ music, etc.), catalogs of recently published music, and catalogs of books about music. Blackwell's will also provide "card-form" announcements of recently published music that fully describe the piece at hand and are most useful. These can be obtained from Blackwell's Music Shop, 35 Holywell St., Oxford OX1 35W, England.

5. May and May provides monthly catalogs listing newly published books along with retrospective offerings in their shop. These monthly lists regularly accompany genre catalogs of available scores. Address: May and May Ltd., Arundel House, Salisbury SP3 6QU England.

European Music Catalog. Wiesbaden: Otto Harrassowitz Buchhandlung, 1974– . 9/year.
Basic trade bibliography covering printed music from Europe, including Soviet bloc.
250–300 citations per issue; yearly index.
Main entry and uniform titles based on AACR2. Complete imprint, series, pricing information.
Handy size and format for quick checking and thorough preorder searching.
Save and bind issues as reference tool.

domestic dealers, the catalogs of European American Retail Music,[6] and the "Front Slips" of the Theodore Front Musical Literature Company have been most useful as first or early indicators of newly published scores.[7] The "recently published" lists of scores issued by the Jerona Music Corporation are a particularly good and succinct means of covering very recent issues of contemporary American art music.[8]

The quarterly journal of the Music Library Association, *Notes*, features in each issue a column of great utility to the music selector. "Music Received" is a genre-ordered list of new titles of printed music with good bibliographic information and prices. The bibliographic column is typically a dozen or more pages in length with more than 250 citations; it has been prepared by Ruth Watanabe and Norma Jean Lamb. George R. Hill's irregular column in *Notes*, "Music Publisher's Catalogues," lists new and current catalogs, but also provides publishers' addresses; regular perusal of this column with appropriate letters requesting admission to publishers'

6. European American Retail Music issues four or five times a year "recently published" lists with special emphasis on new titles worth the attention of research libraries. As the name of the firm indicates, it distributes music published in Europe and America. European American's subject lists, such as those on opera and on American musical theater, are useful aids to selectors engaged in "project" buying. Address: European American Retail Music, Inc., P.O. Box 850, Valley Forge, PA 19482.

7. Through the vigorous efforts of a small but dedicated staff under the direction of Theodore Front, one of America's most distinguished suppliers of printed and recorded music, as well as books on the subject and antiquarian materials, Theodore Front Musical Literature is experiencing a rejuvenation of its services. "Front Slips" were some years ago the standard early warning system for music selectors. Now issued in slip format but in sheet form, "Front Slips" serve the same function for music selectors. Front has an extensive collection of books and scores, so in addition to distributing currently published materials, selectors can direct want-lists for older imprints to this firm. Front offers "out-of-print" record service as well. Approval plan services are also available. Address: Theodore Front Musical Literature, Inc., 16122 Cohasset St., Van Nuys, CA 91406.

8. Joseph Boonin, president of the Jerona Music Corporation, was trained as a music scholar and librarian before entering the trade. As a result, his firm addresses the needs of music collections in institutions with great understanding. Jerona also operates on the "less is more" principle. Nearly everything is available from Jerona, including approval plans and blanket orders, but one is advised to write to and, better yet, talk with Boonin about what one wants and needs. Jerona eschews elaborate marketing devices in favor of dependable, accurate, and timely service. Jerona Music Corporation, 81 Trinity Place, Hackensack, NJ 07601.

Notes, The Journal of the Music Library Association. Canton, Mass.: Music Library Assn., 1933– . Quarterly.

"Music Received" genre ordered list of recent publications. Up to a year lag. Imprints and prices. Regular column.

"Books Recently Published" organized by language. Imprint and prices. Lag time about a year. Regular column.

"Index to Record Reviews" gives general critical impression of phonorecords, manufacturer's name and issue number, in two sections: composers and composite releases (anthologies). Very thorough coverage; up to a year lag time. Biennially.

"Music Periodical Reviews." Topical, lengthy, signed reviews. Lag time a year or more.

"Music and Book Reviews." Short but signed, authoritative reviews of many titles thought to be essential to research music collections. Lengthy lag time makes use as selection tools less likely. Regular columns.

Notes is the best bargain in musical scholarship or librarianship. What other periodical offers 960 pages crammed with information and authoritative opinion in four dependable issues each year for $32?

mailing lists will insure the flow of publishers' catalogs and announcements to selectors. Each March, Hill and Joseph Boonin present an update on music price indexes in *Notes*. These articles, which begin in 1979, document the trends in prices, and the several economic factors influencing prices. They should be required reading for every music selector.

Music selectors occasionally get involved in topical or project acquisitions to support research, new courses, or to strengthen a newly perceived weakness in their collection. In these cases of retrospective buying, recourse to the formidable bibliographic apparatus of music is necessary. First one stops to get an overview of a topic (e.g., art songs, piano quintets, music played in Vienna 1810–30, music emulating or incorporating bird songs . . .). *The New Grove's Dictionary of Music and Musicians* and *Die Musik in Geschichte und Gegenwart* (*MGG*) are encyclopedic surveys of music including selective bibliographies that unfortunately lack complete imprint information. The *Harvard Dictionary of Music* (revised edition) is the invaluable one-volume, English topical dictionary. While the bibliographies following the entries are short, they provide openings for the assiduous selector. Vincent Duckles' *Music Reference and Research Materials; An Annotated Bibliography*, the third edition of the Baedeker to generations of musical scholars and bibliographers, provides more than 1900 citations with pithy comments describing each cited work. These four reference works lead selectors to specialized works directly related to the subject requiring the purchase of retrospective materials.

Having consulted *The New Grove*, *MGG*, Duckles, and the *Harvard Dictionary*, one is ready to dive into the thicket of specialized bibliographies and library catalogs to discover all of what has been published in the genre, by composer or topically, depending upon the project at hand. One of the most useful genre-ordered bibliographies of printed music is the catalog of the BBC Music Library organized into categories: chamber music, piano and organ music, songs, choral and opera music, and orchestral music. The BBC catalogs, and indeed nearly all of the published bibliographies, do not contain citations for very recent publications. However, some printed music tends to stay in-print rather longer than ordinary trade books through frequent unnumbered and unmentioned reissues. And, as stated earlier, much of the repertory is edited and reedited; for the best-known classical and romantic period composers there are usually many editions of any given work.

For more convenient reference to many good editions suitable for research library acquisition, the selector will have to consult the printed catalogs of the New York Public Library (*NYPL*) Music Division, the Boston Public Library (*BPL*) Music Collection, and the British Library Catalog of Printed Music (in progress; up to volume 20, HAE-HARPO, as this is written). The NYPL and BPL catalogs are page-mounted copies of card catalogs and thus include author, title, subject, and added entries. The NYPL catalog is supplemented by annual cumulations beginning in 1975 entitled *Bibliographic Guides to Music*; these volumes have listed all of NYPL's cataloging for the Music Division as well as some added Library of Congress MARC cataloging. The British Library Catalog is in main entry order.

The Library of Congress catalogs, which began in 1954 with the title *Music and Phonorecords* and became in 1973 *Music, Books on Music and Sound Recordings,* present, in a series of multiyear cumulations and most recently yearly issues with mid-year interim issues, the current cataloging of selected titles from the music accessions to the Library of Congress *and* contributed cataloging from a number of important music libraries around the United States. The organization is by main entry; there is a subject index to the cumulations; and the catalogs contain both current and retrospective materials. An important supplement to the Library of Congress catalogs is the *Music Library Association Catalog of Cards for Printed Music 1953–1972*, edited by Elizabeth Olmsted. This catalog reproduces cataloging sent to the National Union Catalog in the period indicated but which were *not* published in the Library of Congress *Music and Phonorecords* catalogs.

The distribution of printed music is made difficult by the lack of a universal numbering system such as ISBN. *Music-in-Print* and other marketplace-oriented lists of music cite edition numbers particular to publishers, some even to the series level.[9] Most dealers find the inclusion of these numbers in orders helpful in providing precisely the right edition in the right version.

Through these very general catalogs and specialized bibliographies, the selector engaged in "project" buying will develop a list of music appropriate for the needs of his or her patrons and then begin to place orders, sending titles presumed to be in-print to music dealers who specialize in currently available scores, and sending "locate and offer" requests to antiquarian music dealers for the titles known to be out-of-print. Most antiquarian dealers prefer "locate and offer" requests on cards rather than in list form, since cards ease their checking and filing procedures.

Current imprint scores usually arrive within two or three months of ordering. Some take longer because most dealers do not maintain extensive inventories. Other scores that have recent publication dates take forever to appear because the initial small print run was sold and the publisher is gathering orders until there are enough in hand to justify another print run. Score orders may not arrive quickly and some music publishers use the device of prepublication announcements with favorable pricing to solicit advance orders, which aids them in deciding the number of copies to print. This practice is not particularly advantageous to the selector except in its financial aspects. Favorable responses to such advertisements are not encouraged unless the publisher's project is extraordinary—a large and elaborate publication, a sorely needed facsimile, reproduction, or edition of some source material, or the like.

Printed music usually provides central acquisitions departments with real trouble. Assignment of orders to book dealers and jobbers claiming broad general capabilities usually results in returned, unfilled orders. The selector should specify dealers in printed music to assure fulfillment of orders. Most research music libraries deal with a few, reliable service-oriented European music dealers for European imprints and similarly inclined American music dealers for American imprints. Acquisitions staff members trained to check in books with distinctive titles and clear imprint information frequently and understandably make errors checking in scores whose titles not only may not match the order, but also lack ISBNs and clear imprint data. Most well-established research music libraries receive

9. *Music-in-Print*: Musicdata Corporation of Philadelphia is making valient attempts to provide exhaustive lists of the products of the international music publishing industry. It have been hampered in its efforts by the lack of consistency in the ways music publishers describe their offerings and from less-than-perfect cooperation on the part of publishers to keep Musicdata informed of its publications of printed music. The resulting volumes require some measure of interpretation, but can be of assistance to patrons and selectors. Volumes released to date cover Choral Music (sacred and secular), Organ Music, and String Music. There are supplement volumes issued to some of these as well as general annual supplements to all of the *Music-in-Print* volumes beginning in 1981. Musicdata is located at 18 W. Chelten Avenue, Philadelphia, PA 19144.

printed and recorded music direct from the vendors and send approved invoices forward to the accounting or acquisitions department for payment.

Recorded Music

Recorded music comes in a wide variety of formats: discs (compact, LP, Digital LP, 45rpm, 78rpm, 16-inch transcriptions, etc.); tapes (reel—in a variety of widths, speeds, and track formats, cassette, cartridge, and video); and occasionally wire, cylinder, and film. Right now the most common formats collected in research music libraries are 78rpm, LP discs, reel-to-reel tapes, and cassettes. Most research music libraries attempt to provide facilities so that all but the most exotic formats can be played back in their audio facility. Many libraries now also are providing video playback equipment so the expanding repertory of videotaped operas, concerts, musical theater, master classes, ethnic music documentaries, and other musical presentations can be used by patrons.

For many years, recorded music was not felt to be material suitable for research. Indeed, the generation of teachers and scholars that began to retire in the early sixties frequently would present musical examples to their classes only by playing piano or bringing in other performers. The generation of musical scholars retiring in the 1980s has generally used recorded music in the classroom and seminars, but it is only in the past decade that the study of performance practices, the investigation of the intentions of composers toward performance of their music, and the exhilarating rise of the study of other than "classical" music (jazz, tribal, ethnic, folk, rock, popular, underground, etc.) has brought the use of recorded music fully into the array of research materials.

In contrast to the situation with printed music, recorded music enjoys status as a consumer commodity. Information about recent releases is readily available and reviews follow in timely fashion, at least in the popular press.[10] Record manufacturers encourage the consumption of their products by mass-marketing techniques including the distribution of free copies to broadcasting organizations, local newspaper reviewers, and to the "hi-fi" press. Manufacturers of records also print lists, catalogs, and brochures of their available recordings; these range from mimeographed order forms to inventory sheets to glossy pamphlets organized by composer, performer(s), genre, or topic. Best of all, there are rough equivalents of *Books-in-Print*.

10. The article by Carol Lawrence (olim Mekkawi),"Music Periodicals: Popular and Classical Record Reviews and Indexes," covers twelve indexes to information on sound recordings and more than two dozen periodicals featuring record reviews. The information and critical judgment in this article is still of great utility. It is found in *Notes* 34: 92–107 (1977/78).

The New Schwann. Boston: Schwann Record and Tape Catalogs, 1983– .
Monthly.
  "Books-in-print" for recorded sound, alternating months of classical and
  pop/jazz lists of musical sound recordings (all formats).
  Manufacturers' names and issue numbers instead of imprint. Anthologies
  not analyzed but listed by title.
  "Occasional Artist Issue" lists recordings by performers (organized by
  performing medium).
  Very timely, but only includes recordings distributed in the United States.
  Check monthly new listings to stay current.
  Occasional special lists and articles.

The New Schwann replaces the monthly *Schwann Record and Tape
Guides* for all stereo, LP recorded music and the semiannual *Schwann 2*
for monophonic music, spoken-word recordings, older popular music, and
miscellaneous other recorded sound materials. *The New Schwann* will
alternate monthly between classical listings and pop/jazz listings. Every
December issue will comprise all listings of all categories. The latest information is in the front of *The New Schwann* in larger type. In this
position are separate lists of new releases, digital compact discs, and recordings scheduled for deletion from manufacturers' inventories. *The New
Schwann* is now a computerized list that has made the catalog more
accurate and more up-to-date. Presumably, the occasional *Schwann Artist
Issue*, a performer-ordered list of currently available classical LPs and
tapes, will continue to appear sporadically.

The Entries in *Schwann* are the most cryptic of all the commercial catalogs,
so the informed selector sometimes must check with a thematic catalog
to assure that the listing in *Schwann* is what it seems. *Schwann* provides
only title entries for recorded anthologies, so one usually must rely upon
intuition, the names of the performers, a review, or another more complete
listing to provide information on contents of collections. *Schwann*'s frequency and its relative completeness for widely distributed discs in the
United States recommend it. It is *not* actually comprehensive and because
the selector's marketplace is the world, reference to the *Schwann* ana-
logues in Europe are important to keep up with more of what is available.

The European equivalents are the quarterly *Gramophone Classical Catalogue* (there are *Popular* and *Spoken Word and Miscellaneous Gramophone Catalogues* as well), the semiannual *Bielefelder Katalog Klassik*
(and the annual *Bielefelder Katalog Jazz*), and the annual *Diapason Catalogue General Classique*. Each of these provide the usual composer/title,
performer(s), manufacturers' names, and issue numbers but each analyzes
recorded collections more completely. Only by reference to all of these
sources will the selector cover most of the available resources. Record

---

Fanfare: The Magazine for Serious Record Collectors. Tenafly, N.J.: Flegler,
1977– . Bimonthly.
Numerous topical articles.
Pithy, authoritative, signed reviews.
Good coverage, occasional handy directories of dealers, some book
reviews.
Jazz and pop listings also, but the main topic is classical music. Timely and
robust.

---

companies occasionally change names and issue numbers of their products
as they market them across national and, more frequently, continental
borders. Issue name and numbers of American releases often bear little
obvious relation to the European original pressings; careful comparison
of titles and performers is a way of discerning duplicate releases.

Dozens of periodical publications feature timely reviews of new releases
of musical recordings. A quick search of the RLIN Serials file on the
subject phrases "Sound Recordings" and "Music-Discography" produced
more than three dozen titles. In addition to the catalogs cited above, four
American publications provide a large number of reasonably critical reviews and are thus most useful to the selector.

The resuscitated *American Record Guide* (*ARG*) is a monthly publication featuring signed reviews of classical music. The reviewers typically
discuss the music and its performance but do not mention the technical
quality of the recording unless there is something vastly amiss. These are
usually well in excess of 100 reviews, each of which is at least several
paragraphs. Occasionally these are round-up reviews covering genres. Most
of the labels covered are commonly available and the reviews are sound.

The bimonthly *Fanfare* is subtitled "The Magazine for Serious Record
Collectors." Amid a number of featured columns, book reviews, and a
few *very* intelligent equipment articles, there are usually more than 175
pages of reviews of recently released classical recordings. *Fanfare* also
includes a fair number of popular, jazz, and sound track reviews. While
the length of the *Fanfare* reviews approximate those in *ARG*, the critical
approach is more intense, especially toward the performances, but also
toward the audio quality of each disc. There is an impressively broad
coverage in each *Fanfare* issue; it is thus well worth the effort of plowing
through the entire magazine each time it arrives. The advertisements in
ARG and *Fanfare* direct the selector to less common labels, to sources
for out-of-print recordings, and to specialty dealers.

Two monthly "newstand" magazines of great use to selectors are *High
Fidelity* (Musical America Edition) and *Stereo Review.* Each focus on the
consumer aspects of recorded sound, namely new home high fidelity, car
stereo systems, and video equipment. Most of the advertisements in these

glossy publications are for equipment, blank tape, and similar products. However, each presents at least three or four articles on music or musicians, a section of reviews of classical music, and a section of reviews of popular music, including jazz. At least a dozen classical and a similar number of popular releases are featured each month. The records reviewed are the sort widely distributed in the United States and are most likely available in local record stores by the time the issues hit the newsstands. While *High Fidelity* and *Stereo Review* are clearly consumer-oriented, the reviewers are knowledgeable and offer trenchant comments on the music as well as the performances. In most cases truly critical remarks are not present; rather, alternative choices are suggested.

Gramophone, the British predecessor to *ARG* and *Fanfare*, is the most useful of all the European recording reviewing periodicals. It is monthly and includes about 175 intelligent, signed reviews in each issue. Most of the titles reviewed are available in the United States, though some have to be imported. *Gramophone*'s thoughtful, understated feature articles and regular columns are highly recommended. Germany's *Fono-Forum* and France's *Harmonie Hi-Fi Conseil* are more like *High Fidelity* and *Stereo Review* and offer many of the same advantages and disadvantages.

Selectors of recordings of classical music cannot afford to ignore Kurtz Myers' "Index to Record Reviews," a regularly featured column since 1949 in *Notes*, the quarterly journal of the Music Library Association. Myers collects opinions of reviewers in seventeen periodicals and one newspaper, the *New York Times*, indicating the reviewers' opinions on the quality of the performance, the presence of mechanical faults, and, in some cases, reviews "of sufficient length and probity to warrant special attention." The index is organized in two sections, the first for composers and the second for "composite releases." Each review is cited in abbreviated form and the review's opinions indicated by symbols. Perusing this column is a very good way of quickly covering a great portion of the current releases and of getting an overview of the critical reception for a recorded performance. The first thirty years of the column have been cumulated into a five-volume work of the same name, published by G. K. Hall. It is a discographic guide as well as an index to record reviews for the first three decades of classical music on LP records. The G. K. Hall cumulation includes a very valuable one-volume index to the composite entries.

There are, of course, Library of Congress CDS Alert Service cards for recorded music, as for printed music.

With these tools at hand, the selector can make informed choices from more than 7000 new records released each year. Most selectors concern themselves with repertory first and performances next. Curricular pressures drive selections for academic collections right now more than immediate research needs, although many selectors are very much aware that research using recorded music, if not upon them, is just around the corner. A good operating principal for all music research libraries is that there should be at least one recorded performance for each title of printed music in the library. For the so-called standard repertory there will need to be more than one title, since the pressure on that portion of our collections is consistently greater than on other portions. It is somewhat easier to provide recorded performances of twentieth-century music to match printed holdings since the music is performed and is printed now when record production is reasonably available. The timely acquisition of any music not in the standard repertory is recommended.

The major record companies are producing fewer new performances of unusual music and more reissues of previous profit makers, while small "cottage-industry" record producers are filling these gaps. These small labels do not have the same marketing outlets as the majors *and* produce records in very small "press runs." Discovering what is available, and then selecting and acquiring desirable recorded music is becoming increasingly more time consuming.

Selectors need to read reviews, peruse pamphlets, watch advertisements, consult with colleagues, follow up leads, and, most importantly, establish cordial working relationships with at least one good local record store. Audio Buff of Athens, Ohio, provides to its customers monthly packets of manufacturers' release sheets and prepares a list of its own unusual offerings.[11] This dealer also can provide any recorded sound title listed in any of the catalogs. Happily, in the record business, discounts to larger accounts are common. One should expect about thirty percent off list prices for records distributed widely in the United States, less for some specialty labels, and cost plus handling for labels imported on request. The best library suppliers also provide a variety of rush order, standing order, approval plan, subscription, and related services. Selectors need to be able to go to a local record store for emergency purchases and to keep their hands on the recorded music business. One needs to know what records are being widely purchased, what new, popular music has affected public listening (and thus buying patterns), and what new performers are appearing. Finally, there is no substitute for listening to recorded music. Selectors of music need to have aural knowledge, if not appreciation, of the music they acquire for their libraries.

11. Audio Buff has become widely known for its devoted service to academic and public libraries. Its search service is legendary. Like Jerona, its advertising is low profile, but it assiduously passes manufacturers' specials on to its customers. It will accept and act upon rush orders by telephone and it does handle subscriptions. Audio Buff can also supply many of the more important record catalogs. Address: Audio Buff, Inc., P.O. Box 2629, Athens, OH 45701-2393.

Video

Research music libraries are coming to grips with the content versus format issue in collection building once again as video forms are becoming consumer-oriented publications. Sound recordings (music and spoken-word) were sufficiently specialized in subject (music and the literatures) not to stimulate debate on this issue. With the onslaught of video and the permeation of video equipment into homes and offices as well as classrooms, the format of knowledge as a characteristic excluding selection must be regarded with more suspicion.

"Video'ed" productions of any of the variety of staged musical forms (opera, ballet, musical theater) are now available, and give students and scholars new insights, new subjects, and new methods for research. In addition, music of non-Western cultures are more easily introduced by the use of video publications. There are about 100 video productions related to music in the RLIN Film (FLM) file as this is written. *The Video Source Book* and the *Media Review Digest* list many musical titles that have little, if any, research value, except as source materials. These "filmographic" compendia apparently serve commercial distributions. Dramatically lowered hardware costs have made possible video productions by academic and ethnic societies; these titles are usually available only through the producer or a sole distributor, but are of greater research value.

Identifying available video publications is difficult for music specialists. Some audio dealers and a number of publishers provide lists. Communication with and reliance upon media specialists is important as the format gains acceptance in research institutions. Placement on appropriate mailing lists already mentioned seems to give the best chance of discovering what is available of interest to selectors of music research materials. Producers and distributors are apparently taking advantage of automated and coded files in order to target their advertisements to most likely consumers.

In evaluating a video publication, all of the questions of content pertinent to printed and recorded music as well as to books about music should be applied to the video. In addition, one should be concerned with the quality of the video image, "scenographic" matters, and the preferred electronic format (which depends in part on playback equipment available in each institution).

Words about Music

For music selectors in most research music libraries, purchasing books about music is the most obvious responsibility, because so many more patrons can and will read words than printed music. With few exceptions music selectors must purchase deeply in some very specialized areas to support current research while somehow buying widely to provide balance. This tightrope feat is crucial because, like printed music, small press runs and almost certain long-term availability problems obtain in nearly every case. A title passed over this year will be most difficult and certainly more expensive to obtain in five years.

The selection of books about music for a research collection is made less demanding than selecting printed or recorded music by the inclusion of most of these titles in the standard bibliographical tools and selection aids. The marketplace for books about music is international in scope and many books have two publishers. The selector can use Library of Congress CDS Alert Service cards, the "Recently Received" lists, and the more timely reviewing media to keep fairly well up-to-date. Major publishers and dealers issue the usual plethora of brochures, fliers, and other advertisements, but particularly in music there seems to be a fair number of "little" presses and organizational publications that enter the bibliographical literature often in eccentric ways and without effective advertising.

The most comprehensive of the "Recently Received" lists is in *Notes* every quarter. David Sommerfield now edits "Books Recently Published," which is organized by the language of the text and is typically about 250 entries long. A most timely list of English language titles appears each month in the *Musical Times*. Reviews in *Choice* and *LJ* may serve the needs of selectors for college-level collections well enough, but are neither deep nor numerous enough to be used regularly by selectors for research collections.

A good portion of any research library's monographs are acquired through standing orders. This is particularly true in the case of books about music because publishers with the desire to produce music titles know all too well that their market is small and their music list will probably never yield a bestseller. To a considerable degree publishers have used the numbered series to insure at least a break-even return on music monographs. Numerous series are direct or derivative versions of doctoral theses; this is particularly true of a large number of German-language monographic series. The annual Harrassowitz catalogs of Composers' Collected Editions (Harrassowitz Special Music Catalog No. 7) and of monographic series and yearbooks (Special Music Catalog No. 8) published in Europe are good lists of available titles. The Music Program Committee of the Research Libraries Group is preparing a list of current standing orders and subscriptions among its members. When complete, this may be the most comprehensive list of available titles in music. European American Retail Music distributes a list of recently published numbers in series it distributes to advertise its products and also alert selectors to new titles as they are issued.

In most cases, individual titles in numbered monographic series are available as separate purchases. With many of the monumental series, especially those edited and published by scholarly societies and with subvention monies, there is a possibility that individual titles are not available without a subscription. Eventually, these come into the antiquarian market and special pleas to one's favorite dealer or even to the publisher directly sometimes produce a single volume in a numbered set. Individual titles are announced through the sources already mentioned and in pamphlets or brochures for the series issued by the publishers.

In the past twenty years selectors have placed, more or less uncritically, subscriptions to monographic series as a way of covering a difficult literature as well as a way of reducing time and effort. With committed funds nearing the majority of available funds each year and with the collection evaluation and coordinated collection development policies/ projects among the community of research libraries in the United States, some critical reviews of institutional standing orders to such series are likely. A correction in the marketplace is overdue.

Music selectors must read reviews fairly widely and ideally in numerous languages to keep track of current research and the current quality of any given publisher's output. Regular review reading, along with constant immersion in the periodical literature, keeps one aware of the directions in musical scholarship. The *Journal of the American Musicological Society, Ethnomusicology, Acta Musicologica,* the *Musical Quarterly, Early Music,* the *Musical Times, American Music, Die Musikforschung, Fontes Artis Musicae, Journal of Music Theory,* the *Latin American Music Review, 19th Century Music, Perspectives of New Music, Revue de Musicologie, Rivista Italiana di Musicologia,* and the *International Review of the Aesthetics and Sociology of Music* are journals one needs to read to stay reasonably afloat in the currents of musical scholarship. One quickly builds a critical sense of which authors, which research institutions, which editors, and which publishers produce the kind of books a research music library needs for its scholars. Such books are characterized by well-focused topics, reliance on and citation of sources, and well-constructed apparatus around the body of the book. Indexes cite topics and titles of compositions; there are thematic locators or indexes; occasionally there are chronological or geographical indexes; there are adequate to extensive introductions justifying a point of view and/or the impetus for the study; there are musical examples, usually printed but occasionally in recorded form; there are illustrations; and in the best cases there are also nice wide margins for annotations (anathema in most libraries most of the time, but important for the individual scholar).

The number of newly published titles has continued or even increased during the past few years. Many of the popular titles and a number of typescript publications might have been left out of the scholarly publishers' lists, but when monographs on star performers, on trendy topics, or promising some new aspect are announced, our clientele generally provide us with suggestions and nudges to purchase such works. Since the popular literature has a wider and less critical audience, this kind of literature will continue and flourish.

Selectors are advised to hone their own critical skills by reading book reviews in the *New York Times*, the *New York Review of Books* and the *Times Literary Supplement.* While these do not publish very many reviews of books about music, those that do appear are really quite important. One should always remember that for most research in music, cultural and intellectual contexts influence scholars, their methods and results, and have influenced composers and performers. Weekly forays into the general critical review publications keep the music selector ever aware of the contexts of music and musical scholarship.

Periodicals

Two substantial subgenres of the category "words about music," music periodicals and reference works, need some special treatment. There are an enormous number of music periodicals, perhaps 3000.

Most research libraries subscribe to at least 200, and some up to 400 or 500. Only the periodical review column in *Notes* has regularly featured critical examinations of new periodical titles, and no one has attempted to bring under control the numerous regional or highly specialized music periodicals.[12] One must ferret out information on music periodicals as best one can; Ulrich's is not in any sense comprehensive. Most research libraries subscribe to the major music periodicals intended for general readers (*Musical Times*, *Musical Quarterly*, etc.), to the publications of the various widely recognized societies (*Journal of the American Musicological Society*, *Die Musikforschung*, etc.) and then purchase other journals to support research. The practice of buying comprehensively in regional and highly specialized music periodicals matching institutional curricular and research interests is recommended for consideration, especially as the development proceeds of the national research collection (incorporating collections and services at the Library of Congress and the other federal libraries, major research universities, and numerous private research institutions). Regional and specialized journals that now may seem ephem-

12. The most recent version of this irregular column is edited by Stephen Fry and found in *Notes* 40, no. 2: 275–78 (Dec. 1983).

eral and perhaps too popular will be considered important sources for twenty-first-century scholars working on twentieth-century topics, just as we are finding similar publications of the eighteenth and nineteenth centuries illuminating and particularly effective in debunking what were considered axiomatic notions.

In considering a periodical for possible addition to one's list of subscriptions, obtaining several specimen copies is the most reliable way to begin evaluating it. Uniqueness of content, relevance to one's collection and patrons, inclusion of substantial factual material, the use of foot- or endnotes, the presence of reviews or lists of new titles, descriptions of contributors, clearly stated editorial policies, quality of production, regularity of issue, and cost are elements to be considered. The maintenance of a backfile of specimens of periodicals evaluated and rejected is perhaps useful in comparing journals with similar goals and/or styles.

Reference Books

Many music reference works receive too little attention in the critical literature of music and general librarianships for variety of good and bad reasons. On one hand, these titles have a limited market and librarians are too busy coping with everyday responsibilities to give them the close examination they need. On the other hand, some reference works slide soundlessly into our reference collections with skewed viewpoints, bad information, too little coverage, and other flaws. For reference works, accuracy, clarity of organization, and type of use are elements that weigh more heavily in addition to those elements for consideration of monographs cited above.

Rare and Antiquarian Material

Music manuscripts, archival materials, early printed music, and old books about music provide most music selectors in research institutions with complex, compelling, and vexing opportunities. Especially for such materials are good, clearly understood selection policies useful. The community of rare and antiquarian music dealers is small but in close touch with their clients. Much to their credit, these dealers generally try to find suitable "homes" for unusual materials. In many cases, the catalogs of musical antiquarians are important reference and research tools. However much assistance the dealers provide, selectors must learn to identify, verify, and describe materials seldom dated and frequently disguised by their originator or publisher, or a subsequent owner. In no other discipline is the adage "every book printed before 1800 is a separate issue" more true. Reliance upon the *Guide for Dating Early Printed Music* and the tools cited therein and on the *Repertoire International des Sources Musicales* (*RISM*) is crucial to the wise selection of unusual and costly items.[13]

Since the availability of rare and antiquarian materials is seldom predictable and almost never long-term, one must be flexible in approach and quick to make a decision. Most selectors need to justify a request for an older and more expensive purchase if not to raise the required funds.

The most prominent antiquarian music dealers advertise in *Fontes Artis Musicae* and in *Notes*. There is a lengthy list of such dealers in the *International Directory of Booksellers*. It is not wise to communicate with any more dealers than are likely to provide the institution with the opportunities needed to continue building the collection in desired areas. Major auction houses regularly conduct sales of manuscript and printed music and books about music, so selectors whose institution is prepared to enter the heady world of bidding (usually through agents) are advised to introduce themselves and specify their areas of interest to the music and/or rare books specialists employed by the principal establishments.

Skimming the antiquarians' catalogs first each day is a good way of gaining as much time as possible once one's interest is piqued. The most organized and successful selectors let their dealers know of specific titles and general areas of interest. Whenever possible communication and even visits between selector and dealer make for better decision making.

The questions to be asked in the process of deciding to purchase or acquire otherwise any unusual title or collections are: Is the material as described (identification and condition)? Does the material "fit" into the collection (complementarity)? Is the material needed for research or for the sake of the existing collection? Is the material available at a reasonable price? What is the provenance of the material? In considering manuscript and archival materials, selectors need to consider also whether and how these materials will be made available to readers.

The usual pace of acquiring current imprint materials is too slow for acquiring unusual materials. Wise selectors establish an understanding with

13. RISM is the acronym for the *Repertoire International des Sources Musicales* (International Inventory of Musical Scores), a project of the International Musicological Society and the International Association of Music Libraries. There are three series of publications resulting from RISM, which is concerned exclusively with the documentation of musical sources created before the first quarter of the nineteenth century:

Series A concerns works ascribable to a single composer—*Einzeldrucke vor 1800* (Kassel, et al.: Barenreiter, 1971–). It is now ready to issue supplementary volumes, and a manuscript catalog is about to be distributed in preliminary form.

Series B concerns anthologies, unattributable works, books about music, and a variety of other source materials.

Series C consists entirely of directories of institutions and persons owning musical source materials.

See the article "Repertoire International des Sources Musicales" in vol. 15 of *The New Grove's Dictionary of Music and Musicians*, ed. by Stanley Sadie, 20v. (London: Macmillan, 1980).

collection development officers and acquisitions librarians on the use of cables, telephone calls, and confirming orders before proceeding with special purchases.

It is in this matter of rare and unusual materials that collection-driven decisions become more prominent. In the best of situations, patrons will stimulate interest and support for such selectors, of course. This area also presents the selector with important responsibilities, since in many cases the titles or materials offered are unique. In purchasing current imprint materials, one can be reasonably assured that several similar institutions will select the same titles much of the time, but in selecting rare titles, one is quite possibly protecting a unique title for universal access and from oblivion. The developments of strong bibliographic skills, a close understanding of the institution's rare holdings, as well as mutual trust and understanding between antiquarian and selector are essential in addition to the other characteristics discussed earlier.

Obtaining microform and photocopies of primary sources from other libraries, particularly those in Europe, presents special problems and procedures. In many cases, prepayment or barter is required. Also, for smaller libraries, long lead times are required, since a company able to microfilm the material is almost never nearby. Many libraries require information about the intended use of the material in question and some will not provide copies without institutional or personal assurances that they will be cited as the owner and that no extensive publication would be prepared without prior permission. The excellent article of Sigrun Folter, "Library Restrictions on the Use of Microfilm Copies" in *Fontes Artis Musicae* discusses this situation in more detail and provides a list of conditions by institution.

Approval Plans and Blanket Orders

After some desultory attempts by a number of music dealers in the 1960s, substantial approval plans and blanket orders for the acquisition of printed music were firmly established by the Otto Harrassowitz agency in the 1970s. Such plans require considerable effort from the selector and the acquisitions librarian to establish a profile of the library's collection policy to guide the dealer(s) in providing titles. Once profiles are set, however, approval plans do save time and effort for the selector. They can make new publications available more quickly; they can assure systematic coverage of the selected publications at a predetermined level. Most of the prominent printed music dealers specializing in the institutional trade welcome the opportunity to develop such plans; most model their efforts on the pioneering work of the firm Otto Harrassowitz in Wiesbaden, Germany.[14]

Approval plans and blanket order profiles can be written to cover broadly or narrowly on several characteristics: date of imprint; date of composition; genre; country of origin; language; performing resources; cost; nature of publication (collected works facsimiles; reprints; excerpt; etc.) performing resources; level of editing; name of composer, editor, publisher. One must also take care to cover the problem of series and series overlaps. We have found broad geographical divisions useful since most dealers specialize in providing scores from their home continent. Europe and America are easily covered with several firms competing for business in these areas. Other continents, particularly Latin and South America, Africa, the Middle East and the various Asian subcontinental areas are less well served. For Latin and South America, our selector colleagues in SALALM (Seminar on the Acquisition of Latin American Library Materials) have been remarkably cooperative in attempting to obtain printed music, but still more work and understanding of Asian and Third World marketplaces is necessary.

Of crucial consequence are the profile, of course; the annual dollar limit of the plan; the possibility of returns for credit; and the provision of bibliographical forms, invoices, and various reports by the dealer. Once the plan is established, the selector then needs to monitor the plan to assure that it is providing what the institution wants with a minimum of returns and/or business problems between the dealer(s) and the acquisitions unit. In addition to regular monitoring some rather formal annual review is recommended to assure that institutional benefits and goals are being met.

As a means of providing the titles that most research libraries will need and of minimizing work in a time of increasing workloads but decreasing staff availability, approval plans and/or blanket orders, particularly for printed music, should be considered.

Conclusion

Underlying the many decisions a selector of music for the larger academic library must make constantly is training and experience in the numerous disciplines mentioned in the introductory paragraphs of this article. Music selectors must be responsive, quickly and effectively responsive, to their clientele and their collections. However, selectors must also be aware of

14. The booklet "European Music Scores; Harrassowitz Approval Plan ... " ought to be consulted by music selectors before embarking upon an approval plan or a blanket order, whether for foreign or domestic imprints. The booklet is available on request from Harrassowitz.

the limitations in *only* being responsive. At the end of the Second World War, the study of non-Western music was limited to a few individuals, some with institutional connections, some without. Today ethnomusicology is an accepted and burgeoning discipline opening the ears and minds of students to musics vastly different from the sounds, aesthetics, and constructs of Western European art music. This expansion is good for cultural understanding, for intellectual development, for world peace. A colleague recently pointed out to me that the transmission of even Western European musical traditions in eighteenth- and nineteenth-century America was through arrangements and reductions. Since most of us have been raised to revere the sources closest to the creators of music, we have simply neglected to concern ourselves with the transmission of musical traditions.

Selectors of music, and probably selectors of any humanistic library materials, must challenge their own assumptions, make convincing arguments, and balance responsiveness with leadership in order to assure that selection for acquisition or preservation assures gathering disparate ideas for the sake of posterity as well as amassing resources for the penetrating musical scholarship now universal in American institutions of higher learning.

Selection Sources

Acta Musicologica. Kassel: Barenreiter, 1928– . Semiannually.
American Music. Champaign: Sonneck Society and Univ. of Illinois Pr., 1983– . Quarterly.
American Musicological Society. 201 S. 34th Street, Philadelphia, PA 19104. Publication: *Journal of the American Musicological Society*. 3/year.
American Record Guide. Melville, N.Y. ARG Publishers, 1934– . 10/year.
Audio Buff, Inc., P.O. Box 2629, Athens, OH 45701-2393.
Apel, Willi, comp. *Harvard Dictionary of Music*. 2nd ed. Rev. and enlarged. Cambridge: Belknap Pr. of Harvard Univ. Pr., 1972. (A completely new edition is in preparation by Don Michael Randel.)
Bibliographic Guides to Music. Boston: Hall, 1975– . (Preceded by Hall's 1974 *Music Book Guide* covering only Library of Congress' cataloging of books about music.)
Bielefelder Katalog Klassik. Karlsruhe: G. Braun, 1952– . Semiannually.
Boston Public Library. *Dictionary Catalog of the Music Collection*. 20 v. Boston: Hall, 1972.
British Broadcasting Corporation. Central Music Library. *Catalogues*. London: BBC, 1965-82. (For chamber music, piano and organ music, songs, choral and opera works, and orchestral music.)
British Library. *The Catalogue of Printed Music in the British Library to 1980*. London and New York: Saur, 1981– . (65v. projected.)
College Music Society. Regent Box 44, University of Colorado, Boulder, CO 80309. Publication: *College Music Symposium*. 1961– . Semiannually.

Diapason Catalogue General Classique. Boulogne: Diapason, 1963– . Annually.

Duckles, Vincent H. *Music Reference and Research Materials; An Annotated Bibliography.* 3rd ed. New York: Free Pr., 1974. (A fourth edition is underway.)

Early Music. London: Oxford Univ. Pr., 1973– . Quarterly.

Ethnomusicology. See *Society for Ethnomusicology.*

European Music Catalog. Wiesbaden: Otto Harrassowitz, 1974– . Request from: Otto Harrassowitz Buchhandlung, P.O. Box 2929, D–6200 Wiesbaden, Germany. 8/year (varies).

Fanfare. Tenafly, N.J.: J. Flegler, 1977– . Bimonthly.

Folter, Sigrun. "Library Restrictions on the Use of Microfilm Copies." *Fontes Artis Musicae* 24, n. 4:207–43.

Fono Forum. (Bielefelder Verlagsantalt.) Postfach 1140, 4800 Bielefeld 1, Germany, Bielefeld. Monthly.

Fontes Artis Musicae. Kassel: Barenreiter, 1954– . 3/year.

Gramophone. Harrow, Middlesex: General Gramophone Publications, 1922– . Monthly.

Gramophone Classical Catalogue. Harrow, Middlesex: General Gramophone Publications, 1953– . Quarterly.

Guide for Dating Early Published Music: A Manual of Bibliographic Practices. Comp. by Donald W. Krummel. Hackensack, N.J.: Joseph Boonin, Inc., 1974; Kassel et al.: Barenreiter Verlag, 1974.

Harmonie Hi-Fi Conseil. Paris: Nouvel Office d'Edition, 1980– . 11/year.

High Fidelity. Great Barrington, Mass.: High Fidelity, 1951– . Monthly.

Hill, George R., and Joseph M. Boonin. "Price Indexes, Foreign and Domestic Music." *Notes* 35: 593–609 (1979) et seq.

Index to Record Reviews. comp. by Kurtz Myers. Boston: Hall, 1978.

International Directory of Booksellers. New York: Saur, 1978. (There is a lengthy index on pp. 844–57 of booksellers offering books on music, printed music, or recorded music. Those marked "ANT *and* MUS" in the directory listings are most likely to be of use in retrospective buying projects.)

International Review of the Aesthetics and Sociology of Music. Zagreb: Press Inst. Jazu, 1970– . Semiannually.

Journal of Music Theory. New Haven, Conn.: Yale School of Music, 1957– . Semiannually.

Latin American Music Review. (*Revista de Musica Latinoamericana.*) Austin: Univ. of Texas Pr., 1980– . Semiannually.

Library of Congress. *The National Union Catalog Music and Phonorecords 1953–57, 1958–62, 1963–67, 1968–72.* Paterson, N.J.: Rowman & Littlefield, 1961, 1963; Ann Arbor, Mich.: J. W. Edwards, 1969, 1973.

Media Review Digest. Ann Arbor, Mich.: Pierian, 1974. Annually.

Mekkawi, Carol Lawrence. "Music Periodicals: Popular and Classical Record Reviews and Indexes." *Notes* 34: 92–107 (1977/78).

Music, Books on Music and Sound Recordings: 1973-77. Totowa, N.J.: Rowman & Littlefield, 1978.

———: *1978– .* Washington, D.C.: Library of Congress, 1979– .

Music Educators National Conference. 1902 Association Drive, Reston, VA 22091. Publications: *Music Educators Journal.* 9/year; *Journal of Research in Music Education.* 1953– . Quarterly.

Music-in-Print. Musicdata, Inc., 18 W. Chelten Avenue, Philadelphia, PA 19144.

Music Library Association. Business Office, P.O. Box 487, Canton, MA 02021. Publication: *Notes.* Quarterly.

Musical America: 1984 International Directory of the Performing Arts. New York: ABC Leisure Magazines, 1984– . Annually.

Musical Quarterly. New York: G. Schirmer, 1915– . Quarterly.

The Musical Times. London: Musical Times, 1848– . Monthly.

Die Musik in Geschichte und Gegenwart. Ed. by Friedrich Blume. 14v. Kassel und Basel: Barenreiter Verlag, 1949-67.

Die Musikforschung. Kiel: Gesellschaft fur Musikforschung. 1948– . Quarterly.

Myers, Kurtz, comp. *Index to Record Reviews.* 5v. Boston: Hall, 1978.

The New Grove's Dictionary of Music and Musicians. Ed. by Stanley Sadie. 20v. London: Macmillan, 1980.

The New Schwann. Dec. 1983– . Boston: Schwann Record and Tape Catalogs. 1983– . Monthly. (Dist. by Schwann Record and Tape Catalogs, 535 Boylston St., Boston, MA 02116.)

New York Public Library. *Dictionary Catalog of the Music Collection.* 30v., covering up to 1963. Boston: Hall, 1964. *Cumulative Supplement, 1964-1971.* 10v. Boston: Hall, 1973.

19th Century Music. Berkeley: Univ. of California Pr., 1977– . 3/year.

Notes; The Quarterly Journal of the Music Library Association. Canton, Mass.: Music Library Assn., 1934– . Quarterly.

Olmsted, Elizabeth, ed. *Music Library Association Catalog of Cards for Printed Music 1953-1972.* Totowa, N.J.: Rowman & Littlefield, 1974.

Perspectives of New Music. Princeton, N.J.: Princeton Univ. Pr., 1962– . Semiannually.

Revue de Musicologie. Paris: Société Française de Musicologie, 1917– . Semiannually.

Rivista Italiana di Musicologia. Firenze: Olschki & Quaderni: Societa Italiana di Musicologia, 1966– . Semiannually.

Society for Ethnomusicology. P.O. Box 2984, Ann Arbor, MI 48106. Publication: *Ethnomusicology.* 1955– . 3/year.

Sommerfield, David. "Books Recently Published." *Notes* 40, no. 3 (Mar. 1984).

Special Music Catalog No. 7: Composers Collected Editions. 2nd rev. ed. Wiesbaden: Harrossowitz, 1984.

Special Music Catalog No. 8: Music Survey 84 Monographic Series and Yearbooks. Wiesbaden: Harrossowitz, 1984.

Stereo Review. Flushing: Ziff–Davis, 1947– . Monthly.

The Video Source Book. 5th ed. Syosset: National Video Clearinghouse, 1983.

Part 3

SOCIAL SCIENCES

Edited by
Beth J. Shapiro

ANTHROPOLOGY

Stephen MacLeod

The etymological root of the word anthropology, literally "the study of man," is consistent with the broad, comprehensive, complex nature of the discipline. Anthropology encompasses research on all aspects of the earth's peoples throughout time and space, and consequently the field is eclectic and interdisciplinary. The field overlaps and incorporates subject matter from other disciplines in the social sciences, humanities, and the natural and physical sciences. Anthropological theory, research, and methodology can be distinguished from other all-encompassing fields that study humankind by its comparative perspective. Anthropologists have historically attempted to identify and interpret differences and similarities among human ethnic groups in the context of the whole of humankind. This is a major concern only of anthropology, and thus distinguishes this discipline from others in the social sciences. Anthropology also is unique among the human sciences in that it seeks to study both our physical and sociocultural aspects.

Anthropology consists of physical and cultural areas of research with four major subfields: social/cultural anthropology, physical/biological anthropology, linguistics, and archaeology. The proliferation of new subdivisions within and outside this structure has increasingly challenged this division of subfields, especially in the last twenty years. An early attempt was the functionalist approach of A. R. Radcliffe-Brown and Bronislaw Malinowski, which in the 1920s and 1930s tried to distinguish social anthropology from cultural anthropology. A more recent example, the use of anthropological data to solve practical social, political, and eco-

The author gratefully acknowledges the useful suggestions and comments of David Perkins of the California State University, Northridge Library; Chris Ferguson of the library at the University of California, Irvine; Bonnie Nelson of the John Jay College of Criminal Justice Library; Gregory Finnegan of the library at Roosevelt University; and Dewitt Durham of Stanford University.

nomic problems, has fostered the field of applied anthropology, which also has challenged the traditional division.

A sample of the subdivisions that have emerged primarily in the second half of this century demonstrate the tremendous expansion and diversification of anthropology: medical anthropology, ethnoarchaeology, urban anthropology, sociolinguistics, educational anthropology, cultural ecology, anthropology of law, visual anthropology, economic archaeology, mathematical anthropology, humanistic anthropology, culture change, psycholinguistics, political anthropology, psychological anthropology, ethnographic futures research, semantics, cognitive anthropology, and clinical anthropology. The history of anthropology, which produced a flurry of publishing in the 1930s, has experienced renewed interest in the last fifteen years. Theoretical and methodological concepts are also of growing importance to the discipline. Yet it is difficult to discern just what the mainstream of anthropology is today, as the discipline has become very fragmented. At the same time as diversification within the field continues, efforts at synthesis increase as anthropologists in all subfields and subdivisions seek universals in their research. At present, it is unclear what these recent trends in anthropology will mean for the future. The expansion of the range of fields to which anthropology is applied might represent the transition of anthropology from a discipline to a theoretical perspective and methodological approach. The interest in the history of the discipline might imply recognition of the decline of anthropology, or it might reflect the search for theories and ideas that will expand the range of fields to which the anthropological approach can be applied.

The Literature of Anthropology

Traditional emphasis on fieldwork as a central method of inquiry makes anthropology unique among the social sciences. Other social sciences incorporate fieldwork methodologies, but anthropology continues to rely heavily on the fieldwork experience. Yet traditional fieldwork among relatively isolated societies might rapidly become an anachronistic model of anthropological inquiry. Fieldwork today quite often occurs in the urban environment, in hospitals, in large industrial organizations, in schools, and in other institutions of modern society. The reports of the results of fieldwork, most often called ethnographies, appear in a somewhat systematic reporting process. The literature of anthropology from the late nineteenth century to the present is influenced to a substantial degree by this methodology. Data gathering, analysis, and reporting from field, site, or experimental laboratory dominates the literature.

Anthropological research may first appear in the literature in working papers, association papers, conference proceedings; next in theses, dissertations, or journal articles; and finally in monographs. It is not unusual for a number of publications to arise from the research done by an anthropologist at one site. Work at one site may continue for a substantial portion of an anthropologist's career. Publications of professional associations, societies, university departments, student organizations, government agencies, and museums are extremely valuable to researchers. Field notes, archaeological site reports, and laboratory reports are also very important. Research in the field tends to focus the literature needs of anthropologists on specific regional areas. This concentration makes important the resources of atlases; federal, foreign, and international government publications; special library catalogs and bibliographies; area handbooks and maps. The accumulated literature of anthropology remains valuable and useful to researchers. Past publications and primary research sources are important to those tracing former work with specific cultural groups or in specific regional areas. Anthropological "readers," which may contain papers, site reports, journal articles, or book extracts (quite often reprints), represent a growing form of publication. They attempt to accumulate relevant publications on a particular subfield or subdivision of anthropology, a particular region, a particular methodology or a particular cultural group. Monographs and monographic series (which are characteristic of the literature) are extremely important to the discipline and remain the standard means of publication for "classic" writings in the field.

The tradition of fieldwork requires that sufficient research in the literature be accomplished before the anthropologist enters the field. This requirement arises from the need of anthropologists to understand the subjects in their physical, cultural, and historical contexts. In addition, the research emphasis in many academic departments of anthropology on specific regional areas requires that many collections be area-specific. The acquisitions problems of the area selector are documented elsewhere, and I will only touch upon them here, but it is important to note that this emphasis requires the anthropology selector to acquire material in non-English and, quite often, non-Western languages (McBride, 1981).* Anthropology has also experienced recent increases in the number of anthropologists from non-Western countries, resulting in a substantial increase in non-Western anthropological publications, many of which are difficult to obtain.

There are a number of other formats of recorded information that are potentially valuable for anthropologists, such as films, videotapes, audio

*For complete information for such citations throughout this chapter, see References, p. 183.

recordings, photographs, and data tapes. The primary uses of these media are to record field, site, and lab data, and to document vanishing societies or endangered customs. They also play an important role in the classroom for conveying the unique nature of the field experience. The extent to which these types of materials are required by a local institution is directly related to the specific requirements of the local clientele; the capacity of the library to process, store, and make available such materials; and budgetary considerations.

The Uses of Anthropological Literature

There have been few published citation or user studies that have included anthropology (Amsden, 1968; Spurling, 1973; Stenstrom and McBride, 1979; Bulick, 1982; Garfield, 1984). Bulick's *Structure and Subject Interaction: Toward a Sociology of Knowledge in the Social Sciences* is a thorough and interesting study but, as the author acknowledges, it fails to include comparative data with the physical and natural sciences. In the case of anthropology, the lack of attention to these disciplines in the study weakens it considerably. The Garfield study, which was originally published in *Current Contents* and reprinted in *Current Anthropology*, shows some of the difficulties in conducting citation studies in a fragmented field like anthropology. The comments on Garfield's study, published with the *Current Anthropology* reprint, offer very interesting opinions not only on Garfield's work but on the current state of anthropological research. With the exception of the studies by Amsden and Garfield, the user studies examine the faculty of individual anthropology departments in specific universities. It is possible to generalize from these analyses, but one should not use the results of user studies from other institutions as the only basis for selection decisions in the anthropology collections of the library. As was stated earlier, the tremendous diversity within the discipline, as well as within individual departments of anthropology, prevent generalizations about the research practices of anthropologists from one department to another. Keeping this in mind, we can conclude the following from these studies:

1. Anthropologists use material from a wide range of disciplines outside anthropology (Spurling, 1973; Stenstrom and McBride, 1979; Garfield, 1984). The most important disciplines are geography, biology, psychology, sociology, geology, zoology, economics, religion, philology, linguistics, and especially history (Amsden, 1968; Bulick, 1982).

2. Foreign-language materials are essential for anthropological study. Anthropologists possess more diversified language skills than other social scientists, and they use foreign-language materials more than other social

scientists (Amsden, 1968; Spurling, 1973; Stenstrom and McBride, 1979; McBride, 1981).

3. The accumulated knowledge of anthropology, at least as published in journals, maintains continuing importance for the discipline. Amsden found that journal articles older than ten years are used only slightly less than those less than one year old (Amsden, 1968; Garfield, 1984).

4. Anthropologists use a wide variety of literature in their research, but monographs and journals publishing original research are used most often. Lack of bibliographic access to unpublished materials and foreign publications continues to be a problem for researchers (Amsden, 1968).

Current Awareness of Anthropological Research

The bibliography of anthropology may be as old as the discipline itself, dating from the mid-nineteenth century, but only in the last thirty years has any measure of bibliographic control in the discipline occurred. A number of books and articles provide the novice selector in anthropology with an overview of the discipline and its bibliography (see the Further Readings section at the end of this chapter for additional sources of information). The best introduction to the bibliography of anthropology is still the "Anthropology" chapter in the second edition of Carl M. White's *Sources of Information in the Social Sciences*. Look at both editions of this work as the descriptions of the subfields of the discipline and recommended readings in these subfields differ in each edition. The first was written by Felix M. Kessing; Bernard Siegel wrote the second to reflect the changes in the discipline during the 1960s. Joseph H. Greenberg's "Anthropology: The Field" in the *International Encyclopedia of the Social Sciences* provides a classic description. Other entries in the encyclopedia under "Anthropology," "Archaeology," "Linguistics," and "Physical Anthropology" also provide excellent descriptions of various aspects of the discipline.

Faculty contact and perusing book reviews can keep one current with changes in the field, but there are several publications that should be read on a regular basis by the selector. The journal *Current Anthropology* supplies a broad interdisciplinary approach to new ideas and trends in the field. Each issue also has a calendar of events, brief news items, conference information, descriptions of new institutions, a list of publications received, and a list of serial publications. The *Annual Review of Anthropology* presents critical bibliographic essays in all branches of anthropology and through these thorough review articles a selector can maintain a knowledge of recent research developments.

Current Anthropology. Chicago: Univ. of Chicago Pr. v.1- . 1960- . 5/year.
  Scholarly journal.
  Approximately 5 lengthy articles per issue.
  Includes a number of responses/comments to each article, with the
    authors' concluding response.
  Occasional book and journal reviews.
This publication provides a forum for a broad interdisciplinary exchange of new
ideas and trends in a wide spectrum of anthropological topics, and is an extremely
useful source for current issues and trends in anthropology. Included in each
issue is a calendar of events, information on forthcoming conferences, descriptions of the activities and publications of new institutions, and a list of serial
and monographic publications received.

There are a number of general and specialized newsletters that should
be read regularly by selectors. *Documentation in Anthropology* is published for the information specialist in anthropology. This publication is
relatively new and not yet well established, but is worthy of support. The
Executive Committee of the International Union of Anthropological and
Ethnological Sciences (IUAES) established a Commission on Documentation in November of 1979. The commission publishes the newsletter
Documentation in Anthropology, which attempts to report activities of
the commission; news of institutions, organizations, and collections of
interest to anthropology bibliographers; bibliographic and documentation
projects; technological developments and projects; reports and reviews of
publications; conference news; and practical assistance for anthropological
bibliographers and information specialists.

Other specialized newsletters abound in the social sciences and in anthropology. Those that will be important to the anthropology selector
are dependent upon local collection policies and research requirements.
Anthropology Newsletter, *RAIN* (Royal Anthropological Institute Newsletter—soon to change to *Anthropology Today*), *History of Anthropology
Newsletter*, and *Practicing Anthropology* are examples of excellent newsletters that can be of use to the selector.

Selecting Material in Anthropology

Given the magnitude of anthropology's scope, the extreme diversification
within the discipline, and the interdisciplinary nature of the field, the
anthropology selector must establish acquisitions strategies that match
anthropology's diversity with the programmatic needs of the institution,
the research needs of that population, as well as any cooperative agreements the library might have. Given the diffuse nature of the field, the

establishment and application of a collection development policy is an essential tool for the anthropology selector. Communication and interaction with other subject selectors in the institution is extremely important in building anthropological collections. This interaction must be maintained to insure that the research needs of anthropologists in the library are being met, and to insure that collecting responsibilities for cross-disciplinary subject areas are understood by all selectors.

CURRENT SELECTION

Basic information about approval plans, alert services, and general selection tools for current publications are described earlier in this book, but it is important to note the primary use of these services by the anthropology selector. If selecting somewhat comprehensively in any area of anthropology, services such as the Library of Congress CDS Alert Services; approval plan alert services; and publications such as the *Weekly Record*, *American Book Publishing Record*, and the *British National Bibliography Weekly List* can provide information regarding new or forthcoming publications. Many new anthropological publications are critical for collections and yet difficult to obtain if not ordered immediately. The CDS Alert Service is particularly useful for advanced notice of material published by associations, research centers, and museums that may become out-of-print soon after publication.

Publishers catalogs and flyers are useful for all selectors in anthropology. Even if collecting comprehensively, a file of publishers—both domestic and foreign—is an important tool for every selector to maintain. Catalogs from major publishers should be kept and updated periodically. Some of the most important publishers of anthropological titles are Holt, Rinehart and Winston; University of California Press; Mouton; Oxford University Press; Aldine; Humanities; Praeger; Academic; University of Chicago Press; Cambridge University Press; Harvard University Press; and Columbia University Press.

General reviewing publications, such as *Choice*, are not particularly useful to selectors for large comprehensive research collections for a number of reasons. Reviews in these sources are usually not current, as there is quite a time lag between date of publication and review. Also most of these sources do not include the more esoteric publications that are so valuable to a research collection, and they only cover a small portion of the anthropology titles published. *Choice* and other general reviewing sources may be useful, however, for building small general collections in a college library or for undergraduate collections.

There are a number of scholarly anthropology journals that provide extensive reviews of books and related research material for general an-

American Anthropologist. v.1- . 1888- . Washington, D.C.: American
  Anthropological Assn. Quarterly.
  Scholarly journal.
  Includes 50–75 reviews per issue.
  Reviews appear 9–24 months after publication.
  "Book Notes" section lists 20–25 additional titles of interest, without
    reviews.
  Signed critical reviews, usually 250–300 words in length, are arranged topically
  under archaeology, linguistics, cultural/ethnology, physical, and general/theo-
  retical anthropology. Scholars in the field submit reviews of books, films, and
  occasionally recordings. Included also are articles on current research topics,
  field reports, commentaries, and usually one to three review articles. Publishers
  announcements and advertisements are particularly useful. This is the most important reviewing source for American anthropology.

thropology and for a variety of anthropology's subfields. A critical problem
with using reviews in academic journals in the selection process is that
there is always a time lag between publication date and appearance of the
review. Academic journals can be valuable as a check on previous selection
decisions by reading reviews, as a source of information about forthcoming
publications through advertising or notices, and as a means of acquiring
information about current trends in the field. The amount of time one
can spend reading journals may be limited, but it is important to check
these sources to make certain that necessary material has been acquired
and that approval plans are providing the library with the research material
needed.

American Anthropologist, Anthropologie, Anthropos, Man, and *Reviews in Anthropology* should be consulted regularly. *American Anthropologist* is the most important journal for American anthropology. Because
it includes in each issue between fifty and sixty authoritative reviews of
books, films, and recordings from all of anthropology's subfields it is also
the most important reviewing source for selectors. Each issue lists from
twenty to twenty-five additional titles that may be of interest, but are not
reviewed. International coverage is not strong in this journal because of
its emphasis on American anthropology.

Reviews in Anthropology publishes reviews of relatively recent books
and related material in all fields of anthropology. By its own admission
this journal covers only about "10% of the annual scholarly output" in
anthropology, but the review essays are quite lengthy and usually comparative.

Anthropologie, Anthropos, and *Man* are the best reviewing sources for
general anthropology publications from publishers outside of North
America. *Anthropologie* covers primarily European and other foreign publications in cultural anthropology, archaeology, and physical anthropology.

Reviews in Anthropology. v.1– . 1974– . South Salem, N.Y.: Redgrave.
   Quarterly.
   Scholarly review journal.
   Approximately 10 major reviews per issue. Signed, critical reviews, usually
      1500–3000 words in length.
   Occasionally includes review essays that critically evaluate several works in
      a comparative manner.
   Reviews appear 1–2 years after publication.
   Commentary section provides a forum for ideas and opinions regarding
      previous reviews.
   Publishers' announcements.
Reviews cover all topics in anthropology. There is a bias toward publications
from the United States, but there is also coverage of a wide variety of inter-
national publications. This publication provides a useful source for keeping
current with important publications and recent trends in the field.

Anthropos provides critical reviews arranged geographically covering titles
in linguistics, cultural anthropology, religious studies, and archaeology.
Articles are published in English, French, or German, and geographic coverage is of Africa, the Americas, Europe, and Oceania. *Man*, the journal
of the Royal Anthropological Institute of Great Britain and Ireland, publishes approximately fifty signed reviews in each issue along with an additional list of titles received. Reviews are arranged in four topical sections:
physical anthropology, archaeology, social anthropology, and general anthropology. Coverage is mainly of British and other European publications.
This is the best source for reviews of British anthropological publications.
   In addition to these general anthropology journals are several specialized
journals that also contribute useful reviews. *Antiquity: A Quarterly Review
of Archaeology* covers much of the field of archaeology. The journal has
traditionally focused on European archaeology, but it has recently begun
to cover Africa, Asia, and the Americas. It reviews approximately sixty
titles every year. *Language*, the journal of the Linguistic Society of Amer-

Man. v.1–65, 1901–65; n.s., v.1– . 1966– . London: Royal Anthropological
   Institute of Great Britain and Ireland. Quarterly.
   Scholarly journal.
   Includes 40–50 signed reviews per issue.
   "Books Received for Review" lists 70–80 additional titles per issue.
   Publishers' announcements.
Signed, critical reviews are arranged in four sections: Physical Anthropology,
Archaeology, Social Anthropology, and General Anthropology. The coverage is
mainly of British and other European publications. This is the best source for
reviews of British anthropological publications.

ica, includes both book reviews and lists of publications received. It provides the single best listing of recent publications in linguistics.

Choosing a list of journals to read regularly as part of a selection strategy is a difficult individual decision. I recommend these additional journals as being useful to the selector in anthropology:

Africa. v.1- . 1928- . London: International African Institute. Quarterly.

American Antiquity. v.1- . 1935- . Washington, D.C.: Society for American Archaeology. Quarterly.

American Ethnologist. v.1- . 1974- . Washington, D.C.: American Ethnological Society. Quarterly.

American Journal of Archaeology. v.1- . 1885- . New York: Archaeological Institute of America. Quarterly.

American Journal of Physical Anthropology. v.1- . 1918- . New York: American Assn. of Physical Anthropologists. Monthly.

Bulletin Signaletique. sec. 521, sec. 524, sec. 526. v.24- . 1974- . Paris: Centre de Documentation de Centre International de la Recherche Scientifique. Quarterly.

Journal of Anthropological Research. v.1- . 1945- . Albuquerque: Univ. of New Mexico, Dept. of Anthropology. Quarterly.

Language in Society. v.1- . 1972- . New York: Cambridge Univ. Pr. Quarterly.

Oceania: Devoted to the Study of the Native Peoples of Australia, New Guinea and the Islands of the Pacific Ocean. v.1- . 1930- . Sydney, New South Wales, Australia: Univ. of Sydney. Quarterly.

Quarterly Review of Archaeology. v.1- . 1980- . Salem, Mass.: Peabody Museum of Salem. Quarterly.

Studies in Visual Communications. v.1- . 1970- . Philadelphia: Society for the Anthropology of Visual Communications. Quarterly.

Urban Anthropology. v.1- . 1972- . New York: Plenum. Quarterly.

Zeitschrift fuer Volkskunde. Bd. 1- . 1905- . Berlin: W. Kohhammer. Biannually.

RETROSPECTIVE SELECTION

Retrospective acquisitions are usually necessary to strengthen weak areas of collections discovered by systematic collection evaluations, by the suggestions of researchers, or by reviewing dealer catalogs. *Anthropological Bibliographies: A Selected Guide*, compiled by the Library-Anthropology Resource Group, lists more than 2500 bibliographies arranged by region and country, and by broad topic. There is a detailed index. This source, along with the *Annual Review of Anthropology* or its predecessor *Biennial Review of Anthropology* (1959–71), provides a variety of important bibliographies for collection evaluations. Rexford S. Beckham's core list of books and journals for undergraduate anthropology collections, "A Basic List of Books and Periodicals for College Libraries" (Beckham, 1963), can also be a basis for collection evaluations. The list is dated, but it can be useful for some collections. The selector should be aware of important current bibliographies as possible evaluation aids also.

Major microform collections, such as the *Professional Correspondence of Franz Boaz*, can represent retrospective acquisitions of great research importance to anthropology. These collections are listed and reviewed in many current selection tools. Reprint and microform selection tools are discussed in other chapters of this book.

Published book catalogs of special research libraries can also be valuable for collection evaluations and ultimately for retrospective purchasing. Examples include the *Peabody Museum of Archaeology and Ethnology Library Catalogue* and the *Dictionary Catalog of the Library of the Bernice Pauahi Bishop Museum*. Bonnie R. Nelson's article "Anthropological Research and Printed Library Catalogs" (*RQ*, 1979) describes a number of important library catalogs of use to anthropology selectors and researchers.

SERIAL PUBLICATIONS

As the diversification and expansion of anthropological research has increased, so have the number of anthropological journals. *Ulrich's International Periodicals Directory* lists, in the anthropology section alone, 59 titles in 1959, 112 titles in 1969, 180 titles in 1979, and 257 titles in 1983 (Clark, 1982). The rapid increase in new journal publications in the 1970s is documented by Nancy J. Schmidt in her article "New Periodicals in Cultural Anthropology" (*Behavioral & Social Sciences Librarian*, 1981/ 1982), which reviews 88 new journals that started publishing between 1975 and 1980.

Core lists of journals can be useful in establishing new collections, building noncomprehensive collections, or evaluating existing collections. Rexford Beckham, Carl M. White, Charles Franz, James Urry, and Bill Katz provide basic lists of journals in anthropology (Beckham, 1963; White, 1973; Franz, 1972; Urry, 1977; Katz, 1982). Barton M. Clark's article "Core Journals in Anthropology: A Review of Methodologies" (*Behavioral & Social Sciences Librarian*, 1981/1982) provides a discussion of these lists and a useful review of methods for the development of core lists.

The most comprehensive list of anthropological serial publications is *Serial Publications in Anthropology* (rev. ed., 1982), which compiles information about over 4500 serial titles published internationally. It includes, for each title, basic bibliographic information, languages of publication, frequency of publication, date of first issue, and sources in which a serial is indexed or abstracted. UNESCO's *World List of Social Science Periodicals* (6th ed., 1983) is updated by the *International Social Science Journal*, which includes information about new periodicals in anthropology.

Serial Publications in Anthropology. 2nd ed. Ed. by F. X. Grollig; S. J. Tax; and Sol Tax. South Salem, N.Y.: Redgrave, 1982.

Lists over 4500 anthropological serial publications.

The arrangement is alphabetical by title, with a detailed subject index.

Each entry provides: basic bibliographic information, languages of publication, frequency of publication, date of first issue, previous title or titles, indexes or abstracts that include each title.

This is the most comprehensive compilation of anthropological serial titles, providing information about titles published internationally. The publication was completed by the Library-Anthropology Resource Group (LARG).

Indexing and abstracting publications can provide information about bibliographic access to specific journals. This can be a selection consideration, especially in less comprehensive library collections. Over 900 serials held by the Tozzer Library of the Peabody Museum of Archaeology and Ethnology at Harvard University are indexed by *Anthropological Literature: An Index to Periodical Articles and Essays. Anthropological Index to Current Periodicals in the Museum of Mankind* indexes over 650 journals and *Abstracts in Anthropology* provides international coverage of about 350 journals.

The American Anthropological Association's annual *Guide to Departments of Anthropology* lists serial publications of American and Canadian anthropological museums, research centers, and university departments. The program and research facilities of each department are described and publications from each are listed. Also included is a list of dissertations submitted in connection with Ph.D. degrees awarded during the previous academic year. The *Directory of the American Anthropological Association* contains listings of official publications of American anthropological associations.

Few professional journals in anthropology review new serials on a regular basis. *Current Anthropology* lists new serials received and occasionally

---

Guide to Departments of Anthropology. 23rd ed., 1984–85. Washington, D.C.: American Anthropological Assn., 1984. Annually.

Lists over 450 academic departments, museum departments, and research departments of anthropology in the United States and Canada.

Each entry includes names of faculty, degrees offered, number of students, degree requirements, special programs, and resources. Also includes statistical breakdown of students, etc.

Index of individuals.

A useful and important listing of publications by academic departments, museums, and research institutes is included in each entry. Also included is a list of all dissertations submitted in connection with Ph.D. degrees awarded in the previous year.

reviews new journals. *Anthropology Newsletter* and *RAIN* (Royal Anthropological Institute of Great Britain Newsletter) frequently announce new journals. As with other disciplines, professional journals usually provide the most current source of new journal information through advertisements and notices. Publishers' flyers or, better yet, sample issues can help with the selection decision. Efficient communication channels with faculty and students can often provide information and opinions regarding important new publications.

ASSOCIATION, MUSEUM, AND RESEARCH CENTER PUBLICATIONS

Association, museum, and research center publications are extremely important to anthropologists. The identification and subsequent acquisitions strategies for this material should be established based on program needs, research requirements, and cooperative agreements. The directories, bibliographies, indexes, and abstracts described here should provide the selector with the tools to compile a list of sources for this material. The list should be updated regularly by scanning notices in newsletters, journals, publishers' catalogs, and new publication flyers; and by maintaining close contact with faculty and researchers. A thorough revision of such a list should be done periodically. Once a list of sources has been established, it is critical that the selector write to each institution to request placement on mailing lists for publication catalogs, free newsletters, and notifications of new publications.

The most efficient way to insure that the publications of a particularly important association, museum, or research center are obtained is to place a standing order for the complete publications of that institution, for specific serial publications of that institution, or to become a member of that institution. Obtaining the services of a vendor who will successfully handle this type of material is sometimes a problem, and most often it is better to place these orders directly with the institution. Much of this material is issued in relatively small editions and quite often goes out-of-print rapidly. It is very important to regularly peruse the publication catalogs, journals, newsletters, and flyers from these institutions, and to place orders quickly to insure acquisition.

There are a growing number of associations, museums, and research centers that publish a variety of valuable material for anthropological research, such as newsletters, conference proceedings, working papers, pamphlets, books, and journals. A few of the more active and important publishing programs come from:

American Anthropological Association
American Ethnological Society
American Museum of Natural History

Archaeological Institute of America
Bernice Pauahi Bishop Museum
Field Museum of Natural History
Harvard University, Peabody Museum of Archaeology and Ethnology
Human Relations Area Files, Inc.
Indiana University Research Center in Anthropology, Folklore and
    Linguistics
International Union of Anthropological and Ethnological Sciences
Royal Anthropological Institute of Great Britain and Ireland
Smithsonian Institution
Societe d'Anthropologie de Paris
Wenner-Gren Foundation for Anthropological Research

The annual *Guide to Departments of Anthropology* and the *Directory of the American Anthropological Association* should be consulted for publications of academic departments, museums, research centers, and associations. These primary sources should be supplemented by the *Encyclopedia of Associations, Association Publications in Print, Research Centers Directory*, the *Official Museum Directory*, the *World of Learning*, and *World Directory of Social Science Institutions*.

The *International Directory of Anthropological Institutions* is a dated but still useful source. Arranged geographically, with a description of the history and scope of research for each country or area, followed by a detailed description of each institution or organization, this directory also includes a list of publications for each institution. This information is updated by the "Fourth International Directory of Anthropological Institutions" (*Current Anthropology* 8:647–751 [1967]).

Two useful anthropological indexes regularly include association, museum, and research center publications. *Anthropological Literature: An Index to Periodical Articles and Essays* indexes journals, books, annuals, proceedings, newsletters, transactions, and reports published internationally. Unfortunately the subject approach to this index is very restricted, but the breadth of coverage of this type of material makes the index valuable. The *International Bibliography of the Social Sciences: Social and Cultural Anthropology* regularly indexes journals, books, research reports, and conference proceedings. The coverage is international, but by no means comprehensive. Author and subject indexes are very thorough in social and cultural anthropology with limited attention given to other subfields. The main limitation of this source is the long time lag between publication date and appearance in the index.

The *Index to Social Science and Humanities Proceedings* indexes papers presented at conferences, conventions, symposia, and institutions, and published subsequently in proceedings. Coverage in this valuable index is international for all of the disciplines in the social sciences and humanities and includes both privately and publicly published proceedings. *Sociological Abstracts* indexes papers given at sociological association conferences, and includes abstracts submitted by the authors. Some of these papers are of interest to anthropologists and are very difficult to obtain otherwise. Copies of papers indexed are only available directly from the author, and many of them never are published elsewhere.

PUBLICATIONS IN OTHER FORMATS

The microfiche collection *HRAF Microfiles*, produced by Human Relations Area Files, Inc., is a unique and invaluable research source for anthropology. Since 1958 HRAF has been issuing this collection of primary source material, which consists of both published and unpublished books, articles, and manuscripts. The collection gathers research on selected cultural groups and topics of importance worldwide. Comparative cultural data is readily available to anthropologists through this collection. There are presently about 270 member institutions that subscribe to the *HRAF Microfiles*. If the institution is unable to acquire this material, the selector should at least be able to provide information about its availability to local researchers.

Films, videotapes, and various other audiovisual materials are increasingly used in anthropology as a means of recording field data, as a way to document vanishing societies or endangered customs, and as a classroom simulation of fieldwork. In collecting audiovisual material, especially films and videotapes, it is very worthwhile to view a preview copy of a work as part of the selection process. Published critical reviews are also important because of the expense involved in this type of collecting. Useful reviews appear in the journals *American Anthropologist, Journal of American Folklore, RAIN, Archaeology*, and the *American Journal of Physical Anthropology*.

The most important listing of anthropological films is *Films for Anthropological Teaching*, which has been edited for several years by Karl G. Heider and published by the American Anthropological Association. The seventh edition compiles information for 1575 titles, with indexes by geographic area and by topic. Each entry includes title, production credits, distribution sources, rental price, sale price, complete film description, and published reviews. *Films: The Visualization of Anthropology* is a catalog of over 1800 films available from the Pennsylvania State University Audio Visual Services. It contains anthropological films selected from both the American Archive of the Encyclopaedia Cinematographica and the PCR (Psychological Cinema Register): Films and Video in the Behavioral Sciences. Other useful compilations are *Africa on Film and Videotape, The*

Middle East and North Africa on Film, Encyclopaedia Cinematographica, PCR: Films and Video in the Behavioral Sciences, UNESCO's *Premier Catalogue Selectif International de Films Ethnographiques sur l'Afrique Noire, Premier Catalogue Selectif International de Films Ethnographiques su la Region du Pacifique, Catalog de Films d'Interet Archeologique, Ethnographique ou Historique,* and *Archaeology on Film: A Comprehensive Guide to Audio-visual Materials.*

Another source for the study of ethnographic film is the Human Studies Film Archives in the Smithsonian Institution, established in 1981 as a national center for collecting and preserving historical and contemporary ethnographic film and videotape for research purposes. Policies for accessing this collection and a brief list of the holdings are available from the Smithsonian.

Conclusion

Anthropology has experienced such rapid growth and diversification in the last several decades that the literature of anthropology has consequently grown and expanded tremendously. Anthropological research, particularly cross-disciplinary research and research generated from developing countries, is growing at an ever-increasing pace. Relatively recent developments in the bibliographic control of anthropology publications have been welcome, but are still not satisfactory. There are numerous fugitive types of material that can provide rich resources for anthropological research. Unpublished field notes, archaeological site reports, working papers, and experimental data have not been adequately collected by libraries in the past. The acquisition of these materials can provide the greatest challenge to the selector.

Access to foreign publications is also a continuing and growing challenge for the selector and researcher in anthropology. We can hope that future efforts by the Commission on Documentation of the International Union of Anthropological and Ethnological Sciences and other international and national social science documentation committees will help to alleviate some of these inadequacies.

This chapter has looked at selection strategies and tools for acquiring research materials in anthropology. I have defined anthropological research in fairly broad terms, but there are numerous literature resources used by anthropologists that are not, strictly speaking, anthropological. Few libraries, even comprehensive research libraries, are able to collect material in all of the subdisciplines of anthropology or in all of the other disciplines that interest anthropologists. In order to develop and maintain a successful selection strategy for anthropology, it is critical for the selector to construct collection policies; to sustain a knowledge of developing trends in the field; to solicit close communication with faculty and researchers; and to initiate constructive communication with other subject selectors in the institution.

References

Amsden, Diana. "Information Problems of Anthropologists." *College and Research Libraries* 29, no. 2:117–31 (1968).

Beckham, Rexford S. "A Basic List of Books and Periodicals for College Libraries." In *Resources for the Teaching of Anthropology*, pp. 77–316. Ed. by David G. Mandelbaum, Gabriel W. Lasker and Ethel M. Albert. Berkeley: Univ. of California Pr., 1963.

Bulick, Stephen. *Structure and Subject Interaction: Toward a Sociology of Knowledge in the Social Sciences*. Books in Library and Information Science, v.41. New York: Dekker, 1982.

Clark, Barton M., and Susan E. Clark. "Core Journals in Anthropology: A Review of Methodologies." *Behavioral & Social Sciences Librarian* 2, no.2/3:95–110 (Winter 1981/Spring 1982).

Franz, Charles. *The Student Anthropologist's Handbook*. Cambridge, Mass.: Schenkman, 1972.

Garfield, Eugene. "Anthropology Journals: What They Cite and What Cites Them." *Current Anthropology* 25, no.4:514–28 (Aug.-Oct. 1984).

Katz, Bill, and Linda Sternberg Katz. *Magazines for Libraries*. 4th ed. New York: Bowker, 1982.

McBride, Ruth B. "Foreign Language Serial Use by Social Science Faculty: A Survey." *The Serials Librarian* 5, no.4:25–32 (Summer 1981).

Spurling, Norman Kent. *Information Needs and Bibliographic Problems of the Anthropology Departments at U.N.C. and Duke University*. Washington, D.C.: ERIC Document Reproduction Service, 1973. (Microfiche).

Stenstrom, Patricia, and Ruth B. McBride. "Serials Use by Social Science Faculty: A Survey." *College and Research Libraries* 40, no.5:426–31 (Sept. 1979).

Urry, James. "The Literature and Sources of Social Anthropology." In *Uses of Social Science Literature*. Ed. by Norman Roberts. Boston: Butterworth, 1977.

White, Carl M. "Anthropology." In *Sources of Information in the Social Sciences*. 2nd ed. Ed. by Carl M. White. Chicago: American Library Assn., 1973.

Further Readings

TRENDS IN ANTHROPOLOGICAL RESEARCH

Franz, Charles, ed. *Ideas and Trends in World Anthropology*. New Delhi: Concept Publishing, 1981.

Freedman, Maurice. *Main Trends in Social and Cultural Anthropology*. New York: Holmes & Meier, 1979.

Goldschmidt, Walter. "Anthropology and America." In *Social Science in America: The First Two Hundred Years.* Ed. by Charles M. Bonjean, Louis Schneider, and Robert L. Lineberry. Austin: Univ. of Texas Pr., 1976.

Greenberg, Joseph H. "Anthropology: The Field." In *International Encyclopedia of the Social Sciences.* Ed. by David L. Sills. New York: Macmillan, 1968.

Harris, Marvin. *The Rise of Anthropological Theory.* New York: Crowell, 1968.

Hoebel, Adamson; Richard Currier; and Susan Kaiser; eds. *Crisis in Anthropology.* New York: Garland, 1982.

Hymes, Dell. *Reinventing Anthropology.* New York: Pantheon, 1972.

Rogge, A. E. "A Look at Academic Anthropology: Through A Graph Darkly." *American Anthropologist* 78, no.4:829–43 (1976).

Stocking, George W., Jr. *Race, Culture, and Evolution: Essays in the History of Anthropology.* New York: Free Pr., 1968.

TRENDS IN ANTHROPOLOGICAL BIBLIOGRAPHY

Amsden, Diana. "Information Problems of Anthropologists." *College and Research Libraries* 29, no.2:117–31 (Mar. 1968).

Beckham, Rexford S. "Anthropology." *Library Trends* 15, no.4:685–703 (Apr. 1967).

Clark, Barton M., and Susan E. Clark. "Core Journals in Anthropology: A Review of Methodologies." *Behavioral & Social Sciences Librarian* 2, no.2/3:95–110 (Winter 1981/Spring 1982).

Currier, Margaret. "Problems in Anthropological Bibliography." *Annual Review of Anthropology* 5:15–34 (1976).

Franz, Charles. *Student Anthropologist's Handbook.* Cambridge, Mass.: Schenkman, 1972.

Hass, Marilyn L. "Anthropology: A Guide to Basic Sources." *Reference Services Review* 5, no.4:45–51 (Oct./Dec. 1977).

Kane, Deborah. "Resources in Psychological Anthropology." *Collection Building* 5, no.4:23–30 (Winter 1984).

Nelson, Bonnie R. "Anthropological Research and Printed Library Catalogs." *RQ* 19, no. 12:159–70 (Winter 1979).

Perkins, David. *Bibliographic Control for Recently Published Books in Anthropology.* Master's thesis, California State Univ., Northridge, Calif., 1973.

Perry, Paula, and Bonnie R. Nelson. "Anthropology: Haas Revisited." *Reference Services Review* 11, no.3:67–70 (Fall 1983).

Pitt, David C. *Using Historical Sources in Anthropology and Sociology.* New York: Holt, 1972.

Schmidt, Nancy J. "New Periodicals in Cultural Anthropology." *Behavioral & Social Sciences Librarian* 2, no.2/3:57–93 (Winter 1981/Spring 1982).

Urry, James. "The Literature and Sources of Social Anthropology." In *Uses of Social Science Literature.* Ed. by Norman Roberts. Boston: Butterworth, 1977.

White, Carl M. "Anthropology." In *Sources of Information in the Social Sciences.* 2nd ed. Ed. by Carl M. White. Chicago: American Library Assn., 1973.

Selection Sources

Abstracts in Anthropology. v.1– . 1970– . Farmingdale, N.Y.: Baywood. Quarterly.

Africa. v.1– . 1928– . London: International African Institute. Quarterly.

American Anthropologist. v.1- . 1888- . Washington, D.C.: American Anthropological Assn. Quarterly.
American Antiquity. v.1- . 1935- . Washington, D.C.: Society for American Archaeology. Quarterly.
American Ethnologist. v.1- . 1974- . Washington, D.C.: American Ethnological Society. Quarterly.
American Journal of Physical Anthropology. v.1- . 1918- . Philadelphia, Pa.: American Assn. of Physical Anthropologists, Wistar Institute of Anatomy and Biology. Bimonthly.
Annual Review of Anthropology. v.1- . 1972- . Palo Alto, Calif: Annual Reviews, Inc. Annually.
Anthropological Bibliographies, A Selected Guide. Ed. by Margo L. Smith and Yvonne M. Damien. South Salem, N.Y.: Redgrave, 1981.
Anthropological Index to Current Periodicals in the Museum of Mankind. v.1- . 1963- . London: Royal Anthropological Institute. Quarterly.
Anthropological Literature: An Index to Periodical Articles and Essays. v.1- . 1979- . South Salem, N.Y.: Redgrave. Quarterly.
Anthropologie. v.1- . 1890- . Paris: Masson. Quarterly.
Anthropology Newsletter. v.1- . 1960- . Washington, D.C.: American Anthropological Assn. 9/year.
Anthropos: International Review of Ethnology and Linguistics. v.1- . 1906- . Fribourg, Switzerland: Anthropos Institute. Biennially.
Archaelogy. v.1- . 1948- . New York: Archaeological Institute of America. Bimonthly.
Archaeology on Film: A Comprehensive Guide to Audiovisual Materials. Ed. and comp. by Peter S. Allen and Carole Lazio. Boston: Archaeological Institute of America, 1983.
Association Publications in Print. New York: Bowker, 1981- . Annually.
Bernice Pauahi Bishop Museum, Honolulu. Library. *Dictionary Catalog of the Library.* 9 v. Boston: Hall, 1964. 1st supplement, 1967, 1 v.; 2nd supplement, 1969, 1 v.
Biennial Review of Anthropology. Stanford, Calif.: Stanford Univ. Pr., 1959-71. (see *Annual Review of Anthropology.*)
British National Bibliography. Weekly List. London: Council of the British National Bibliography. British Museum, 1950- . Weekly.
Choice. v.1- . 1964- . Middletown, Conn.: Assn. of College and Research Libraries. Monthly.
Current Anthropology. v.1- . 1960- . Chicago: Univ. of Chicago Pr. 5/year.
Directory of the American Anthropological Association. Washington, D.C.: American Anthropological Assn., 1975- . Annually.
Documentation in Anthropology. no. 1- . 1980- . Paris: Commission on Documentation, International Union of Anthropological and Ethnological Sciences. (Distributed free to subscribers to *Anthropological Index to Current Periodicals in the Museum of Mankind.* Also available from the editor: Anne Akeroyd, Dept. of Sociology, Univ. of York, Heslington, York YO1 5DD, England.)
Encyclopaedia Cinematographica. University Park, Pa.: Audio-Visual Services, Pennsylvania State Univ., 1981.
Encyclopedia of Associations. 18th ed. Detroit: Gale, 1984.
Films for Anthropological Teaching. 7th ed. Ed. by Karl G. Heider. Special Publication no. 13. Washington, D.C.: American Anthropological Assn., 1983.
Films: The Visualization of Anthropology. University Park, Pa.: Audio-Visual Services, Pennsylvania State Univ., 1977.

"Fourth International Directory of Anthropological Institutions." *Current Anthropology* 8:647–751 (1967).

Guide to Departments of Anthropology. 23rd ed. 1984–85. Washington, D.C.: American Anthropological Assn., 1984.

Harvard Univ. Peabody Museum of Archaeology and Ethnology Library. *Catalogue: Authors.* 26v. Boston: Hall, 1963. *Catalogue: Subjects.* 28v. Boston: Hall. 1st supplement (author and subject), 1970, 12v.; 2nd supplement, 1971, 6v.; 3rd supplement, 1975, 7v.; 4th supplement, 1979, 7v.

History of Anthropology Newsletter. v.1– . 1973– . Chicago. Irregularly. (Available from: Prof. George W. Stocking, Jr., Dept. of Anthropology, Univ. of Chicago, 1126 E. 59th St., Chicago, IL 60637.)

HRAF Microfiles. New Haven, Conn.: Human Relations Area Files, 1958– .

Journal of American Folklore. v.1– . 1888– . Washington, D.C.: American Folklore Society. Quarterly.

Index to Social Sciences and Humanities Proceedings. v.1– . 1979– . Philadelphia: Institute for Scientific Information. Annually.

International Bibliography of the Social Sciences: Social and Cultural Anthropology. v.1– . 1955– . London: Tavistock. Annually.

International Directory of Anthropological Institutions. Ed. by William L. Thomas, Jr., and Anna M. Pickelis. New York: Wenner-Gren Foundation for Anthropological Research, 1953.

International Social Science Journal. v.1– . 1949– . Paris: UNESCO. Quarterly.

Language. v.1– . 1925– . Arlington, Va.: Linguistic Society of America. Quarterly.

Man. v.1–65, 1901–65; n.s., v.1– . 1966– . London: Royal Anthropological Institute of Great Britain and Ireland. Quarterly.

McClintock, Marsha Hamilton. *The Middle East and North America on Film: An Annotated Filmography.* Garland Reference Library of Humanities, v.159. New York: Garland, 1982.

The Official Museum Directory 1984. Washington, D.C.: American Assn. of Museums, 1983.

PCR: Films and Video in the Behavioral Sciences. University Park, Pa.: Audio-Visual Services, Pennsylvania State Univ., 1981– . Irregularly.

Practicing Anthropology. v.1– . 1978– . Washington, D.C.: Society for Applied Anthropology. Quarterly.

RAIN; Royal Anthropological Institute of Great Britain and Ireland Newsletter. no.1– . 1974– . London: Royal Anthropological Institute of Great Britain and Ireland. Bimonthly. (Title will soon change to *Anthropology Today.*)

Research Centers Directory. 9th ed., 1984–85. Detroit: Gale, 1984.

Reviews in Anthropology. v.1– . 1974– . South Salem, N.Y.: Redgrave. Quarterly.

Serial Publications in Anthropology. 2nd ed. Ed. by F. X. Grollig, S. J. Tax, and Sol Tax. South Salem, N.Y.: Redgrave, 1982.

Sociological Abstracts. v.1– . 1953– . San Diego, Calif: Sociological Abstracts, Inc. 5/year.

UNESCO. *Catalogue de Films d'Interet Archeologique, Ethnographique ou Historique.* Paris: UNESCO, 1970.

_____. *Premier Catalogue Selectif International de Films Ethnographiques su la Region du Pacifique.* Paris: UNESCO, 1970.

_____. *Premier Catalogue Selectif International de Films Ethnographiques sur l'Afrique Noire.* Paris: UNESCO, 1967.

_____. Social Science Documentation Centre. *World Directory of Social Science Institutions: Research, Advanced Training, Documentation, Professional Bod-*

ies. 3rd rev. ed. World Social Science Information Series, 2. Paris: UNESCO, 1982.

———. ———. *World List of Social Science Periodicals*. 6th rev. ed. World Social Science Information Series, 1. Paris: UNESCO, 1983.

Weekly Record. New York: Bowker, 1974– . Weekly.

Wiley, David. *Africa on Film and Videotape. 1960–1981*. East Lansing: African Studies Center, Michigan State Univ., 1982.

World of Learning. 34th ed., 1983–84. London: Europa, 1983.

Zeitscrift fuer Volkskunde. Bd. 1– . Berlin: W. Kohhammer, 1891– . Biennially.

SOCIOLOGY

Beth J. Shapiro

Sociology, as a discipline, covers a wide range of topics and issues that focus on social systems, institutions, groups, and social structures. But since it has not been characterized by a distinctive subject matter or methodology, defining sociology precisely is difficult. Like other social sciences, sociology examines the social world. What distinguishes sociology from other social sciences is, however, its concern with the relationship between all types of social situations and their outcomes. Put another way, sociology studies social groups and institutions and their influence on individual behavior, studies the relationship between social structure and social change, and, ultimately, looks for explanations of social causes for social phenomena.[1]

Because of its cross-disciplinary nature, sociology exhibits enormous range and scope. Sociological literature encompasses scholarly studies concerned with such social institutions as family, government, education, health care, industry, religion, law, arts, and sport, and such social processes as urbanization, community development, migration, rural development, and collective behavior. Sociology presents critiques of social processes and institutions perceived as problematic by social groups such as minorities, women, the unemployed, the colonized, and the politically dispossessed. In addition, it addresses theoretical and methodological issues.

Librarians responsible for selecting sociology materials must be concerned with the discipline's relationship to such other disciplines as anthropology, education, psychology, political science, and economics. Consequently, the Library of Congress (LC) classification scheme (HM and HN) is an inadequate guide to the literature of sociology.

The contributions of Marcia Pankake, Patti McClung, and Ray McInnes are gratefully acknowledged.

1. Albert J. Reiss, Jr., "Sociology: The Field," in *International Encyclopedia of the Social Sciences*, 15:1 (New York: Macmillan, 1968); C. C. Harris, *Fundamental Concepts and the Sociological Enterprises* (London: Croom Helm, 1980), pp. 8–22.

In this essay, I will address selection issues as they relate specifically to sociology. However, I would like to begin with a discussion of the bibliographic structure of sociological literature, as an understanding of it is central to the selection process.

Bibliographic Structure of Sociological Literature

Numerous citation and readership studies for sociology describe a consistent and clear picture of the structure of sociological literature:[2]

1. Fifty to sixty-two percent of all citations from scholarly research in sociology are from nonserial publications (e.g., monographs, documents, reports, etc.).
2. Ninety to ninety-three percent of all citations are from English-language sources.
3. Fifty to seventy percent of all citations are from sources less than ten years old.

Brown and Gilmartin also found that seventy-five percent of all sociological research focuses on the United States.[3]

As a result, a core collection in sociology consists of both monographic and serial publications published primarily in English during the last ten years. French and German sociologists also contribute significantly to the discipline, especially in methodology and political sociology, and research level collections should include their works.

Subjects covered by sociology include the following: sociological theory and methodology; social stratification; race and ethnicity; work and organizations; family and feminist studies; demography; social psychology; mass phenomena; law and society; health care; dependency and development; urban/rural/community development; political sociology; and education. Specific subject and/or geographic emphases necessarily will depend upon local needs. In many instances, retrospective collection development may play a part in your overall strategy.

In addition to trade and scholarly books and periodicals, sociologists often need alternative or nontraditional research materials such as pam-

2. Shirley A. Fitzgibbons, "Citation Analysis in the Social Sciences," in *Collection Development in Libraries: A Treatise*, Part B. (Greenwich, Conn.: JAI Press, 1980), pp. 291–344; Robert N. Broadus, "The Literature of the Social Sciences: A Survey of Citation Studies," *International Social Science Journal* 23:236–43 (1971); James C. Baughman, "A Structural Analysis of the Literature of Sociology," *Library Quarterly* 44: 293–307 (Oct. 1974); William Satarino, "Journal Use in Sociology: Citation Analysis Versus Readership Patterns," *Library Quarterly* 48:293–300 (July 1978); Nan Lin and Carnot E. Nelson, "Bibliographic Reference Patterns in Core Sociological Journals, 1965–66," *American Sociologist* 4, no. 1:47–49 (Feb. 1969); Julia A. Brown and Brian G. Gilmartin, "Sociology Today: Lacunae, Emphases, and Surfeits," *American Sociologist* 4:283–90 (Nov. 1969).
3. Brown and Gilmartin, p. 287.

phlets and small press monographs from community or social action groups, government publications (local, state, federal, and international), research publications from institutes and academic departments, audiovisual materials, and data files. All such material may have a place in one's library, again depending upon local needs.

Selection and Acquisition of Library Materials

Before developing a selection strategy, selectors must understand not only the bibliographic structure of a discipline, but also the specific bibliographic needs of their clientele. For example, the faculty of some sociology departments may specialize in small group research, educational sociology, and family studies. At another institution, faculty research interests may emphasize critical theory, urban political economy, and social problems. Because few institutions are able to comprehensively collect material in all areas of sociology, you should be familiar with both your institution's special areas of concern and its financial limitations.

The selection process itself is discussed sufficiently elsewhere and will not be repeated in this essay.[4] Nevertheless, several points should be emphasized. Selectors ought to consider the types and levels of course offerings, publishing and research activity of the faculty and staff, strengths and weaknesses of existing collections, cooperative arrangements with other institutions, technical services support for processing and storing alternative materials (e.g., audiovisual materials, data files, pamphlets, etc.), and relationships with other subjects, particularly if other selectors are involved.

The selection and acquisition of materials in sociology can be an exciting and challenging experience. Frequently, those unfamiliar with either collection development or with selection in the social sciences perceive the selection process as routine and mundane. But, contrary to these perceptions, the social science selector must take unique and frequently radical approaches to building collections that reflect not only the contemporary trade and scholarly market but also the more esoteric and ephemeral publications of small presses, social action groups, and research centers.

Monographs. In "Selection Sources and Strategies" Patricia McClung discusses the basic selection tools that selectors regularly consult. In addition to her fine comments, I would like to suggest a word of caution concerning the *Weekly Record* as a current selection tool. Unlike a number

4. Jean Boyer Hamlin, "The Selection Process," in *Collection Development in Libraries: A Treatise*, Part B, pp. 185–201; Sheila F. Dowd, "The Formulation of a Collection Development Policy Statement," in *Collection Development in Libraries: A Treatise*, Part A. (Greenwich, Conn.: JAI Press, 1982), pp. 67–68; American Library Assn., Collection Development Committee, *Guidelines for Collection Development* (Chicago: ALA, 1979).

Contemporary Sociology. v.1– . 1972– . Washington, D. C.: American
Sociological Assn. Bimonthly.
Review journal for sociology and related disciplines.
60–70 book reviews and 15 review essays, survey essays, or symposia per
issue.
9–12-month lag between book publication and review.
Evaluative book reviews, written by scholars, are arranged under 30 topics. The
journal is particularly useful for selecting materials in areas that overlap with
sociology.

of other disciplines, publishing output in sociology consists of a relatively
large number of popular secondary books, many of which are of questionable quality. Yet, due to interest and contemporary relevance, many
secondary books must be purchased. This anomaly adds to the complexity
of selecting sociological materials.

In order to insure complete coverage of social science trade monographs, consult *Contemporary Sociology*, which devotes its pages exclusively to book reviews and review essays. About 150 books are reviewed
in each issue. Unfortunately, *Contemporary Sociology* is not extremely
current. Books are generally reviewed nine to eleven months after publication.

To identify seminal sociological works published in Europe, two sources
are available. Neither, unfortunately, provides up-to-the-minute coverage.
Bulletin Signaletique. 521. Sociologie. Ethnologie provides international
coverage of both monographs and journal articles. Annotated, this quarterly arranges entries under nineteen subject categories. A major drawback
is the delay in its publication. But when you need to identify French and
German works on a narrow topic, *Bulletin Signaletique's* subject index
can be an invaluable tool.

Unlike the *Bulletin Signaletique*, *L'Annee Sociologique* provides evaluative reviews of monographs published in Europe. Even though *L'Annee*
is published annually, its coverage is a bit more current than the *Bulletin*.
All reviews are written in French and are arranged under eight major
subject categories.

To supplement more traditional library selection tools, consult the following periodicals that regularly publish book reviews. Because of the
time lag, these periodicals serve as back-up to other sources. In addition,
they confirm (hopefully) that you have covered your subject adequately.
Listed below are a number of journals I find particularly useful:

American Journal of Economics and Sociology
American Journal of Sociology
Journal of Conflict Resolution
Journal of Marriage and Family

Women's Review of Books. v.1– ; 1983– . Wellesley, Mass.: Center for
 Research on Women. Monthly.
 Review periodical concerned exclusively with women's studies.
 Tabloid format.
 10–20 lengthy reviews per issue.
 2–12-month time lag between book publication and review.
Each issue contains long, informed reviews in all fields, including sociology.
Reviews are written by specialists.

Social Forces
Social Science Quarterly

Because sociological literature encompasses so many different subjects,
it is also useful to look at the book review sections of more specialized
journals. Below are listed several other journals that provide additional
coverage of publishing output in such related fields as ethnic studies, feminist studies, and war and peace:

Current Research on Peace and Violence
Ethnic and Racial Studies
Feminist Studies
Human Rights Quarterly
Journal of Black Studies
Women's Review of Books

The time lag for book reviews in all of the sources mentioned above
is significant. Consequently, primary selection tools should consist of traditional library reviewing journals and publishers' catalogs, flyers, and advertisements. In addition, standing order or approval plans help insure that
a solid core of materials will be ordered and received in a timely fashion.
   Annual reviews of the literature have some utility for selectors. *The
Annual Review of Sociology* and *Current Sociology. La Sociologie Contemporaine* contain original bibliographical essays. While of high quality,
the essays themselves have marginal value in the selection of specific titles.
Nevertheless, review essays provide concise discussions of current research
and trends in sociology.

Current Sociology. La Sociologie Contemporaine. v.1– . 1952– . Beverly Hills,
 Calif.: Sage, 3/year.
 Scholarly sociological journal.
 International coverage of trends in sociological research.
Each issue is devoted to a trend report on a topic of interest to the international
sociological community. By regularly reading this journal, the selector is kept
up-to-date on new trends. Many essays are written in French. The bibliographies
appended to each essay are useful for retrospective and back-up selection.

Periodicals. Because of rising subscription costs, librarians are increasingly selective when considering periodical subscriptions. Thus, to develop and maintain viable periodical collections, communication with faculty, familiarity with their research habits, and familiarity with bibliographic access to periodical literature is essential. Satariano, Brown and Gilmartin, and Baughman identify core lists of journals in sociology.[5]

Though primarily intended for use by scholarly writers and reviewers, *Political and Social Science Journals: A Handbook for Writers and Reviewers* is also useful for identifying journals for possible subscription. It lists more than 400 English-language journals published throughout the world. Arranged alphabetically by journal title, complete bibliographic information is provided. *Sociology: An International Bibliography of Serial Literature*, compiled by Jan Wepsiec, is a comprehensive listing of more than 2000 serial titles from sociology and its related fields. Ceased, as well as current, publications are listed. Numerous foreign-language periodicals are included.

The "Source Index" section of *Sociological Abstracts (SA)* should be consulted as well. This abstracting service covers all English-language sociological journals as well as selected foreign-language journals. In addition, it covers many journals with related or multidisciplinary coverage. The "Journal Citation Reports" section of *Social Sciences Citation Index (SSCI)* ranks journals by the number of times each is cited annually. Since citation activity is one measure of past use, this tool is useful to consult, particularly if your library cannot support a comprehensive periodical collection in the social sciences.

Proceedings and Conference Papers. In the last several years, bibliographic access to proceedings and conference papers has improved. The *Index to Social Sciences and Humanities Proceedings* comprehensively indexes published proceedings. Before its appearance, many of these publications were not indexed. This source, published three times a year, should be reviewed annually. While time-consuming, it is time well spent, as the *Index* includes proceedings published both commercially and privately. Even though the commercially published proceedings almost always are listed in the *Weekly Record* when they are first published, privately published proceedings typically are unique to this source.

Sociological Abstracts (SA) indexes and abstracts papers presented at meetings of the International Sociological Association, American Sociological Association, Society for the Study of Social Problems, and regional sociological associations. Conference papers are indexed and abstracted separately from the main portion of *SA*. Unfortunately, these papers rarely are compiled and published. The only way to obtain them is to write

5. Satariano, p. 297; Brown and Gilmartin, p. 286; Baughman, p. 300.

directly to the authors. Nevertheless, if your library collects preprints and unpublished conference papers, *SA* is an indispensable selection tool.

Alternative and Nontraditional Materials. Alternative and nontraditional materials such as pamphlets, working papers, and reports are essential components of social science collections. However, bibliographic access to these materials is fragmented. The *Weekly Record* sporadically lists alternative publications and most traditional library reviewing media ignore them. Typically, materials that are not reviewed or indexed are not purchased.[6] Given the difficulties in identifying this material, selecting and acquiring alternative and nontraditional publications is often an exciting and rewarding challenge. It requires creativity, perseverance, and enthusiasm.

A number of alternative library reviewing sources do exist and you are urged to review them regularly. One such source is *Sipapu*, a newsletter published twice a year for librarians and others interested in alternative and radical publications. Noel Peattie, the editor, provides ordering information for pamphlets and other publications concerned with the Third World, dissidents, feminism, racism, classism, and other nonestablishment issues.

An indispensable tool is *Alternatives in Print*, the "books in print" of alternative publishing. Including books, pamphlets, periodicals, and audiovisual material, its coverage is international. Alternative publications frequently go out-of-print soon after publication and may be out-of-print by the time they are listed in *Alternatives in Print*. Consequently, I suggest that you use this source to build your file of publishers from whom you wish to receive "blurbs," newsletters, and catalogs. The *Small Press Record of Books in Print* and its companion volume, the *International Directory of Little Magazines and Small Presses* are also useful.[7] Each has a subject index that enhances its value. When using these sources, the following subject headings help identify publishers of sociology related materials: Asian American; Black; Chicano; Native Americans; Third World Minorities; Gay; Lesbianism; Society; Energy.

The *U. S. Progressive Periodicals Directory* is a fine source that lists 500 progressive periodicals published in the United States by associations and community groups. This is a useful tool for retrospective selection of periodicals. For current alternative periodical selection, I have found *Serials Review, Serials Librarian,* and Bill Katz's "Magazines" section of *Library Journal* to be enormously helpful.

6. James Danky, "The Acquisition of Alternative Materials in Libraries," in *Alternative Materials in Libraries* (Metuchen, N. J.: Scarecrow, 1982), pp. 12–30.

7. *Small Press Record of Books in Print*, 11th ed. (Paradise, Calif.: Dustbooks, 1982); *International Directory of Little Magazines and Small Presses*, 18th ed. (Paradise, Calif.: Dustbooks, 1982).

But it is unwise to rely solely on reviews for alternative material. To keep current with new publications, you must be on the mailing lists of neighborhood associations, community and social action groups, professional associations, and other special interest organizations. Newsletters from these groups are excellent sources for information on their publications.

Two standard reference sources can assist you in this endeavor and should be used in conjunction with *Alternatives in Print*. The *Encyclopedia of Associations* is a valuable source for identifying specific voluntary groups, even indicating if the groups in question are engaged in any publishing activity. The entries are listed under broad subject categories and a keyword index is also provided. Several relevant categories to consult include Social Welfare Organizations, Public Affairs Organizations, and Educational Organizations. But it, too, is incomplete.

A supplement is the relatively new source, *Associations Publications in Print*, published by Bowker. It identifies previously difficult to access materials from thousands of national, state, regional, local, and trade associations. Materials listed include pamphlets, newsletters, journals, and free materials. In the broad subject index, sociology publications are listed under "Sociology, Anthropology, Archaeology—Sociology." A title index, publisher/title index, and an association name index providing addresses and telephone numbers are provided as well.

The Center for Association Publications, creator of *Associations Publications in Print*, serves as a purchasing agent or vendor for association publications.[8] Since traditional approval plans do not cover this type of material adequately, working with the center can save you time and can insure complete coverage.

To identify other potential listings, also consult the *Directory of Directories*. Arranged by broad subject categories, it identifies specific published directories of organizations, publishers (including small press publishers), and special interest groups. Relevant subject categories include Law and Government; Education, Social Science and Humanities; and Public Affairs and Social Concerns.

Publications of independent and university affiliated research centers and academic departments are difficult to identify and are rarely indexed or reviewed. Fortunately, the *Research Centers Directory* lists more than 6000 institutes and research centers. Entries, arranged under broad subject categories, describe how the organization's research results are disseminated. In addition, a good subject index is provided. Again, review this source and develop a list of centers to whose mailing lists you wish your name to be added. UCLA's Center for Afro-American Studies and the

8. Center for Association Publications, Inc., P. O. Box 2410, Falls Church, VA 22042.

Research Centers Directory. Detroit: Gale, 1976– . Irregularly.
> A directory of more than 6000 institutes and research centers in the United States.
> Good subject index.
> Entries are arranged under broad subject categories. Primary use for selectors is to identify publishers that are not listed in more traditional reviewing sources. Many excellent reports are not reviewed or indexed. Useful to identify centers to contact in order to be placed on mailing lists.

University of Wisconsin's Institute for Research on Poverty are examples of the types of centers listed in this directory. Both have active research programs, yet their publications rarely are reviewed in standard sources.

Once you identify alternative publications, an acquisitions strategy must be developed. Some organizations place libraries on a mailing list to receive copies of their publications at no charge. But many others charge a small fee, which must be prepaid. In addition, many alternative groups do not accept orders through jobbers, thus requiring libraries to order directly. These restrictions frequently give acquisitions departments fits and require the development of specific procedures.[9]

Multidisciplinary and Alternative Format Materials. As mentioned above, sociology touches many other disciplines. Consequently, as a selector you must keep a handle on the literature of such other disciplines as anthropology, political science, psychology, education, law, medicine, economics, and business. In some institutions, one person is responsible for selection in all of the social sciences. But in many others, selectors are responsible for only one or two disciplines. When the latter is the case, it is important to develop excellent communication links with the other selectors to avoid duplication of effort.

Government documents are primary resource materials for a number of the subfields of sociology. If your institution does not have a government publications unit, to select appropriate documents for your collection you should review the *Monthly Catalog of U. S. Government Publications*. Publications of the departments of Education, Health and Welfare, and Housing and Urban Development are particularly relevant.

A number of microform projects are available that contain documents related to sociological concerns. The ERIC microfiche for education, the *Statistical Reference Index* microfiche collection, and NTIS documents all contain useful information. These sets can be subscribed to, or individual documents can be ordered as needed. If your library does not subscribe to the microfiche collections, you can select needed documents from their published indexes: *Resources in Education* (ERIC), *Statistical Reference Index* (SRI), and *Government Reports Announcements* (NTIS).

9. Danky, pp. 14–15.

Conclusion

The literature of sociology is exciting, interesting, and related to current social issues. Because of its cross-disciplinary focus, it is important to communicate regularly with selectors in other fields.

Few libraries are able to collect comprehensively in all of sociology's subfields. It is, therefore, imperative that you know what your library users need. One way to accomplish this is to maintain regular contact with faculty and researchers in sociology. Another is to keep current with the professional literature of sociology by subscribing to a number of key journals or by having a number of journals routed to you on a regular basis.

Alternative and nontraditional materials are rich sources of information but are difficult to identify, as they are not reviewed in traditional sources. Thus, attempt to have your name added to as many mailing lists as possible.

Selection Sources

Alternatives in Print. New York: Neal-Schuman, 1971– . Biennially.

American Journal of Economics and Sociology. v.1– . 1941– . New York: American Journal of Economics and Sociology. Quarterly.

American Journal of Sociology. v.1–. 1895– . Chicago: Univ. of Chicago Pr. Bimonthly.

L'Annee Sociologique. v.1–12, 1896–1912; n. s., v.1–2, no. 2, 1923–24, 1924–25; 3rd ser., v.1– , 1948– . Paris: Alcan, 1896–1925. Presses Universitaires de France, 1948– . Annually.

Annual Review of Sociology. v.1– . 1975– . Palo Alto, Calif.: Annual Reviews, Inc. Annually.

Associations Publications in Print. New York: Bowker, 1981– . Annually.

Bulletin Signaletique. 521. Sociologie. Ethnologie. v.24– . 1974– . Paris: Centre International de la Recherche Scientifique. Quarterly.

Contemporary Sociology. v.1– . 1972– . Washington, D.C.: American Sociological Assn. Bimonthly.

Current Research on Peace and Violence. Tampere, Finland: Tampere Peace Research Institute, 1971– . (Address: Hameenkatu 13B, Box 447, Tampere, Finland 33101.) Quarterly.

Current Sociology. La Sociologie Contemporaine. v.1– . 1952– . Beverly Hills, Calif.: Sage. 3/year.

Directory of Directories. 2nd ed. Detroit: Gale, 1983.

Encyclopedia of Associations. 18th ed. Detroit: Gale, 1984.

Ethnic and Racial Studies. v.1– 1978– . Oxon, England: Routledge & Paul. Quarterly.

Feminist Studies. v.1– . 1972– . College Park: Women's Studies Program, Univ. of Maryland. 3/year.

Government Reports Announcements and Index. v.74– . 1974– . Springfield, Va.: NTIS. Biweekly.

Human Rights Quarterly. v.1– . 1974– . Baltimore, Md.: Johns Hopkins Univ. Pr. Quarterly.

Index to Social Sciences and Humanities Proceedings. v.1– . 1979– . Philadelphia: Institute for Scientific Information. Quarterly.

Journal of Black Studies. v.1– . 1970– . Beverly Hills, Calif.: Sage. Quarterly.

Journal of Conflict Resolution. v.1– . 1957– . Beverly Hills, Calif.: Sage. Quarterly.

Journal of Marriage and Family. v.1– . 1939– . Minneapolis: National Council on Family Relations. Quarterly.

Monthly Catalog of U. S. Government Publications. Washington, D. C.: Government Printing Office, 1859– .

Political and Social Science Journals: A Handbook for Writers and Reviewers. Santa Barbara, Calif.: ABC-Clio, 1983.

Research Centers Directory. 8th ed. Detroit: Gale, 1983.

Resources in Education. Washington, D. C.: Government Printing Office, 1966– . Monthly.

Serials Librarian. New York: Haworth Pr., 1976– . Quarterly.

Serials Review. Ann Arbor, Mich.: Pierian, 1975– . Quarterly.

Sipapu. Winters, Calif.: Sipapu Konocti Books, 1970– . Biennially.

Social Forces. v.1– . 1922– . Chapel Hill: Univ. of North Carolina Pr. Quarterly.

Social Sciences Citation Index. Philadelphia: Institute for Scientific Information, 1969– . 3/year.

Social Science Quarterly. v.1– . 1920– . Austin: Univ. of Texas Pr.

Sociological Abstracts. San Diego: Sociological Abstracts, Inc., 1953– . 5/year.

Statistical Reference Index. Bethesda, Md.: Congressional Information Service, 1981– . Monthly with quarterly and annual cumulations.

U. S. Progressive Periodicals Directory, 1982–83. Nashville: Progressive Education Service of the South, 1982.

Weekly Record. New York: Bowker, 1974– . Weekly.

Wepsiec, Jan. *Sociology: An International Bibliography of Serial Literature, 1880–1980.* Bronx: Mansell, 1983.

Women's Review of Books. Wellesley, Mass.: Wellesley Center for Research on Women, 1983– . Monthly.

ECONOMICS AND POLITICAL SCIENCE

Robert Goehlert

This chapter outlines the development of a selection methodology for economics and political science. First I will enumerate some issues a subject specialist must address, and I will describe how to design a collection development strategy for the fields of economics and political science. Next will follow a discussion of some of the specific tools that can be used for identifying materials in the general social sciences, economics, and political science.

Before one can begin to develop a selection methodology for economics and political science, it is important to consider the dimensions of both the process and the disciplines involved. Basically there are three factors that affect collection development in economics and political science. First, one must consider the amount of time one can devote to collection development. Second, it is crucial to consider the materials budget in order to determine how many materials one can acquire. While these factors may apply to any field, it is important to keep them in mind when selecting in economics and political science, because the amount of material published in these fields is extensive, exceeding all other disciplines in the social sciences in publishing output. The amount of time and money available will, to some extent, determine whether or not one follows a narrow or comprehensive selection strategy. In addition, it will determine the extent the selector can search for out-of-print materials and conduct evaluations of the collection.

Knowing the structure of the literature in economics and political science is also crucial to developing a collection development strategy. While both disciplines are highly developed, they are also interdisciplinary. In addition, researchers are especially concerned with current materials.

In economics, research is disseminated primarily in journals, and fifty percent of all citations are no more than six years old.[1] The literature of

---

1. John Fletcher, "A View of the Literature of Economics," *Journal of Documentation* 28: 283–95 (1972); Richard E. Quandt, "Some Quantitative Aspects of the Economics Journal Literature," *Journal of Political Economy* 84:741–55 (1976).

Journal of Economic Literature. v.1– . 1969– . Pittsburgh: American
Economics Assn., Quarterly.
Review journal for economics and its subfields.
50 book reviews and 250 author-written abstracts per issue.
12-month time lag between book publication and reviews.
Several-month time lag for book publication and annotations.
The book reviews in the *Journal* are critical and written by economic scholars.
Comprehensive coverage of English-language scholarly production is provided.

political science reflects a much higher usage of monographs, about sixty
percent.[2]

It is not unusual for the political science and economics subject spe-
cialists to select materials that fall within a number of Library of Congress
(LC) classes, including the B, D, E, H, J, K, Q, R, T, U, and V schedules.
Within both disciplines, the field of policy sciences is growing rapidly.

Most important of all, it is necessary to know where the boundaries
will be drawn with respect to the responsibilities of selectors for sociology,
business, history, law, philosophy, and area studies so that the gray areas
do not go unnoticed or unnecessarily duplicated. Therefore, it is critical
to design a detailed collection development policy that details those aspects of the discipline to be collected and at what intensity.

To develop a collection development policy for economics that will
reflect the structure of the literature, one can use the classification scheme
developed by the *Journal of Economic Literature.* While there is no such
classification scheme developed by the American Political Science Association, there are several possible tools available; Frederick Holler's *Information Sources of Political Science* includes a useful introductory essay
on the literature of political science.[3]

A most useful book for someone starting as a selector in the field of
political science is *Political Science: The State of the Discipline.* This
volume, published by the American Political Science Association in 1983,
includes nineteen chapters on present and future research directions. Unfortunately, no similar volume exists for economics. While the new *Encyclopedia of Economics* (McGraw-Hill, 1982) presents a good overview
of economic theory and research, it was not intended, nor does it serve,
as a survey of the literature.

Despite the development of a comprehensive selection policy and strategy, numerous problems will often be encountered. For example, iden-

2. William C. Baum et al., "American Political Science before the Mirror: What Our
Journals Reveal about the Profession," *Journal of Politics* 38:895–917 (1976); June Stewart,
"The Literature of Politics: A Citation Analysis," *International Library Review* 2:329–53
(1970).
3. Frederick Holler, *Information Sources of Political Science,* 3rd ed. (Santa Barbara,
Calif.: ABC-Clio, 1981).

tifying reprints is difficult. Likewise, in the field of economics, numerous edited works and collections of essays are published. Often these materials are collections of published journal articles, while others may include a substantial number of original essays. Unless this is indicated in a review or catalog, it is impossible to tell which is the case. For works in both economics and political science it is frequently difficult to tell if a volume is a text or a research monograph.

General Selection Tools for Monographs

Essentially the task of selection in economics and political science follows two processes. The first involves the designing of a selection strategy that goes from general to specific tools. The second process involves the identification of specialized publishers, including both commercial and research-oriented. During the discussion of various tools, an effort will be made to describe how one goes about these tasks. The tools discussed in this essay are presented in categories that give the process more coherence than is actually the case; in the actual process of selection, a bibliographer does not move from one tool to another in a sequential fashion, but employs a variety of tools daily.

Alert Services. The CDS Alert Service is invaluable for selection in economics and political science, particularly since cataloging in publication has increased dramatically in recent years.[4] Also, LC cataloging of materials in economics and political science is broad and up-to-date, including a wide range of materials in French and German, the two most important foreign languages with which the selector must be concerned. LC proof slips can be used as a primary selection tool as well as a check on materials that should have been selected already. The slips may be used to develop a list of specialized publishers and research centers publishing materials in economics and political science. As LC does catalog a large amount of material published by foundations, institutes, research centers, and the like, the proof slips are instrumental in helping a selector keep abreast of publishing trends.

Many vendors and publishers, such as Blackwell North America, Nijhoff, and Casalini Libri, distribute alert services.[5] As the "half-life" of materials in economics and political science is so short, it is important to acquire materials as fast as possible. Alert services are valuable in providing advance notice of publications in a convenient format. While there are

4. CDS Alert Service, Customer Services Section, Cataloging Distribution Services, Library of Congress, Building 159, Navy Yard Annex, Washington, D. C. 20541.
5. Addresses for these vendors are as follows: Blackwell, 10300 S.W. Allen, Beaverton, OR 97005; Martinus Nijhoff Booksellers, Box 269, 2501 AX, The Hague, Netherlands; Casalini Libri, Via B da Maiano, 50014 Florence, Italy.

no alert services specific to economics and political science, the three mentioned above provide excellent coverage.

Publishers' Catalogs. If your institution does not participate in an approval plan for university or trade publications, it is important to review as many publishers' catalogs as possible. Clearly, the best way to keep up with the literature is to ask to be placed on mailing lists for catalogs and advance notices.

As with alert services, there is no quick way to identify all the publishers in economics and political science, nor is there a single directory or listing of the major publishers in those areas. The *Book Publishers Directory* does have a subject index that will direct you to a number of publishers in political science and economics.[6] Another approach is to develop one's own file of publishers, including the address, types of publications specialized in, subjects covered, and the date the last catalog was received. As publishers are identified, a form letter should be sent asking to be put on specific mailing lists for catalogs and announcements. You might also inquire at this time if the publisher provides any type of alert service.

The process of building a publisher's file can be done as a regular part of the selection process. When perusing advertisements in journals or when reviewing selection tools, check to see if you already have a card for a particular publisher. By using this method, it is possible to identify and maintain a file of both domestic and foreign publishers. I have also found it particularly useful to communicate regularly with acquisitions librarians and other bibliographers, as well as with students and faculty. Faculty can be especially useful, as they often receive publications or catalogs from more specialized publishers and associations.

Finally, you should attend the publishers' book displays at conferences, including those of the American Library Association, American Political Science Association, and the American Economics Association. In my own work, I have found the following publishers to be among the most important for economics and political science: Sage, Lexington, Westview, Praeger, Academic, Pergamon, Nijhoff, and Greenwood.

Standard Bibliographic Tools. Every bibliographer will undoubtedly employ a wide range of standard selection tools such as *Publishers Weekly*, *Library Journal*, *New York Times Book Review*, the *New York Review of Books*, and the *Times Literary Supplement* for their reviews and advertisements. An in-depth discussion of standard bibliographic tools is provided in "Selection Sources and Strategies" and will not be repeated in this essay. However, I do wish to emphasize an important point concerning the selection of foreign-language materials that are already somewhat out-of-date by the time they are reviewed in these tools. It is im-

6. *Book Publishers Directory*, 4th ed. (Detroit: Gale, 1982).

Economic Books: Current Selections. v.1- . 1974- . Fairfield, N. J.: Augustus
M. Kelley. Quarterly.
Some 900 abstracts of books, special studies, reports, and periodical
articles in each issue.
International coverage.
Arranged by subject.
Abstracts are not critical, but excellent coverage of book production in eco-
nomics is provided. Each abstract provides form of publication, level (e. g.,
popular, university, etc.), and language of publication. Produced by the De-
partment of Economics and the libraries of the University of Pittsburgh.

portant to receive information from foreign publishers as materials are
published. This can be done only by writing for catalogs, being placed on
mailing lists, or by subscribing to approval plans or alert services. The best
way to effectively purchase older foreign-language materials is to establish
contacts with a variety of out-of-print dealers who specialize in those
areas.

Economics Bibliographic Tools. For the field of economics, the following tools are useful in selection: *Journal of Economic Literature, Economic Books: Current Selections*, and *Economic Titles/Abstracts*. These
tools provide excellent coverage for economics materials published around
the world in various languages, including special reports and shorter monographs.

Political Science Bibliographic Tools. Unlike economics, there are no
comprehensive bibliographic tools for political science. There is, however,
one source that does review approximately 250 political science books
annually: *Perspective*. It is published ten times a year, and attempts are
made to review books as they are published, so the reviews are somewhat
timely. Other than these and traditional library reviewing sources, the
selector must rely on journals within each of the disciplines to insure
complete coverage.

Perspective. v.1- . 1971- . Washington, D. C.: Heldref. 10/year.
Review journal for political science and related fields.
International coverage with emphasis on United States.
25–30 book reviews per issue.
1–3-month time lag.
Signed book reviews by subject specialists with doctorates in political science
are featured in this journal. While most items covered are published in the
United States, items from all parts of the world are reviewed. Books reviewed
cover political theory, international relations, political methodology, and comparative politics.

Institutes and Centers. As in all social science disciplines, there are a large number of institutes, research centers, and think-tanks that publish varying amounts of material. Many are associated with universities while others are private institutes. There are basically two ways of selecting materials from such groups: by having a standing order or by selectively acquiring the publications.

Standing orders or memberships with institutions considerably simplify the selection process. This is particularly true for the more prestigious organizations such as the Rand Corporation, Brookings Institution, American Enterprise Institute, National Bureau of Economic Research Institute for Contemporary Studies, and Cato Institute, which have extensive publishing programs. The problem is determining how many standing orders one can afford and whether all the publications an institution produces fulfill the needs of a collection. If you purchase materials selectively, you will have to receive catalogs, publication lists, notices of new publications, and so forth. The only effective way to insure receipt of these materials is to write to the institutes, maintain regular contact, and periodically double check to see if you have the latest catalog.

While some of this material is listed or reviewed in standard tools and journals, it is impossible to rely on them to adequately cover all the literature. Since these small publications go out-of-print rapidly, it is necessary to be persistent and thorough. Consequently, it is important to keep an eye open for notices in journals, association newsletters, and other sources that might provide information on such institutions and their publications. There is no easy way to keep abreast of this type of material except to review and scan a wide variety of journals and newsletters within the discipline. Periodically, one should also review the standard institutional and research centers directories, such as the *Encyclopedia of Associations* and the *Research Centers Directory*, to make sure that all the major sources are covered.

Two particularly useful tools for identifying the publications and addresses of associations and institutes are *PAIS* and *PAIS Foreign Language Index*. Both regularly index a variety of publications from research centers, professional organizations, and associations. Again, faculty and students can be invaluable sources of information regarding the publications of smaller centers and institutes, especially those having academic affiliations. When one comes upon an institute or association that issues a series of working papers or research reports, it is always best to write for an examination copy and to inquire whether the series can be obtained gratis or whether a subscription or membership is required.

Abstracts and Indexes. There are several indexes and abstracting services that are useful in the selection process. Among these are *Human Resources Abstracts, Sage Urban Studies Abstracts, Sage Public Admin-*

istration Abstracts, and *Quarterly Strategic Bibliography.* All of these tools index or abstract books and research publications. Again, the time factor is a problem. But these tools can be useful as a back-up and for selecting items that might not appear in the more general tools.

Foreign-language Materials. This section does not treat the selection of foreign-language materials as a separate process. This is as it should be, for the selection of foreign-language materials should be incorporated in the normal review of publishers' catalogs, national bibliographies, journals, and the like.

The level of acquisition of foreign-language materials needed at your institution will affect your selection strategy. While English is the primary language for both economics and political science, the number of titles published in German and French is considerable, followed by Spanish and Italian. To a large extent, the amount of these materials acquired will depend on the curriculum and research endeavors of your institution. The collection of foreign-language materials is especially important for economics and political science if your library is at an institution that offers Ph.D. programs.

Without the resources to acquire large amounts of foreign-language materials, acquisition must be very selective. While there is no way to compensate for the lack of materials in a particular language, one can provide consistency and thought to the kinds of materials to be selected with a precise collection development policy in place.

Though the policy a selector follows will depend on the institution, there are some general guidelines to consider. It is important to collect materials by leading authors and "schools of thought." Preference should be given to acquiring materials about specific countries written in that country's language as opposed to, for example, a German or French study of the United States. The selector should be very careful in acquiring foreign-language materials, the substance of which transcends any geographical area. An example of such would be a theoretical work on econometrics, or formal modeling, written in French.

Another consideration is the acquisition of materials that focus on some special institution, issue, policy, or process related to a foreign country or area. For example, foreign-language materials on federalism in Switzerland, the welfare state and industrial democracy in Scandinavia, the European Parliament, and the European Economic Community are definite areas of research for which foreign-language materials are a primary resource. Above all else, without a definite plan for the acquisition of foreign-language materials, the end result will be little more than a smorgasbord of titles.

Journals. Journals are valuable primarily for four reasons: book reviews, book advertisements, notices and news items, and the content that enables a bibliographer to keep abreast of a discipline. The trick is to develop a list of journals that will provide all four categories of information.

Several general social science journals should be consulted regularly. These fall into three categories: review journals, academic journals, and contemporary journals. *The Literature of Liberty*, and two journals that provide excellent coverage of German-language materials, *Philosophy and History* and *Modern Law and Society*, are useful review journals. The second category, academic journals, includes *Social Science Quarterly*, *Social Forces*, and *Social Science Journal*. Journals such as these provide numerous reviews, advertisements, and general information about developments in the social sciences. Finally, contemporary journals such as *Society*, *Dissent*, *Commentary*, and *Encounter* are also quite useful; their reviews, advertisements, and contents make them invaluable. They help to keep the selector up-to-date on controversies, current trends, and developments in research.

Journals specifically related to economics should be scanned because they include a significant number of reviews, lists of materials received, and/or extensive advertisements. When developing a list of such journals, it is important to identify those that focus on various subfields within economics and cover a number of languages, particularly French and German. Below is a highly selective list of journals I've found to be particularly useful:

American Economic Review. v.1– . 1911– . Nashville: American Economics Assn. Quarterly.

Economica. v.1– . 1921– . London: London School of Economics. Quarterly.

Economia Internazionale. v.1– . 1948– . Genoa, Italy: Camera di Commercio, Industria, Artigianato e Agricoltura di Genova. Quarterly.

Economic History Review. v.1– . 1927– . Cambridge: Economic History Society. Quarterly.

Economic Journal. v.1– . 1891– . Cambridge: Cambridge Univ. Pr. Quarterly.

Economic Record. v.1– . 1925– . Bundvora, Australia: Economic Society of Australia and New Zealand. Quarterly.

Journal of Comparative Economics. New York: Academic Pr., 1977– . Quarterly.

Journal of Political Economy. Chicago: Univ. of Chicago Pr., 1892– . Bimonthly.

Review of Social Economy. v.1– . 1944– . Chicago: Assn. for Social Economics, DePaul Univ. 3/year.

Southern Economic Journal. v.1– . 1934– . Chapel Hill: South Economic Assn., Univ. of North Carolina. Quarterly.

For political science, a large number of journals provide reviews and bibliographies. Rather than provide a comprehensive list, I will list those I've found to be particularly useful in my own work:

American Journal of International Law. v.1– . 1907– . Washington, D. C.: American Society of International Law. Quarterly.

American Political Science Review. v.1- . 1906- . Washington, D. C.: American Political Science Assn. Quarterly.

Foreign Affairs. v.1- . 1922- . New York: Council on Foreign Relations. 5/ year.

International Review of Administrative Sciences. v.1- . 1928- . Brussels: International Institute of Administrated Sciences. Quarterly.

Journal of Politics. v.1- . 1939- . Gainesville: Univ. of Florida. Quarterly.

Political Science Quarterly. v.1- . 1886- . New York: Academy of Political Science. Quarterly.

Political Studies. v.1- . 1953- . Surrey, England: Butterworth. Quarterly.

Il Politico. v.1- . 1950- . Milan, Italy: Universita degli Studi di Pavia, Istituto di Scienze Politiche. Quarterly.

Politische Vierteljahresschrift. v.1- . 1960- . Wiesbaden: Westdeucher Verlag GmbH. Quarterly.

Revue Administrative. v.1- . 1948- . Paris: F. Bureau 203. Bimonthly.

Revue Francaise de Science Politique. v.1- . 1951- . Paris: Presses de la Fondation Nationale des Sciences Politiques. Bimonthly.

Beyond this core of journals, it is important to develop additional lists of titles covering the subfields of political science. For instance, if an area of specialization is public administration you should scan *Public Administration* and *Public Administration Review*. Or if legislative research constitutes a particular focus, you should review *Congress and the Presidency*, *Journal of Constitutional and Parliamentary Studies*, and *Legislative Studies Quarterly*.

A good bibliographer will develop a sizeable list of journals, possibly as many as fifty titles, to be reviewed. As with standard bibliographic tools, the time lag is a problem. Consequently, journals should be used primarily to keep you informed of activity in the discipline and to back up your selection from other more current sources. In essence, journal reviews fill the gap.

Selection of Reports, Papers, and Documents

The tools discussed in this section may be the most important but are the hardest to describe. They include acquisitions lists distributed by other libraries, specialized bibliographies published on a regular basis, extensive review articles, and newsletters published by relatively small associations. There is no single method available to identify these sources, as the selector usually comes across them by serendipity. Nevertheless, they can be invaluable.

In economics, identifying and selecting published working papers is facilitated by *Economics Working Papers Bibliography*. This reference tool lists working papers of academic departments in the United States and England. Many papers eventually appear as articles or are expanded into monographs at a later date. Consequently, the selector must have a clear idea of the kinds of materials to be collected.

Similarly, conference proceedings in economics are quite important, but may change publishers from year to year or not be published at all for some years. The *Directory of Published Proceedings Series SSH—Social Sciences/Humanities* is of some help in identifying published proceedings, but is not comprehensive.

Whether or not the selector is responsible for selecting reference works in economics and political science, it is important to keep aware of new tools, handbooks, statistical sources, and so on. A related problem is the growing trend towards the publication of data only in electronic or machine-readable form. In the future, this area of collection development is going to be a major concern.

The publication of documents directly related to collections of economics and political science is becoming more complicated, as many such documents are now published by commercial presses. Often it is difficult to determine if an item actually *is* a document, and if it is, how the responsibility for selection is to be handled. Another problem is the publication of materials by small presses, ideological organizations, public interest groups, political parties, and similar kinds of organizations. Many, if not most, of these publications fall outside the range of most standard tools and journals. Identifying publications of this sort is an enormous problem for which there is no easy solution. Ultimately, it requires the time and effort of a bibliographer to research these areas.

In addition to the problem of the interdisciplinary nature of the social sciences, there are traditional categories of literature that often necessitate special attention. One area is the collection of biographies, memoirs, letters, and essays, and works by politicians, economists, public figures, and theorists. Because this material frequently is not listed with other economics and political science material in selection tools, the selector must review other sections, such as history or biography, or risk missing excellent material. These problems are difficult to solve, and ultimately require periodic attention, review, and collection evaluation.

Selection of Journals

A particularly troublesome problem for any selector is keeping abreast of new journals. *Choice* regularly reviews a number of new journals, as does the *Journal of Economic Literature* and *PS*. Another useful strategy is to scan the advertisements appearing in the major journals of a discipline, especially those issued by Sage, Butterworths, North-Holland, Pergamon, and Blackwell. While somewhat time-consuming, one could also review each supplement of *New Serial Titles* to identify new journals.

When considering subscribing to a new journal it is always best to review a sample issue and seek the advice of other librarians and faculty. Publishers usually will send a complimentary copy if requested. To determine if your periodical collection is complete, I recommend consulting *Political and Social Science Journals: A Guide for Writers and Reviewers,* the *Journal of Economic Literature,* as well as a variety of indexes and abstracting services, to get a sense of the most heavily indexed journals.

Conclusion

This chapter has provided a rather broad discussion of selection strategies for economics and political science. While there are some specific tools one can use for economics and political science, the majority are standard bibliographic tools. The key to selection in economics and political science is knowledge—knowledge of the disciplines and their subfields, knowledge of important authors and works, and knowledge regarding the publishers in the field. Such knowledge goes beyond the reading of reviews and the reliance on selection tools; it requires an understanding of the disciplines themselves, their history, scope, methodologies, and philosophies.

Clearly, depending on how much time one can devote to the selection of materials, a selection strategy can be either simple or complex. In addition to reviewing publishers' catalogs, alert services, a wide array of general tools, and a well-chosen core of journals in the disciplines, there is no substitute for a knowledge of the disciplines themselves, their prominent authors and researchers, trends in the professions, new methodologies, and important new developments.

Selection Sources

Commentary. v.1- . 1945- . New York: American Jewish Committee. Monthly.
Congress and the Presidency. v.1- . 1972- . Washington, D. C.: Center for Congressional and Presidential Studies, American University. Biennially.
Directory of Published Proceedings. Series SSH—Social Sciences/Humanities. Harrison, N.Y.: Interdok, 1968- . Quarterly.
Dissent. v.1- . 1954- . New York: Dissent Publishing. Bimonthly.
Economic Selections. Pittsburgh: Dept. of Economics, Univ. of Pittsburgh, 1962- .
Economic Titles/Abstracts. v.1- . 1974- . The Hague, Netherlands: Martinus Nijhoff. Semimonthly.
Economics Working Papers Bibliography. Dobbs Ferry; N.Y.: Transmedia, 1976- . Annually.
Encounter. v.1- . 1953- . London: Encounter, Ltd. Monthly.

Encyclopedia of Associations. 18th ed. Detroit: Gale, 1984.
Foreign Language Index. New York: Public Affairs Information Service, 1972- . Quarterly.
Human Resources Abstracts. Beverly Hills, Calif.: Sage, 1966- . Quarterly.
Journal of Constitutional and Parliamentary Studies v.1- . 1967- . New Delhi: Institute of Constitutional and Parliamentary Studies. Quarterly.
Journal of Economic Literature. v.1- . 1963- . Pittsburgh: American Economic Assn. Quarterly.
Legislative Studies Quarterly. Iowa City: Comparative Legislative Research Center, 1976- . Quarterly.
Literature of Liberty. Menlo Park, Calif.: Institute for Humane Studies, 1978- . Quarterly.
Modern Law and Society. Tübingen, W. Germany: Institut fuer Wissenschaftliche Zusammenarbeit, 1968- . Biennially.
PAIS (Public Affairs Information Service Bulletin). New York: Public Affairs Information Service, 1915- . Bimonthly with quarterly and annual cumulations.
PS. Washington, D. C.: American Political Science Assn., 1968- . Quarterly.
Perspective. v.1- . 1971- . Washington, D. C.: Heldref. 10/year.
Philosophy and History. Tübingen, W. Germany: Institut fuer Wissenschaftliche Zusammenarbeit, 1968- . Biennially.
Political and Social Science Journals: A Handbook for Writers and Reviewers. Santa Barbara, Calif.: ABC-Clio, 1983.
Public Administration. v.1- . 1923- . London: Royal Institute of Public Admin. Quarterly.
Public Administration Review. v.1- . 1948- . Washington, D. C.: American Society for Public Admin. Bimonthly.
Quarterly Strategic Bibliography. v.1- . 1975- . Boston: American Security Council Foundation.
Research Centers Directory. 8th ed. Detroit: Gale, 1983.
Sage Public Administration Abstracts: Beverly Hills, Calif.: Sage, 1974- . Quarterly.
Sage Urban Studies Abstracts. Beverly Hills, Calif.: Sage, 1973- . Quarterly.
Social Forces. v.1- . 1953- . Chapel Hill: Univ. of North Carolina Pr. Quarterly.
Social Science Journal. v.1- . 1963- . Fort Collins, Colo.: Western Social Science Assn. Quarterly.
Social Science Quarterly. v.1- . 1920- . Austin: Univ. of Texas Pr.
Society. v.1- . 1953- . New Brunswick, N. J.: Rutgers Univ. Bimonthly.

PSYCHOLOGY

by Raymond G. McInnis

Psychology, perhaps the most wide-ranging of disciplines, embraces subjects from philosophy to physiology. "Currently," Kenneth E. Clark and George A. Miller observe, "psychology is concerned with organisms from the flatworm to man, with phenomena ranging from prenatal conditioning to brain changes in senility, and with processes as simple as the eye blink or as complex as man's adaptation to an environment in outer space."[1] Given the broad character of today's psychology, some might have difficulty understanding that, originally, psychology emerged as an offshoot of philosophy. Even its name, "which means the study of the soul or mind," Clark and Miller note, no longer adequately defines the discipline's fields of interest.

Currently, psychology has three main levels of research and/or practice: behavioristic, humanistic-existential, and psychoanalytic.[2] The discipline, Richard W. Coan observes, is "a peculiarly heterogeneous science with a far-flung and shifting boundary line." Within psychology, theoreticians and practitioners follow careers that are very close to physiology, sociology, or philosophy. Individuals occupy themselves with "factual research data," with "abstract theoretical issues," or with "immediate qualities and experiences of the people" with whom they associate or treat. Continues Coan, "one may take any number of sharply contrasting stances with

The contributions of Diane Parker, library director at Western Washington University; Topsy Smalley, reference librarian at State University of New York at Plattsburgh; Donna Packer, acquisitions librarian at Western Washington University; Walter Lonner, professor of psychology at Western Washington University; Robert Lawyer, former library director at Western Washington University; Beth Shapiro, assistant director of Reader's Services, Michigan State University; and Ed Mignon, professor of librarianship at the University of Washington are gratefully acknowledged.

1. Kenneth E. Clark and George A. Miller, *Psychology* (Englewood Cliffs, N.J.: Prentice-Hall, 1970).
2. For more on the three levels, see Benjamin B. Wolman, ed., *Dictionary of Behavioral Science* (New York: Van Nostrand Reinhold, 1973), p. 296–97.

respect to the theoretical assumptions and methods that are deemed appropriate for psychologists."[3]

Psychology occupies a crucial position among the disciplines that endeavor to understand humans and animals scientifically, a characteristic that makes it similar to other sciences. Its subject matter ranges from such observable behavioral processes as gestures, speech, and physiological changes, to such processes that can only be inferred, like thought and dreams. Because it deals with behavior in complex social environments, as a social science psychology relates to anthropology, sociology, and political science. But because it studies the behavior and mental functions of living organisms, it is also a life science, closely related to biology and psychiatry. It is, finally, a profession dedicated to the application of psychological knowledge and techniques to human problems.

In what follows we discuss first the research literature of psychology, including the use of citation studies and psychology's relationship to other disciplines, and how to identify and evaluate local needs. Then, in selecting materials, we address problems with journal and other serial literature, monographic literature, reference literature, and microform collections. Finally, we examine approval plans, book and serial prices, and the specific publishers of the literature of psychology. (Throughout, our discussion takes a broad view of psychology's fields of knowledge. This view includes, for example, psychiatry, sometimes considered a branch of medicine, and educational psychology. The governing criteria for inclusion is the range and scope of topics covered in the classification scheme of *Psychological Abstracts*.)

The Research Literature of Psychology

From this brief outline of the range and scope of psychology's research interests, we must distinguish the forms and the formulations in which the literature of psychology appears. The literature in which psychologist's report their original research occurs in several forms. These forms include journals, monographs, conference proceedings, and technical reports. There is another body of literature in which psychologists reformulate research done by others. Common examples of this second type are review articles, handbooks, and encyclopedias. Essential in the production of knowledge, these latter publications, primarily review literature, are designed to evaluate and synthesize new research findings.

Information scientists Gabriel Pinski and Francis Narin confirm that within a scientific community, the accepted formal communication net-

---

3. Richard W. Coan, *Psychologists: Personal and Theoretical Pathways* (New York: Irvington, 1979), p. 25, discusses these divisions in terms of the decisions psychologists make as they develop their professional careers.

work for transmitting new information is the journal literature.[4] However, citation studies based upon frequency of citation lead Shirley A. Fitzgibbons to caution that books too "were an important form of material" for research by psychologists.[5]

Necessarily, of course, material appears in monographs later than in journals. And necessarily, too, attention must be given to psychology's report literature, a large percentage of which is distributed in microform, by such institutions as Educational Resources Information Center (ERIC), the American Psychological Association's *Psychological Documents*, and the National Technical Information Service (NTIS).

When psychology's report literature is broken down into its different forms, we can address the following question: What proportion of a budget should go for purchasing monographs, and what proportion of it for journal subscriptions? Suppose the formula is sixty percent for journals, forty percent for monographs. (This hypothetical budget ratio could change, depending upon how a library budgets for reference materials, including reference serials.[6]) Citation studies can be used to help determine what is realistic for dollars budgeted for monographs and for journals. Fitzgibbons, in her review of citation analyses in the social sciences, surveyed twenty-seven studies in psychology. In these studies, she notes, journals accounted for as much as sixty-nine percent of all citations in psychology's literature.[7] With the evidence gained from such analyses, it is possible to develop ideas about budget proportions for monographs and for journals.

Despite the problems inherent with citation analyses, they tell what journals are most highly cited, and thus the most likely to be needed by scholars. Pinski and Narin, for example, discovered that in psychology there are seventy-one highly cited journals.[8] The annual *SSCI Journal Citation Reports* is a useful compendium of journal citation frequencies.

4. While no studies of the situation are known, sufficient recent evidence suggests that increasing numbers of "multiauthored" monographs are being published. One can speculate on the reasons: (1) rising costs of publication and (2) increased numbers of individuals engaged in research combine into a need for the kind of integrative publications that make up the material in much of the titles. That is, to a large extent, chapters in these volumes are designed to evaluate, assess, or otherwise develop a "state-of-the-art" view, topic by topic, of trends and developments in psychological research. (Gabriel Pinski and Francis Narin, "Structure of the Literature of Psychology," *ASIS* 30:161 [May 1979].)

5. Shirley A. Fitzgibbons, "Citation Analysis in the Social Sciences," in *Collection Development in Libraries: A Treatise*, ed. by Robert D. Steuart and George A. Miller (Greenwich, Conn.: JAI Press, 1980), p. 302. But, Fitzgibbons cautions, wide variation exists between different social sciences: in general, in the social sciences, "a range of 31% to 46% of all citations were to books, while a range of 29% to 43% were to periodicals."

6. At some institutions, for example, for at least the last decade reference materials, other than reference serials, and monographs are purchased out of the same acquisitions funds.

7. Fitzgibbons, p. 316.

8. Pinski and Narin, p. 164–65; Louis C. Buffardi and Julia A. Nichols, "Citation Impact, Acceptance Rate, and APA Journals," *American Psychologist* 36: 1453–56 (Nov. 1981), present still another citation analysis of psychology journals. They attempt to compare the impact of ninety-nine APA and non-APA titles.

But the significance of our concern for citation patterns in specific areas of research is perhaps made most impressive by the citation analysis of educational psychology literature. Conducted by Paul Barron and Francis Narin, that study analyzes 140 heavily cited, widely circulating journals, and demonstrates that psychology is the primary source of knowledge for research in education. Represented graphically, research literature in educational psychology clusters around the dominant journal, the *Journal of Educational Research*. In addition, two subclusters link educational psychology with special education and clinical psychology, while other journals provide links with the social sciences and guidance.[9]

Critics note at least four disadvantages to the use of citation analyses in collection development, however. Fitzgibbons, for example, claims "because of the low frequencies of citations in the sciences, including psychology, where most of these studies were conducted," monographs receive less attention than journals.[10] A second disadvantage, according to Robert N. Broadus, is that citation analyses measure use of journals and monographs "by sophisticated scholars." Citation analyses, he stresses, cannot "be expected to correlate strongly with undergraduate and popular demands." Another disadvantage in the application of citation analyses, also touched on by Broadus, comes from the realization that the information derived from them comes from studies that are out-of-date.[11] That is, these studies reflect literature needs of an earlier period, not necessarily those of today. And, concludes Broadus, a fourth disadvantage of applying citation analyses in collection development "is the difficulty in applying the data." A much easier method of selecting journals for a library, he argues, are the lists of titles indexed by abstracting and indexing services.[12]

But we question Broadus's suggestion that citation studies are more up-to-date than records derived from interlibrary loan data. In many institutions there are mechanisms for informing librarians responsible for purchasing materials in specific areas what is being requested by library users. And similar arrangements can, of course, be utilized for requests for online searches.

Identifying and Evaluating Local Needs

Besides citation studies, in selecting materials in psychology for academic libraries' collections there are other matters to consider.[13] What is the

9. Paul Barron and Francis Narin, *Analysis of Research Journals and Related Reasearch Structure in Education* (Chicago: Computer Horizons, 1972).

10. Fitzgibbons, p. 294.

11. Robert N. Broadus, "Application of Citation Analyses," *Advances in Librarianship* 7: 315 (1977).

12. Ibid., p. 324.

13. This section owes much to Sheila Dowd's discussion of how to formulate a collection development policy statement. See Sheila Dowd, "The Formulation of a Collection Development Statement," in *Collection Development in Libraries: A Treatise*, pp. 67–87.

focus of the instructional curriculum for the department? What are the individual research interests and needs of the psychology faculty? To help answer some of these questions and avoid unnecessary problems, it is recommended that libraries develop a collection policy.

In general, a collection development policy statement outlines the department's instructional curriculum and research areas in the discipline in which faculty members in the department have interests. But the details in a collection development policy should be specific enough to allow the librarian responsible for collection development to operate with the confidence and cooperation of the department and, ideally, with a minimum of administrative supervision. The statement describes the fields of knowledge in psychology that are in the institution's area of interest. Next, it states the desired intensity or comprehensiveness of the library's collection of materials in psychology.[14]

In addition, such a statement seeks to answer some of the following questions. Among psychology materials published in languages other than English, what languages are included in the collection? What languages are excluded?[15] What policy does the library take toward materials in the history of psychology? What is the library's policy toward "pop" psychology publications? What is the library's policy toward "textbook" materials (that is, publications specifically dedicated to student purchase for courses)? In psychology, new research areas can develop rapidly. What is the library's policy toward collecting publications on new research topics? Recent examples are behavioral medicine and cross-cultural psychology.[16]

14. Collection Development Committee, Resources Section, Resources and Technical Services Div., American Library Assn., "Guidelines for the Formulation of Collection Development Policies," *Library Resources and Technical Services* 21:40–47 (Winter 1977).

15. *Contemporary Psychology* occasionally reviews a work in psychology written in a language other than English, most likely French, German, or Russian. One notices, however, that time after time the same handful of individuals are called upon to do the reviews, which suggests that out there only a few psychologists possess a command of another language. In many middle-sized institutions, faculty members in psychology with foreign-language skills do not exist. What is true for monographs, however, evidently is not true for journals. Several prominent psychological journals, for example, are published in German by West German publishers.

There is, nonetheless, empirical evidence to back up the notion that American psychologists make little use of foreign-language materials. At five-year intervals, between 1945 and 1970, social psychologists Lorenz J. Finison and Charles L. Whittemore, "Linguistic Isolation of American Psychology: A Comparative Study of Journal Citations," *American Psychologist* 30:513–16 (1975), sampled citation patterns in nine American journals of social psychology. Over that period, their findings show percentages that range from less than eight percent to one percent, figures of such startling results that Finison and Whittemore speak of the situation as the "linguistic isolation of American social psychology."

16. As an indication of increasing maturity of the discipline, the history of psychology and allied subjects is a growing field, but evidently has not yet become well defined, department by department, as a subdiscipline. For collection development in the history of the behavioral sciences and psychology, consult Wayne Viney et al. and Robert I. Watson. The International Society for the History of Behavioral and Social Sciences, *Directory of the Membership [of] the CHEIRON Society* (Akron, Ohio: Archives of the History of American Psychology, Univ. of Akron, 1982) arranges the society's almost 400 members by country and state, and broadly indicates their special interests.

And the history of psychology is not the only area of increasing interest. Henry C. Weinstein

Selection of Materials

Journals and Serials in Psychology and Allied Fields. For selecting journals for a library, Broadus's advice is sound: select from the lists of titles indexed in abstracting and indexing services. But also utilize information from citation studies, faculty suggestions, and whatever other sources are available.[17]

For information on journals in psychology, turn to (1) the "PsycInfo Coverage List" (annual) in *PsycInfo's* "User's Reference Manual"; (2) the equivalent for *Index Medicus* (1960–); or (3) the "Guide and Lists of Source Publications" in the *Social Sciences Citation Index* (1966–) or the *Science Citation Index*, both of which are published as part of these indexes. As well as annotating 800 titles, Margaret Tompkins and Norma Shirley's 1976 guide to serials in psychology and allied fields aids selection by indicating the abstracts and indexes in which particular titles are included. The list of nineteen serials Joan K. Marshall gives for psychology is incomplete; far more complete for the discipline's serials is Tompkins and Shirley's list of serials in psychology and allied fields. Not as useful as Tompkins and Shirley, since it includes just over half as many titles, is Allan Markle and Roger C. Rinn's 1977 guide to psychology journals. (Markle and Rinn designed their annotated listing as an aid to getting published, not as a list of journals for libraries.) Available through the American Psychological Association's (APA) *Psychology Documents*, Noel W. Smith's directory of psychology journals throughout the world lists 727 titles by country and region. Although the *Research Guide for Psychology* contains more titles of "serials" in psychology than the sources above, the serials listed publish almost exclusively only literature review articles, a topic covered below in the section "Psychology's Reference Literature."

In addition to consulting regularly featured descriptions of new journals in standard review periodicals, other sources of new journal titles in psychology are *Psychological Abstracts* and the *Social Sciences Citation Index* "Guide and Lists of Source Publications" (annually). Experience suggests that, as new journals are established in psychology, they themselves invite subscribers through promotional mailings.

Monographic Literature. As review sources for selecting books in psychology, the key titles are *Contemporary Psychology* and *Choice*. Con-

---

recommends books for "Mental Health and the Law," a topic that will continue to grow. Behavioral medicine, too, is gaining in the amount of research concerns by psychologists. For a discussion of this new subdiscipline, see Joseph D. Matarazzo, "Behavioral Health and Behavioral Medicine: Frontiers for a New Health Psychology," *American Psychologist* 35: 807–17 (Sept. 1980). For cross-cultural psychology, another emergent subdiscipline, Harry C. Triandis and William W. Lambert's handbook, a six-volume set, is the best source from which to select materials. The listings at the end of the set's fifty-odd chapters are "the key findings of cross-cultural psychologists."

17. Broadus, p. 324.

Contemporary Psychology: A Journal of Reviews. v.1– . 1956– . Washington,
D. C.: American Psychological Assn. Monthly.
Review journal for psychology.
Evaluates nearly 1000 monographs and selected serials, films, and tapes
annually.
12-month time lag between book publication and review.
CP is considered one of the most prestigious journals in which to be reviewed.

temporary Psychology, a monthly published by the American Psychological Association, devotes its pages exclusively to extensive, evaluative reviews
of current books. It contains by far the greatest number of reviews of
books on psychology each year. According to the editors, *Contemporary
Psychology* reviewed an average of 955 books annually for the last five
years. Of that number, the editors "do not know how many are textbooks," but approximately sixty textbooks are received each year.[18] We
doubt that any other of the social sciences possesses a review journal that
covers its monographic publications as comprehensively as does *Contemporary Psychology*. In *Contemporary Psychology*, the time lag is a year
or so. Of the sixty-three titles in the February, 1984, issue, for example,
the bulk were published in 1982. Most of the rest (twenty-six) were published in 1983. The remaining two titles are 1981 imprints.

The difference between the number of books reviewed in *Contemporary
Psychology* and the approximately 100 fewer titles distributed by Blackwell North America (BNA) (noted below), is understandable. In selecting
books for review, *Contemporary Psychology* casts a broader net, and
therefore includes books that fall outside the BNA "profiles" for psychology and psychiatry.

Contemporary Psychology consistently reviews the discipline's multiauthored volumes, including handbook-type publications, and the numerous recurrent literature reviews, such as *Advances in . . . , Progress in
. . . ,* and so forth. As a rule, experience suggests that no other review
journal, including *Choice*, is as consistent or as inclusive in covering multiauthored literature. *Contemporary Psychology* significantly contains brief
information on the credentials of *both* authors and reviewers, a feature
not characteristic of *Choice*.

Choice, published by the American Library Association (ALA), is specifically intended as a source of reliable reviews for academic libraries.
Choice reviewers are instructed to be comparative when they evaluate
specific titles. In practice, this policy means that, in addition to selecting
or rejecting the book being reviewed, you can check your holdings for
the books with which it is compared. According to the editors, between

18. Personal correspondence from *Contemporary Psychology*.

1979/80 and 1982/83—until recently, *Choice*'s "volume-year" was March through February—*Choice* reviewed between 160 and 186 psychology books each year. And, the editors explain, we should recognize that additional volumes appropriate to the discipline are reviewed in the reference section and in such other sections as the cross-disciplinary "Social and Behavioral Sciences" section.[19] Time lag for the appearance of a review in *Choice* is a little less than *Contemporary Psychology*, about six to twelve months after a book's publication.

In addition to reviews, *Choice* is a source of bibliographic essays specifically intended for collection development. Called "In the Balance," so far in the 1980s this section of *Choice* has included bibliographic essays by Karen Fisher on wolf ecology and behavior, Frances Cordasco on bilingual education in American schools, Mary Casata and Thomas Skill on the literature of television, Richard Picard on the new religious right, and Norman Bell on child abuse.

British Book News, at least the equal to *Choice* in the standard achieved for excellence of reviews, is of course oriented strongly toward books with materials written by British psychologists. This characteristic does not hurt its value, however. If perhaps there is anything disappointing about *British Book News*, it is that too few books in psychology are reviewed.

As a source of reviews of books in psychology appropriate for academic library collections, *Library Journal* is not very satisfactory. In choice of titles for review, it is evidently more concerned with "pop" psychology. Perhaps more than in any other category of books *Library Journal* reviews, the psychology section primarily addresses the needs of public libraries. *Booklist*, an ALA publication, also addresses the needs of public libraries; nonetheless, for serious, well-considered reviews by nonpsychologists of books in psychology designed for popular consumption, *Booklist* is recommended.

Psychology's Reference Literature. In psychology, research topics are small, usually confined to two variables. That is, in general psychologists approach their topics in terms of the focus of their investigation, ordinarily consisting of an independent variable and a dependent variable, such as the effect of the intensity of shock (the independent variable) on learning in a shuttle box (the dependent variable). With such small topics, in an academic library, the card catalog's subject headings are frequently not very useful in exposing appropriate literature on the library's shelves. Unfortunately, from the perspective of the card catalog, research literature on this matter is scarce. John M. Christ's study in sociology is one, but, as Thelma Friedes suggests, it is not entirely satisfactory.[20]

19. Personal correspondence from *Choice*.
20. John M. Christ, *Concepts and Subject Headings* (Metuchen, N. J.: Scarecrow, 1972); Thelma Freides [Review of John Christ's *Concepts and Subject Headings*], *Library Journal* 98: 1096 (Apr. 1973).

Perhaps more than any one scientific study, however, experience confirms this notion about the card catalog's limitations for disciplines such as psychology. For example, in a completely unscientific survey in connection with this chapter, questions to both faculty and graduate students received the same responses. When psychologists use the card catalog, it's from a position of knowing something in advance—for example, an author's name, found in another source. Seldom, these people say, is a subject search in the card catalog successful. Moreover, these same faculty members report that when students' papers are done completely with materials exposed through the card catalog, more often than not these papers are unfocused, off the subject, or are generally considered unsatisfactory.

Among indexes, the two mainly used by psychologists for locating research literature are *Psychological Abstracts* and the *Social Sciences Citation Index (SSCI)*. In other institutions, however, the pattern may be different. More emphasis, for example, may be on literature accessed in *Index Medicus*, or its online version, *Medline*, or with ERIC, or the *Science Citation Index*. Any of these major indexing services, however, through their subject indexes, serve as selection sources, especially to meet specific local needs.

For the most part, *Psychological Abstracts* covers research literature published in journals. At the moment, the evidence suggests little or no coverage of psychological literature published in monographs.[21] But, according to officials at APA's Washington, D. C., headquarters, there is promise that monographs reviewed in APA journals will be abstracted and entered in the PsycInfo database. Among these titles, of course, will be many of the *Handbook of . . .* , *Advances in . . .* , *Annual Review of . . .* publications reviewed in *Contemporary Psychology*.

Since 1978, what their editors call "multiauthored" books are indexed in the *Science Citation Index* and the *Social Sciences Citation Index*. Since then, better indexing coverage is given an important segment of psychology's literature: namely articles of larger scope published as book chapters and literature reviews published in *Handbook*-type volumes or as recurrent titles, such as *Advances in . . .* , *Progress in . . .* , etc.

Psychology's *Handbooks*, *Reviews*, etc., function much like encyclopedias in other disciplines. Part of a scholarly community's means of arriving at a consensus, this group of publications provides authoritative appraisals of research advances in a given field. This practice is a feature

21. Since 1980, citations from *Dissertations Abstracts International* appear only in the database. For empirical studies that compare *Psychological Abstracts* with other literature sources, see Topsy Smalley, "Comparing *Psychological Abstracts* and *Index Medicus* for Coverage of the Journal Literature in a Subject Area in Psychology," *ASIS: Journal of the American Society for Information Science* 31; 143–46 (1980); and George V. Baranowski, "A Comparison of the *Psychological Abstracts* and National Institute of Mental Health Databases," *Behavioral and Social Sciences Librarian* 2: 13–24 (Fall 1980). (Smalley's study is on the literature of operant conditioning.)

Social Sciences Citation Index. v.1– . 1966– . Philadelphia: Institute for
   Scientific Information. 3/year.
   Periodical and citation index for international social science research
      literature.
   Since 1979, the *SSCI* has indexed annually about 300 "multiauthored" books,
   many of which constitute psychology's reference literature. Other entries in these
   lists, a lesser number, make up part of psychology's report literature. Because
   chapters in these multiauthored volumes are frequently located by psychologists
   conducting literature searches, these lists become aids to selecting titles for your
   library shelves. A listing of these materials is in the colored pages at the beginning
   of the *Source Index* portion of each set. Other ISI publications, such as the
   Science Citation Index and the *Index to Scientific Review*, are also useful.

---

well suited to and possibly developing from psychology's characteristically
narrow research topics. And, too, these types of publications are legion
in psychology. In the *Research Guide for Psychology*, for example, the
index lists almost 100 entries for titles beginning with *Handbook* alone.
But, to give us an idea of the numbers of these multiauthored publications,
even more impressive is the 400-odd *Handbook* titles in psychology listed
in the Research Libraries Information Network (RLIN) in spring, 1983.
Some entries are duplicates, of course, but this information lets us see the
extent of this growing trend among publishers who concentrate on psychological literature.[22]

   To update the McInnis guide, use the lists of multivolume publications
indexed in the citation indexes and related publications of the Institute
for Scientific Information in Philadelphia, the *Index Medicus* spinoff, *Bib-*

McInnis, Raymond G. *Research Guide for Psychology*. Reference Sources for
   the Social Sciences and the Humanities, no. 1. Westport, Conn.:
   Greenwood, 1982.
   Comprehensive single-volume source for indexes, abstract journals,
      bibliographies, encyclopedias, dictionaries, handbooks, and so forth.
   1200 reference sources evaluated.
   This is an excellent retrospective selection tool for psychology reference materials. In its compilation, psychology's "literature review" publications, including serials, and single and multivolume sets are stressed.

---

22. In a personal conversation, Henry Small, an information scientist at ISI, observed that
the usefulness of citation analyses is pretty well ended. That is, in his view, just about every
aspect of citation patterns, or citing behavior, has been exhaustively studied. In our view,
however, there is one important area that still needs attention: why, and how, psychologists
cite review literature. Experience suggests, for example, that it is a characteristic among
authors of articles in the *Annual Review of . . .* series, published by Annual Reviews, Ltd.,
of Palo Alto, California, to cite preceding review articles, not only published in that series'
volumes, but in other locations as well. Such information is good to have at hand, yes, but
it only begins to scratch the surface of the information that citation analyses can give about
how and why psychologists, as an identifiable group of researchers, cite literature reviews.

Psychological Documents. v.1- . 1971- . Washington, D. C.: American
Psychological Assn. Quarterly.
Abstracts of report literature and other fugitive material in psychology.
200 new publications abstracted annually.
Formerly entitled *Catalog of Selected Documents in Psychology: The Journal
Supplement Abstract*, this publication attempts to "bridge the gap between formal journal publications and informal information exchange." Full texts of the
approximately 200 items abstracted annually are available in microfiche or "pa-
per-copy" format, either by subscription or by individual order.

---

liography of Medical Reviews, H. W. Wilson's *Bibliographic Index*, and
APA's *Contemporary Psychology*. In general, as a source of information
about new publications for psychology, the *American Reference Books
Annual* is disappointing.

Microform Collections in Psychology. Listed in its own abstract journal,
Resources in Education (RIE), the ERIC system comprises some 200,000
publications (about 1200 items are added each month). Subject matter
contained in publications in the ERIC system cannot be easily summarized.
Along with a broad range of miscellaneous writings related to education,
there are many research and project reports. Most material included is
not readily available elsewhere. For an idea of the range of publications
contained in ERIC, perhaps the best suggestion is to consult the "publication type index" in any issue of *Resources in Education* since July,
1979.[23] And for libraries without a depository arrangement for receiving
ERIC materials, *RIE* is a guide to selecting materials not adequately covered in monographic or journal literature.

Much like *Resources in Education*, the quarterly *Psychological Documents* is designed to "bridge the gap between formal journal publication
and informal information exchange." *Psychological Documents* is the new
name for the APA's *Catalog of Selected Documents in Psychology: The
Journal Supplement Abstract*. Publications abstracted represent the "fugitive" literature in psychology—technical reports, invited addresses, bibliographies, literature reviews, "well designed studies with negative results," major works in progress, "fresh looks at controversial issues,"
management of psychological resources, proceedings of annual meetings
of the regional psychological associations, and psychology-related material
not available through conventional communication channels. Currently,
this source contains about 2400 items, with 200 items added annually.

Similar to *Resources in Education*, *Government Reports Announcements and Index (GRAI)* lists and abstracts research and development
reports of U. S. government-sponsored projects and selected other similar

23. For more details, see Robert M. Simmons, *Library User's Guide to ERIC* (Syracuse,
N. Y.: ERIC Clearinghouse on Information Resources, 1978), or McInnis.

materials that the National Technical Information Service (NTIS) distributes in microfiche. *GRAI* arranges entries first in the service's twenty-two subject fields, and then breaks them down into narrower categories.

For psychology, most materials in *GRAI* fall in field five, "Behavioral and Social Sciences." Field five, in turn, contains eleven categories. As well as in *GRAI*, materials in this category are listed and abstracted in the weekly *NTSI Abstracts Newsletter: Behavior and Society* or its sister publications on administration and management, biomedical technology and human factors engineering, and medicine and biology.

In the material it distributes, NTIS is rich and rapidly reflects the changes in concerns of researchers and practitioners. Military psychology, behavioral medicine, and industrial psychology are just a few of the subdisciplines NTIS contains. Furthermore, its consistency in coverage of materials is subject to rapid, volatile changes. Bibliographies on subjects of current social concern appeared frequently until about the beginning of 1982. Since then, evidently because of budgetary reductions, some curtailment of these services has been necessary. At the moment, bibliographies on subjects that relate to psychology appear only infrequently.[24]

Among these microfiche services, working without ERIC seems impossible to consider. Given the range and scope of information needs expressed by today's faculty and students, it seems inconceivable not to have this source at hand. For most academic libraries, it is essential. Besides the obvious connection it has with educational psychology, much material in this collection relates to psychology. All of its materials are listed in *Resources in Education*. A similar argument exists for material in *Psychological Documents*, especially since it is indexed in *Psychological Abstracts*.

The case for NTIS is different. Access to NTIS materials comes primarily from *GRAI*, which is also filled with the large quantity of other reports that *GRAI* lists. Because of the quantity, access to NTIS is more efficient through online searches. Given these considerations, and the specialized nature of the psychological research publications NTIS contains, libraries will have to determine for themselves whether they need comprehensive coverage of research materials from NTIS. Far better, it seems, is to recognize that *GRAI* is an excellent source from which to select items in psychology that fall in a given library's field of interest.

24. For a directory of libraries with NTIS microfiche holdings, see Mary G. Chitty, *NTIS: Concept of the Clearinghouse, 1945–1979* (master's thesis, Chapel Hill: Univ. of North Carolina, 1979), pp. 57–62; or Nancy Cline and Jaia Heymann, eds., *Directory of Government Document Collections and Librarians* (Washington, D. C.: Congressional Information Service, 1978). Cline and Heymann's *Directory* indicates subject specialities of individual libraries, but Chitty does not indicate the extent of holdings.

Acquisition of Materials

Book and Journal Prices in Psychology and Psychiatry. In the last two decades, costs of both books and journal subscriptions have risen at steep rates. The following figures, for example, come from Blackwell North America (BNA), one of several approval plan vendors specializing in services to academic libraries.[25]

In 1981/1982, BNA handled 584 titles in psychology; among these, 557 were new titles, and cost an average of $25.09 per volume. The rest, 27, were reprints, with an average cost per title of $24.61. As a general rule, we can assume that reprints cost more than new titles.

In the same period, BNA handled 313 titles in psychiatry; among these, 310 were new titles, with an average cost of $26.37 per title. There were 3 reprints, at an average cost of $36.63 per title.

In 1981/1982, if one had purchased all of these books, the cost would have been, for psychology, $14,639.60, for psychiatry, $8,284.59, or for both groups, a total of $22,924.19. Of the titles included above, university presses published 59 in psychology (average cost, $26.68), and 16 in psychiatry (average cost $25.20).

Gerald R. Lowell indicates that in 1982 Faxon, one of several journal subscription services that cater to academic libraries, supplied 257 journals in psychology, with an average price of $61.10 per title. Lowell also reports that the average price per title increased 12.3 percent from the previous year, compared with the overall average price increase of 9 percent for all titles bought by college and university libraries. If a library subscribed to all these titles, the total cost for 1982 would be about $15,700.00.[26]

Even as we write this chapter, the above statistics are dated. They can serve, however, as a means of roughly indicating for the 1980s publishing patterns, approximate costs, and inflation rates for both monographs and journals for the discipline and its related fields.

Approval Plans. To ease the problems of monograph acquisitions, many libraries, especially in the late 1960s and early 1970s, turned to "approval programs" with such vendors as BNA and Baker and Taylor. While approval plans offer a number of advantages, as a selector you should be aware of some of the disadvantages. For example, with an approval pro-

25. Blackwell North America, *Approval Plan Coverage and Cost Study (1980–1982)* (Portland, Ore.: Blackwell North America, 1982). Vendors such as BNA handle the majority of titles published in the United States and Canada by university presses, trade publishers, society publications, small presses, some government publications, and so forth, that meet the requirements of most academic library collection development specifications. All types of books are distributed, including encyclopedias, dictionaries, atlases, and other reference books, but not undergraduate textbooks.
26. Gerald R. Lowell, "Periodical Prices 1980–1982 Update," *The Serials Librarian* 7: 75–83 (Fall 1982).

gram, since books arrive automatically, experience suggests that one no longer reads book reviews with the same serious dedication one does when selecting books, title by title, for the library shelves. As a result, you may find that you lose touch with current trends and that your command of the field diminishes. Fortunately, in psychology we are blessed with *Contemporary Psychology*, which, perhaps better than any other discipline-oriented review journal, approaches near comprehensiveness in its coverage of English-language monographic literature. With a source of this type, even if the time lag between publication and review is greater than you would prefer, the need for an approval plan is greatly reduced. But in the end, of course, each institution must weigh the advantages/disadvantages of whether to utilize an approval program to help develop their collection.[27]

Publishers Specializing in Psychology. If you, as a librarian responsible for collection development in a specific knowledge field, become informed about the range and scope of a particular discipline's published materials, you will recognize that certain publishers specialize in subject areas. American publishers who specialize in issuing materials for various aspects of psychology include: Academic Press; Brunner/Mazel; Lawrence Erlbaum; Free Press; Greenwood; Grune and Stratton; Jossey-Bass; Pergamon; Plenum Press; Raven Press; Saunders; Springer-Verlag; Van Nostrand Reinhold; and Wiley. As a selector of materials in psychology, direct your acquisitions department to forward to you catalogs and other promotional material they receive. And get on the mailing list of publishers who concentrate most heavily in psychology and related fields. As you gain more skill and background knowledge about psychology, you will begin to recognize authors' names, topics, and publishers, and on that basis will be able to select from advance notices of publishers' materials without having to wait for reviews.

Summary

As a discipline, psychology is rich and diverse. Its fields of interest stretch from philosophy to physiology.

The findings derived from citation analyses suggest that close to seventy percent of psychology's literature comes from journals. Armed with this knowledge, selectors for psychology in academic libraries need to be as concerned with journal literature as monographic literature. Collection development in psychology, then, unlike other social sciences, closely

27. For more on approval plans, see Peter Spyers-Duran and Daniel Gore, eds., *Advances in Understanding Approval and Gathering Plans in Academic Libraries*. Second International Seminar on Approval and Gathering Plans in Large and Medium Size Academic Libraries (Kalamazoo: Western Michigan Univ., 1970).

resembles the "hard" sciences. Furthermore, because of the great many "literature review" publications increasingly indexed in the citation indexes, psychology's reference literature, perhaps to a greater degree than any other social science, is indexed in a unique way.

Selection Sources

American Reference Books Annual. v.1– . 1970– . Garden City, N.Y.: Literary Guild.

Bell, Norman W. "Abusing the Child." *Choice* 21:931–39 (Mar. 1984).

Bibliographic Index. v.1– . 1938– . New York: Wilson. Biennially.

Bibliography of Medical Reviews. v.1– . 1955/1960– . Washington, D. C.: National Library of Medicine.

Booklist. v.1– . 1905– . Chicago: American Library Assn. Semimonthly.

British Book News. v.1– . 1940– . London: British Council. Monthly.

Casata, Mary, and Thomas Skill. "The Literature of Television." *Choice* 19:584–97 (Jan. 1982) and 19:721–36 (Feb. 1982).

Choice. v.1– . 1964– . Middletown, Conn.: Assn. of College and Research Libraries, American Library Assn. Monthly.

Contemporary Psychology. v.1– . 1956– . Washington, D. C.: American Psychological Assn. Monthly.

Cordasco, Francesco. "Bilingual Education in American Schools." *Choice* 19:1517–26 (July–Aug. 1982).

Fisher, Karen. "Wolf Ecology and Behavior." *Choice* 20:36–42 (Sept. 1982).

Government Reports Announcements and Index. v.1– . 1946– . Washington, D. C.: U. S. National Technical Information Service. Semimonthly.

"Guide and Lists of Source Publications." *Social Sciences Citation Index.* Philadelphia: Institute for Scientific Information. 1966– . Annually.

Index Medicus. Bethesda, Md.: National Library of Medicine, 1960– . Monthly.

Journal of Educational Research. Washington, D.C.: Heldref, 1920– . Bimonthly.

Library Journal. v.1– . 1876– . New York: Bowker. Weekly.

Markle, Allan, and Roger C. Rinn. *Author's Guide to Journals in Psychology.* New York: Haworth, 1977.

Marshall, Joan V. *Serials for Libraries.* New York: Neal-Schuman; Santa Barbara, Calif.: ABC-Clio, 1979.

McInnis, Raymond G. *Research Guide for Psychology.* Westport, Conn.: Greenwood Pr., 1982.

NTIS Abstracts Newsletter: Behavior and Society. Washington, D. C.: U. S. National Technical Information Service. Weekly.

Picard, Richard V. "The New Religious Right." *Choice* 19:863–79 (Mar. 1982).

Psychological Abstracts. v.1– . 1927– . Washington, D. C.: American Psychological Assn. Monthly.

Psychological Documents. v.1– . 1971– . Washington, D. C.: American Psychological Assn. Quarterly.

PsycInfo Psychological Abstracts Information Services Users Reference Manual. Rev. ed. Washington, D.C.: American Psychological Assn., 1984.

Resources in Education. v.1– . 1956– . Washington, D. C.: Government Printing Office. Monthly.

Smith, Noel W. *Psychology Journals throughout the World.* Washington, D. C.: American Psychological Assn., 1981, MS 2151. 1982 supplement, MS 2467.

Social Sciences Citation Index. v.1- . 1966- . Philadelphia: Institute for Scientific Information. 3/year.

Social Sciences Citation Index Journal Citation Reports. Philadelphia: Institute for Scientific Information. Annually.

Tompkins, Margaret, and Norma Shirley. *Serials in Psychology and Allied Fields*. Troy, N. Y.: Whitston, 1976.

Triandis, Harry C., and William W. Lambert, eds. *Handbook of Cross-Cultural Psychology*. 6v. Boston: Allyn & Bacon, 1980.

Viney, Wayne, et al. *History of Psychology: A Guide to Information Sources*. Detroit: Gale, 1979.

Watson, Robert I., ed. *The History of Psychology and the Behavioral Sciences: A Bibliographic Guide*. New York: Springer, 1978.

Weinstein, Henry C. "Mental Health and the Law." *Library Trends* 30:557–75 (Spring 1982).

Part 4

SCIENCE AND TECHNOLOGY

Edited by
Stanley P. Hodge
and
William Hepfer

SCIENTIFIC AND TECHNICAL MATERIALS: A GENERAL OVERVIEW

Stanley P. Hodge and William Hepfer

All library materials should be selected thoughtfully and acquired promptly. This is a truism for every subject area, of course, but it is especially important for scientific and technical publications. Scientists rely on the latest research findings for their professional enhancement and to prevent duplication of effort in their own work.

This chapter will offer some practical advice based on the authors' collective experience in dealing with collection development and acquisition of the primary sources of information for members of the scientific community. Although some of the formats used by those in science and technology are identical to those used in other fields, the librarian should be aware that the methods of disseminating information and the patterns of use for books and serials often differ from those in the humanities and social sciences. For instance, in a study for Earle and Vickery, the percentage of citations to the monograph literature was twelve percent in the sciences, fourteen percent in technology, and forty-six percent in the social sciences. For periodicals it was eighty-two percent, seventy percent, and twenty-nine percent, respectively. Citations to other formats were six percent in the sciences, sixteen percent in technology, and twenty-five percent in the social sciences.[1]

In addition to monographs and journals, certain other formats are important in science and technology, depending on the discipline and the stage of development that characterizes the research. The early written forms of a scientist's or engineer's findings often consist of technical reports, reports of research in progress, review letters, preprints, and the proceedings of conferences or symposia. Garvey and Griffith's description of the communication of research findings determined that the median

The authors wish to thank Sally Donaldson and Jay Martin Poole for their assistance.

1. Penelope Earle and Brian C. Vickery, "Subject Relations in Science/Technology Literature," *Aslib Proceedings* 21:237–43 (June 1969).

times for the dissemination of a research scientist's work after initiation of a project was one-and one-half to two years at a conference, two years in a technical report, two-and-a-half to three years in a journal (assuming initial acceptance of the manuscript), and five years in an annual review. When accumulated research data were synthesized and transformed into scientific "knowledge" in a treatise or text, a median time of thirteen years had elapsed.[2]

Most collection development librarians are concerned with the selection and acquisition of books, serials, and conference proceedings, and that will be the major focus of this chapter. Other formats may also play a major role in the formal patterns of communication within the scientific and technological disciplines. In some cases, their selection and control may be assigned to a specialized library unit outside of a subject bibliographer's jurisdiction. Examples are: hundreds of thousands of technical reports of sponsored research published each year, and U. S. government documents. In some cases, as in the earth sciences, federal and state geological surveys and publications assume a major role. In agriculture, thousands of state agricultural experiment station and extension service bulletins, circulars, miscellaneous publications, and reports are disseminated. Patents are a useful source of information in chemistry, as are standards and specifications in engineering. Librarians should recognize the uniqueness of these primary sources of information and adapt their procedures accordingly.

In addition, it should be noted that keeping current with the changing scene in collection development strategies and maintaining an awareness of new developments in building sci-tech collections will be enhanced by perusing some specialized library journals. The quarterly journal *Science & Technology Libraries* is highly recommended in this regard.

Serial Publications: Journals and Continuations

Journals are the predominant information source for scientists. They can be prepared and produced in a much shorter time than monographs; thus, they are better able to fulfill scientists' needs for reports of current research.

Continuations share the serial nature of journals, but are seldom able to match their currency of information. Rather, their main virtue is that libraries can issue standing order instructions to collect all volumes in the series. This saves librarians from having to select and order each volume

2. William D. Garvey and Belver C. Griffith, "Scientific Communication as a Social System," in *Communication: The Essence of Science*, pp. 148–64. Ed. by William D. Garvey (Oxford: Pergamon, 1979).

individually and enables them to acquire the volumes as soon as they are published. Since volumes in a series usually share a common subject or point of view, an intelligently chosen standing order represents no more risk of bringing in unwanted publications than a periodical subscription does.

The high cost of science-oriented serial publications is a major factor in the huge sums that many large academic libraries allocate for their serials. (Average prices ranged from $70.74 in zoology to $207.94 in chemistry and physics for 1983 subscriptions.[3]) Figures in excess of $1 million, representing sixty to eighty percent of the total materials expenditures, are not uncommon at universities belonging to the Association of Research Libraries (ARL).

Since library budget allocations rarely keep pace with inflation, institutions must sometimes impose serial cutbacks lest the cost of renewals take over the total amount. This leaves collection development librarians with the ironic and unpleasant task of deselecting current titles, rather than adding new ones.

SELECTION CRITERIA

Dhawan and others have developed a model of three techniques for determining which scientific journals are primary candidates for selection, retention, or deselection from the library's collection.[4] Their recommended criteria include: (1) frequency of citations in the primary literature; (2) frequency of indexing/abstracting in the secondary literature; and (3) actual use in a particular library. Individually, each criterion has certain disadvantages, so a judgment should be based on all three whenever possible.

Several sources for determining ranked frequency of citation in the primary literature are available. There are some, such as the Institute for Scientific Information's *Journal Citation Reports*, that cover the broad area of science and technology, and the *Chemical Abstracts Service Source Index* (CASSI), that lists the 1000 journals most frequently cited in *Chemical Abstracts*. Others, such as Harris's *Annotated World List of Selected Current Geographical Serials*, cover a specific discipline. The implication here is that the more frequently a journal is cited, the greater will be its importance. However, the librarian should be aware of some of the caveats associated with relying solely on citation analysis for selection/deselection purposes. These have been summarized by Smith and include such factors as high quality news journals being infrequently cited, due to their purpose,

3. Norman B. Brown and Jane Phillips, "Price Indexes for 1983: U. S. Periodicals and Serial Services," *Library Journal* 109:1659–62 (Sept. 1, 1983).
4. S. M. Dhawan and others, "Selection of Scientific Journals: A Model," *Journal of Documentation* 36:24–32 (Mar. 1980).

or journals being highly cited as a function of their accessibility, which is reflected by their form, place of origin, age, and language.[5]

Scientific journals that are indexed or abstracted provide another basis on which a selection, retention, or deselection decision may be determined. Indeed, some librarians try to acquire most of the journals covered by the major indexing services, assuming that those titles will be the ones sought most frequently by library users. This is usually true at the undergraduate level, but it does not always follow for all of the scientific community. In surveys described by Meadows, for instance, the two most important methods physicists and chemists have for acquiring information are from citations in relevant papers and from reading current publications.[6] The use of abstracting and indexing journals ranked fifth and third, respectively, for these two groups.

Use is a third criterion. Ideally, the person responsible for selecting/ deselecting will be familiar enough with the collection and library users to do this without checking further. Realistically, however, such a project will have to be based on user surveys or reshelving statistics. Neither of these methods is foolproof, but they can suffice in the absence of circulation data (usually not available because periodicals traditionally do not circulate).

The price and the library's ability to borrow a title are additional factors to consider, along with how much a journal is used. Some publications will need to be retained at any price to support strong curricula or programs, while others might be justifiable at a modest cost but not if the price doubles. Some little-used titles may have to be retained simply because they are not held by another institution that is willing to lend or photocopy for a reasonable fee. In those cases, the least used should not necessarily be the first canceled. The plight is then worsened when cancellations force the publishers to increase the prices, and this in turn leads to more cancellations at other libraries.

Libraries should not despair of ever being able to add a new subscription or standing order, however. Journal and continuation selection need not become a lost art, because conscientious librarians should always be comparing the titles in their present collections with everything else that is available. An institution's needs are constantly evolving as new programs are introduced and old ones are dropped or reduced; a library's collection should likewise be evolving if it is to serve the current needs of its users.

Academic librarians who pay attention to the shifting foci of the curricula are in the best position to recommend cancellations and new titles. Money is finite, and there will be few arguments if collection manipulation is based on substantive data such as enrollment figures and the number

5. Linda C. Smith, "Citation Analysis," *Library Trends* 30:83–106 (Summer 1981).
6. A. J. Meadows, *Communication in Science* (London: Butterworths, 1974).

of courses offered. It is usually advisable, however, to head off dissent by involving appropriate faculty members in the decision making process insofar as it is possible.

REVIEWS

Finding reviews and bibliographic information pertinent to many scientific journals can be accomplished readily by following the guidelines set forth in Marcia Tuttle's chapter on serials. All of the standard periodicals directories and review sources—*Ulrich's, Serials Review,* etc.—include science-oriented publications as part of their regular coverage. An additional, excellent source for reviews of science periodicals, however, is an annual issue of *Nature.* One issue each year (usually in the fall) devotes extensive coverage to reviewing new periodical titles of recent origin. In 1984, for example, fifty-six journals were evaluated in the September 27 issue. Most of the reviews were by British scientists, but the scope was international (although limited to English-language periodicals) and, all-in-all, their roundup was far superior to other review media in currentness and thoroughness.

Approval Plans

Approval plans are now recognized by many libraries as an efficient and effective method for obtaining many current publications. Over eighty-five percent of ARL libraries and seventy-one percent of the engineering libraries surveyed by Smith utilize one or more approval plans to some extent.[7]

The major features, advantages, and disadvantages of approval plans are discussed elsewhere in this book, as well as in other recent publications.[8] This section will minimize duplication of information, therefore, by concentrating on their strengths and weaknesses as they pertain to scientific and technical publications.

Timeliness, while not as significant for books as for journals, is nonetheless an important factor in the acquisition of all science materials. Approval plans are able to nicely accommodate this requirement by saving librarians from the chores of selection, preorder searching, and purchase order preparation.

7. Assn. of Research Libraries, Office of Management Studies, *SPEC Kit 83, Approval Plans in ARL Libraries* (Washington, D. C.: ARL, 1982); Charles R. Smith, *Approval Plans—Their Directions and Alternatives* (College Station: Texas A&M University, 1982).

8. Peter Spyers-Duran, ed., *Shaping Library Collections for the 1980's* (Phoenix: Oryx, 1980); Jennifer S. Cargill and Brian Alley, *Practical Approval Plan Management* (Phoenix: Oryx, 1979); Association of Research Libraries, *SPEC Kit 83.*

Book dealers offering approval plans are usually able to provide discounts, because they buy publications in quantity as soon as they are published. With science books averaging $44.44 each in 1982, this can represent substantial savings.[9]

These materials are promptly processed by the dealer according to a customer-established collection development profile and shipped within a short period of time. The authors have found by working with the two major approval plan dealers, Baker and Taylor and Blackwell North America, that both have been able to supply over eighty percent of the science and technology titles reviewed by *Choice* before the *Choice* review cards were received. Other librarians, however, have expressed much satisfaction with the domestic approval plans of Ballen Booksellers International, Coutts Library Services, Midwest Library Service, and Yankee Book Peddler.

Some foreign book dealers such as B. F. Stevens & Brown, B. H. Blackwell, Otto Harrassowitz, and Martinus Nijhoff offer plans that can be used to provide European coverage based on selected subjects, countries, and language requirements. Publisher approval plans like Elsevier North-Holland and Springer-Verlag (both with American sales offices) are often used by librarians to acquire the numerous science and technology publications of these firms.

Most dealers offering books on approval also supply book selection forms that are imprinted with author, title, price, and selected bibliographic information. These forms are used to notify librarians about the availability of titles that fit their profile. Librarians sometimes request only the slips to keep abreast of what is being published in marginal collection areas or to avoid duplication between domestic and foreign approval plans. There are also cases where the slips are initiated by the dealer in lieu of sending nonreturnable publications. The latter situation, while understandable from a dealer's viewpoint, can be frustrating to librarians because it negates the major advantages of an approval plan: the material cannot be examined beforehand, nor is it provided as promptly as desired. Unfortunately, the number of scientific and technical publishers with no-return policies seems to be growing.

Librarians who are trying to build comprehensive coverage in a scientific or technical field should temper their expectations with the knowledge that no plan will provide *everything*. Even an unrestrictive profile will be limited by publishers who insist on direct sales, and book dealers who cannot afford to supply low-profit publications against a stated discount. Impressive monographs that are issued by learned societies, institutes, or research centers are frequently omitted for purely economical reasons.

9. Chandler B. Grannis, "U. S. Title Output, Average Prices: Final Figures for 1982," *Publishers Weekly* 224:29–32 (Sept. 23, 1983).

It has been the authors' experience that all of the scientific and technical publishers listed on dealers' approval plan prospecti are not always fully represented in the books that they supply. The smaller houses seem more likely to be overlooked, and librarians should monitor them carefully until confidence in the vendor has been established. The dealers will usually honor claims, but if delays persist they should be reminded of their responsibility to automatically supply materials in accordance with the profile.

Discount, service, and the breadth and depth of coverage must be weighed by any library contemplating establishing an approval plan or changing to a different dealer. Smith's survey of engineering libraries suggests that no book dealer has a decided advantage over the others for providing inexpensive, exacting coverage of scientific and technical materials.[10] The authors have even found that different dealers will supply substantially different publications against very similar profiles. For example, Baker and Taylor's coverage of scientific materials appears to be much broader, yielding a higher number of items, while Blackwell North America's is perceived to be more "quality conscious." Both of these firms approach profiling differently, however, and librarians are advised to interview and compare several dealers to determine which one is most able to meet their individual needs.

Selection Guidelines for Firm Orders

Firm orders are required for those desired publications that will not be received as part of an approval plan, standing order, or comprehensive/package arrangement. They frequently account for over half a library's monograph acquisitions. Librarians charged with collection development responsibilities can save themselves much time and effort by being thoroughly familiar with the approval plan profile and other avenues of automatic receipt. This will enable them to maximize their effectiveness at selecting titles to be firm ordered and will also save the preorder searchers from the unnecessary trouble of handling and rejecting many requests for titles that are already in the library.

Collection development policies covering all subject areas are also helpful to librarians trying to deal with the quandaries of book selection. In academic libraries these policies are ideally the result of mutual effort between collection development librarians and the teaching faculty and are usually formulated on the basis of academic disciplines or subject collections. Such policies should describe who the collection is intended to serve, language restriction, chronological and geographical boundaries,

10. Smith, *Approval Plans.*

important formats of material to be collected, treatment, and desired levels of collecting intensity by specific subfields, e.g., research, graduate, undergraduate, or basic.

In the absence of subject policies, the inexperienced librarian will have to rely on common sense about what material will be most useful to the library's users. Meanwhile, experience can be gained by observing book request patterns and trends. Other useful approaches for making decisions involve looking at collection management reports that can be provided by approval plan dealers or at circulation statistics that show which areas in the collection are the most heavily used. In order to anticipate future needs, librarians should also develop faculty contacts and get on mailing lists to receive appropriate reports about new curricular and research developments in specific areas.

Selection Tools

Farina and Snyder identified publishers' flyers and catalogs, advertisements in journals, and book reviews in scholarly journals as book selection tools common to both librarians and members of the teaching faculty.[11] The major difference in the approaches between librarians and teaching faculty was that the former also used professional review publications such as *Library Journal, Choice, Publishers Weekly,* and *New Technical Books.*

Many selection tools are available, and collection development librarians may want to consult all or depend on just a few fairly reliable sources, rather than dealing with all the overlapping information. The choice of what to look at should be based on such factors as the time available for selection, the depth of coverage required in specific subject fields, and the objectives of an individual selection tool, e. g., the intent of a publisher's prepublication announcement is quite different from that of a review in *Choice.* Confidence in a particular publisher's offerings may come with experience, but until then, some librarians may find authoritative reviews worth the wait.

The following section discusses the advantages and disadvantages of various types of selection tools as they pertain to scientific and technical material.

PUBLISHERS' FLYERS AND CATALOGS

The advantage to be gained from selecting scientific and technical publications from publishers' flyers and catalogs is that orders can be placed

11. Alfred J. Farina and Monroe B. Snyder, *Decision-Making in the Selection of Science Library Materials for Higher Education: Empirical Findings and Guidelines* (Washington, D.C.: ERIC Document Reproduction Service, 1967) (ERIC Document ED 047 708).

early, sometimes before the material is actually published. This presumes that current advertisements are forwarded to the appropriate librarians who will make prompt decisions. Prepublication orders occasionally qualify for larger discounts, but the biggest point in their favor is that libraries will receive the materials as soon as they become available.

Collection development librarians who may lack confidence in their teaching faculty's selections from publishers' brochures might find reassurance in a National Enquiry Survey of scholars' book buying patterns. The study revealed that scholars based over half of their decisions to purchase a book on a publisher's announcement or advertisement in a journal, and that they were seldom disappointed in their purchase.[12]

Complete reliance on brochures for selection purposes would hardly be satisfactory, however, as many small publishers cannot afford to print and distribute enough brochures to flood the market. Also, some nonprofit organizations will only provide catalogs on request, and librarians should develop a list of useful resources if they intend to build comprehensive collections in particular subject areas. Two useful sources for locating the names and addresses of this type of publisher are the *World Guide to Scientific Associations* and *Scientific and Technical Books and Serials in Print, 1984.* The former offers a subject approach to the organizations listed. After identifying the relevant organizations, libraries may then write and request that they be put on mailing lists for current publication announcements or comprehensive catalogs of materials in print.

Selecting from new brochures and catalogs in conjunction with an approval plan may cause a serious duplication problem unless librarians exercise great caution.[13] In some cases, it may not be evident that some titles will fall within the library's profile, and in others the inclination to order early at a savings might be too tempting.

PROFESSIONAL LIBRARY TOOLS

The advantage of selecting library materials on the basis of information in professional library tools is that the listings have usually been subjected to editorial screening, and several of them provide a fairly broad approach to scientific and technical literature. *American Book Publishing Record* (APBR), which is issued monthly, is unselective and does not provide reviews. Rather, citations are based on Library of Congress cataloging or CIP and arranged in Dewey Decimal Classification order for a convenient subject approach. A typical issue will cite 400–600 scientific and technical books from 150–220 publishers.

12. *Scholarly Communications; The Report of the National Enquiry* (Baltimore: Johns Hopkins Univ. Pr., 1979).

13. Stanley P. Hodge, "Duplicates, Delivery Times, and Claims: Three Related Factors in Approval Plan Effectiveness," in *Shaping Library Collections for the 1980's*, pp. 74–78, ed. by Peter Spyers-Duran (Phoenix: Oryx, 1980).

New Technical Books. New York: Research Libraries, the New York Public
   Library, 1915– . 10/year.
   Review journal.
   75–100 reviews an issue.
   Time lag varies from 6 months to 2 years or more.
   Descriptive reviews are by the professional staff at the Science and
      Technology Research Center of the New York Public Library or an
      occasional guest reviewer.
Books in this source are arranged by Dewey Decimal Classification; there is also
an "Author Index" and "Subject or Catchwork Index" in each issue. *New
Technical Books* is primarily a selective listing of "noteworthy English-language
books" and occasionally a few foreign-language works as well.

APBR cumulates the information from the *Weekly Record* that provides
the information sooner but does not offer the classified arrangement. The
intention of both publications is to list most books published or distributed
in the United States exclusive of government documents, technical reports,
dissertations, pamphlets, periodicals, and primary/secondary school textbooks. Juvenile books and reprints are easily identified from the bibliographical information, but undergraduate textbooks may be indistinguish-
able from higher level materials unless the titles themselves indicate the
intended audience.

New Technical Books features reviews of books by the Research Center
Staff of the New York Public Library. The ten issues a year average 130
reviews each covering books in the pure and applied sciences, mathematics,
engineering, industrial technology, and related disciplines. The level of
coverage ranges from introductory college to the advanced research level.
Entries are arranged by Dewey classification heading and provide full bibliographic descriptions. The reviews are brief, intelligent statements regarding each book's contents, purpose, intended audience, and other relevant attributes. They frequently appear six months after a book is published
but can be useful to science librarians for monitoring approval plans or
ensuring that some recommended titles were not overlooked in *ABPR*.
New Technical Books is also a good investment for libraries with limited
budgets because it enables librarians to be more discriminating and confident during the selection process.

Technical Book Review Index is similar in purpose to *New Technical
Books*. It is a monthly publication divided into sections covering agriculture, life sciences, medicine, pure sciences, and technology. Entries provide
author, title, publisher, place, date, pagination, price, and LC card number
and are arranged alphabetically within the five subject groups. Excerpts
of recent book reviews from a wide variety of scholarly journals are also
given. *Technical Book Review Index* suffers as a selection tool because

Technical Book Review Index. v.1– . 1935– . Pittsburgh: JAAD Publishing.
   Monthly.
   Indexing service.
   Technical Book Review Index provides extracts from published book
      reviews spanning most of the scientific disciplines. Its broad coverage
      encompasses over 2000 journals.
   Reviews are arranged alphabetically by the last name of the author/editor
      within 5 broad categories: pure sciences, life sciences, medicine,
      agriculture, and technology.
   A cumulated author/editor listing appears in the December issue.

the issues usually follow the reviews by three to five months, and it is not
unusual for the reviews to appear six months or a year after a book's
publication. It is more comprehensive than *New Technical Books*, however, covering more than 2700 books a year.

Still another review source specializing in scientific materials is *Science
Books and Films*. Published five times a year by the American Association
for the Advancement of Science, each issue contains around 180 brief
book, film, and video reviews arranged under two dozen topic headings.
The nontechnical reviews are written by scientists in academia and industry
about materials ranging from an elementary to university level. Most of
the titles have been published or produced within the past twelve months.

Choice, both the journal and the review cards, is very popular in libraries
for selecting or checking holdings in most subject fields. Its focus is on
undergraduate materials, including some textbooks in the science and
technology section. There are usually around sixty reviews of scientific
and technical books arranged by subject in each issue. There is no agriculture section, however. *Choice*'s reviews were previously unsigned, although written by persons knowledgeable in the subject. This policy was
changed to one of signed reviews in September of 1984.

Science Books and Films. Washington, D. C.: American Assn. for the
   Advancement of Science, 1965– . 5/year.
   Review journal.
   200–250 signed, critical reviews per issue.
   Most reviews cover materials published during the past 12 months.
   Reviews are arranged by Dewey Decimal Classification within the listings
      by format.
   Broad coverage includes books, films, videocassettes, and filmstrips appropriate
   for elementary, junior high, and senior high school students, as well as college
   students, general audiences, and professionals. Evaluations cover content, ac-
   curacy, currency, scope, clarity, technical quality, audience level, and interest.
   An overall rating is also provided.

Library Journal reviews such a limited number of science and technology books that the regular book reviews are hardly adequate unless used in conjunction with other sources. Some issues feature announcements of forthcoming science books, though, and a list of 100 outstanding scientific and technical books from the previous year appears each March.

Academic librarians responsible for selecting science books for a curriculum collection will find a relevant section in *School Library Journal*, which is arranged similar to its companion, *Library Journal*. It is much more current, but not as thorough as *Appraisal: Science Books for Young People*. The latter is published three times a year by the Children's Science Book Review Committee. Approximately 200 books a year are rated on a scale of one to five (unsatisfactory to excellent), and each title is discussed by a children's librarian and a science specialist.

SCHOLARLY JOURNALS

Another category of selection tools is the science journals that attempt to cover the broad spectrum of science and technology monographs through book reviews or selective listings. In her study of biomedical, scientific, and technical book reviewing tools in the early 1970s, Chen determined that the "time lag in book reviewing is generally longer in the specialized journals than in the general ones and the reviews tend also to be longer and more comprehensive in the former."[14] She also concluded that during that period considerable duplication occurred between the general science journals and the specialized ones. However, there was a minimum of duplication of books selected for review among general science journals. The general science tools described below are those that currently include the largest number of reviews in a wide variety of science and technology subject fields.

Science, a weekly journal published by the American Association for the Advancement of Science, includes about 240 authoritative reviews each year. A cumulative annual index appears in May. In addition, it also lists about fifty titles of "books received" in each issue. Good bibliographic information is provided. This review source is stronger in the biological than in the physical sciences. Conference proceedings and some nontrade material are also included.

New Scientist annually provides 300–400 signed, critical reviews of science and technical books in its weekly issues. Compared with *Science*, coverage of British books is much stronger—as would be expected. The reviewed books are less technical, and the selection is also more evenly divided across all of the subject fields.

Nature is another good British source of reviews. The material is more specialized than that covered by *New Scientist* and the lag time between

14. Ching-chih Chen, *Biomedical, Scientific, and Technical Book Reviewing* (Metuchen, N. J.: Scarecrow, 1976), p. 124.

Science. v.1- . 1880- . Washington, D. C.: American Assn. for the
  Advancement of Science. Weekly.
  Scholarly journal.
  Four signed, critical reviews in most issues plus a listing of 100–50 "Books
    Received."
  Reviews follow publication by 12–18 months; "Books Received" titles are
    more recent, 3–6 months.
English-language monographs, serials, volumes of monographic series, and con-
ference proceedings from all scientific disciplines are cited alphabetically by title
in the "Books Received" section. This is one of the most comprehensive listings
of recent scientific and technical materials available. *Science* can serve bibliographers as a selection tool and as a checklist to monitor approval plans.

New Scientist. v.1- . 1956- . London: Commonwealth House. Weekly.
  General interest science journal.
  5–8 signed, critical book reviews in each issue.
  Most of the reviewed titles were published in the past 6–24 months.
This well-written, British-flavored journal features short articles and news features on a wide variety of scientific and technical topics. Bibliographers can
benefit from its informative coverage of current scientific developments. Request
U. S. subscriptions from IPC Magazines, Ltd., 205 E. 42nd St., New York, NY
10017.

the book's appearance and the review is short compared to other general
review sources. This weekly journal includes about 350 signed, critical
reviews each year.

American Scientist has a scientist bookshelf column in each bimonthly
issue. About 450 critical 100–400 word reviews of primarily commercial
and university press books appear under the fields of physical, earth, life,
and behavioral sciences; mathematics; computer science; engineering; and
the history and philosophy of science. This source would provide a good
selective holdings check by discipline of both popular and technical books.
The November/December issue has an annual author index of books
reviewed. The major drawback to this source is that about half the books
reviewed have been out a year or more.

Science News (weekly) has very brief annotations for from six to twelve
popular science books in each issue.

Science and Children (monthly during the school year) reviews ten to
twenty science books in each issue. These books are directed primarily
toward the primary and secondary school levels.

Conference Proceedings

Conference proceedings are frequently cited by scientists as a preferred
information source second only to journals in importance. Although sev-

eral bibliographic tools exist to help librarians select, verify, and order conference proceedings, acquiring these reports of meetings and presentations can still be a formidable chore. Typical problems include variations in the form of entry and frequent changes in publisher. Indeed, conference proceedings frequently spark controversy in libraries over whether they should be handled as monographs or serials, a decision not helped by the Library of Congress when it catalogs the same publication both ways.[15]

Another problem stems from the limited number of copies that are printed of some specialized conference proceedings: it is not uncommon for them to be out-of-print by the time they are cited in the standard bibliographic tools. On the other hand, some proceedings may be published in a professional or scholarly journal and also reprinted as a separate publication. It is fairly obvious how unintentional duplication may occur despite careful efforts to guard against it.

Conference proceedings may be acquired as a part of an approval plan, but most require a more active approach such as: (1) contacting a conference sponsor regarding publication plans; (2) selecting from a specialized bibliographic tool; or (3) placing a standing or blanket order.

The first method usually involves scanning brochures or reference tools for information about meetings. The *Encyclopedia of Associations* frequently mentions an organization's regular meetings, as does *World Meetings*. A librarian can then send a form letter inquiring about ordering information.

The second, more prevalent method is to select from a bibliographic tool specializing in identifying and providing information about conference proceedings. The *Directory of Published Proceedings: Series SEMT* (science, engineering, medicine, technology) is one of the most useful sources in terms of currency, comprehensiveness, and ordering information. It has been published ten times a year since 1965 and is cumulated annually and quinquennially; over 4000 titles were listed in the 1980–81 cumulation. Proceedings information may be accessed in the issues by date or location of a conference, and the editor in the monthly issues. The cumulations also provide a subject/sponsor approach. Publishers' and distributors' addresses are listed separately.

The *Directory* is not an easy tool to use, and it is sometimes difficult to formulate a probable main entry based on the information given. The LCCNs and ISBNs that are included in many entries, however, can be used in conjunction with an online bibliographic utility to determine access points.

Interdok, the publisher of the *Directory of Published Proceedings*, handles orders—both firm and standing—for conference proceedings. They

15. Jim E. Cole, "Conference Publications: Serials or Monographs?" *Library Resources & Technical Services* 22:168–73 (Spring 1978).

Directory of Published Proceedings. Series SEMT—Science, Engineering, Medicine, and Technology. Harrison, N. Y.: Interdok, 1965– . 10/year with 3 cumulated index supplements and annual and quinquennial cumulations.

Indexing Service

Over 3000 conferences are indexed each year by the Sciences, Engineering, Medicine, and Technology Section. Coverage of proceedings in books, serials, NTIS Reports, international and government documents.

Indexing of citations is by keywords in the name of the conference, sponsors, title, editor, and location.

Information may include month and year of publication, conference title, editor(s), publisher, series, date, price, pagination, ISSN or ISBN, and LC card number. In recent years, publishers' and distributors' addresses have been listed separately in the front of each issue.

---

cannot provide everything that they list, but they do seem to have a higher percentage of success than libraries that order direct. Librarians dealing with Interdok should be aware that they will probably have to pay a service charge and that ordered materials may not be returned.

The Institute for Scientific Information's *Index to Scientific and Technical Proceedings (ISTP)* is published monthly, with semiannual cumulations since 1978. *ISTP* covers individual papers as well as the conferences themselves. Many proceedings are cited several months after publication.

The user can look up information by several approaches: category (subject), sponsor, author/editor, location, corporate body, and keyword in the title. Complete bibliographic information, usually including price and distributor, is provided with the categorized entries; proceedings appearing in journals are easily identifiable.

Approximately thirty-five percent of *ISTP*'s coverage deals with engineering, technology, and applied sciences; twenty-one percent with clinical medicine; twenty percent with life sciences; twelve percent with physical and chemical sciences; and twelve percent with agricultural, biological, and environmental studies.

Index to Scientific and Technical Proceedings. Philadelphia: Institute for Scientific Information, 1978– . Monthly with semiannual cumulations.

Indexing service.

80,000–90,000 papers from over 3000 conferences are indexed each year.

Coverage extends to conference proceedings that appear in journals as well as books.

Multiple approaches are possible from six different access points: author's name, conference sponsor, subject category, meeting location, title words, and author's corporate affiliation. This tool can be very helpful to bibliographers and acquisitions personnel as well as reference librarians.

Numerous access points and currency make this a preferred bibliographic tool for most libraries to use for selection purposes. It is considerably more expensive than the *Directory*, however, and libraries that cannot afford both should compare them carefully to determine which is better suited to their specific needs.

Other specialized guides to proceedings information include *Proceedings in Print* (2000 conferences indexed in 1982) and G. K. Hall's *Bibliographic Guide to Conference Publications*. Most large libraries probably have all four.

Standing orders are the third method of acquiring conference proceedings. Many regularly held conferences make their proceedings available on a standing order basis, and librarians may acquire them like serial publications. An agent, such as Interdok, that specializes in proceedings can be very helpful here. Albert J. Phiebig, Inc., specializing in current and out-of-print foreign materials, is also very good at supplying proceedings singly and on standing order.

When comprehensive coverage is desired for specific professional societies a blanket order (this may be called a "standing order" by some societies) for all of their conference symposia and proceedings may sometimes be placed. Advantages, in addition to automatic and timely receipt, are favorable discounts and a yearly billing. The Institute of Electrical and Electronics Engineers (IEEE) and the American Society for Mechanical Engineers (ASME) are examples of professional societies offering this service to libraries.

Technical Reports

Technical reports are a specialized form of literature that are largely, but not exclusively, devoted to science and technology. Although reports have long been a traditional source of information for the geological sciences, the report literature did not begin to appear in quantity for the technical and physical sciences until after World War II. They are now typically produced by persons working in the applied sciences and engineering, more often than in the pure sciences. The total number of technical reports issued worldwide annually is a difficult figure to estimate, but it may exceed one-half million.[16]

A technical report typically contains only one paper, rather than a collection of papers, and is not refereed like many scholarly journals. The purpose of a report is to provide information on the progress or results of research and development, particularly for government-sponsored research. As noted earlier, such reports appear very early in the information

16. Charles P. Auger, *Use of Reports Literature* (Linnet, Conn.: Archon, 1975).

dissemination process, so their utilitarian value may be lessened by the subsequent appearance of a journal article that is more accessible and more current. This is so in almost half of the cases, and several studies have demonstrated the "half-life" of technical reports to be less than two years.[17]

Despite this handicap, a technical report is likely to contain more complete technical information about the research conducted. Garvey contends that "any scientist who is especially interested in a journal article would likely benefit from examining its technical report counterpart."[18]

The magnitude and diversity of issuing bodies for technical reports makes bibliographic access to them multifarious. Fortunately, much national effort has been spent in providing timely distribution and access to technical reports. The primary sources of information on unclassified reports of interest to scientists and engineers include National Technical Information Service's (NTIS) *Government Reports and Announcements Index* for the United States, which categorizes reports in twenty-two subject fields. This tool provides author, title, contract number, sponsoring agency, contractor, report number, order number, and an abstract. Other domestic agency-sponsored bibliographic sources include *Scientific and Technical Aerospace Reports (STAR)*, *Energy Research Abstracts*, and *INIS Atomindex*. Citations to the report literature also appear in the major abstract journals, i.e., *Chemical Abstracts*, ERIC's *Resources in Education*, and *Engineering Index*, to name a few.

In addition, databases are used to provide selective dissemination of information, i.e., STAR cite technical reports.

Acquiring individual technical reports requires procedures much different from those used to obtain the other formats mentioned. Initially, technical reports are usually distributed by the sponsoring agency to those considered to have a "need to know." After distribution to interested researchers, reports are deposited in large clearinghouses for distribution on a national scale. Reports are not handled by book trade dealers and it is best to go directly to a national clearinghouse in the case of government-sponsored reports. In such cases, it is helpful to have deposit accounts or to prepay. Complete bibliographic information, including accession number, should always be provided, and the use of the supplier's specific order form is highly recommended. It is always advisable to follow these guidelines when dealing with any publication clearinghouse, i.e., NTIS, ERIC, UNESCO, or HMSO. Technical reports are also issued by

17. Gordon E. Randall, "Literature Obsolescence at a British and an American Aeronautical Library," *Special Libraries* 50:477 (Nov. 1959); D. A. Fuccillo, *The Technical Report in Biomedical Literature* (Washington, D. C.: National Institutes of Health, 1967); and C. W. J. Wilson, "Report Literature Used among Aerodynamicists," *Aslib Proceedings* 10:194 (Aug. 1958).
18. Garvey, *Communication*, p. 60.

> *Government Reports Announcements and Index.* v.75, no. 7– . Washington,
> D. C.: National Technical Information Service, April 4, 1975– . Biweekly
> with annual cumulations.
> Indexing service.
> Comprehensive coverage of 70,000 American and foreign unclassified
> technical reports each year.
> International in scope.
> *GRA&I* provides report summaries arranged in twenty-two subject fields: aer-
> onautics; agriculture; astronomy and astro physics; atmospheric sciences; be-
> havioral and social sciences; biological and medical sciences; chemistry; earth
> sciences and oceanography; electronics and electrical engineering; energy con-
> version; materials; mathematical sciences; mechanical, industrial, civil, and ma-
> rine engineering; methods and equipment; military sciences; missile technology;
> navigation, communications, detection, and counter-measures; nuclear science
> and technology; ordnance; physics; propulsion and fuels; and space technology.
> Access points include subject, personal author, corporate author, contract num-
> ber, and accession/report number.

a wide range of nonfederal agency organizations and these often must be
acquired directly from the agency. Libraries usually obtain them through
exchange agreements, subscriptions to specific series, or by ordering single
titles directly.

A Look at the Future

In addition to the formats covered in the preceding sections, there are a
few others that are also important to some of the science and technology
disciplines. These are: government documents, treated separately in Judy
Horn's chapter; standards and specifications (especially important to engineers) covered in Edwin Posey's essay on the engineering literature; and
patents, discussed in John Pinzelik's essay on the chemical literature.

New types of media are now rapidly emerging to carve out a place
among the more traditional forms of printed literature. Their proportion
to the total may now be small, but this will change as the cost effectiveness
of their utilization begins to match the already present technological feasibility. In one study, for instance, a group of publishers, technologists,
and librarians forecast that fifty percent of all newly published technical
reports would be available only in electronic form by the year 1995. That
same percentage of indexing/abstracting services would be only available
electronically by the year 2000.[19]

19. F. W. Lancaster and others, *The Impact of a Paperless Society on the Research Library
of the Future.* Final Report to the National Science Foundation (Urbana: Univ. of Illinois,
Graduate School of Library Science, 1980).

As of June 1983 the full text of eighteen American Chemical Society (ACS) journals were available online from Bibliographic Retrieval Services, Inc., and new documents by the ACS were being updated every two weeks. This portends another factor in favor of the electronic journal—namely *timeliness*. In the fields of applied research, where currency of information is a critical problem, the economic advantages of the new technologies will result in new services to help alleviate the delay and high cost of traditional printed formats.[20]

Seiler and Raben note that several varieties of the electronic library are now emerging.[21] One type consists of a combination electronic and print form—indexes and abstracts in the former, and primary information in the latter. A second type utilizes computers for indexing and abstracting, and microfiche for information. A third type—or total electronic library—is viewed as offering the greatest potential for flexibility, speed, and accuracy.

Various combinations of technology are also being developed to locate and retrieve information more quickly. The Optical Stored Computer Assisted Reference Service (OSCAR), which utilizes microcomputers, optical disks, and satellite technology to deliver digital data to libraries, is now being tested.[22]

While there is always some resistance to new developments, and some rethinking about the role of the scholarly journal has already begun, those in the scientific community have already indicated a favorable attitude toward such developments as the online journal. A Royal Society Committee's survey of 592 British scientists revealed that although fewer than half had used online computer-based methods of information retrieval, a substantial majority wished to do so. These scientists also advocated the growth in certain types of online information systems, although the maintenance of scientific standards and the reputation of journals were clearly a concern.[23] In surveying departments for the purpose of developing local subject collection policies, it has also been the observation of the authors that there is more receptiveness toward online journals by scientists and engineers in academia than in the humanities and social sciences.

One thing is clear: librarians who will be collecting and providing information in the areas of science and technology will be doing so in diversified information environments. In some cases, it will be the librarians who take the initiative to persuade their clientele to use the new formats.

20. Edward M. Walters, "The Future of the Book: A Historian's Perspective," *Information Technology and Libraries* 1:15–21 (Mar. 1982).
21. Lauren H. Seiler and Joseph Raben, "The Electronic Journal," *Society* 18:76–83 (Sept./Oct. 1981).
22. "News and Announcements," *Information Technology and Libraries* 2:324–29 (Sept. 1983).
23. J. F. B. Rowland, "The Scientist's View of His Information System," *Journal of Documentation* 38:38–42 (Mar. 1982).

If the reverse is the case, unresponsive librarians may find that their collections will not only lag behind the state of the art, but that their role in the information network may become obsolete.

Selection Sources

American Scientist. v.1- . 1913- . New Haven, Conn.: Scientific Research Society. Bimonthly.

Appraisal: Science Books for Young People. v.1- . 1967- . Boston: Children's Science Book Review Committee. 3/year.

Bibliographic Guide to Conference Publications. Boston: Hall, 1974- . Irregularly.

Chemical Abstracts. v.1- . 1907- . Columbus, Ohio: Chemical Abstracts Service. Weekly.

Chemical Abstracts Service Source Index. Columbus, Ohio: Chemical Abstracts Service, 1969- . Quarterly supplements.

Directory of Published Proceedings. Series SEMT—Science, Engineering, Medicine and Technology. v.1- . 1965- . Harrison, N. Y.: Interdok. 10/year, with annual and quinquennial cumulations.

Encyclopedia of Associations. Detroit: Gale, 1956- . Annually.

Energy Research Abstracts. v.1- . 1976- . Oak Ridge, Tenn.: U. S. Department of Energy. Annually.

Engineering Index Monthly and Author Index. v.1- . 1884- . New York: Engineering Information, Inc. Monthly.

Government Reports Announcements and Index. v.74- . 1974- . Springfield, Va.: National Technical Information Service. Biweekly; cumulated annually by *Government Reports Annual Index.* (This NTIS database of technical reports is also available online through several vendors.)

Harris, Chauncey D. *Annotated World List of Selected Current Geographical Serials: 443 Current Geographical Serials from 72 Countries with a Study of Serials Most Cited in Geographical Bibliographies.* 4th ed. Chicago: Univ. of Chicago Pr., 1980.

INIS Atomindex. v.1- . 1970- . Vienna: International Atomic Energy Agency; dist. by UNIPUN. Semimonthly with semiannual cumulations.

ISI Journal Citation Reports. v.1- . 1973- . Philadelphia: Institute for Scientific Information.

Index to Scientific and Technical Proceedings. Philadelphia: Institute for Scientific Information, 1978- . Monthly with semiannual cumulations.

Irregular Serials and Annuals. New York: Bowker, 1967- . Annual.

Katz, William A. *Magazines for Libraries.* 4th ed. New York: Bowker, 1982.

Nature. v.1- . 1869- . London: Macmillan Journals Ltd. Weekly.

New Scientist. v.1- . 1956- . London: IPC Magazines Ltd. Weekly.

New Technical Books. v.1- . 1915- . New York: New York Public Library. 10/year.

Proceedings in Print. v.1- . 1964- . Arlington, Mass.: Proceedings in Print, Inc. Bimonthly.

Resources in Education. v.1- . 1966- . Washington, D. C.: Dept. of Education. Monthly with annual cumulations.

SCI Journal Citation Reports. v.1- . 1977- . Philadelphia: Institute for Scientific Information. Annually.

STAR (Scientific and Technical Aerospace Reports). v.1– . 1963– . Baltimore-Washington International Airport, Md.: U. S. National Aeronautics and Space Administration.

School Library Journal. v.1– . 1954– . New York: Bowker. Monthly.

Science. v.1– . 1880– . Washington, D. C.: American Assn. for the Advancement of Science. Weekly.

Science and Children. v.1– . 1963– . Washington, D. C.: National Science Teachers Assn. Monthly during academic year.

Science and Technology Libraries. v.1– . 1980– . New York: Haworth. Quarterly.

Science Books and Films. v.1– . 1965– . Washington, D. C.: American Assn. for the Advancement of Science. 5/year.

Science News. v.1– . 1921– . Washington, D. C.: Science Service. Weekly.

Scientific and Technical Books and Serials in Print, 1984. New York: Bowker, 1983. Irregularly.

Serials Review. v.1– . 1975– . Ann Arbor, Mich.: Pierian. Quarterly.

Technical Book Review Index. v.1– . 1935– . Pittsburgh: JAAD Publishing. Monthly.

Ulrich's International Periodicals Directory. v.1– . 1932– . New York: Bowker. Annually supplemented by *Ulrich's Quarterly.*

Wilson Library Bulletin. v.1– . 1914– . Bronx: Wilson. Monthly.

World Guide to Scientific Associations. 3rd ed. New York: Saur, 1982.

World Meetings: Outside United States and Canada. v.1– . 1968– . New York: Macmillan. Quarterly.

World Meetings: United States and Canada. v.1– . 1963– . New York: Macmillan. Quarterly.

BIOLOGY

Bill Robnett

The scope of research in biological science is vast, and the body of literature that has evolved to report experimental and observational data in this discipline is correspondingly so. The *Quarterly Review of Biology* routinely reviews published materials in all subdisciplines of biological science, including history, philosophy and ethics, general biology, paleontology, molecular biology, cellular biology, genetics and evolution, reproduction and development, microbiology, botanical sciences, zoological sciences, aquatic sciences, environmental sciences, neural sciences, animal behavior, human biology and health, and biomedical sciences.

The Division of Biology and Agriculture of the National Research Council includes representatives from more than fifty societies, each representing a generally similar field of research in biological science. These are anatomy, laboratory animal science, genetics, physiology, phytopathology, cell biology, microbiology, biological chemistry, ichthyology and herpetology, limnology and oceanography, mammalogy, parasitology, plant physiology, plant taxonomy, zoology, biometry, biophysics, botany, ecology, mycology, paleontology, phycology, nematology, protozoology, systematic zoology, and wildlife.[1]

The advent of new research fronts throughout the history of biological science has often necessarily been accompanied by the development of more sophisticated instrumentation or has been dependent upon borrowed techniques from other disciplines, such as chemistry. For example, Leeuwenhoek's microscope enabled for the first time observation and some experimentation at the cellular level of organisms. Previously biological scientists had been observers of systems within individual organisms or observers of the complete organism itself. The limitation was the resolution capabilities of the unaided human eye.

1. A. G. Atkins, ed., *Guide to World Science*, v. 23, *United States of America*, pt. 2. (Guernsey, U. K.: Francis Hodgson, 1975), p. 389–91.

Increasingly sophisticated instruments and concomitant manipulative experimental techniques have enabled investigation of the subcellular milieu. The optically advanced light microscope, used in conjunction with chemical fixatives, preservatives, stains, and dyes, and later the development of the transmission and scanning electron microscopes with their extremely minute resolution power, heralded the development of cell biology. And finally the molecular level has been breached. Three noteworthy examples are the discovery of the structure of deoxyribonucleic acid, DNA, using X-ray diffraction techniques by Watson and Crick in 1953; the use of nuclear magnetic resonance techniques for living systems; and genetic engineering, the manipulation of the molecular genetic structure of organisms to produce chemicals outside the living system that normally produces those chemicals.

It is at this molecular level of investigation that biological research enters that "gray" area of the research spectrum where biology, chemistry, and physics merge. Biology of the human organism, at the opposite, or organismal, end of the spectrum, is another research area that shares characteristics of other disciplines, especially anthropology, psychology, and medicine. In the area of plant research, weed science, phytopathology, and crop physiology make the distinction between agriculture and botany difficult to make.

Garland Allen, in his characterization of contemporary biology, points out two major aspects: that all biological problems are assumed to be examinable at the molecular level and that the approach in contemporary biology is highly experimental in both mode of thinking and method. He goes on to describe twentieth-century biology as experimental, analytically rigorous, and integrative, and the approach in the preceding century as descriptive, speculative, and mechanistic, the latter characteristic especially true in the physiological research of that period.[2] Physiology was one of the few areas of experimentation before the twentieth century.

The rigor of biological investigation in the twentieth century can also describe continued specialization of research areas (subdisciplines of those areas aforementioned) and concomitant development of new journal titles that ostensibly rapidly communicate new findings and interpretations in these developing areas. Such bifurcation is one of the significant challenges to successful collection development in the discipline. This specialization and the reality of "publish or perish" in research institutions have led to a discipline that is highly dependent on periodical literature and occasionally on conference proceedings. Emphasis is on editorial scrutiny by recognized authorities in the field before publication.

2. Garland Allen, *Life Science in the Twentieth Century* (New York: Wiley, 1975), p. xiv.

Overview and Guides

Biological research heavily emphasizes current primary literature for points of clarification and bases of comparison. The vast majority of citations in biology publications refer to recent articles published in biological periodicals.

Monographs, with the exception of symposia proceedings, usually contain secondary information and are seldom cited. Biologists do utilize monographic publications, however, when they want to review the research being done beyond their specialized field of interest. Such compilations frequently contain the most important results and conclusions of several years of investigative research. Researchers can then expand on matters of interest by consulting the original journals that are referenced in the text.

Students are more likely to consult secondary sources, since these often provide a good synthesis of a subject. Despite the time lag in getting them published, biological monographs are very useful sources of biological information that collection development librarians should not overlook.

Smith's Guide to the Literature of the Life Sciences provides an excellent overview of the structure of biological literature and how researchers utilize it. Another useful publication is *Science and Engineering Literature: A Guide to Reference Sources* by Malinowsky and Richardson. Both guides discuss primary and secondary literature sources. In addition, Sheehy's *Guide to Reference Books*, with its two supplements, and *Walford's Guide to Reference Material* both describe the standard reference works in biology. New reference sources or new editions of standard works are periodically reviewed in *RQ, Reference Services Review*, and *Booklist*.

Major trade publishers in biology include Academic Press, Elsevier Science Publishers, Springer-Verlag New York, Pergamon Press, John Wiley & Sons, Annual Reviews, and Plenum Publishing. Scholarly and professional groups also sponsor or publish biology publications. In the United States the major groups are the Botanical Society of America (BSA), the Ecological Society of America (ESA), the American Association of Anatomists (AAA), the American Society of Plant Physiologists (ASPP), and the American Society of Zoologists (ASZ). European groups engaged in publishing include the Zoological Society and the Royal Society of London, the Academie des Sciences and the Centre National de la Recherche Scientifique (France), the Academy of Sciences of the USSR (Akademiya Nauk SSSR), and the Federation of European Biochemical Societies (FEBS). The Max Planck Society should be mentioned because of its very active support of scientific research in the Federal Republic of Germany. An overview of scientific societies, foundations, and associations is given in Trevor Williams's *Guide to World Science*.

Biology Journals

Reviews of biology journals are far less common than reviews of monographs and other publications in series. They do exist, though, and selectors should check *Nature* and *Current Advances in Plant Science* regularly for announcements of new periodicals. These announcements are more descriptive than critical, however.

In many instances faculty members will recommend new biology periodicals before reviews are available. Their sources of information include publishers' advertisements, members of the "invisible college," and contacts at regional or national meetings.

Many publishers will provide the names of the editors and editorial board members for forthcoming periodicals in their prepublication announcements. Sample issues usually give these names inside the front or back covers or within a few pages of the title page. Since the editors and board members will ultimately determine the quality of the publication, selectors can review their names with faculty members to help determine the potential quality of a biology journal and whether or not it belongs in the collection.

The *Academic Press Journal Catalog*, published annually, gives names and institutional affiliations of journal editors and includes a description of the features and scope of each title. The Kluwer Academic Publishers Group provides their *Descriptive Journal Catalogue*, which also lists editors and advisory groups. S. Karger and Pergamon Press publish similar catalogs. Complimentary examination copies of new journals are available from most publishers. The Journal Information Center of Elsevier Science Publishers provides preaddressed tear-out postcards in their *New and Forthcoming Books and Journals* to request copies.

JOURNAL TRANSLATIONS

English translations of scientific Russian-language journals can represent a significant monetary commitment for periodicals in the biological sciences. For example, Consultants Bureau, a subsidiary of Plenum, currently publishes English translations of seventeen Russian journals directly related to the biological sciences. These titles include *Doklady Biological Sciences*, *Doklady Botanical Sciences*, *Soviet Journal of Developmental Biology*, *Soviet Journal of Ecology*, and *Soviet Plant Physiology*, ranging in price from $145 to $460 in 1984.

In smaller bioscience collections, where purchasing some or all translated titles is not feasible, the *Translations Register Index*, compiled by the National Translations Center at the John Crerar Library, is a far less expensive source for locating foreign-language articles translated into En-

Translations Register Index. Chicago: John Crerar Library, National
   Translations Center. 1967–. Monthly.
   Indexing Service.
   International in scope.
   Indexed publications are available from the center for a nominal
      photocopying and service fee.
English translations deposited at the center by societies and institutions around
the world are listed under 22 subject fields. The *Index* also lists government-
sponsored translations announced in *Government Reports Announcements and
Index*. Coverage extends to the natural, physical, medical, and social sciences.

glish. The *Index* includes the location of the translated article and the
cost. Provision of access to individual translated articles is certainly more
involved than processing regular subscriptions. However, annotating the
Index to indicate articles added to the collection or creating an easily
edited and updated list of purchased translated articles on a word processor
or personal computer is uncomplicated.

In larger collections with many translated journals, the annotated *Index*
or a list can provide user access to owned non-Russian-language biology
journals that have no English-language translation available. It should be
noted that only selected papers are translated and included in the *Translations Register Index*.

INDEXING SERVICES

Access to the international biology literature is provided by some of the
most extensive indexing services currently published: *Biological Abstracts*,
Biological Abstracts/RRM, *The Zoological Record*, and *Current Awareness in Biological Sciences* (formerly *International Abstracts of Biological
Sciences*). Whether a journal is covered by an available index is an important factor to consider when evaluating new titles for a collection.

Literature Reviews

Biological literature reviews published in periodicals and in other serials
and annuals are another source of information when making collection
development decisions. These bibliographic essays on specific subjects can
serve as checklists against which the current periodical titles in a biological
collection can be compared. Since such a large number of serials are
mentioned in these checklists, they are not listed in the Selection Sources
bibliography at the end of this essay. However, complete bibliographical
information may be obtained from *Ulrich's*.

Biology journals that regularly publish literature reviews include *Quarterly Review of Biology, BBA Reviews on Bioenergetics, Aquatic Botany, Biological Reviews, Botanical Review, Experimental Mycology, Cell, Journal of Histochemistry and Cytochemistry, Journal of Human Evolution, Microbiological Reviews, Journal of Cell Science, Physiological Reviews, Comparative Biochemistry and Physiology,* and *BBA Reviews on Biomembranes.*

Several titles beginning *Annual Review of . . .* and *Advances in . . .* contain extensive literature reviews on various subjects within the scope of the individual titles. In the *Annual Reviews,* major biological concepts are reviewed every five to eight years, since a wide variety of topics is considered. Titles of importance in biology include *Annual Review of: Biochemistry, Biophysics and Bioengineering, Ecology and Systematics, Entomology, Genetics, Immunology, Microbiology, Physiology, Phytopathology,* and *Plant Physiology.* There are *Advances in: Anatomy, Embryology and Cell Biology, Biology, Applied Biology, Applied Microbiology, Botanical Research, Cell Culture, Comparative Physiology and Biochemistry, Ecological Research, Genetics, Insect Physiology, Parasitology, the Biosciences,* and *Virus Research,* among others.

Literature reviews on specific subjects are indexed in the *Index to Scientific Reviews.* This tool is very useful for continuing evaluations of a biological collection, when new degree programs are initiated, or when faculty members representing new research interests in the biological sciences join an institution.

Published bibliographies such as the *Photosynthesis Bibliography* or *The Lynn Index: A Bibliography of Phytochemistry,* and series such as the *Benchmark Papers in: Biological Concepts, Ecology, Systematic and Evolutionary Biology,* and *Genetics* can be used in a similar assessment process. The *Benchmark Papers* series offer a historical approach and are mainly useful for retrospective collection development.

Several biology series should be noted because of their consistently high quality. These include *Methods in Enzymology, Virology Monographs, Ciba Foundation Symposia, Developments in Endocrinology, Symposia of the Society for General Microbiology, Cambridge Monographs in Experimental Biology, Current Topics in Microbiology and Immunology, Progress in Botany, Molecular Biology, Monographs on Theoretical and Applied Genetics, Monographs of the Physiological Society, Ecological Studies, Ultrastructure in Biological Systems,* and *Wildlife Behavior and Ecology.* Others are *Cell Biology Monographs, Encyclopedia of Plant Physiology* (new series), *Handbook of Physiology, Zoophysiology* (formerly *Zoophysiology and Ecology*), *International Series on Pure and Applied Biology* (biology, plant physiology, zoology and physiological sci-

> *Quarterly Review of Biology.* Stony Brook, N.Y.: Stony Brook Foundation,
> Inc., State Univ. of New York, 1926– . Quarterly.
> Scholarly journal.
> 150 or so reviews and listings an issue. Some publications are "merely
> listed, others are given brief notices, most receive regular critical reviews,
> and a few are featured in lead reviews."
> 12–24-month time lag between publication date and most reviews.
> Reviews are classified in broad subject categories such as history, philosophy
> and ethics; general biology; molecular biology; etc. Monographs, volumes in
> series, and conference publications spanning the biological sciences are included.

ences divisions), *Developments in Cell Biology, Developments in Plant Biology,* and *Cold Spring Harbor Symposia on Quantitative Biology.*

PERIODICALS FEATURING REVIEWS

The *Quarterly Review of Biology* is the outstanding review source for biological sciences. The publication covers approximately 150 reviews and listings per issue in a subject-classified arrangement including history, general biology, paleontology, cellular, genetics and evolution, reproduction and development, microbiology, botany, zoology, and environment. Relatively inexpensive, it is an exceptional source of timely comments on biological publications. Longer reviews are given to publications of special significance, and all regular reviews are signed. Newly published books are listed without comments, and the editors provide brief notices for symposia volumes. Each issue includes an index to books received.

Bioscience publishes up to twenty signed reviews and a list of books received in each monthly issue. *Nature* and *Science* also publish numerous scientific book reviews, including many of bioscience publications. These weeklies are quite prompt in reviewing most materials soon after publication.

Biologisches Zentralblatt features fifty to eighty reviews of mongraphs, serials, and proceedings in each bimonthly issue. Most are in German, although an occasional review in English can be found. The coverage is international in scope. *Ecology* reviews five to twenty books per bimonthly issue, and the listings of books received indicate which titles are currently in review. Reviews are critical and signed by the reviewer.

The quarterly issues of the *Transactions of the Biochemical Society, London,* except those with abstracts of the society's symposia, contain signed reviews of biochemistry and physiology monographs, series, and symposia, as well as a list of publications received. Some of these are reviewed in subsequent issues.

FEBS Letters publishes numbered lists of monographs and series received, and book reviews of biological chemistry-oriented publications.

Nature. London: Macmillan Journals Ltd., 1869- . Weekly.
   Scholarly journal.
   4–6 signed, critical reviews in each issue.
   Reviews usually follow publication by 3–6 months.
   A classified checklist of recent scientific publications is included
      periodically.
A *Nature* review supplement focuses primarily on biological science journals but covers other sciences as well, and has appeared annually since 1981. English-language monographs, volumes in series, and a few videocassettes dealing with all aspects of science and technology are possibilities for *Nature*'s "Book Reviews" column. *Nature*'s timely articles on all branches of science are a good source of information for librarians trying to keep abreast of recent scientific developments.

Trends in Biochemical Science has book review supplements in approximately two issues per volume with fifteen to twenty reviews; in other issues fewer reviews are published. Annuals and symposia proceedings receive good coverage by members of the international scientific community.

In the field of botany, *Current Advances in Plant Science* publishes announcements of new journal titles, as well as more descriptive reviews of monographs, series, and symposia proceedings. For all publications listed, the reviewers indicate the audience to be served by the publication, the frequency, if applicable, and a contents listing. Monthly issues of the *Journal of Experimental Botany* review three to twelve works, including reference titles and symposia. The *Bulletin of the Torrey Botanical Club*'s quarterly issues cover a total of about twenty reviews per year. An additional feature is the "Index to American Botanical Literature" in each issue, which may serve as a checklist for collection development in botany.

Three noteworthy periodicals feature book reviews about genetics and evolution. The *American Journal of Human Genetics* reviews about thirty titles per year, including symposia. A separate list of books received for review is published in most issues. *Evolution* includes two to six signed reviews in each bimonthly issue. Each bimonthly issue of *Heredity* also contains reviews and books received.

The *Journal of Applied Bacteriology* includes five to ten reviews of monographs and series in each bimonthly issue. The publication also lists books received for review, and occasionally presents abstracts of papers from symposia. *Comparative Biochemistry and Physiology, Pt. A. Comparative Physiology* publishes approximately thirty reviews per year of titles in physiology.

Ornithology publications are well reviewed by *Auk*, *Condor*, *Ibis*, and the *Wilson Bulletin*. Since coverage does overlap, reviews of the same title can be compared. *Auk* reviews about fifty titles per year; *Condor* includes three to twenty reviews in the "Recent Publications" section of each issue; *Ibis* reviews five to twenty monographs, series, proceedings, etc., in each issue; and the *Wilson Bulletin* covers about forty titles per year. A great variety of materials are reviewed, probably due to the more popular nature of birding. Sound recordings, exhibits, checklists, directories, etc., are included for review.

In addition to reviews of titles in ornithology, *Auk* publishes the feature "Recent Literature" under the auspices of the American Ornithologists' Union, and *Ibis* includes a section in each issue of periodical article citations arranged by subject. The use of such lists as checklists was discussed above.

Systematic Zoology extensively reviews approximately twenty monographs, published proceedings, etc., per year. Some reviews refer to earlier publications and may be useful in retrospective purchases. In each volume the *Journal of Protozoology* publishes about twenty reviews of titles on the biology of unicellular organisms. The German journal *Zeitschrift fuer Tierpsychologie* has approximately thirty reviews per volume. The reviews are signed, and some are in English.

Technical Reports

Government Reports Announcements and Index of the National Technical Information Service (NTIS) compiles reports in the biological and medical sciences in category six of the *Index*. Approximately eight of the subcategories are directly related to biological science. A selective dissemination of information (SDI) service, Selected Research in Microfiche (SRIM), is available for all subject categories, or individual reports can be ordered from NTIS. The SRIM service includes a quarterly index and an annual cumulation for the SDI profile.

Retrospective Monographic Selection

Retrospective purchasing may be necessary to support a history of science program or to fill gaps in some of the collections that do not become rapidly outdated. Natural history, descriptive taxonomy, morphology and anatomy, and paleontology are some of these areas in which information remains useful for long periods of time.

Bibliographies that may be useful when considering retrospective purchases include *A Guide to the History of Science* and *History of the Life Sciences*. The latter has excellent annotations. *Isis*, a history of science journal, publishes bibliographies in each volume, and these are cumulated in the *Isis Cumulative Bibliography*. Biographical information is often available in *Biographisch-literarisches Handwörterbuch zur Geschichte der exakten Wissenschaften* and *Biographisch-literarisches Handwörterbuch der exakten Naturwissenschaften.*

Summary

Numerous new serial titles and monographs in biology are published each year. Researchers and instructors will require access to that new information promptly, because biological research depends on current and timely information. Collection development librarians must thus be able to identify appropriate materials before or soon after they are published so that they can be acquired when the information is most useful. Building a balanced collection that effectively supports instruction and research requires selectors to utilize numerous sources of information about biological publications.

Selection Sources

Current Advances in Plant Science. v.1– . 1972– . Oxford: Sciences, Engineering, Medical, & Business Data, Ltd. Monthly.

Government Reports Announcements and Index. v.75– . 1975– . Springfield, Va.: National Technical Information Service. Biweekly; cumulated annually by *Government Reports Annual Index.*

Index to Scientific Reviews. v.1– . 1974– . Philadelphia: Institute for Scientific Information. Semiannually.

Malinowsky, H. Robert, and Jeanne M. Richardson, *Science and Engineering Literature: A Guide to Reference Sources.* 3rd ed. Littleton, Colo.: Libraries Unlimited, 1980.

National Translations Center. *Translations Register Index.* v.1– . 1967– . Chicago: The Center. Monthly.

Neu, John, ed. *Isis Cumulative Bibliography, 1966–1975.* v.1– . 1980– . London: Mansell. Irregularly.

Poggendorff, Johann C. *Biographisch-literarisches Handwörterbuch der exakten Naturwissenschaften.* v.7. Ed. by R. Zaunick, H. Salie, and L. Weichsel. Berlin: Akademie-Verlag, 1955– .

———. *Biographisch-literarisches Handwörterbuch zur Geschichte der exakten Wissenschaften.* 6v. Leipzig: Barth, 1863–1904; Verlag Chemie, 1925–40.

Quarterly Review by Biology. v.1– . 1926– . Stony Brook, N.Y.: Stony Brook Foundation, Inc. Quarterly.

Sarton, George. *A Guide to the History of Science.* Waltham, Mass.: Chronica Botanica Co., 1952.

Sheehy, Eugene P., comp. *Guide to Reference Books.* 9th ed. Chicago: American Library Assn., 1976. Supplements, 1980 and 1982.

Smit, Pieter. *History of the Life Sciences.* New York: Hafner Pr., 1974.

Smith, Roger C. *Smith's Guide to the Literature of the Life Sciences.* 9th ed. Minneapolis: Burgess, 1980.

Walford, A. J., ed. *Walford's Guide to Reference Materials.* 4th ed. London: Library Assn., 1980.

Whitrow, Magda, ed. *Isis Cumulative Bibliography.* 5v. London: Mansell, 1971–82.

Williams, Trevor I., ed. *Guide to World Science.* 2nd ed. 24v. Guernsey, U. K.: Francis Hodgson, 1974–76.

CHEMISTRY

John Pinzelik

Chemistry is the science that attempts to describe and explain the composition of matter and the changes matter undergoes. As a discipline, chemistry has two primary functions: first, to determine and to elucidate the chemical and physical properties of substances, and second, to develop and to control chemical processes for specific goals.

Chemistry is sometimes called the fundamental science because it rests on the foundation of mathematics and physics, and in turn underlies the sciences of life: biology and medicine. One fully understands a living system when one understands the chemical reactions and the chemical influences that operate within it.

There are two major divisions of chemistry: organic chemistry and inorganic chemistry. Organic chemistry is the chemistry of carbon compounds; inorganic chemistry is the chemistry of the noncarbon compounds. The sheer size of this body of knowledge, however, requires a more systematic organization. One may subdivide chemistry into areas based on related compounds, methods or systems such as alkaloid chemistry, analytical chemistry, or industrial chemistry. A more detailed organization of the subject of chemistry is found in *Chemical Abstracts*, a publication of the American Chemical Society. Today, *Chemical Abstracts* divides its coverage of the world's chemical literature into five major sections: Biochemistry; Organic Chemistry; Macromolecular Chemistry; Applied Chemistry and Chemical Engineering; and Physical and Analytical Chemistry. This classification system reflects the current publication coverage of the Chemical Abstracts Service; thus, it is a reasonable mirror of the structure of the discipline of chemistry of today.

The profession of chemistry had its roots during the nineteenth century, when scientists began to specialize. A pattern of research and chemical education was established in Germany that soon became imitated throughout the Western world. Along with this growth was the development of chemical societies and journals devoted to chemistry. The scientific journal became the major medium for the communication of information.

Direction of Research

Chemists study systems of atoms and molecules from temperatures near absolute zero to temperatures as high as those found on the sun. Properties of matter are also investigated both at very low pressures, as that found in intersteller space, and at very high pressures, as that found at the earth's core. The diversity of research chemists undertake is evident in the problems that underlie many aspects of modern life: human health, food and energy needs, and increasing environmental concerns. New chemical findings concerning AIDS or diabetes or the synthesis of a gene are as exciting as the discovery of insulin more than sixty years ago. Chemists continue to use their skills to find answers to questions concerning the creation of life, energy, and the environment. The variety of information resources for chemists is therefore as diverse as the directions of their research. The many resources for selecting chemistry library collections that follow are evidence of this diverse nature of chemistry and the large body of literature that supports its research.

Overview and Guides

Selection decisions are particularly challenging in chemistry collections because of the variety of primary, secondary, and tertiary sources; increasing specialization; expansion of interdisciplinary research; and escalating costs. For these reasons, a strong collection development program is a necessity. The role of individual chemistry faculty members or a faculty advisory committee is vital in suggesting titles for a collection, but the librarian must accept the responsibility for all library purchases.

The goals of a good collection development policy are determined by the needs of users and use of the materials. The strengths and weaknesses of the collection, the available fiscal resources, and the amount of clerical support are important considerations in determining the magnitude of this program.

The discipline of chemistry has had guides to the literature for more than sixty years. Several important ones have been published recently. The *Guide to Basic Information Sources in Chemistry* is primarily bibliographic in nature. *Use of Chemical Literature, Literature Matrix of Chemistry, How to Find Chemical Information, Chemical Publications; Their Nature and Use, Die Chemische Literatur: ihre Erschliessung und Ben-*

utzung, and *Chemical Information; A Practical Guide to Utilization* are more specific sources devoted to this subject. These titles will be helpful to anyone responsible for developing a collection in chemistry.

Undergraduate and graduate textbooks also may provide useful bibliographies if they are not too limited in scope or out-of-date.

In charting a collection program, it is quite sensible to look first to the American Chemical Society (ACS) for direction. Its *Guidelines and Suggested Title List for Undergraduate Chemistry Libraries* gives practical advice for building an undergraduate chemistry collection. In addition, this compilation provides a list of over 700 books in the areas of analytical, biological, inorganic, organic, and physical chemistry, and should certainly be a checklist for any library devoted to chemistry.

Earlier editions of some of these guides are helpful in retrospective collection development. A useful list of books about chemical literature is found in Antony's *Guide to Basic Information Sources in Chemistry* and Mellon's *Chemical Publications: Their Nature and Use.* A list of the major, recently published reference works and books is found in Skolnik's *Literature Matrix of Chemistry.*

Journals

Since over ninety percent of citations by chemists are to journals, the acquisition, maintenance, and evaluation of this primary source should have first priority in any collection development policy.[1] The importance of journals becomes more obvious when one discovers that a major proportion of an acquisition budget for a chemistry library is usually devoted to periodicals.

Selection decisions become particularly difficult with every announcement of a new chemistry journal title and the subsequent request by an interested researcher. Price indexes for periodicals for 1983 showed that titles in chemistry and physics are again the most expensive in the twenty-four subject categories reported.[2] The average 1983 subscription price for all categories was $50.23; the average cost for chemistry and physics journals was $207.94! Although the *SCI Journal Citation Reports (JCR)* and *Chemical Abstracts Service Source Index*'s "List of 1000 Journals Most Frequently Cited in Chemical Abstracts" can be helpful in identifying the rankings of chemistry journal titles, they must be treated only as guides. The selector who is familiar with the existing collection and the library users' needs is still the best judge.

1. Richard Heinzkill, "Characteristics of Reference in Selected Scholarly English Literary Journals," *Library Quarterly* 50:352–65 (July 1980).
2. Norman B. Brown and Jane Phillips, "Price Indexes for 1983: U. S. Periodicals and Serial Services," *Library Journal* 108:1659–62 (Sept. 1983).

Online Services

Another matter for chemistry librarians to deliberate is the possible role of electronic journals in collection development. A small but growing number of journals and indexing services is now available online. The American Chemical Society, for example, now provides electronic access to the full text of eighteen of its journals, while Chemical Abstracts Service offers its *Chemical Abstracts Condensates* database online. These services are not inexpensive, to be sure, but they do respond to the chemist's need for up-to-date information. Whether they will ever replace paper and microform subscriptions remains to be seen.

Review Journals

The review literature is vital to the scientific community today. Timely overviews of research areas and the evaluations of the literature are of immeasurable value to scientists and scholars. These titles at one time were few in number; today titles with *Advances*, *Annual Review*, *Special Report Series*, or even *Topics* seem to proliferate on library shelves. Their selection for a chemistry collection is not a simple matter, and many of the same concerns as with primary journals must be faced when making decisions for the acquisition of this secondary source.

Chemical Reviews has been published by the American Chemical Society since 1924 and is the standard for review titles. On the same level are the titles of the Specialist Report Series published by the Royal Society of Chemistry. Nearly fifty different titles to date have been published, with some volumes exceeding $150.

The Royal Society's *Index of Reviews in Organic Chemistry* (*IROC*) and *Index of Reviews in Analytical Chemistry* (*IRAC*) may also be useful in the decision making for purchasing reviews. These compilations index all the titles in the Specialist Report Series published by the society in addition to many review, monographic, and conference titles found in the world's chemical literature.

Monographs

Perusing announcements and catalogs from the major publishers in chemistry is one of the best means to keep up with the publication of new books in chemistry. Ten of the major publishers who are quite productive in chemical publication are: Academic Press, Butterworths, CRC Press, Chapman & Hall, Marcel Dekker, McGraw-Hill, Pergamon Press, Sprin-

Journal of Chemical Education. v.1– . 1924– . Easton, Pa.: American
   Chemical Society, Div. of Chemical Education. Monthly.
   Professional Journal.
   3–5 signed, critical book reviews plus a listing of several "Titles of
      Interest" are included in each issue.
Most reviews cover chemistry textbooks that were published within the past
three to twelve months. Some of the "Titles of Interest" citations include descriptive annotations. Monographs, symposia publications, new periodical titles,
and volumes from continuing series are likely to be announced in this section.
Timely articles and features about new products and services make this an
informative source about developments in the field of chemical education.

ger-Verlag, Verlag Chemie, and John Wiley & Sons. The major society
publishers, the American Chemical Society and the Royal Society of Chemistry, also distribute announcements of current books and catalogs of
interest to the collection builder in chemistry.

Book reviews in selected journals are also important to the selection
process for specialized collections. Reviews found in *Science, Nature,
Journal of Chemical Education*, and the *Journal of the American Chemical
Society* should be read by the librarian and routed, if necessary, to appropriate members of the library committee and/or chemistry faculty for
recommendation. Unfortunately, some of the reviews do not appear until
months or longer after publication and may have only limited value in
the selection process for current books.

The journals listed above also print lists of recently received books
without reviews. These are particularly useful because, unlike the announcements received from publishers, they are fairly reliable indicators
of availability.

The titles and the tables of contents of many review/monographic
volumes in the "Recent Reviews" section of the *Journal of Organic Chemistry* are helpful additions to this primary journal. A similar feature found
in weekly issues of *Current Contents: Physical, Chemical & Earth Sci-*

Journal of the American Chemical Society. v.1– . 1879– . Washington, D. C.:
   American Chemical Society. Biweekly.
   Scholarly journal.
   1–25 reviews per issue; most are less than a column in length.
   Lag time between publication and review varies from 6 months to 5 years.
Monographs, volumes in series, and conference proceedings relating to all areas
of chemical research are reviewed. Although most reviews appear too late to
meet current collection development needs, they do serve as a useful checklist
for titles that may have been overlooked earlier.

CA Selects: New Books in Chemistry. Columbus, Ohio: Chemical Abstract
Service. (Numerous sections are available.) Biweekly.
Alerting service.
"New Books in Chemistry" is one of the publications in the *CA Selects* series.
All monographs, volumes in series, and conference publications dealing with
chemistry and chemical engineering containing at least forty-nine pages and cited
in *Chemical Abstracts* are listed.

ences, published by the Institute for Scientific Information, are listings of
tables of contents and ordering information for selected science books.

"New Books in Chemistry" appears in *CA Selects*, a biweekly publication from the Chemical Abstracts Service. Information on new books,
monographs, series publications and conference proceedings in chemistry
and chemical engineering cited in *Chemical Abstracts* is reported.

A selector's confidence is heightened when deciding with a book in
hand, so chemistry librarians may want to consider an approval plan.
Librarians and faculty could then examine appropriate categories of books
soon after publication and return the titles they deem unsuitable for the
collection. The vendors of approval plans expect libraries to keep most
of the books, of course, or to modify the guidelines about what types of
materials should be sent.

Browsing the book exhibits at professional conferences is another way
to get to see materials before actually purchasing them. Sales representatives are usually there to answer questions and to help resolve problems.
Occasionally, conference attendees can buy books from the exhibits at
substantial discounts.

Patents

Copies of United States or foreign patent publications are generally given
a lower priority in collection development programs in university libraries
than journals and monographs, although patents are important to chemistry collections. Both United States and foreign patents can be found in
one of the more than fifty patent depository libraries. A list of these
libraries appears in the year's first issue of the *Official Gazette of the United
States Patent and Trademark Office.* Copies of both foreign and domestic
patent publications may be obtained from the commissioner of patents
at the Patent and Trademark Office in Washington, D. C. The first issue
of each volume of *Chemical Abstracts* provides information about patents
and how to acquire them.

The New York Public Library and the Sunnyvale, California, Patent
Information Clearinghouse handle requests for patents efficiently, and a

number of commercial organizations also provide rapid services. Research Publications, Inc., in Arlington, Virginia, is the official distributor for U. S. patents on microfilm. In addition to supplying patents dating back to 1790, they maintain a Rapid Patent Service for U. S. and non-U. S. patent publications. INFO/DOC, in Washington, D. C., is still another source for patents. Meanwhile, DIALOG and other online vendors are offering electronic patent delivery services.

Conclusion

No single method of selection can satisfactorily identify all the publications or services that will satisfy the needs of the teaching or research chemist. The complexity and growth of chemical information, increasing specialization, and escalating costs are major factors affecting the management of collections in chemistry. The librarian must continually monitor the entire corpus of chemical information, evaluate the available resources, and revise the collection development program to accommodate the changing needs of users and their patterns of use. The increasing availability of electronic technologies such as the online primary journals from the American Chemical Society, the online access of documents, and the development of networks will certainly alter the perceptions and procedures of chemistry selectors in years to come.

Selection Sources

Antony, Arthur. *Guide to Basic Information Sources in Chemistry*. New York: Wiley, 1979.

Bottle, R. R. *Use of Chemical Literature*. 3rd ed. Boston: Butterworths, 1979.

Brasted, Robert C., and Leallyn B. Clapp, eds. *Guidelines and Suggested Title List for Undergraduate Chemistry Libraries*. Washington, D. C.: American Chemical Society, Div. of Chemical Education and Dept. of Educational Activities, 1982.

Chemical Abstracts. v.1– . 1907– . Columbus, Ohio: Chemical Abstracts Service. Weekly.

Chemical Abstracts Service Source Index. v.1– . 1969– . Columbus, Ohio: Chemical Abstracts Service. Quarterly supplements.

Chemical Reviews. v.1– . 1924– . Columbus, Ohio: Chemical Abstracts Service. Bimonthly.

Current Contents: Physical, Chemical & Earth Sciences. v.1– . 1961– . Philadelphia: Institute for Scientific Information. Weekly.

Index of Reviews in Analytical Chemistry. v.1– . 1983– . Nottingham: Royal Society of Chemistry. Annually.

Index of Reviews in Organic Chemistry. v.1– . 1971– . Nottingham: Royal Society of Chemistry. Annually.

Journal of Chemical Education. v.1- . 1924- . Easton, Pa.: American Chemical Society, Div. of Chemical Education. Monthly.

Journal of Organic Chemistry. v.1- . 1936- . Washington, D. C.: American Chemical Society. Biweekly.

Journal of the American Chemical Society. v.1- . 1879- . Washington, D. C.: American Chemical Society. Biweekly.

Maizell, Robert E. *How to Find Chemical Information.* New York: Wiley, 1979.

Mellon, M. G. *Chemical Publications: Their Nature and Use.* 5th ed. New York: McGraw-Hill, 1982.

Mucke, Michael. *Die Chemische Literatur: ihre Erschliessung und Benutzung.* Deerfield Beach, Fla.: Verlag Chemie, 1982.

Nature. v.1- . 1869- . London: Macmillan Journals Ltd. Weekly.

Official Gazette of the United States Patent and Trademark Office. v.1- / 1872- . Washington, D. C.: U. S. Patent and Trademark Office, U. S. Department of Commerce. Weekly.

SCI Journal Citation Reports. v.1- . 1977- . Philadelphia: Institute for Scientific Information. Annually.

Science. v.1- . 1880- . Washington, D. C.: American Assn. for the Advancement of Science. Weekly.

Skolnik, Herman. *The Literature Matrix of Chemistry.* New York: Wiley, 1982.

Wolman, Yecheskel. *Chemical Information: A Practical Guide to Utilization.* New York: Wiley, 1983.

COMPUTER SCIENCE

Stanley P. Hodge

Overview and Problems

Information about computer science is growing and changing as rapidly as the technology itself. The literature, while primarily only twenty-five years old and occupying but a very small portion of any library's holdings, nevertheless describes a field that has touched nearly every facet of our lives and most academic disciplines. The use of computers is widespread in college coursework for many subjects today, and the library's collection of computer science literature will be used by those seeking information on such diverse topics as selecting a personal computer, automating an office, setting up a budget system, solving a tough programming problem, or determining the proper equations for multifactor data analysis in engineering.

As a discipline, computer science is broad in scope, heterogeneous in nature, relatively new, and rapidly changing. There is no general agreement about its structure and it is difficult to describe within well-defined boundaries. It is because of these attributes and the potentially broad applications of the library's computer science collection that a primary dictum of materials selection—know the collection's users and their interests—is a challenge.

Another formidable task that confronts the librarian embarking on a collection development project in computer science is devising an organized approach to the terminology and subject content of the field. This becomes a very real problem for those who attempt collection evaluation or strengthening projects. Several sources mentioned in this chapter provide different choices of key computer science terms and organize those terms in different arrangements.

The author gratefully acknowledges comments and suggestions from Harry Llull.

A third challenge is the wise use of a library's budget, whether limited or generous. The cost of acquiring the literature, until recently, has exceeded the inflation rate. This, combined with an explosion in computer science books and journals, makes selection more difficult. For instance, one major approval plan vendor handled 346 computer science titles in 1978. The number tripled to 1021 titles in 1983, while the average list price rose from $18.44 to $24.53.[1] The annual publication, *ACM Guide to Computer Literature*, has cited about 1000 selected computer science monographs and conference proceedings during each of the past few years.[2] In the most rapidly expanding computer science area, microcomputing, *LAMP; Literature Analysis of Microcomputer Publications* cited about 1000 reviewed books in this subfield alone in its 1983 issues.[3] These indicators, and the fact that new journals in computer science are also rapidly multiplying, demonstrate the need for a sound approach to selecting and acquiring material in computing science in order to maintain a core collection and to respond to and anticipate the needs of an expanding base of specialized users.

Terminology for Organizing the Field

Classification schemes and standard guides to computer science literature take a variety of approaches to categorizing major components and subfields of the discipline. A collection policy statement that articulates the levels of importance the various subfields have for the library's users is useful as a first step in collection development. One approach to classification is represented by using subject descriptors associated with the Library of Congress classification schedules. This is particularly useful when evaluating the strength of a library's present collection or selecting new material from various sources, e.g., *American Book Publishing Record* or *Pure and Applied Science Books, 1876–1982*, which include LC classification numbers and subject descriptors. In addition to the QA76 classification, incorporating most computer science subfields, terminology associated with the following class numbers should also be considered:

HD9696   Computer industry
HF5547.5   Office automation

1. *Approval Program Management Information Report (Subject Station)*, (Sommerville, N. J.: Baker & Taylor, 1978 and 1983).
2. *ACM Guide to Computer Literature*, v.1– . 1964– . New York: Assn. for Computing Machinery.
3. *LAMP; Literature Analysis of Microcomputer Publications*, v.1– . 1983– . (Mahwah, N. J.: Soft Images).

HF5548–48.2	Electronic data processing in business and management, word processing
HF5548.2	Computer crimes
HF5548.3	Real time processing
HF5548.5	Programming languages—business applications
KF390.5	Computer laws and legislation
LB1028.43–.5	Computer-assisted instruction
T57.6–.62	Operations research
T58.6	Management information systems
T385	Computer graphics
TA173–74	Engineering design
TK5105	Computer networks
TK7883.3	Miniature computers
TK7885	Computers—congresses, miniature computers, catalogs, etc.
TK7887	Computers—maintenance and repair, input-output equipment ·
TK7887.6	Analog-to-digital converters
TK7887.8	Computer terminals
TK7888	Electronic analog computers
TK7888.3–.4	Electronic digital computers, mini- and micro-computers—Design and construction
TK7889–95	Special computers and computer components

A second classification scheme is that found in *Computing Reviews* (*CR*), a monthly review source published by the Association for Computing Machinery (ACM). This classification system evolved from a major effort by the Taxonomy Committee of the American Federation of Information Processing Societies, which studied the structure and terminology of computer science for three years.[4] There are eleven major categories and hundreds of minor categories subdivided down to a fourth level in *CR*'s classification scheme. It is possible to synthesize and incorporate the *CR* classification table into a collection policy statement, although it is longer and much more detailed than most libraries would realistically need. However, a selection guide organized around this classification scheme would be useful for special or technical libraries or if major reliance on *CR* for current or retrospective selection is preferred. Full listings of this schedule are found in the January issues, and it is periodically expanded to reflect the latest developments in the field.

4. American Federation of Information Processing Societies, Taxonomy Committee, *Taxonomy of Computer Science & Engineering* (Arlington, Va.: AFIPS, 1980).

A more manageable list of terms that covers the broad field of computer science may be found in Darlene Myers's *Computer Science Resources; A Guide to Professional Literature.*[5] Eighty-nine important terms are used by Myers, and selected monographs and journals are categorized under these terms. The thesaurus is an alphabetical, rather than classified, arrangement. In *Library List on Undergraduate Computer Science, Computer Engineering and Information Systems,* ACM and the Institute of Electrical and Electronics Engineers (IEEE) use only twenty-eight categories to classify the literature.[6]

The taxonomical arrangements or number of terms the collection development librarian finally settles on depends on how they will be used, the depth of the collection that is desired, and familiarity with the terminology. Should teaching faculty be involved in collection policy formulation and/or materials selection, they may be more comfortable with a particular organizational arrangement or level of detail. Should only one or two selection aids be used, practicality dictates the use of their terms. It is also possible to select a broad and detailed scheme, to refine and cross-reference it in order to reflect an institution's specialized needs, and to use it in conjunction with the selection tools that will be used over time.

Serials Selection

Analyses of the computer science literature indicate that journal articles account for approximately half of the citations referenced.[7] This indicator of relative importance of primary journals is a factor that should be considered when funding priorities are considered for developing a computer science collection where research is a primary focus.

Several sources for core serial lists are available, or lists may be developed from selected abstracting/indexing sources. Although the limitations of core lists developed from citation analysis have been alluded to in Hodge and Hepfer's essay on general science and technology (pp. 231–32), these lists may provide a useful starting point for evaluating or modifying the library's present collection. If nothing else, the failure to hold a title that is on a core list can be noted for future consideration based

5. Darlene Myers, *Computer Science Resources; A Guide to Professional Literature* (White Plains, N. Y.: Knowledge Industry Publications, 1981).
6. *Library List on Undergraduate Computer Science, Computer Engineering and Information Systems* (New York and Long Beach, Calif.: Assn. for Computing Machinery and Institute of Electrical and Electronics Engineers, 1978).
7. Mary J. Culnan, "Analysis of the Information Usage Patterns of Academics and Practitioners in the Computer Field: A Citation Analysis of a National Conference Proceedings," *Information Processing & Management* 14, no. 6: 395–404 (1978); K. Subramanyam, "Core Journals in Computer Science," *IEEE Transactions on Professional Communication* PC-19: 22–25 (Dec. 1976).

on its usefulness as perceived by the collection development librarian or teaching faculty liaisons. Conversely, the presence in a collection of a serial not on any recommended source list, together with a reliable method for determining its nonuse and perceived need, may give one justification to consider its cancellation.

Core lists of journals in computer science, however, become somewhat obsolete because there is a proliferation of new journal titles in the field. For example, the twentieth (1981) edition of *Ulrich's International Periodicals Directory* lists about 500 titles categorized in the computer science subject area. In the twenty-second edition (1983) the number grew to 680 periodicals in these areas. Furthermore, some specialized titles on older core lists would no doubt have been upgraded or downgraded as various subfields in computer science strengthened or declined in their importance.

A useful and fairly current list of computer science journals is found in Darlene Myers's *Computer Science Resources: A Guide to Professional Literature.* Over 450 journals are listed by subject and title. Bibliographic information is also noted, and 100 titles are selected by Myers as an important, yet inexpensive, core group. The method for selecting these titles was not provided, however. A shorter list (62 periodicals) compiled as recommendations for an undergraduate computer science collection is found in *Library List on Undergraduate Computer Science, Computer Engineering and Information Systems.*

Some core lists based on citation analysis have also been developed. K. Subramanyan has attempted to overcome some of the drawbacks of lists based on frequency citation in his article "Core Journals in Computer Science."[8] The author combines the use of a secondary journal, *Computing Reviews*, with a primary journal, *IEEE Transactions on Computers.* The result is a list of a "few (65) very productive and highly cited primary journals" that are "indispensable in any specialized collection of computer science literature."

Hirst and Talent used five source journals and an "impact factor" based on *Journal Citation Reports* to develop a list of forty-one computer science journals. The first twenty-one titles are considered a core computer science list; the remaining twenty are noted as being important in applications fields and could be considered by librarians if interest in those applications existed. The authors also provide some suggested additions to the core list.

In order to update core lists, it is suggested that the librarian note those serials covered by recent issues of the important abstracting/indexing tools in most reference collections. For instance, the 1980 edition (published

8. K. Subramanyam, "Core Journals in Computer Science," p. 22.

Computing Reviews. v.1– . 1960– . New York: Assn. for Computing
  Machinery. Monthly.
  Reviews of current monographs and journal articles.
  20–35 critical book reviews an issue. 6–12-month lag between book
    publication and review.
  Periodical titles received listed in November issue.
Featured are signed critical book reviews by and for those in the field, reviews
that range from one to several paragraphs in length. Reviews are arranged according to a detailed and evolving topical classification. An excellent, although
highly selective source for professional and scholarly material by specialized
topics. Excludes programming and other "popular" books for the lay person.
Complete bibliographical information, including price, is provided.

in 1982) of the annual publication *ACM Guide to Computing Literature*
had 163 serial titles cited five or more times. (One's own criteria for
frequency citation can be established, of course.) The November issues
of *Computing Reviews* also list all periodical titles received, including
those not indexed in that source.

In developing the serial collection for the popular new field of microcomputing, recent issues of indexes such as *LAMP* or *Microcomputer
Index* may be used as a source for journal titles to consider. Librarians
will find that one of the most useful and inexpensive sources on microcomputer journals is *Microcomputing Periodicals: An Annotated Directory*. Revised about twice each year through the microcomputer production of camera-ready copy, this source provides an alphabetized list of
microcomputer indexes, periodicals, journal name changes, and cessations.
Although this source attempts to be comprehensive (843 active titles cited
in its tenth edition) rather than selective, the subject and geographical
indexes, as well as brief annotations, provide some guidance for selecting
titles appropriate to specific topics, computers, and program languages.
Current publishers' addresses and journal frequencies and prices are also
noted for each entry.

The purchase of retrospective holdings is always a consideration when
selecting serials. A note of caution is advisable with regard to the importance of backfiles in computing science. One study of the journal citations
made by academicians and practitioners indicated that the median age of
the computer science journal literature cited was only two years. These
data also indicated that the frequency of citations to journal articles in
computer science fell off very sharply at around five to six years.[9]

9. Culnan, "Analysis of the Information Usage Patterns," p. 402.

Monographs and Conference Proceedings Selection

AIDS AND REVIEW SOURCES

Monographs and conference proceedings are second only to journals in the computing science field. These will be covered by focusing first on those selection tools that cover the very current literature but are less selective, and then turning to those more selective, but devoted primarily to retrospective collection development.

Forthcoming book announcements by publishers are often a primary method of current awareness for teaching faculty and subject bibliographers. Certain publishers are notable for a high output of titles in computing science, and announcements or periodic catalogs devoted to computer science material from these publishers would be useful if selection before or concurrent with publication date is important. Based on a survey of the monographic literature covered by the 1982 edition of the *ACM Guide to Computer Literature*, the following are the most prolific publishers of computer science monographs and conference proceedings:

Academic Press
Addison-Wesley
American Federation of
   Information Processing
   Societies (AFIPS)
Association for Computing
   Machinery (ACM)
Auerbach
Cambridge University Press
Creative Strategies International
Elsevier North-Holland
Hemisphere Publishing
Heydan & Sons
Infotech
Institute of Electrical and
   Electronics Engineers (IEEE)

International Federation for
   Information Processing (IFIP)
MIT Press
Osborne/McGraw-Hill
Petrocelli Books
Plenum Press
Prentice-Hall
Reston Publishing
Howard W. Sams
Springer-Verlag
TAB Books (Blue Ridge Summit,
   Pa.)
Van Nostrand Reinhold Co.
Wadsworth Publishing Co.
John Wiley & Sons
Winthrop

For a listing of important computer science institutes, societies, etc., that publish, refer to Myers's *Computer Science Resources.*

A review of current issues of the *American Book Publishing Record* in the 001.64 classification provides another unselective, but current, source of domestically distributed monographs in computer science. The best current sources with bibliographic information on conference proceedings are Interdok's *Directory of Published Proceedings: Series SEMT* and the

Institute for Scientific Information's *Index to Scientific and Technical Proceedings*. The latter is more selective. Monthly issues of *Computer & Control Abstracts* also provide a fairly current "subsidiary index" of conference papers.

The major review sources fall between the unselective current awareness tools and selective bibliographies. The delay factor inherent in these tools may range from a few months to over a year. *Computing Reviews* has previously been mentioned as the major source of reviews for computer science. This monthly journal aims to furnish computer-oriented persons with critical information about current publications in all areas of the computing sciences. It includes often lengthy and signed reviews of seventeen to thirty-five books per issue. Citations are divided by topics such as hardware, software, theory, applications, computing milieu, etc. Books on electronics and computer science are also covered by *Institute of Electrical and Electronics Engineers Proceedings*. These monthly issues have authoritative and lengthy book reviews reprinted from other IEEE publications as well as brief descriptions of additional books on these topics.

Useful, but less comprehensive, are the "telegraphic reviews" in issues of *American Mathematical Monthly*. Each issue includes up to twenty-five very short, signed, critical book reviews of computing science monographs. Books are identified as being texts, supplementary or professional reading, or as being suitable for undergraduate libraries. More extensive reviews may appear in the *Monthly*'s book review section. Reviews lag about one year after publication date. Classification is very general: computer programming, computer literacy, computer science, or software systems. The primary advantage of this source is the provision of a quick, convenient, authoritative check of commercially published books and their suitability for a library's collection rather than as a tool for developing specific areas of a collection.

An excellent index to reviews on microcomputer publications is found in *LAMP; Literature Analysis of Microcomputer Publications*. This bimonthly index began in 1983 and includes reviews for books as well as periodicals, educational courseware, films, hardware, software, and video and computer games. The majority of reviews are accompanied by one to five stars that indicate the reviewers' ratings, ranging from poor to excellent. Complete bibliographical information for both the review journal and the material being reviewed is provided. This is an excellent aid in selecting more popular material sometimes neglected in scholarly review sources.

RETROSPECTIVE SELECTION

The field of computer applications is rapidly changing, and much of the popular literature becomes quickly dated. Selective guides to retrospective

Myers, Darlene. *Computer Science Resources: A Guide to Professional Literature.* White Plains, N. Y.: Knowledge Industry Publications, 1981. Guide to the literature.

    Over 800 recommended books. Over 450 recommended journals. Over 140 recommended technical report series. Over 100 recommended indexes, abstracts, and other reference tools. Sources of computer center newsletters. Selected listing of major computer science conference proceedings.

    Index to major computer science publishers.

Serials and monographs are categorized by important subject terms and full bibliographic information is provided for these two formats. An excellent resource tool and overview of the types of literature. Recommendations could be used to build a retrospective core collection. Names and addresses of important computer science institutes, societies, and publishers are listed.

---

monographs have limited value here, but this is less the case in some theoretical areas. However, those interested in selecting a core collection or strengthening retrospective holdings in specific subfields will find the following bibliographic tools still quite useful. Fairly recent selective lists appear in the *Library List on Undergraduate Computer Science, Computer Engineering and Information Systems.* This source selects nearly 1300 monographs categorized under twenty-eight topics. Imprint dates are primarily in the early and mid 1970s.

Darlene Myers's *Computer Science Resources: A Guide to Professional Literature* provides more than 800 titles (most published in late 1970s), categorized under about ninety subject headings. Selection for inclusion was based on patron usage at the University of Washington.

The seventeenth edition of the *Annual Bibliography of Computer-oriented Books* contains about 1200 recently published books divided into over sixty categories. This bibliography, also published in the January issues of *Computing Newsletter for Instructors of Data Processing*, provides author, title, publisher, date, pagination, and indicates whether the book is a text, reference source, or handbook. It provides the librarian with an inexpensive, updated, selective guide, and is highly recommended as a tool to assist in building a large core collection of current titles or to strengthen specific parts of the collection. Its focus is on business and social science applications, programming languages, systems design, and microcomputers, rather than on theory and scientific/engineering applications. Each succeeding edition adds a few hundred new titles and drops older ones.

The *ACM Guide to Computing Literature* provides a listing by author of about 1000 monographs each year. It is international in scope and emphasizes scholarly, rather than popular, material. There are two disadvantages to this source: there is no convenient subject arrangement for

Annual Bibliography of Computer-oriented Books. v.1- . 1967?- . Colorado
Springs: Center for Cybernetics Systems Synergism. Annually.
Recommended list of 1200 recently published monographs.
Organized by subject categories. Updated annually. Basic bibliographic
information, type, and style of book indicated.
A selective guide to recently published titles that may be used as a checklist or
to build a core collection. Emphasis is on business applications, programming
languages, systems design, and microcomputing. A convenient, inexpensive, and
fairly current source.

books, and the *Guide* has been published two years following the material
it covers. ACM has promised to correct this delay in the future, however.

The references included at the end of each chapter of the *Encyclopedia
of Computer Science and Technology* provide selective sources on the
hundreds of specialized computer topics covered by this encyclopedia.

Another helpful tool is a new addition from R.R. Bowker's subject
databases—*Computer Books and Serials in Print, 1984*. Although unselective, this source provides bibliographic data on nearly 12,000 U. S. and
foreign books, government publications, pamphlets, and about 1500 serial
titles relating to some aspect of computer science. Citations are arranged
under LC subject headings, and indexed by author and title. Another
section provides publishers' names and addresses. This tool is a convenient
source for locating bibliographic information or gaining access to in-print
material by subdiscipline.

In addition to the above retrospective selection tools, in-depth collection building in specific areas of computer science will be aided by referring
to specialized bibliographies, many of which cite monographs and conference proceedings. An excellent source that conveniently lists bibliographies on computer science subfields that may be "hidden" in journals
is the monthly listing in *Computer & Control Abstracts'* "Bibliography
Index of Articles." An example of one such article cited is Gunther F.
Schrack's "Gaining Access to the Literature of Computer Graphics."[10] Not
only does the article include a seventy-five item selective bibliography, but
it surveys the literature of computer graphics in a bibliographic essay.

Conclusion

Librarians should be aware of prevailing trends having an impact on materials selection in computer science. For example, "hot topics" such as

10. Gunther F. Schrack, "Gaining Access to the Literature of Computer Graphics," *IEEE
Transactions on Education* E-26: 7–10 (Feb. 1983).

robotics, CAD/CAM, speech systems, and vision will stimulate more demand for current literature on these subjects.

Automation itself is affecting reference tools and accessibility to the literature of computer science. Several online databases may now be used to access computing science literature by subject, and in some cases may be successfully employed in conjunction with collection development. Some of the major ones pertinent to computer science include *Inspec, NTIS, Compendex, Electrical Engineering Meetings, Mathfile, Computer Database,* and *Microcomputer Index.* Details on these databases are provided in the *Directory of Online Databases.*

Automation is also changing the methods of communication between those within the field. And, despite the fact that computing science continues to evolve and develop specialized subfields, its literature is becoming more interdisciplinary as the application of computing science expands into other subjects.

Selection Sources

ACM Guide to Computer Literature. v.1- . 1964- . New York: Assn. for Computing Machinery. Annually.

American Book Publishing Record. v.1- . 1960- . New York: Bowker. Annually.

American Mathematical Monthly. v.1- . 1894- . Washington, D. C.: Mathematical Assn. of America. Monthly.

Annual Bibliography of Computer-oriented Books. v.1- . 1967?- . Colorado Springs: Center for Cybernetics Systems Synergism. Annually.

Computer & Control Abstracts. Science Abstracts, Section C. v.1- . 1966- . Piscataway, N. J.; Herts, England: Inspec I.E.E.

Computer Books and Serials in Print, 1984. New York: Bowker, 1984.

Computing Reviews. v.1- . 1960- . New York: Assn. for Computing Machinery. Monthly.

Directory of Online Databases. v.1- . 1979- . Santa Monica, Calif.: Cuadra Associates. Quarterly.

Directory of Published Proceedings: Series SEMT. v.1- . 1965- . Harrison, N. Y.: Interdok Corp. 10/year with annual and quinquennial cumulations.

Encyclopedia of Computer Science and Technology. 16v. New York: Dekker, 1975–81.

Hirst, Graeme, and Nadia Talent. "Computer Science Journals—An Integrated Citation Analysis." *IEEE Transactions in Professional Communication* PC–20: 233–38 (Dec. 1977).

Index to Scientific and Technical Proceedings. v.1- . 1978- . Philadelphia: Institute for Scientific Information. Monthly with annual cumulations.

Institute of Electrical and Electronics Engineers Proceedings. v.1- . 1913- . Piscataway, N. J.: I.E.E.E. Monthly.

LAMP; Literature Analysis of Microcomputer Publications. v.1- . 1983- . Mahwah, N. J.: Soft Images. Bimonthly.

Library List on Undergraduate Computer Science, Computer Engineering and Information Systems. New York and Long Beach, Calif.: Assn. for Computing Machinery and Institute of Electrical and Electronics Engineers, 1978.

Microcomputer Index. v.1– . 1980– . Santa Clara, Calif.: Microcomputer Information Services. Bimonthly.

Myers, Darlene. *Computer Science Resources; A Guide to Professional Literature*. White Plains, N. Y.: Knowledge Industry Publications, 1981.

Pure and Applied Science Books 1876–1982. New York: Bowker, 1982.

Shirinian, George. *Microcomputing Periodicals: An Annotated Directory*. 10th ed. Toronto, Ont.: G. Shirinian, 1984. (Available from author, 53 Fraserwood Ave., #2, Toronto M6B 2N6.)

GEOLOGY

Russell Fulmer

We live on the earth and constantly experience its presence around us. From it comes our food, the raw materials for our clothes, shelter, and civilization. Mankind has used and abused the earth throughout history. The earth is far older than human history and people, for all their time on the earth, have marveled at the presence around them. The earth is old, and seems changeless but, in an instant, cataclysmic forces can erupt. Explanations have been sought from the gods for these changes since our earliest predecessors could comprehend the effect of earth's forces in their lives, and it is from such speculation that the modern scientific theories and laws comprising geology have evolved. In the quest for the rational explanation of why things are as they are, history has come from the supernatural to the natural. Geology is the rational study of the earth and the forces affecting the changes observed on and within the planet. The modern quest for a rational explanation of the universe takes this study to extraterrestrial worlds, and new chapters are now being written for history of the moon, planets, and the cosmos.

In the beginning, geology confined itself to the study of rocks and how they developed. Specialization began as individual aspects of the earth and its history were studied. Petrology, mineralogy, sedimentology, stratigraphy, and geomorphology have now become distinct disciplines within the framework of geology. The effects of water and air on the earth have created hydrology, oceanography and marine geology, soil science, and weathering. The physical forces active upon the planet are now investigated in geophysics, while geochemistry studies the chemical changes that natural phenomena bring to the earth. Interest in the history of the earth and life itself is covered in paleontology, paleoclimatology, paleogeography, and historical geology. The uses of geology are not limited to the academic

The author wishes to thank Judy Rieke and Marilyn M. Stark for their helpful comments and suggestions.

281

study of why the earth is as it is, but also include practical applications to benefit mankind and civilization. Engineering applications in geophysics enable us to cope with life in earthquake and volcanic zones, economic geology studies the uses to which the earth can be put, and environmental geology studies ways to prevent abuse to this fragile world and all life on it.

The diversification of studies under the general heading of geology goes even further than listed here, but for purposes of this essay is confined to those areas closest to the original meaning of geology, the study of the earth and the forces acting upon it. More detail is given to the various forms in which geologic information comes than in an analysis of geology's academic disciplines. Curricula and depth of study on the graduate and undergraduate level determine the breadth of coverage needed by a university, as does research.

Guides to the Geological Literature

The basic principles of material selection apply to the geological sciences, and these are well covered in the general sections of this book. This essay will focus on the major in-print sources for identifying and selecting appropriate library materials including field guides, government documents, maps, proceedings, and those "class" publications that must be acquired for study and research in the geological sciences. The use of exchange and gift programs and antiquarian book dealers is also discussed, as these material sources help insure adequate coverage. The strategies proposed may apply primarily to the institution in which this author has experience, but they do suggest that imagination and a positive attitude for the task at hand are the first requirements for successful selection in geology—and everything else.

Space does not permit an exhaustive bibliographic listing, and this essay should not be considered a comprehensive text for sources in the geological sciences; the titles listed below, however, cover the vast majority and will be very useful to any selector aspiring to build a large research collection. John W. Mackay's *Sources of Information for the Literature of Geology: An Introductory Guide* is a good, if brief, review of the field, although it is now a decade old. *Geological Reference Sources* by Dederick C. Ward, Marjorie W. Wheeler, and Robert A. Bier, Jr., provides an easy-to-use classified guide and includes a survey divided by geographic regions. The first ten pages are an excellent introduction to acquisitions in this subject area. If a lengthier text is desired, the *Use of Earth Sciences Literature*, edited by D. N. Wood, is most useful.

Bibliography and Index of Geology. v.32– . 1968– . Boulder, Colo.:
Geological Society of America in cooperation with the American
Geological Institute. Monthly with annual indexes.
Indexing service.
International in scope.
Author and subject indexes provide access to entries divided into 29 broad
categories. Coverage includes books, papers, and maps on geology. The bibli-
ography continues *Bibliography and Index of Geology Exclusive of North
America* (v.1–31. 1933–68).

For current reviews and information on what is happening in the field,
the librarian in the geological sciences can find much help in journals such
as *Geoscience Documentation*, published bimonthly by Geosystems in
London. Another information resource is the Geoscience Information
Society's *GIS Newsletter*, containing articles, news, meeting announcements, and lists of new maps, books, and serials. The society also publishes
pertinent papers annually in its *Proceedings*.

The *Bibliography and Index of Geology*, called the "Bib," of the American Geological Institute is the major bibliographic tool covering monographs (including dissertations, serials, proceedings, etc.) for the geological
sciences. It is published monthly and was formed by combining the coverage of the Institute's *Bibliography and Index of Geology Exclusive of
North America* and the United States Geological Survey's (USGS) *Bibliography of North American Geology*, which ceased publication in 1970.
There are indexes in each issue as well as an annual index. For all practical
purposes, complete world coverage is gained by combining the "Bib" with
the relevant sections of the French *Bulletin Signalétique*, published by the
Centre National de la Recherche Scientifique and Bureau de Recherches
Géologiques et Minières, and the *Referativnyi Zhurnal* of the Academy
of Sciences of the USSR. Because of the language factor and the complex
structure of the two foreign sources, the "Bib" is the easiest and most
definitive of the bibliographic and abstracting sources for the various disciplines. Others, such as *Petroleum Abstracts*, a weekly published by the
University of Tulsa's Division of Information Services since 1961, and the
quarterly *Mineralogical Abstracts*, produced for over sixty years by the
Mineralogical Society of Great Britain and the Mineralogical Society of
America, are also important.

Listings for the different subject bibliographies and abstracting sources
in the subdisciplines are found in the guides to the literature. Because the
publishing schedules of the sources delay access to the materials listed in
them, these tools are really only useful for retrospective acquisitions, and
then only if the material is still available. They need to be used in con-

junction with R. R. Bowker's *Scientific and Technical Books and Serials in Print.*

Current Selection of Monographs and Serials

The most common method of selecting books and serials is by wading through the mail with its load of publisher's catalogs and brochures, reading the review sections of the current scholarly and trade journals in the field, and going over the more current reviewing tools. Serials have not been treated separately in this essay because they are frequently reviewed in the same sources as are books. The American Geological Institute's monthly *Geotimes, Geotitles Weekly* from Geosystems in London, and *Eos*, the weekly of the American Geophysical Union, should be regularly checked because they contain the timeliest reviews. Also useful, but not as current, are *Episodes*, the quarterly official newsletter of the International Union of Geological Sciences, and *Economic Geology*, published eight times a year by the Economic Geology Publishing Company. Besides listing new books, serials, and maps, all of these are excellent sources of news, meetings, etc. Other helpful sources for identifying books and serials are accession lists from other libraries collecting in the same areas; the *Accessions List* of the USGS Library in Reston, Virginia, for example, can be very useful. Reviews of the current literature can be found in many trade journals such as *Oil and Gas Journal* or *Engineering and Mining Journal (E&MJ)*, as well as some scholarly publications like *GIS Newsletter.*

Geotimes. Alexandria, Va.: American Geological Institute, 1945– . Monthly.
   20–30 descriptive book reviews and 8–25 map citations an issue.
   6–18-months between publication and citation in the journal.
   Reviews are frequently brief statements taken from a book's preface or
      introduction.
   Relevant monographs, reference tools, conference proceedings, and maps are
   cited. The news items, articles, and advertisements in *Geotimes* provide solid
   information for librarians wishing to keep up with recent developments in the
   geological sciences.

Sources of Other Important Formats

TECHNICAL REPORTS AND CONFERENCE PROCEEDINGS

The strategies and tools for collecting technical reports are covered in Hodge and Hepfer's essay on general science and technology. This approach works well for developing an important aspect of a solid geological sciences collection.

Conference proceedings are also dealt with nicely in that chapter. They are extremely important information sources, and the geological sciences selector should make special efforts to obtain as many as are appropriate. Memberships in various societies is one way to get informed about conference proceedings and related publications. Brochures and announcements in professional journals such as *Geotimes* can also be very informative. It is also a good idea to set up a file about new conferences because, occasionally, selectors will have to initiate correspondence to determine if proceedings were actually published and, if so, how to acquire them.

FIELD TRIP GUIDEBOOKS

Field trip guidebooks are important in every geological collection. The *Union List of Geologic Field Trip Guidebooks of North America*, published by the Guidebook and Ephemeral Materials Committee of the Geoscience Information Society, is not an acquisitions tool per se, but does provide the names of the associations and societies that publish these guidebooks. Some can be acquired on standing order either through the issuing group or a jobber, but others must be ordered direct. Many field trip guidebooks do not stay in-print for very long, so ordering must be systematically maintained to prevent spotty coverage. A good, commercially available series published since 1975 is the *K/H Geology Field Guide Series*.

GOVERNMENT GEOLOGICAL PUBLICATIONS

A tremendous amount of material necessary in the geological sciences comes from the national and regional governments of the world. For the United States, the publications of the United States Geological Survey and the Bureau of Mines are a must. The easiest course of acquisitions is to be a depository library. All documents are not depository items, however, and, for those the reader is directed to the chapter on economics and political science.

No library should be without *New Publications of the U. S. Geological Survey*, published monthly with annual cumulations, or the annual *List of Bureau of Mines Publications and Articles*. The latter has ordering information after each abstract for its "Open File Reports."

State geological survey documents present acquisitions problems because there is so much inconsistency. Some states publish efficient catalogs, some accept standing orders, some participate in exchange programs, while others offer little, if any, information on what they do. Fortunately, each August issue of *Geotimes* has a listing of state agencies so librarians can

New Publications of the U.S. Geological Survey. List 1– . 1907– . Reston,
   Va.: U.S. Geological Survey. Monthly.
   Indexing service.
   200–400 entries an issue.
   Time lag between publications and citations varies from 1–2 months to 1–
      2 years.
Relevant books, bulletins, papers, circulars, periodicals, periodical articles, maps,
etc., are categorized by type of publication in this source. Subject and author
indexes provide detailed access.

correspond and build a file listing what each agency can provide. Monitoring and follow-up is recommended.

For other nations, the *Worldwide Directory of National Earth-Science
Agencies and Related International Organizations* is a good source for
locating the correct government agency for geological matters; it is updated
periodically. Federal and provincial Canadian documents can be obtained
by writing to the Geological Survey of Canada for their publication lists
and then to the responsible provincial department.

MAPS

Maps are indispensable in geological sciences collections. Luckily, most
of the important ones are listed in catalogs of materials available from
the USGS and the Geological Survey of Canada. There are also several
geological societies that publish map series that can be obtained on standing order. Numerous maps are reviewed in *Geotimes*, *Episodes*, and *Eos*.

Some vendors specialize in handling maps. One of the best in terms of
coverage and reliability is the GeoCenter Internationales Landkartenhaus
in Stuttgart, Germany. Another good source is the Geological Map Service
of the Telberg Book Corporation in Sag Harbor, New York. Experience
is the best teacher for someone trying to learn when to order maps directly
and when to use a vendor.

Exchange and Gift Programs and Out-of-Print Materials

A useful means of obtaining serials and special publications is an exchange
program. Often, one institution's publications can be exchanged with another's for a considerable savings. The problem is to determine which
institutions are publishing materials appropriate to your needs and then
to develop an exchange program that is mutually beneficial. In addition
to serials, nongovernmental technical reports can sometimes be obtained
in this manner.

A well-publicized gift solicitation program will sometimes garner significant additions to the collection. Not all donations will be valuable, of course, but worthwhile categories of materials can be acquired by making the library's needs known. Although geology librarians will inevitably have to sift through many duplicates and outdated materials in order to find the serendipitous "gems," alumni, their heirs, faculty, and the general population can usually be counted on to provide some welcome items that could not have been acquired any other way. Each librarian must decide whether the end result is worth the effort required.

Even strong geological sciences collections will need the services of an out-of-print or antiquarian bookseller occasionally. Many older publications, such as Louis Agassiz's *Studies on Glaciers* or some USGS *Bulletins* are referred to regularly, so they wear out in time and need to be replaced. Two dealers who specialize in out-of-print geological materials are: James G. Leishman, Bookseller (P. O. Box A, Menlo Park, CA 94025), and Albert G. Clegg (312 W. Broad Street, Eaton Rapids, MI 48827).

Conclusion

Sensible collection development for the geological sciences requires common sense coupled with a knowledge of bibliographic resources and the needs of the library users. It is beneficial to utilize suggestions from the latter whenever possible.

Good communication links with library users provide useful information about forthcoming new programs and changes within existing programs. Anticipating and preparing for these changes in direction will better enable the librarian to acquire maximum materials when they are most readily available.

Selection Sources

Accessions List. U. S. Geological Survey. Reston, Va.: U. S. Geological Survey Library, 1978– . Monthly.

Agassiz, Louis. *Studies on Glaciers.* New York: Hafner, 1967.

Bibliography and Index of Geology. Falls Church, Va.: American Geological Institute, 1969– . Monthly with annual indexes.

Bibliography and Index of Geology Exclusive of North America. Washington, D. C.: Geological Society of America, 1933–68.

Bibliography of North American Geology. Washington, D. C.: U. S. Geological Survey. Dist. by Washington, D. C.: Government Printing Office, 1907–70.

Bulletin Signalétiques. Paris: Centre National de la Recherche Scientifique, Centre de Documentation Scientifique et Technique, Bureau de Recherches Géologiques et Minières, 1972– . (Numerous sections may be appropriate.)

Eos. Washington, D.C.: American Geophysical Union, 1919– . Weekly.

Economic Geology. Duluth, Minn.: Economic Geology Publishing Co., 1906– . 8/year.

Engineering and Mining Journal. New York: McGraw-Hill, 1866?– . Monthly.

Episodes. Ottawa: International Union of Geological Sciences, 1978– . Quarterly.

GIS Newsletter. Alexandria, Va.: American Geological Institute, 1966– . Bimonthly.

Geoscience Documentation. London: Geosystems Publications, 1969– . Bimonthly.

Geoscience Information Society. Guidebook and Ephermeral Materials Committee. *Union List of Geologic Field Trip Guidebooks of North America.* 3rd ed. Alexandria, Va.: American Geological Institute, 1978.

_____.*Proceedings.*Washington,D. C.:GeoscienceInformationSociety,1969– .

Geotimes. Alexandria, Va.: American Geological Institute, 1956– . Monthly.

Geotitles Weekly. London: Geosystems Publications, 1969– . Weekly.

K/H Geology Field Guide Series. Dubuque, Iowa: Kendall/Hunt Publishing Co., 19– . Irregularly.

Mackay, John W. *Sources of Information for the Literature of Geology: An Introductory Guide.* 2nd ed. Edinburgh: Scottish Academic Pr. for the Geological Society of London, 1974.

Mineralogical Abstracts. London: Mineralogical Society of Great Britain and Mineralogical Society of America, 1920– . Quarterly.

New Publications of the U. S. Geological Survey. Reston, Va.: U. S. Geological Survey, 1900– . Monthly with annual cumulations.

Oil and Gas Journal. Tulsa, Okla.: Penn Well Publishing, 1902– .

Petroleum Abstracts. Tulsa, Okla.: Univ. of Tulsa, 1961– . Weekly.

Referativnyi Zhurnal. Moscow: Vsesoyuznyi Institut Nauchno-Tekhnicheskoi Informatsii (VINITI). (Several sections may be appropriate.)

Scientific and Technical Books and Serials in Print. New York: Bowker, 1978– . Annually.

United States Bureau of Mines. *List of Bureau of Mines Publications and Articles . . . with Subject and Author Index.* Washington, D. C.: The Bureau; dist. by Government Printing Office, 1960– . Annually.

[U. S.] Geological Survey. *Bulletin.* Washington, D. C.: Government Printing Office, 1884– . Irregularly.

Ward, Dederick C.; Marjorie W. Wheeler; and Robert A. Bier, Jr. *Geologic Reference Sources: A Subject and Regional Bibliography of Publications and Maps in the Geological Sciences.* 2nd ed. Metuchen, N. J.: Scarecrow, 1981.

Wood, D. N., ed. *Use of Earth Sciences Literature.* Hamden, Conn.: Archon Books, 1973.

Worldwide Directory of National Earth-Science Agencies and Related International Organizations. Geological Survey Circular 934. Washington, D. C.: Government Printing Office, 1984.

MATHEMATICS

Jack Weigel

Mathematics is traditionally associated with numbers and quantitative measurements, but it is also concerned with shape and arrangement in an abstract sense. Thus, mathematics consists of the logical and systematic study of these concepts, their interrelationships, and the various levels of abstraction resulting from these factors.

In ancient civilizations arithmetic and geometry were the earliest areas of mathematics to be developed. At first, they were highly practical subjects, useful in commerce and land measurement. Later, especially with the ancient Greeks, mathematics was perceived as an abstract, pure aspect of knowledge.

The next field of mathematics to emerge was algebra, a generalization of arithmetic. Beginning in the seventeenth century analysis, which deals with the concepts of continuity and limits and includes calculus, was rapidly developed. During the twentieth century the study of similar structures in different fields of mathematics has reached a level of abstraction such that the once-discrete areas of algebra, analysis, and geometry have overlapped to a considerable degree.

Throughout its history, mathematics has been closely tied to research and progress in science and technology. The strongest connections of all have been with physics and astronomy, where advances in mathematics have often led to new scientific discoveries, and where new scientific discoveries have often led to new mathematics. Recently, mathematics has also become more closely involved with research in the biological sciences and the new field of computer science.

Mathematics, so intertwined with science and technology, is often referred to as "applied mathematics." By contrast "pure mathematics" consists of research into abstract areas not presently known to have immediate applications in other fields of knowledge. However, there have been repeated instances in which the "pure" mathematics of one generation has provided very fruitful applications for later generations.

Although computers have been employed for mathematical research, including the occasional solution of problems in pure mathematics, most new mathematics is still created by human thought unaided by technology. Since the only requisites for mathematical creation are a brain and some writing tools, mathematics can be developed without resort to expensive machinery, laboratories, or other advanced technology. Hence, although most mathematical research comes from centers of excellence in the technically advanced nations, it is also possible for mathematicians in less-developed countries to make significant contributions to the field.

This fact has obvious implications for library selectors in mathematics; a mathematical research collection must include publications in numerous foreign languages as well as in English. Also, as noted later in this chapter, nearly all of the significant mathematical research information is in the form of journal articles, books, and other print formats such as technical reports and preprints. Information in electronic and other nonprint media is thus far relatively limited and little used.

Not surprisingly, the literature of mathematics shares certain characteristics with the literature of other scientific and technical disciplines. Among these are the great importance of serials and conference proceedings and the relatively high cost of both books and serial publications. On the other hand, there are certain distinctive features that developers of mathematics collections should keep in mind. The "half-life" of mathematical literature is somewhat longer than that in some other areas of science and technology. Also, foreign-language contributions tend to be more valuable in mathematics than in such fields as physics and engineering. The Soviet Union, in particular, has many mathematicians of high international repute; hence, mathematical research libraries in North America need to collect some Russian-language publications to supplement the available English-language translations of major Soviet works. Finally, although technical reports and preprints in mathematics do exist, they are not generally as important as the formally published journal and book literature.

There are several guides to mathematics literature that contain useful information for selectors. The best-known, Parke's *Guide to the Literature of Mathematics and Physics*, is unfortunately also the oldest; the second (and last) edition was published in 1958.[1] It is aimed primarily at practitioners in science and engineering, but the bulk of the volume consists of bibliographies of major books in various subfields of physics and mathematics. Given the age of the data, these lists should be used with con-

---

1. Nathan Grier Parke, *Guide to the Literature of Mathematics and Physics Including Related Works on Engineering Science*, 2nd ed. (New York: Dover, 1958).

siderable caution. However, a selector who is building a new mathematics collection or is charged with improving a weak one will find that some of the listed classics are still available as reprints or in the form of later editions.

Pemberton's *How to Find Out in Mathematics* and Burrington's *How to Find Out about Statistics* are both reference guides for mathematical and statistical practitioners.[2] They do not include substantial lists of books, but library selectors will find a few key reference works and journals mentioned.

Dick's *Current Information Sources in Mathematics* contains, by contrast, extensive bibliographies of more than 1600 significant English-language books and periodicals published from 1960 to 1972.[3] The entries for books include author, title, imprint, collation, price, and summarized table of contents. Special lists of professional societies and publishers further augment the volume's value for selectors. Again, even this guide is handicapped by the fact that its contents are more than a decade old.

Societies and Commercial Publishers

There are several mathematical organizations in the United States of particular importance to library selectors. The American Mathematical Society (AMS) emphasizes research in pure mathematics and publishes several of the world's leading mathematics journals, some important monographic series, *Mathematical Reviews,* and miscellaneous other publications. The Mathematical Association of America (MAA) specializes in mathematics education, especially at the college level. It publishes three journals, four monographic series, and numerous nonserial monographs. The National Council of Teachers of Mathematics (NCTM) is also concerned with education, but particularly at the primary and secondary levels. It publishes four journals and dozens of booklets. The Society for Industrial and Applied Mathematics (SIAM) concentrates chiefly on applied mathematical research. It publishes about ten journals and some assorted books. Each of these organizations will supply on request a list of its publications.

Two U. S. organizations publishing important statistical journals are the American Statistical Association and the Institute of Mathematical Statistics. Lists of equivalent mathematical and statistical societies in other countries may be found in the books by Burrington and Pemberton.

2. John E. Pemberton, *How to Find Out in Mathematics,* 2nd ed. (New York: Pergamon, 1969); Gillian A. Burrington, *How to Find Out about Statistics* (New York: Pergamon, 1972).
3. Elie M. Dick, *Current Information Sources in Mathematics; An Annotated Guide to Books and Periodicals, 1960-1972* (Littleton, Colo.: Libraries Unlimited, 1973).

In addition to the professional organizations listed above, there are several commercial publishers who issue a substantial fraction of the new mathematical literature. Among these are Springer-Verlag, Birkhauser, Academic, Dekker, Wiley, Pitman, Addison-Wesley, Plenum, and North-Holland. Sundry academic publishers also produce some significant mathematical books and journals. Examples include the presses of Princeton University, Johns Hopkins University, Cambridge University, and the Massachusetts Institute of Technology.

Serials

Serials, particularly those known to researchers as "journals," are the predominant publications in advanced mathematics. A university mathematics library is likely to receive from 300 to 700 current serial titles. Because of their importance and their high cost, serials typically consume eighty to ninety percent (or more) of the acquisitions budgets of mathematical research libraries. Tables presented in the *Bowker Annual* and the Lowell article cited in the selection sources section give some idea of the rank order of serial costs in various disciplines.[4] Mathematics serials are not as expensive as those in physics, chemistry, and, possibly, medicine. On the other hand, they are a bit more expensive than those in other areas of science and technology, and far more costly than serials in humanities and the social sciences.

As suggested in the beginning of the chapter, significant mathematics serials are published in many countries. Although North America, Western Europe, and Japan account for most of the major publications, the Slavic countries and Third World nations such as China and India also issue valuable serials. Many of the serials from foreign academies and universities may be obtained on exchange; a large mathematics library that can supply copies of serials from its own institution may be able to obtain as many as forty percent of its serial titles on exchange.

Because of the aforementioned importance of mathematics publications from the Soviet Union, there are cover-to-cover English-language translations of approximately twenty-five Russian-language mathematics serials currently offered by publishers such as the American Mathematical Society, the London Mathematical Society, and several commercial firms, e.g., Allerton Press and Consultants Bureau. In the past few years Chinese-language journals have begun to flourish and may also begin to appear in English-language translations.

4. *Bowker Annual of Library and Book Trade Information*, 28th ed. (New York: Bowker, 1983); Gerald R. Lowell, "Periodical Prices 1980–1982 Update," *Serials Librarian* 7:75–83 (Fall 1982).

In addition to periodicals, there are a number of monographic series that many mathematics libraries obtain on standing orders. Examples are: *Lecture Notes in Mathematics, Ergebnisse der Exacten Wissenschaften, Grundlehren der Mathematischen Wissenschaften,* and *Graduate Texts in Mathematics* (Springer-Verlag); *Pure and Applied Mathematics: A Series of Monographs and Textbooks,* and *Probability and Mathematical Statistics* (Academic); *Lecture Notes in Pure and Applied Mathematics,* and *Statistics: Textbooks and Monographs* (Dekker); *North-Holland Mathematical Library, North-Holland Mathematical Studies,* and *Studies in Logic and the Foundation of Mathematics* (North-Holland); *Monographs and Studies in Mathematics* and *Research Notes in Mathematics* (Pitman); and *Pure and Applied Mathematics: A Wiley-Interscience Series of Texts, Monographs, and Tracts* and *Wiley Series in Probability and Mathematical Statistics* (Wiley).

There is no review medium specializing in mathematics serials; the sources cited in Hodge and Hepfer's essay on general science and technology do, of course, include some reviews of mathematical serials. If critical reviews are scarce, there are at least a variety of listings of serial titles and their publishers. For a selector who must build up from a small or nonexistent collection, the serials lists in the previously cited book by Dick and in the mathematics section of *Ulrich's International Periodicals Directory* and *Irregular Serials and Annuals* are good starting points. A more comprehensive listing of currently published serials may be found in the annual author index to *Mathematical Reviews.* Also, a set of details concerning American mathematical research journals was published in a 1983 issue of the *Notices of the American Mathematical Society.*[5] In the case of serials that have ceased publication, a selector would do well to obtain the serials holdings lists of two or three established large mathematics libraries. Recent serial titles may often be detected first, as are the books, in publishers' mailings and advertisements in other publications. For a comprehensive listing of new serials, selectors should check each issue of *Current Mathematical Publications,* which has a special serials section near the back.

Approval Plans

In this writer's experience, an approval plan can be a very useful means for acquiring a core collection of mathematics books. In addition to providing a welcome discount from high list prices, approval plans also provide insurance that many important publications *will* be received before

5. "Survey of American Mathematical Research Journals," *Notices of the American Mathematical Society* 30:715–19 (Nov. 1983).

they go out-of-print. Beyond the elementary text level, mathematics books are generally issued in small printings; any substantial delay in sending out firm orders is likely to result in a large fraction being returned with the disappointing notation "O. P."

Generally, it is not essential to set up a special West European mathematics approval plan. The largest mathematics publishers from that area have branch offices in the United States and can thus be covered by a program devoted to U. S. imprints. Approval plans with individual major publishers may not be as effective as a multipublisher plan with an experienced approval plan vendor; single-publisher plans tend to have subject profiles that are too broad and imprecise.

Book Selection Tools

For library selectors concerned with mathematics books at the undergraduate level, the Mathematical Association of America (MAA) offers some helpful publications. *A Basic Library List for Four-Year Colleges* should be useful for retrospective development collection, although the latest edition is several years old. Two journals published by the MAA— the *American Mathematical Monthly* and the *College Mathematics Journal*—have book review sections. Even though only a few titles are given full-scale reviews, a great many more are covered by "telegraphic reviews," providing bibliographic details along with very brief descriptive statements.

With respect to books at a more advanced level, we have already noted that the published lists in handbooks are too old to be fully satisfactory. Perhaps the best way to get usable retrospective information is to go back through the past several years of the "current" selection tools discussed below.

Often the first description of a new publication comes by way of publishers' announcements and advertisements; these arrive directly in the mail or appear in professional periodicals. The direct mailings often come unsolicited, but the selector can strengthen this information by writing to all major mathematics publishers to request future catalogs and circulars.

Although not as early as the prepublication announcements from selected publishers, *Current Mathematical Publications* (CMP) is far more comprehensive, since it provides worldwide coverage to new mathematics titles from every sort of publisher. The contents of *CMP* consist mostly of citations for publications received at the editorial office of *Mathematical Reviews*; tables of contents from the latest issues of key journals are also included. All entries in the main list are arranged according to the subject classification also used in *Mathematical Reviews*. Even though most entries are for articles in journals and conference proceedings, mon-

Mathematical Assn. of America. Committee on the Undergraduate Program
in Mathematics. *A Basic Library List*. 2nd ed. Washington, D. C.:
Mathematical Assn. of America, 1976.
Recommended list of 700 retrospective monographs for an undergraduate
collection.
Citations arranged under 16 general subject headings that are further
subdivided. Recommends 17 essential journals for an undergraduate
library.
Indexed by author.
Recommended monographs are drawn largely from "Telegraphic Reviews" that
appeared in the *American Mathematical Monthly* between 1964 and 1974.
Subdivisions in each field include, for example: histories; readings; introductory,
intermediate, and advanced titles; and special topics. May serve as a checklist
or tool for retrospective collection building if used judiciously. Complete bibliographic information is provided, and the list will usually offer alternative
selections in each subdivision.

American Mathematical Monthly. v.1– . 1894– . Washington, D. C.:
Mathematical Assn. of America. Monthly.
Scholarly journal.
50–100 new book notices an issue.
2–12-month lag between book publication and announcement.
Brief narrative descriptions and coded information.
"Telegraphic reviews" are provided in a separate center section "to give prompt
notice of all new books in the mathematical sciences." Only English-language
books are included, however. Short descriptive contributions by mathematicians
and codes to designate textbooks, supplementary or professional reading, and
reading level are provided, along with the book's basic topic in boldface type.
A good current and conveniently formated source to select from for those with
limited time.

ographic entries are easy to pick out because they are marked with a
prominent black star. The data for monograph entries include author,
title, imprint, series note (where applicable), ISBN, and price (when available).

In *Mathematical Reviews* (*MR*) the same data are given, usually combined with a review signed by a professional mathematician. Monographs
are generally reviewed in *MR* from several months to several years after
publication, thus limiting its usefulness as a current selection tool. If a
selector rejects a book at the time of its listing in *CMP*, the added information available later in *MR* may reverse the initial decision. Also, as
noted earlier, *MR* is very useful for a systematic program of retrospective
selection. The *Zentralblatt fuer Mathematik und ihre Grenzgebiete* is very
similar to *MR* in subject coverage and in worldwide comprehensiveness;
it can be employed for selection in the same fashion as *MR*. (Despite its
German title, the *Zentralblatt* is now written mostly in English.)

Current Mathematical Publications. v.1– . Providence, R. I.: American
Mathematical Society. Biweekly.
Specialized alerting service.
100–250 book citations an issue.
2–24-month lag between book publication and announcement. Worldwide
coverage.
Over 90 subject categories are used.
Monographic entries are marked with a star to distinguish them from journal
article citations. Despite occasional long delays, many foreign-language books
are included within a few months after their publication. Complete bibliographical information, including price, ISBN, and series, is provided. Foreign titles
indicated in both original language and in English. A comprehensive and fairly
current selection tool that will provide information before that of *Mathematical
Reviews*.

It is wise to review the selection information in at least a few other
serials besides the *CMP-MR* combination. The *American Mathematical
Monthly*'s telegraphic reviews include some titles at a higher level than
the undergraduate books mentioned earlier. The *Journal of the American
Statistical Association* is a good source for signed reviews of statistics
books. As in other disciplines, the *Weekly Record* provides a good checklist
of new U. S. imprints.

One more source of information is, of course, other selectors working
in the same subject field. Many mathematics libraries issue periodic new
acquisitions lists, and the librarians in charge are usually quite willing to
exchange these lists with other mathematics and science librarians. Another means of exchanging mathematics selection information is provided
by the Physics-Astronomy-Mathematics (P-A-M) Division of the Special
Libraries Association (SLA). At each SLA annual conference one of the
meetings sponsored by the P-A-M Division is a mathematics librarians'
workshop; much of the roundtable discussion there is relevant to collection development. The P-A-M Division's *Bulletin*, issued quarterly, will
sometimes contain notes of interest to mathematics selectors.

"Difficult" Publications

For many years mimeographed lecture notes have been an important form
of expository writing about recent progress in mathematics. In the past,
some of these note sets would eventually emerge as formally published
books, but many remained in their original format, available, if at all,
from a university mathematics department or research institute. Fortunately, due to the enterprise of Springer-Verlag, Inc., the problem of identifying and acquiring mathematics lecture notes has been reduced. In 1964

Springer-Verlag launched a new monograph series called *Lecture Notes in Mathematics*, offering relatively rapid commercial publication of notes in typescript. The series now contains over 1000 volumes and continues to grow at the rate of several dozen volumes per year. Other publishers, such as Dekker, have followed suit. Nevertheless, some lecture notes are still issued outside the normal publishing channels, and information on them is still elusive. The *CMP-MR* combination does not cover formally unpublished lecture notes comprehensively, and the notes are ignored by all of the other standard bibliographic sources. Selectors can obtain word-of-mouth information on the availability of informal lecture notes from mathematicians and from other librarians. Also, most mathematics libraries include lecture note sets in their acquisitions lists. This writer has been able to obtain further lecture note information by compiling a list of mathematics departments and institutes known as past producers of lecture note sets and then sending them an annual letter, requesting data on available note sets. One subset of mimeographed material—French mathematical seminar proceedings—has been given excellent retrospective coverage in Anderson's *French Mathematical Seminars; A Union List.*

As previously stated, Soviet mathematical publications are important for research collections in the United States. Unfortunately, these publications are issued in very limited editions; only prepublication orders offer a reasonable chance of success. For prepublication information on books, the weekly *Novye Knigi* is the best source, and a few additional mathematics titles appear in the separate catalogs of Nauka Press. There is also available a periodicals catalog entitled *Gazety i zhurnaly SSSR.* All of these catalogs may be obtained from Les Livres Etrangers S. A., 10 Rue Armand-Moisant, 75737 Paris CEDEX 15, France. Soviet periodicals must also be ordered in advance; if a periodical is ordered in the middle of a volume, the Soviets will expect payment for the full volume but will generally not supply the back issues. This situation is somewhat mitigated for libraries with exchange-worthy publications; Soviet science academies and universities are frequently amenable to exchange agreements.

Even though preprints and technical reports are not nearly as important in mathematics as in certain other areas of science and technology, there are still some that are of interest to selectors for research libraries. The Mathematics Institute at Aarhus University (Denmark) and the Mathematics Center in Amsterdam are examples of preprint producers, and the Mathematics Research Center, Madison, Wisconsin, issues a well-known technical report series. Since both of these forms of the literature lack comprehensive bibliographic control, they must be discovered by the same ad hoc methods used for informal lecture note sets. Once identified, preprints and technical reports can often be obtained as gifts or exchange items.

The Future

In attempting to foresee the future of mathematical literature and related collection development, one is led to contemplate again the differences between mathematical researchers and other scientific and technical researchers. The number of researchers and the amount of published research in mathematics is less than in chemistry, biology, physics, medicine, or engineering. Therefore, mathematicians are less likely than other researchers to adopt a subject-search approach to their literature; many feel that they already know all the significant people working in their specialty. Also, many researchers in pure mathematics are conservative in applying modern technology, especially computers, to their professional work and to their use of research information. It is no coincidence that *Mathematical Reviews* became publicly available to online searchers long after *Chemical Abstracts*, *Physics Abstracts*, and *Engineering Index*.

Yet another factor influencing the pace of development is the already noted importance of mathematical contributions from the Slavic countries and some Third World nations; these countries are not leaders in the electronic transfer of information. In summary, it appears that the methods of information transfer and usage in mathematics will change at a slower pace over the next one to two decades than will be the case in disciplines like physics, chemistry, or engineering. Although some alterations should be apparent by the year 2000, most information in mathematics will still be conveyed in traditional published books and serials.

Selection Sources

American Mathematical Monthly. v.1- . 1894- . Washington, D. C.: Mathematical Assn. of America. Monthly.

Anderson, Nancy. *French Mathematical Seminars; A Union List.* Providence, R. I.: American Mathematical Society, 1978.

College Mathematics Journal. v.1- . 1970- . Washington, D.C.: Mathematical Assn. of America. 5/year.

Current Mathematical Publications. v.1- . 1969- . Providence, R. I.: American Mathematical Society. Biweekly.

Dick, Elie M. *Current Information Sources in Mathematics; An Annotated Guide to Books and Periodicals, 1960-1972.* Littleton, Colo.: Libraries Unlimited, 1973.

Journal of the American Statistical Association. v.1- . 1888- . Washington, D.C.: American Statistical Association. Quarterly.

Mathematical Assn. of America. Committee on the Undergraduate Program in Mathematics. *A Basic Library List for Four-Year Colleges.* 2nd ed. Washington, D. C.: Mathematical Assn. of America, 1976.

Mathematical Reviews. v.1- . 1940- . Providence, R. I.: American Mathematical Society. Monthly.

Special Libraries Assn. Physics-Astronomy-Mathematics Div. *Bulletin*. v.1– . 1973– . n. p.: SLA.

Zentralblatt fuer Mathematik und ihre Grenzgebiete. v.1– . 1931– . Heidelberg and New York: Springer-Verlag.

PHYSICS AND ASTRONOMY

Donald J. Marion

Physics is the study of the most fundamental properties of matter and radiation, and their interactions. What we comprehend of physics provides the basis for our understanding of other, larger, and more complex systems of matter anywhere in the universe. At one time physical science was known as "natural philosophy," and many of its practitioners, who were designated "scientists," were in fact doing physics. As time went on, various specialties within natural philosophy broke off, becoming autonomous disciplines while continuing, in varying degrees, to utilize physics as a foundation. For example, modern chemistry has leaned heavily for its own development on the ideas of physics, most notably quantum mechanics and electromagnetic theory. Similarly, other sciences are indebted to physics for their development, such as earth science and its applied areas, meteorology and geophysics; all fields of engineering; the newer areas of research interest, including environmental science; and in recent years the life sciences, particularly biology. The lone exception to this pattern of development is mathematics, which with physics stands alone as a basic science.

The subfields of importance to physicists engaged in research have undergone a revolutionary change once in history, and appear to be on the threshold of a second change, one no less profound. Traditionally, physics could be divided into a few broad topics: mechanics, electromagnetism, heat, light, and sound. These subfields are still known collectively as "classical physics," and they are still a part of the basic scientific and technical curriculum. As research topics, however, they are branches of applied physics and technology, rather than inherent branches of physics itself.

The major subfields of modern physics are largely divided along the lines of particular types of structure in nature. *Elementary particle physics*, for example, deals with the most fundamental constituents of matter and

300

energy, their interactions with one another, their behavior under extreme conditions, and the mathematical laws that underlie this behavior. As an experimental science, this branch is referred to as *high energy physics*, reflecting the massive energies required to do laboratory research on elementary particles. Closely connected with elementary particle physics, and really its parent, is *nuclear physics*, which involves the structure of atomic nuclei and their interactions with each other, as well as the whole spectrum of elementary particles. *Atomic physics* is concerned with the structure of the atom, its dynamical properties, and its interactions with particles and fields. *Condensed matter (solid state) physics* involves the study of solid, liquid, glassy, and other amorphous substances, their electronic, optical, magnetic, thermal, and mechanical properties. This field interacts strongly with chemistry and metallurgy, as well as with the broad area of materials science.

These are the principal areas of physics research today. But it is also important to bear in mind that within each of these subfields, there are those physicists whose research is carried out in the laboratory—the experimentalists—and those for whom the library is the lab: the theoreticians. It is this latter group that has brought physics to the brink of the revolution alluded to earlier. Simply put, theoretical physics is the description of natural phenomena in mathematical form. It has two goals: the discovery of the fundamental laws of nature and the derivation of conclusions from these laws. The ultimate goal of all theoretical physics is the reduction of these laws to an absolute minimum, with a unified theory of the universe. At the time this is written, such a theory is believed achievable, if not imminent. The theoreticians are heavily reliant on the literature for their research, and consequently it is with this group that the librarian will come into most frequent contact. The selector will also find that the theoretical group is the one that will make the bulk of book and journal recommendations, and because of its knowledge of the literature, will be the most helpful for advice on purchasing decisions.

Overview of Physics Literature

The selector in physics is fortunate in that, while the subject is both intellectually stimulating and challenging, it does not carry with it some of the frustrations one finds in other scientific and technical fields, where a sizable part of the literature may be out of the mainstream or otherwise not readily accessible. Physics research does not require a wide variety of literature types: for example, physicists do not ordinarily use technical reports, patents, or dissertations in their research. (Although high-energy physicists rely heavily on preprints for current information, these are almost always exchanged directly between physics departments). Also, the great majority of the world's important physics research is published in English, either originally or in translation, so foreign-language acquisition is not the problem it is in some fields. Basically, selectors can focus on the books and journals that constitute the bulk of physics literature. However, within these two broad categories there are specific types of material that need to be distinguished.

The challenges to the selector arise from two characteristics of the subject that have a strong impact on collection development. First, the researcher's need for timely information is paramount; therefore, the librarian can seldom enjoy a leisurely approach to book selection, relying on reviews as a guide to what's needed. Second, physics is a basic science, and applications of it are often the focus of research in a variety of other scientific and technical fields. This can lead to confusion in terminology: for example, we have "reliability physics," which is an engineering specialty, and "molecular physics," which is a branch of chemistry. In addition, physics is also a frequent part of inter- and multidisciplinary research and the publications resulting from this.

These problems can both be easily resolved. While the researcher's need for the newest information forces the selector to order many materials with no prior evaluation, the actual chance of selecting something totally worthless is quite small: the refereeing standards of physics are very high for those publications of scientific societies and the major science publishers. And when considering a title from a lesser-known source, the recommendations of faculty are most helpful. The best solution to the question of whether a particular item belongs in the physics collection or is the concern of another selector is, simply, to know one's constituency. The beginning physics selector should get to know from the outset the interests of the research groups in the physics department he or she works with.

GUIDES TO THE LITERATURE

A characteristic of guides in general is that they usually become dated too quickly to be of much use in current collection building; in physics this is very much the case. Since physics research places such a heavy emphasis on the latest findings in the field, the guides will usually help with retrospective collection development only. Even here, however, collection development might not be possible on a large scale because science materials often go out-of-print soon after they are published. Some important works that are cited in guides, therefore, may not be so easy to acquire. Chronologically, the most prominent guides to physics literature are: Nathan Grier Parke, *Guide to the Literature of Mathematics and Physics,*

Coblans, Herbert, ed. *Use of Physics Literature*. London and Boston: Butterworths, 1975.

Guide to literature.

Important works in all formats covered in bibliographic essays. The "minimum elements for identification have been provided for each item cited."

The aim of this guidebook is to include a selection of the most useful printed sources. Bibliographic essays by physicists and librarians indicated the principle journals, regularly held conferences, series, and standard works in each of nine areas of physics. Reference works and indexing/abstracting services are included. Chapters also describe the history and recent developments of each field. A good source for developing a core collection or to use as a checklist of standard works through the early 1970s.

Including Related Works on Engineering Science (1958). This book is notable for its extensive bibliographies of physics literature up to the guide's year of publication. In addition to book citations, it lists many journal articles that were landmarks in modern physics. As the title indicates, it encompasses closely related fields for which the physics selector may also be responsible. Parke's *Guide* includes a great many non-English works from the golden years of German and French physics earlier in this century. Although it is too out-of-date for collection building, Parke is still useful for deaccessioning and storage decisions.

Robert H. Whitford's *Physics Literature* (1968) is basically an update of Parke, although the arrangement is different. Again, it is too dated to be of much use in collection development.

Herbert Coblans edited the *Use of Physics Literature* (1975), a work of collective authorship; it is exactly what its name says: a guide to the *use* of the literature. For an overview of how physics research is done through the literature, this is probably the best source available. Particularly noteworthy is the introductory chapter by John Ziman, the British physicist and frequent writer on scientific literature and communication. The book's major drawback is its relative neglect of the major areas of contemporary research: three chapters are devoted to classical physics, whereas solid-state and high-energy physics are mentioned only in passing in a chapter on "Theoretical Physics." The bibliographies in Coblans' guide are intended to be illustrative only, so they are much less extensive than those in the other guides.

The "Dissemination and Use of the Information of Physics," chapter thirteen in the first volume of *Physics in Perspective* (1972), is an essay on physics literature that provides valuable background reading for the physics selector. While only this chapter deals specifically with that aspect of physics of most interest to librarians, *Physics in Perspective*, a massive three-volume report, will reward the effort one puts into reading it. Commonly referred to as "The Bromley Report," it is still the most comprehensive overview of the physics profession today: who physicists are, where they come from, and what they do. There is a one-volume student edition that can make the task considerably less grueling, but the information chapter is not included.

JOURNALS

Journals constitute the main source, the essential day-to-day material, of the physicist's library research. Whether the contents are lengthy review articles or brief communications ("letters"), the journal article is the indispensable literature form. What particular titles a library holds is another matter, largely determined by the budget, within the context of the physics department's research involvements. This is even more the case with journals than with books, as the physics journal is used almost exclusively for research, whereas the book is primarily employed as a teaching tool.

The journals in a physics collection must be scrutinized closely because they represent a large investment of library resources. Many institutional subscriptions to physics journals are very expensive and, while it may be desirable to subscribe to as many titles as possible, few libraries can afford to support a costly publication that is seldom used.

In general, most large academic libraries will want to subscribe to all journals published by the American Institute of Physics (AIP), including its series of translations of Russian physics journals, and all titles published by the Institute of Physics (IOP) in the United Kingdom. Both of these societies publish major continuation series as well as journals, but those will be discussed with conference proceedings.

In addition to the AIP and IOP journals, there are a large number of physics journals published by trade publishers and by or for physical societies in other countries, e.g., the Physical Society of Japan, the Società Italiana di Fisica, and the Société Française de Physique, etc. A comprehensive listing of these organizations, with addresses, can be found in *International Physics & Astronomy Directory 1969/70*. The best approach to physics journal selection is to apply the guidelines outlined in Hodge and Hepfer's essay on sci-tech materials in conjunction with local faculty recommendations. The same is true when considering a monographic series standing order. Note, however, that the publishers of these often have a very broad interpretation of "physics," and some titles in a series might fall outside of a particular physics department's curricula and research involvements.

There is no adequate list of the "best" physics journals. The most comprehensive is the *List of Journals* covered by Inspec, publishers of

Physics Abstracts. This list attempts to be as comprehensive as possible, including many works from chemistry, mathematics, and several engineering fields, as well as all titles in computer science and electrical engineering. The list is frequently updated by a "Supplementary List of Journals" in individual issues of *Physics Abstracts.* This is a brief and handy way to identify new titles. Perhaps the closest thing to a "best" listing is the one in *Current Contents: Physical, Chemical and Earth Sciences;* it indicates those that are most requested by customers using the publisher's article provision service.

CONFERENCE PROCEEDINGS

The comments about conferences in the essay on sci-tech selection are very pertinent to the field of physics. The physics selector must deal with a great quantity and variance in quality in this burgeoning sector of the literature. Unfortunately, a number of major bibliographic tools, such as *Index to Scientific and Technical Proceedings,* list the contents of individual proceedings but fail to discuss quality. Some conference series, on the other hand, have a proven track record: a good example is the *NATO Advanced Study Institute Series B, Physics.* Selectors should note, however, that a few of the titles in this series are really chemistry or engineering conferences. Two other series of consistently high quality are *Studies in the Natural Sciences (Orbis Scientiae)* from Plenum, and the Enrico Fermi Summer Schools from Elsevier. The AIP's Conference Proceedings series is another that most physics collections will want to receive on a standing order basis. Even though some of the individual titles in the series may be outside the scope of some narrow collections, the overall quality of the series, coupled with its relatively low cost, makes a standing order attractive.

The IOP Conference Series calls for considerably more selectivity: unlike its AIP counterpart, the IOP series includes predominantly applied physics conferences that may be inappropriate for "pure" physics collections.

Selection Sources for Books and Conference Publications

Selection sources for books and conference publications can be considered together because they overlap in so many cases. Publishers' catalogs and advertisements head the list for physics, of course, as they do for all of the scientific disciplines. The conscientious physics selector will try to get on mailing lists to receive announcements and catalogs from all of the following:

Academic Press

Adam Hilger Ltd. (publishing arm of the Institute of Physics)
Addison Wesley Publishing Co.
Birkhäuser, Boston
Cambridge University Press
Elsevier Science Publishing Co.
Heyden & Son
McGraw-Hill Book Co.
Oxford University Press
Pergamon Press
Plenum Publishing Corp.
Princeton University Press
Springer-Verlag, New York
Taylor & Francis, Philadelphia
John Wiley & Sons
World Scientific Publishing Co. Ltd. (distributed in the United States
   by Taylor & Francis)

These are by no means the only publishers of physics books, but they do produce (or distribute in the United States) the bulk of the most important works in the field. For the output of other publishers, the general bibliographic sources are helpful.

Physics book reviews are of little use for selection purposes. The best reviews are those in *Physics Today*, the general physics news magazine of the AIP. These are signed reviews by physicists for physicists, but they generally appear a year or more after publication of the book; most of the candidates for purchase have already been identified by other sources and acquired. Also, there are only a few reviews in each issue, a small fraction of the annual output. A better approach for selectors is the "Books Received" listing at the end of the review section; this is far more timely, and includes all the major publications in the field. Most citations carry a short note indicating the level of the work and whether it is part of a series, a reprint, etc.

Other journals that feature good reviews of physics books are: *Contemporary Physics*, a British journal that carries reviews of the same high quality as those in *Physics Today*, and more of them per issue. However, it is subject to the same problem of lateness. The citations in the books received section are usually a bit slower than *Physics Today*'s, but they provide good bibliographic information, including ISBN.

In *Nature*, the physics books reviewed are mostly undergraduate level or intended for the layman; the *New Scientist* features the same type of material as that found in *Nature*.

The *American Journal of Physics* and *Physics Education* are intended for the college-level teacher of physics in the United States and United

Physics Today. v.1– . 1948– . Woodbury, N. Y.: American Institute of
Physics. Monthly.
Scholarly journal.
2–5 reviews an issue with more than 1-year lag between book publication
and review.
30–100 new book alerts an issue with a 2–6-month lag between book
publication and alert.
Selected books that have a wide potential readership or a political impact are
covered by signed, lengthy, and critical reviews by physicists. More comprehensive coverage of specialized material is offered in new book alerts categorized
into major fields, i.e., energy, quantum electronics, theoretical and mathematical
physics, or student texts. Brief notes may indicate readership level or source of
reprinted articles. Bibliographic information includes author, title, series, pagination, publisher, place, imprint date, and price. Some foreign, noncommercial
publications are occasionally included.

Kingdom, respectively. These journals carry several reviews in each issue,
with an emphasis on textbooks, while the *Physics Bulletin* is the British
counterpart of *Physics Today.*

All these journals should be a part of the physics book selector's reading
program. Regular scanning of the news items, editorials, and advertisements will keep the selector up-to-date on trends and events in physics
worldwide.

As physics research continues to thrive, the literature grows accordingly,
mirroring the health and vigor of the science. While most physics publications are still being issued in monograph and journal formats, the need
for the most recent information possible is bringing less traditional forms,
such as the conference paper, into a more prominent role than is the case
in some other fields. Many more drastic format changes are certainly in
store as developing technologies facilitate improved information delivery
systems. How these developments will affect or change collection development in physics or the role of the physics selector is not yet clear,
however.

Astronomy

A university library's astronomy collection will frequently be an added
responsibility for the physics bibliographer. As a subject for academic
research, the emphasis in astronomy has moved away from the traditional
concept, i.e., the observation of the positions and motions of astronomical
objects, towards astrophysics, the study of the physical properties of those
objects. There are several parallel branches of astrophysics, and the selector should be aware of these, as they impact greatly on collection
development.

The first and most obvious of these branches is the type of object studied: the sun, planets, stars, galaxies, or the universe as a whole (cosmology), etc. Within these categories there is likely to be a wavelength bias in research: infrared, radio, ultraviolet, gamma-ray or x-ray sources. And, finally, one should note whether the researcher's approach is observational or theoretical: if the former, then the researcher will rely heavily on compilations of data, such as catalogs; if the latter, more traditional sources will be required. This is one subject where a high degree of selectivity may be called for. Even a relatively large institution may have a very small group of astronomers; and it serves little purpose to build a collection of, say, star catalogs if the astronomy group consists of two people interested solely in planetary atmospheres. As with physics, the selector must be well acquainted with the constituency.

There are several excellent sources to assist in collection development in astronomy, and the selector should be aware of them. For a good, brief overview of the communication system of astronomy, highlighting its differences from that of physics, see A. J. Meadows and J. G. O'Connor's "Astrophysics" in the *Use of Physics Literature.*

GUIDES TO THE LITERATURE

Robert A. Seal's *A Guide to the Literature of Astronomy* is the best introductory guide, with lengthy annotations, ISBN and LC numbers, and prices as of 1977. D. A. Kemp's *Astronomy and Astrophysics: A Bibliographical Guide* (1970) is a landmark work, *the* classic in astronomy bibliography, designed primarily for astronomers and other scientists working outside their specialties. Every librarian working with astronomy literature should be familiar with Kemp, but will probably find it more useful as a

---

Seal, Robert A., and Sarah S. Martin. *Bibliography of Astronomy, 1970–1979.* Littleton, Colo.: Libraries Unlimited, 1982.
   Guide to key works in the field.
   Divided into 75 subject areas.
   Full bibliographic information except price. Covers 500 monographs or conference proceedings.
This bibliography covers the literature of astronomy and astrophysics for the decade of the 1970s and some earlier works not included by its predecessor—*Astronomy and Astrophysics: A Bibliographical Guide,* by D. A. Kemp. Arrangement is by author within subject areas, so monographs and proceedings are included with journal articles, technical reports, and review chapters. There is, however, a monographic title/conference proceeding index. Brief notes intended to denote subject matter, readership, emphasis, or special features are included. The book is intended to be a selective record of key works; its comprehensiveness makes it a useful tool to check gaps in areas of an astronomy collection or as a bibliographical source for retrospective collection building.

reference tool than as an aid to collection development. It has been updated by a recent work by Robert A. Seal and Sarah S. Martin, *A Bibliography of Astronomy, 1970–1979.*

These works constitute an excellent starting point for any self-education
program in the literature of astronomy.

Selection Sources

American Journal of Physics. v.1– . 1933– . New York: American Institute of
Physics. Monthly.

Coblans, Herbert, ed. *Use of Physics Literature.* London and Boston: Butterworths,
1975.

Contemporary Physics. v.1– . 1959– . Basingstoke, England: Taylor & Francis.
Bimonthly.

Current Contents: Physical, Chemical and Earth Sciences. v.1– . 1961– . Philadelphia: Institute for Scientific Information. Weekly.

"Dissemination and Use of the Information of Physics." In *Physics in Perspective,*
vol. 1, pp. 890–966. Ed. by National Research Council, Physics Survey Committee. 3v. Washington, D. C.: National Academy of Sciences, 1972–73.

Index to Scientific and Technical Proceedings. v.1– . 1978– . Philadelphia: Institute
for Scientific Information. Monthly with annual cumulations.

International Physics & Astronomy Directory 1969/70. New York: Benjamin-
Cummings, 1969.

Kemp, D. A. *Astronomy and Astrophysics: A Bibliographical Guide.* London:
Macdonald Technical and Scientific; Hamden, Conn.: Archon Books, Shoe String,
1970.

List of Journals and Other Serial Sources. Hitchin, England and Piscataway, N.J.:
Inspec, the Institution of Electrical Engineers, 1983– . Annually. (Also printed
in annual Author Index to *Physics Abstracts.*)

Meadows, A. J., and J. G. O'Connor. "Astrophysics." In Colbans, *Use of Physics
Literature,* pp. 122–39.

National Research Council. Physics Survey Committee. *Physics in Perspective.* 3v.
Washington, D. C.: National Academy of Science, 1972–73.

――――. *Physics in Perspective. Student Edition.* Washington, D. C.: National
Academy of Sciences, 1973.

Nature. v.1– . 1869– . London: Macmillan. Weekly.

New Scientist. v.1– . 1956– . London: IPC. Weekly.

Parke, Nathan Grier. *Guide to the Literature of Mathematics and Physics, Including Related Works on Engineering Science.* 2nd rev. ed. New York: Dover,
1958.

Physics Abstracts. Science Abstracts. Section A. v.1– . 1898– . Hitchin, England.
Semimonthly.

Physics Bulletin. v.1– . 1950– . Bristol, England: Institute of Physics. Monthly.

Physics Education. v.1– . 1966– . Bristol, England: Institute of Physics. Bimonthly.

Physics Today. v.1– . 1948– . New York: American Institute of Physics. Monthly.

Seal, Robert A. *A Guide to the Literature of Astronomy.* Littleton, Colo.: Libraries
Unlimited, 1977.

――――, and Sarah S. Martin. *A Bibliography of Astronomy 1970–1979.* Littleton,
Colo.: Libraries Unlimited, 1982.

Whitford, Robert H. *Physics Literature.* 2nd ed. Metuchen, N. J.: Scarecrow, 1968.

Part 5

SPECIAL FORMATS
AND SUBJECTS

Edited by
John Whaley

GOVERNMENT PUBLICATIONS

Judy Horn

Government organizations are the world's most prolific publishers, and the large number of governmental agencies further complicates acquisition success. This chapter covers some of the basic elements in selection, evaluation, and acquisition of materials published by the United States government, state governments, international governmental organizations, foreign governments, and local governments.

The same factors that govern selection of material for the library's collection apply to the selection of government publications. In the past, many large libraries attempted to acquire as complete a collection of government publications as possible. This provides a sense of security for the librarian and the researcher, but in an era of declining resources it is no longer possible or cost effective. We must carefully determine the levels of government and subject areas to be collected so that materials will complement the library's collection and be integrated into it. Their physical location within the library, either housed separately or merged into the collection, is irrelevant.[1]

Preparation of a written collection development policy helps to guide selection decisions that meet the needs of users. It also provides a yardstick for measuring selection activities. In addition to defining subject fields, the collection development policy should identify the levels of government to be collected. While these levels will vary depending upon the community needs, academic programs, and the resources of other libraries in the area, most larger libraries will acquire publications from local city and county jurisdictions, their state, the United States government, and selected international organizations. Publications from other states or foreign governments will usually be limited, since they tend to receive little use.

1. Charles R. McClure, "An Integrated Approach to Government Publications Collection Development," *Government Publications Review* 8A:5–15 (1981).

Before attempting to draft a collection policy, you should survey the literature on collection development. The book *Developing Collections of U. S. Government Publications*, by Peter Hernon and Gary Purcell, contains an overview of collection development issues and includes sample collection development policies for government publications.[2]

Government publications, for the most part, are not evaluated in standard collection development review media. However, a growing number of periodicals include review columns on government publications. These reviews, in addition to evaluating publications, also indicate where they may be obtained. Some of the periodicals currently containing evaluative reviews of government publications include *Government Publications Review* (Pergamon Press), *Documents to the People* (ALA Government Documents Round Table [GODORT]); *RQ* (ALA Reference and Adult Services Division); *Booklist* (ALA); *Serials Review* (Pierian Press); *Serials Librarian* (Haworth Press); and *Wilson Library Bulletin*.

In many instances evaluation is irrelevant since the author (issuing agency) is authoritative and the only producer of certain information. Examples include the material produced by Congress or the annual reports of various agencies. In some cases—for example, census publications—the librarian will need to evaluate compilations published by private publishers and decide whether the library should select the material as published by the government, the private publisher, or both. The sources listed above, including *Microforms Review*, evaluate and frequently offer comparisons of works issued both by the government and private publishers.

Unfortunately, relatively few publications are reviewed. If a government publication appears to fall within the collection policy parameters, select it. While you are waiting for a review to appear in the literature, the publication will probably go out-of-print. The choice in selecting large series, especially technical report series that can be quite voluminous, may not be quite so simple. Unless the library has a strong program in the subject field covered by the series, selection should be on a title-by-title basis. Before deciding to acquire the entire series, order one or two titles most pertinent to the collection policy and evaluate them. If it is a new series, wait for a number of titles to appear before making a decision. If it appears that over half the titles in the series will be heavily used by the library, you will save time and money in collecting the entire series, unless it is a very bulky collection.

The availability period for government publications will affect your selections. Few government publications are available after five years and most go out-of-print within two. The increase in government publications

2. Peter Hernon and Gary R. Purcell, *Developing Collections of U. S. Government Publications* (Greenwich, Conn.: JAI Press, 1982).

titles in microform, issued both by governments and private publishers, has extended the purchase period.

Resource sharing options will also impact on selection decisions, especially if there are two or more large libraries within a fifteen- to twenty-mile radius, or if several libraries are part of a larger system. An article by Bruce Morton and J. Randolph Cox describes a cooperative program for two smaller selective U. S. depository libraries that may serve as a model for larger libraries.[3] The University of California's shared acquisitions program has made it possible for government publications departments in the system to share the costs and use of large sets, primarily microforms. Before making recommendations for purchase, the government publications librarians consult and decide the most appropriate holdings and locations; each campus receives an index. Direct loans between government publications departments facilitate the use of the materials. This has worked successfully; turnaround time among the southern campuses varies from one to three days.

General Considerations

Deciding how to acquire government publications is one of the major decisions that needs to be made. There are four basic methods of acquiring government publications: (1) exchange; (2) gift; (3) purchase; (4) depository arrangements. Using combinations of these methods increases the available options.

1. *Exchange.* Your initial request to a foreign government for free materials may result in their asking for an exchange agreement. In all except rare instances this method should be avoided. The costs involved in establishing and maintaining exchange agreements far exceed the return. Most libraries seldom have a title or collection of publications consistently available for exchange. The basic question to ask is "Do I have a steady supply of publications that can be exchanged on a regular basis?" If the answer is not an unequivocal "yes," it is best to avoid establishing exchange agreements for government publications.

2. *Gift.* In the past, many large government publication collections were developed through this method. This, in general, is no longer possible, although you may still be able to acquire many publications by getting your library on the agency's mailing list. No publication has yet been issued that lists all free publications from all government jurisdictions; such a publication does not even exist for materials issued by the U. S. government. This is the collection method most subject to change. What

3. Bruce Morton and J. Randolph Cox, "Cooperative Collection Development between Selective U. S. Depository Libraries," *Government Publications Review* 9:221–29 (1982).

is offered free today may have a price tag on it tomorrow. The major indexes of the government jurisdictions discussed below normally indicate which items are free of charge. Write to the agency whose publications you wish to acquire and request to be put on the mailing list for free publications. Some agencies will regularly send you their free publications; some maintain mailing lists for only certain periodical titles; and others do not maintain mailing lists. When an agency does not maintain a mailing list but has free items, each publication must be requested separately. This information about mailing lists is also not published, but is discovered by trial and error. When requesting free items, be careful to request only titles that are compatible with the collection development policy. It is easy to fall into the trap of getting on the mailing lists for publications just because they are free. Gift items frequently require more record keeping and careful monitoring.

3. *Purchase.* In the last few years the number of government jurisdictions requiring that publications be purchased has increased dramatically. No longer can we assume that a government publications collection can be built around gratis publications. Many government agencies are even requiring prepayment. To facilitate orders, some governments and vendors have deposit account options in which money is deposited in advance and drawn upon as needed. Methods of purchasing publications from each of the levels of government are described later in the chapter.

4. *Depository Arrangements.* Various government jurisdictions, including local, state, national, regional, and international governmental organizations, have established depository arrangements with libraries. Libraries designated as depositories generally receive the publications free of charge.[4] Depository types range from full (regional) to partial (selective). Designation as a full depository does not mean that the library will automatically receive everything published by that government jurisdiction, however. Many categories of publications are excluded from depository programs and, since each government jurisdiction establishes its own policies and procedures, the categories of inclusion are seldom uniform. Thus, while a library may participate in one or more depository programs, a separate arrangement will be needed for each.

Depository programs generally provide the greatest return for the least investment of time and effort required by the various acquisitions methods. However, depository arrangements may not be the best means of acquiring publications. Comparing standing order plans and individual purchases to depository receipts will help to identify potential problems. If the depo-

4. United Nations depositories, since 1975, with the exception of one in each country, pay a fee. See Luciana Marulli-Koenig, "Collection Development for United Nations and Documents," in *Collection Development and Public Access of Government Documents,* Proceedings of the First Annual Library Government Documents and Information Conference, Boston, 1981, ed. by Peter Hernon (Westport, Conn.: Meckler, 1982), p. 93.

sitory plan includes a large amount of material outside the subject areas of the collection policy and does not offer selection options, the depository arrangement will probably not be the best acquisition method. Your analysis in making this decision should also consider the costs associated with acquisitions, processing, cataloging, and space requirements of possibly extraneous materials.

Each of the methods outlined above may apply to an individual library's program. At times you may find it desirable to experiment with a combination of methods. The strategy you employ will depend upon the government jurisdiction involved.

U. S. Government Publications

Depository Libraries. There are currently over 1300 U. S. government depository libraries. Depository libraries are allocated primarily on the basis of Congressional and Senatorial districts. The *U. S. Code*, Title 44, Sections 1905–07, lists other means by which a library may become a depository. The depository library program is administered by the Library Programs Service under the superintendent of documents in the Government Printing Office (GPO).

Forty-nine regional depositories receive all items issued in the depository program. There is a limit of two regionals per state. Regionals are responsible for retaining depository materials permanently and for providing interlibrary loan and reference service for the region served.

The other libraries are selective depositories. They have the option of selecting, from approximately 6000 item numbers, the material that the library will receive. Each depository library is required to select a minimum of twenty-five percent of the available item numbers. An item number may be for one specific title, a subject group, a type of publication, or a catchall category, such as "general publications." New item selections are sent to depository libraries at least once a month. Selection of an item number establishes a "standing order" for the material included in that item number. Each depository receives an item number printout twice a year. This printout indicates each item number and notes whether the library has selected it or not, and item selections may be revised with the receipt of each printout. The "List of Items for Selection by Depository Libraries," available from the superintendent of documents, outlines the assigned item numbers, categories, and titles.

Each depository shipment contains one or more *Depository Shipping Lists* listing the items sent to depository libraries by superintendent of documents classification number, title, and item number. Libraries receive only those items on the list that they have selected. The *Daily Depository*

Shipping List may be used by depository libraries to acquire items not selected for deposit. When publications are available for sale from the Government Printing Office (GPO) this information is usually indicated on the *Daily Depository Shipping List*. However carefully the item number selections are tailored to the collection development policy, most libraries will receive some publications that would not be selected if the material were available title by title, or by subject. This is because some item numbers are very broad. For example, the *Federal Reserve Bulletin* was recently assigned a separate item number after previously being included as part of the "general publications" item for the agency. Libraries desiring to select this one title had to take everything included in the general publications category. Although GPO has been refining item numbers to make them more specific, a choice must still be made between selecting an item number that provides material extraneous to the collection and not selecting the item number but acquiring only those titles relevant to the library's collection. This choice must be made on a library-by-library basis. Space availability, staffing resources, proportion of the material outside the parameters of the collection policy, ease of acquiring the publications if not received on deposit, and the availability of the publications at another area institution must be considered.

Each government agency is responsible for sending to GPO all publications except those for official use only or for strictly administrative purposes. The publications GPO receives are included in the depository program. However, not all agencies cooperate fully with this requirement, especially those with multiple regional offices, so all government publications do not get into the depository program. The publications from two large agencies, the National Technical Information Services (NTIS) and Educational Resources Information Center (ERIC) are not included in the depository program. The indexes to the publications for NTIS and ERIC are available on deposit but the publications must be purchased. There are varying degrees of overlap between what is included on deposit and what is included under the rubric of NTIS or ERIC. Technical reports from the Department of Energy are now included in the depository program.

It is difficult to outline precisely what is and what is not included in the depository program. You can safely assume that all administrative reports, such as annual reports of agencies or reports of established entitlement programs, are included. Also included on deposit are public information programs. The gray areas, in which titles will sometimes be included on deposit and sometimes will not, usually involve publications resulting from scientific and technical research, especially those done under government contract. Also included in this gray area are publications issued by regional offices.

The depository program is very active and constantly changing. Regular perusal of *Administrative Notes* from GPO and *Documents to the People*, issued by GODORT, plus attendance at meetings such as the Depository Library Council and the Acquisitions and Bibliographic Control Work Group of the GODORT Federal Documents Task Force, will keep depository librarians abreast of new changes.

Philosophically, in selecting item numbers I prefer to select only those that fulfill academic program/patron needs, but during the last few years it has become increasingly difficult to acquire materials not selected on deposit. Rising costs and the substitution of microfiche for paper copy has created problems. The traditional means of acquiring nonselected items has been to scan the *Daily Depository Shipping List* and acquire a copy from the issuing agency or from the GPO Sales Program. All publications offered for sale by GPO are in the depository program. However, the sales program includes only about ten to fifteen percent of the titles issued by GPO. The remaining titles must be acquired on deposit or from the issuing agency, and many issuing agencies are not retaining copies for distribution because of budget cuts. Many of these agencies are now selling their publications or charging a user or handling fee.[5]

An additional consideration is microfiche. Nearly half of the publications in the depository program are now issued in microfiche. Some item categories are available only in microfiche; others are available in dual format. Microfiche offers cost savings, especially in space. However, in the selection of microfiche, libraries should be careful to stay within the parameters of the collection policy. Microfiche cabinets take space, and a growth rate of two or more cabinets per year requires as careful consideration as creating new shelving space. The same selection criteria should be applied to microfiche as to paper with the added considerations of usage and format, when choice is available. Libraries will want to select heavily used items and reference tools in paper copy.

Individual Title Selection. Since even depository libraries must occasionally request or purchase individual titles, the following information can be used by both depository and nondepository libraries to select and acquire U. S. government publications. As noted earlier, in addition to the depository program the GPO has a sales program. Through this program publications may be purchased from GPO in Washington, D. C., or from GPO bookstores located in major cities. The bookstores do not, however, stock all of the publications included in the program. Libraries will find it most convenient to send orders directly to the superintendent of doc-

5. The Department of Housing and Urban Development is an example of an agency charging a handling fee based on the number of titles requested. The Department of Defense Directorate for Information Operations and Reports has a set fee for each of its reports and requires prepayment. These defense publications recently became part of the depository program (*Daily Depository Shipping List*, Survey 82–55, Dec. 28, 1982).

Publications Reference File. Washington, D. C.: Government Printing Office. Bimonthly.
  Microfiche index to U. S. government publications and subscription services offered for sale by the Government Printing Office (GPO).
  Bimonthly cumulation with biweekly updates of new titles (1–2 microfiche).
  Titles appear in *PRF* a minimum of 3–4 weeks after listing on the *Daily Depository Shipping List.*
  Access is by GPO stock number, Superintendent of Documents Classification Number, and title/keyword.
This source is the most up-to-date compilation of publications available from GPO, but is more of an acquisitions tool than a selection tool because each edition cumulates. Out-of-stock titles may remain on the list for up to two years. *Subject Bibliographies* are the paper equivalent of *PRF* but are not as up-to-date. For selection purposes, *New Books* and *U. S. Government Books* are easier to access.

uments in Washington, D. C. To facilitate ordering, a deposit account of at least fifty dollars may be established with GPO. The GPO bookstores will charge your orders to your deposit account.

With the exception of promotional material, GPO does not provide publications gratis. The titles of the publications that GPO has for sale appear in the *Publications Reference File* (*PRF*). This is a microfiche index arranged in three parts; GPO stock number, superintendent of documents classification number, and title/keyword. This contains the most current information available to libraries. However, there is a minimum delay of at least three weeks between a title's appearance on a *Daily Depository Shipping List* and the receipt of a microfiche *PRF* with that title. The *PRF* is now being sent to depository libraries bimonthly with biweekly updates of new titles added. The *PRF* may be purchased from GPO and is valuable as a reference tool as well as a selection tool.

When ordering from the *PRF*, be sure to check the status line carefully. Some titles are still included in the list but are out-of-stock. This is indicated on the left-hand side of the beginning of each entry in the *PRF*. Each entry receives an individual stock number. This is the number that should be used in ordering publications. Do not try to save time by using the stock number of a previous edition of a title in order to receive the most recent edition. Except in a few instances, this will not work. The *PRF* is also available online through DIALOG/DIALORDER. Material can be ordered directly from GPO on DIALORDER.

The *Daily Depository Shipping List* may also be utilized as a selection tool by both depository and nondepository libraries. While depository libraries may quickly scan the list for nonselected item numbers, nondepository libraries may find the *Daily Depository Shipping List*, which can be purchased on subscription, to be awkward and cumbersome to use.

Selection tools issued by the GPO include *Subject Bibliographies*. Issued free by GPO, these bibliographies provide subject access to GPO sales publications. *Subject Bibliographies* are issued on an irregular basis and, because the coverage is limited to GPO sales publications, they may be updated using the *PRF*. The GPO has discontinued *Selected New Publications* and is now issuing two titles, *New Books* and *U. S. Government Books*. These are both free titles. *New Books* is issued bimonthly and contains titles added to GPO sales since the previous issue, while *U. S. Government Books* appears quarterly and includes the 1000 most popular government publications. The information in both of these titles duplicates the *PRF* but they are easier to access for selection and contain brief annotations. The *Consumer Information Catalog* is a source for quickly locating available consumer information. Issued quarterly, this catalog contains titles of publications available from a number of federal agencies through the Consumer Information Center in Pueblo, Colorado. Less than half of the publications are free and there is a user fee for processing an order of two or more free titles. The publications with sales prices indicated are part of the GPO sales program. Those that are offered free of charge are publications for which the publishing agency has paid the printing and distributing costs. A mailing list for individual copies of the *Consumer Information Catalog* is not maintained. However, libraries may get on the bulk mailing list (twenty-five copies or more) by writing to the Consumer Information Center, Dept. 83, Pueblo, CO 81009.

The old standby, the *Monthly Catalog*, is also a useful selection tool because it contains both depository and nondepository publications. The value of this catalog has diminished as the lag between the publication date and the receipt of the *Monthly Catalog* has widened. Recently, however, an improvement in currency has been noted. Publications identified in the *Monthly Catalog* should be searched in the *PRF* to verify availability. If the title does not appear in the *PRF* and if the *Monthly Catalog* citation does not indicate that it is sold by GPO, try obtaining the publication from the issuing agency. Individual copies of congressional hearings may be obtainable from your Congressman or woman.

Another source of government publications is the National Technical Information Service (NTIS). Many government publications done under contract are included in the *Monthly Catalog* and are available from the NTIS. NTIS often makes out-of-print GPO publications available. The selection tool for titles available from NTIS is the *Government Reports Announcements and Index*.

Serials may be purchased on subscription and annuals on standing order from GPO. The *Monthly Catalog* has a separate volume containing bib-

Monthly Catalog of U. S. Government Publications. v.1– . 1895– .
Washington, D. C., Government Printing Office. Monthly.
Index to U. S. government publications.
Entries in MARC format according to AACR2 rules arranged by
Superintendent of Document Classification Number. Entry includes
issuing agency, title, GPO stock number, and price (if for sale).
6–12-month time lag between the publication date and entry in index.
Hearings appear in index an average of 6 months after receipt by
depository libraries.
Separate indexes by author, title, subject, series/report, contract number,
stock number, and title keyword.
Monthly indexes cumulated in semiannual and annual indexes.
Separate serials volume issued annually containing titles issued three times
or more per year and selected annual and monographic series titles.
This is the basic selection tool for U. S. government publications. Time lag for
indexing is the major disadvantage. It also contains some publications available
only from National Technical Information Service (NTIS).

liographic information for serial titles. The best selection tool is *Price List
36*, "Government Periodicals and Subscription Services." This is available
free from the superintendent of documents. Not all periodicals in the
depository program are available on subscription. Titles not sold by GPO
or available on the depository program will not be included in the *Price
List*. Some titles may be obtained through mailing lists while some, such
as the *Federal Reserve Bulletin*, must be ordered from the issuing agency
rather than GPO. These titles and ordering information are included in
the *Monthly Catalog Serials Supplement*, issued at the beginning of each
year. Commercial publishers are selling a small but growing number of
titles. A recent example is the *Naval Research Logistics Quarterly*, which
is being sold by John Wiley & Sons. This title is no longer available on
deposit.

Nondepository libraries and depository libraries that require multiple
copies of annual compilations should acquire from GPO a copy of the
"Standing Order Item List." This list does not include all annual publications but does contain many of the basic reference publications, such
as the *Congressional Directory*, *U. S. Code*, *Statistical Abstract*, and *Oc-
cupational Outlook Handbook*. Information on GPO standing orders may
be requested from Department 40, Superintendent of Documents, Washington, D. C. Standing orders and out-of-print publications may also be
acquired through government publications dealers and jobbers.[6]

Nondepository and regional publications continue to be elusive, but
access tools issued by commercial publishers are of assistance in selecting,

6. Ed Herman, "Directory of Government Document Dealers and Jobbers, 1981," *Documents to the People* 9:229–34 (1981).

American Statistics Index (ASI). v.1- . 1974- . Bethesda, Md.: Congressional
Information Service, Inc. Monthly with annual and quarterly cumulations.
Abstract and index of U. S. government statistical publications issued in
two sections:
Abstracts give full description of the content and format of each
publication. Aranged by ASI accession number. Issuing agency,
availability and price given.
Index section includes subject and name category, title, and report
number indexes. Keyed to *ASI* accession numbers.
Microfiche collection of all publications included in *ASI* available.
Also retrospective *ASI* issued in 1974 covering publications issued 1960–
73.
The *ASI* is an excellent selection source for both depository and nondepository
titles. Out-of-print materials may be acquired through *ASI* Documents on Demand Service. Companion titles by the same publisher are *CIS Index* and *Statistical Reference Index (SRI)*.

---

evaluating, and acquiring both depository and nondepository publications.
Two primary indexes for United States government publications are *CIS
Index* and *American Statistics Index (ASI)*. *ASI* is especially useful in
identifying nondepository serials and in providing the source from which
the title may be obtained. The abstracts serve as an evaluation tool and
assist in selection. A large number of serial titles in *ASI* are available on
subscription in microfiche from the publisher (Congressional Information
Service). This is an excellent means of assuring that nondepository titles
are received on a regular basis, especially from those agencies that are
rather casual about maintaining mailing lists. *Public Affairs Information
Service Bulletin (PAIS)* is another useful selection tool for current titles.
Government Reference Books, a biennial guide, is valuable for identifying
reference materials on specific topics.

State Publications

Collections of out-of-state publications in most libraries are underutilized,
yet much effort is needed to acquire and house these materials. All large
libraries should collect publications from their own state. These will have
a high frequency of use and, if possible, the library should participate in
a depository program. However, not all states have a depository program.
A 1978 article in *Documents to the People*, "Recent Developments in
Depository Systems for State Government Documents," lists those states
that have depository programs.[7] This information has been updated in

7. Robert F. Gaines, "Recent Developments in Depository Systems for State Government
Documents," *Documents to the People* 6:229–30 (1978).

various issues of *Documents to the People.* The updates are on a state-by-state basis and appear whenever changes have occurred. Material collected from other states should be based closely on the subject parameters defined in the collection policy. The availability of such material in another nearby library should be considered. Also, federal publications sometimes summarize state information. There is an astonishing wealth of information about states in the U. S. publications, covering a wide range of topics.

Whenever possible, larger libraries should attempt to acquire a blue book for each state. These government manuals commonly contain an overview of state activities, agencies, and addresses. A problem is that they are frequently not issued on a regular basis. However, they provide a good beginning point. A list of state blue books is included in David Parish's *State Government Reference Publications.*[8]

There is no one overall comprehensive index to all state publications, and bibliographic control varies considerably from state to state. Most states issue checklists of their publications. A list of general reference sources including state checklists can be found in *State Government Reference Publications* and also in "State Reference Sources."[9] *State Government Reference Publications* is a standard reference source that will assist libraries both with and without state collections in identifying publications issued by state governments. This volume also includes agency addresses and a subject core of state publications. If the state does not issue a checklist, contact the agencies within the state that publish material in your field of interest. If both these methods fail, the old, reliable, *Monthly Checklist of State Publications* is the next best source. This is currently the most comprehensive list of state publications available since Information Handling Service's *Checklist of State Publications* is no longer being published. The incomplete coverage of the *Monthly Checklist* lessens its value as a selection tool, however. Although it only includes state publications issued within the last five years, the time lag is such that many publications are out-of-date before their existence is known through the *Monthly Checklist.*

In addition to using the state checklist and lists of agency publications, newspapers, especially those issued in the capital city, will contain useful articles about new reports and government activities. To assist in obtaining these reports, a telephone directory of state offices is invaluable. The best and quickest way to obtain new and popular state publications is to telephone the appropriate state agency.

8. David Parish, *State Government Reference Publications: An Annotated Bibliography* (Littleton, Colo.: Libraries Unlimited, 1981).
9. Peter Hernon, "State Reference Sources," *Government Publications Review* 7A:47–83 (1980).

Government Publications Review. v.1- . 1973- . New York: Pergamon. Bimonthly.
Research articles covering the field of government publications.
Book review column in most issues.
5–20 book reviews an issue.
Signed reviews by librarians and scholars of commercially published books on topics of interest to government publications librarians.
Government publications are reviewed in annual Notable Documents Section that appears in November-December issue. Includes publications issued during previous year from local, state, and national governments and international organizations. Includes availability and price.
This review provides information on both government publications and commercially published information of interest to government publications librarians. Volumes 7–8 (1980–81) were divided into two parts: Part A—Research and Part B—Acquisitions Guide.

State acquisition and distribution programs are well covered in the literature. A recent issue of *Government Publications Review*, devoted to state publications, contains a "state-of-the-art" article on "Distribution of State Government Publications and Information" by Margaret Lane, and David Parish's "Into the 1980's: The Ideal State Document Reference Collection."[10] A valuable article focusing upon collection development is Terry Weech's "Collection Development and State Publications."[11]

An excellent nongovernmental source for acquiring statistical information published by the states is *Statistical Reference Index (SRI)*, published by the Congressional Information Service. This is not a comprehensive index but it is a good selection and acquisition tool. The material indexed in *SRI* is available on microfiche from CIS.

International Governmental Organizations

Selection, evaluation, and acquisition of the publications of some 300 international governmental organizations (IGOs) that issue publications is a challenge. The *Yearbook of International Organizations* includes a general description of an organization, its address, publications, governmental status, and assists in determining appropriate IGOs.[12] However, biblio-

10. Margaret Lane, "Distribution of State Government Publications and Information," *Government Publications Review* 10:159–72 (1983); David Parish, "Into the 1980's: The Ideal State Documents Reference Collection," *Government Publications Review* 10:213–19 (1983).
11. Terry L. Weech, "Collection Development and State Publications," *Government Publications Review* 8A:47–58 (1981). See also Margaret Lane's column in *Documents to the People*, "Scattered Notes for State Documents Librarians."
12. *Yearbook of International Organizations*, 19th ed. (Brussels and Paris: Union of International Assns. and International Chamber of Commerce, 1981).

graphic control of international governmental publications is generally unsatisfactory, as there is no single bibliographic source for all IGOs. Sales brochures are available for most organizations but only the larger publishers, such as the United Nations, UNESCO, and the Food and Agriculture Organization are bibliographically controlled.[13]

International publications are included in selection journals and notices in professional and technical journals that review government publications. A selection tool for publications of international organizations is *International Bibliography: Publications of Intergovernmental Organizations* (UNIPUB). Issued quarterly, the coverage includes all publications sold by UNIPUB as well as other sales or unpriced publications sent by IGOs to the editorial office of *International Bibliography* for inclusion. Arranged by broad subjects, each issue contains information on how to acquire publications, including addresses and a separate periodicals record. Several books and articles are useful in the selection and acquisition of international publications, especially the writings of Luciana Marulli-Koenig, whose column, "International Documents Roundup" in *Documents to the People* is mandatory for keeping informed about IGO activities and publications, especially the United Nations.[14]

International publications are acquired primarily by purchase or deposit. Except for ephemeral or promotional material, little is available free of charge. To facilitate the sale of their publications, the major IGOs have established sales offices or designated sales agents in the United States. International publications are not cheap; prices are comparable to trade publications. The sales program for most of these agencies provides for the establishment of blanket or standing orders. This is definitely the best method if the categories available for purchase meet your collection needs. In ordering United Nations sales publications, you have a choice of three vendors, the United Nations Sales Office, UNIFO, and UNIPUB. The United Nations provides a quarterly billing and list of publications shipped; UNIFO sends a monthly checklist of materials that have been shipped from the UN; and UNIPUB provides packing lists of the materials they have shipped and a monthly billing. UNIPUB is the largest of the IGO vendors, handling deposit accounts and standing orders for approximately fourteen IGOs.

13. Indexes issued by these IGOs include: *UNDOC: Current Index, UNESCO List of Documents and Publications,* and *FAO Documentation: Current Bibliography.*

14. Luciana Marulli-Koenig, "Collection Development for United Nations Documents," *Government Publications Review* 8A:85–102 (1981); Luciana Marulli, *Documentation of the United Nations System* (Metuchen N. J.: Scarecrow, 1979); Peter Hajnal, *Guide to the United Nations Organization, Documentation and Publishing* (Dobbs Ferry, N. Y.: Oceana, 1978); Peter Hajnal, "Collection Development: United Nations Material," *Government Publications Review* 8A:89–109 (1981); Peter Hajnal, "UNESCO Documents and Publications as Research Material: A Preliminary Report," in *Collection Development and Public Access of Government Documents,* pp. 102–33. Also see *International Documents for the 80's: Their Role and Use.* Proceedings of the Second World Symposium on International Documentation, Brussels, 1980 (Pleasantville, N. Y.: UNIFO, 1982).

International Bibliography. v.1- . 1973- . New York: UNIPUB. Quarterly.
(Title of v.1–10, 1973–82, was *International Bibliography, Information, Documentation*.)
Index to publications of international organizations.
6–12-month time lag between publication date and entry in *International Bibliography*.
Each issue in two parts:
  1. Bibliographic record. Arranged by title of publications under broad subject headings. Entry includes full bibliographic citation (publishing organization identified by acronym), availability, and price. Brief annotations.
  2. Periodicals record. Lists by title periodicals received at the editorial office of *International Bibliography*. Provides publisher and subscription information.
Subject and title indexes.
International Bibliography is a good source for libraries interested in collecting a broad range of international publications. Annotations, while brief, are helpful. Includes not only the larger international organizations but also some of the smaller and lesser-known ones.

To further complicate the selection process, external publishing and copublishing are increasing. According to the annual report of the director general of UNESCO for 1979/80, over thirty percent of the titles issued by UNESCO were published by, or copublished with, a commercial publisher.[15] A similar picture is appearing for the United Nations. The proceedings of conferences and several periodicals are available only from private publishers. Each IGO handles this type of publishing differently. UNESCO includes most copublished titles in its standing order plan; the World Bank provides information on titles published by Johns Hopkins University and others in its *World Bank Catalog*. The United Nations primarily relies upon the commercial publisher for publicity. Some of the major publishers for the UN include Kraus (for reprints), Pergamon, UNIFO, and Walker.[16]

Another interesting aspect of the selection process for international organizations is the difference between "publications" and "documents." At all other levels of government, these two terms are used interchangeably; at this level, however, documents refer to meeting records or internal memoranda. As examples, UNESCO has a separate subscription for documents; the European Communities Commission documents (COM) are not sent to depositories but are available on subscription from the Eu-

15. UNESCO. Director General. *UNESCO 1979–1980* (Paris: UNESCO, 1983), p. 205.
16. Some UN titles issued cooperatively by commercial publishers include: *World Trade Annual* (Walker), *Economic Bulletin for Europe* (Pergamon), *Proceedings of the World Conference of the International Women's Year, 1975* (UNIFO), *Statistical Journal of the U. N. Economic Commission for Europe* (North–Holland).

Index to International Statistics (IIS). Bethesda, Md.: Congressional
Information Service, Inc., 1983– . Monthly with quarterly and annual
cumulations.
Guide and index to statistical publications of 80–90 of the world's major
international governmental organizations.
English-language publications.
Issued in two parts:
Abstracts provide full bibliographic and availability information.
Complete description of format and contents of publications.
Index section includes subject, names, geographic areas; categories;
issuing sources; title; and publication number indexes.
Full text of most publications available on microfiche from the publisher.
Abstracts enhance the value of this publication as a selection tool. All major
IGOs, including the United Nations system, Organization for Economic Co-
operation and Development, European Community, Organization of American
States, commodity organizations, development banks, and other important in-
tergovernmental regional and special purpose organizations are included.

ropean Communities; the World Bank documents are not included in the
World Bank Catalog and are difficult to access; documents from organizations such as NATO are confidential.[17]

Official records of the United Nations are available on standing order.
Not included are records designated "limited" and provisional records of
the plenary minutes of the General Assembly. The provisional minutes of
the committees of the General Assembly are included on standing order,
as are the final verbatim records of the plenary meetings of the General
Assembly. The provisional meeting records of the General Assembly are
available on a separate subscription. This is worthwhile if the library needs
current information, beyond that given in the *UN Chronicle*, since the
UN is several years behind in issuing these minutes in the final form.

Documents of international organizations are also available in microform. Readex Corporation, which for many years issued on microprint
the most complete collection of UN materials available, has now switched
to microfiche. Libraries that serve Model United Nations groups will want
to consider this option. The United Nations Sales Office is offering many
of its series in microfiche and UNIFO also has microfiche available for
United Nations publications. Congressional Information Service is now
publishing *Index to International Statistics (IIS)* and provides microfiche
copies of the publications indexed. *IIS*, although not comprehensive, is
valuable as a selection and acquisitions tool.

17. Peter Hajnal, "IGO Documents and Publications: Volume, Distribution, Recent Developments, and Sources of Information," *Government Publications Review* 9:121–30 (1982).

Foreign Publications

Of all of the levels of government, foreign government publications are most appropriate for resource sharing. Collecting foreign government publications is an area in which "one's aim will all too often exceed one's grasp."[18] Fluctuating exchange rates and shrinking library budgets can play havoc with the development of a foreign collection. Before beginning to develop a foreign collection, you should familiarize yourself with the literature on foreign government publications. With the exception of J. J. Cherns's *Official Publications: An Overview*, most articles or books cover only one specific country. Cherns's book covers the history and current government publishing practices of twenty countries as well as providing a general overview. The countries included are primarily developed countries in various parts of the world.[19] The available literature on some countries, such as Australia, Canada, Great Britain, and France, is abundant.[20] For less developed countries, it is practically nonexistent. In these instances, discussing selection and acquisition methods with colleagues who have had actual experience with these countries is invaluable. The meetings of the Foreign Documents Work Group of the GODORT International Documents Task Force are also helpful.

There is considerable overlap of information contained in foreign government publications with that found in United States and international publications. Before making a decision about what to acquire from foreign countries, become familiar with the information in international publications. You should also consider the information found in U. S. publications, not only the well-known sources, such as the *Department of State Background Notes*, *Country Surveys*, and *Foreign Economic Trends and Their Implications for the United States*, but also the publications of the Foreign Information Broadcast Service, and the Joint Publications Research Service.[21] The detail of information in these nonforeign publications will not be as great as that in sources published by the foreign government, but you should carefully consider whether your patrons and programs

18. Theodore Samore, ed., *Acquisitions of Foreign Materials for U. S. Librarians*, 2nd ed. (Metuchen, N. J.: Scarecrow, 1982), p. 113.
19. J. J. Cherns, *Official Publishing: An Overview* (Oxford: Pergamon, 1979).
20. Numerous articles have appeared in *Government Publications Review*. Some examples include: Barbara Smith, "British Official Publications: Publications and Distribution," 5:1–12 (1978); Genevieve Boisard, "Public Access to Government Information: The Position of France," 9:203–19 (1982); Gloria Westfall, "Access to French Publications," 8A:161–73 (1981); Frances Rose, "Publishing and Information Policies of the Government of Canada: Some Recent Developments," 5:391–97 (1978). Pergamon Press is issuing a series of "Guides to Official Publications." Some of the titles published in this series include: Olga B. Bishop, *Canadian Official Publications* (1981); Howard F. Coxon, *Australian Official Publications* (1980); Arthur Malthby and Brian McKenna, *Irish Official Publications* (1980); and Gloria Westfall, *French Official Publications* (1980). Also, *Documents to the People* contains columns on foreign government publications, especially Australian and Canadian publications.
21. Indexes to the Foreign Broadcast Information Service are published by Newsbank. Bell & Howell indexes the Joint Publications Research Service publications in *Transdex*.

require the greater detail. If you are uncertain whether the U. S. and international material is sufficient, visit a library that has a strong collection in foreign government publications. Also, once a decision has been made about which countries or areas you will cover, contact librarians in institutions similar to yours to discuss acquisition methods.[22]

Bibliographic control of foreign government publications is on a country-by-country basis and ranges from nonexistent to excellent. The developed countries have national bibliographies and government printers who also issue lists of publications. Publications lists, when available, should be acquired. Also, foreign government organization manuals or blue books are useful in providing information about the organization of the government and how and where to obtain material.

Depository arrangements, with a few exceptions, are not available for foreign government publications. Deposit accounts will meet with varying success. Some countries will take the deposit and continue to send material long after the money has obviously been exhausted; others will take the money but the publications never arrive. The problems are primarily with the undeveloped countries, especially in Africa or in countries with unstable political conditions. One acquisitions method that can work well is to add foreign government publications to existing standing order or approval plans with vendors supplying material from various parts of the world. This method is probably the most cost effective, especially for undeveloped countries.

The best source of evaluation of foreign government publications is *Government Publications Review*. This is an excellent acquisitions tool and can be used to acquire a limited collection of basic foreign publications. Ordering information is normally included.

Many commercial publishers are offering foreign government materials, especially legislative and statistical material, in microform. These publications are good candidates for resource sharing. Evaluative reviews appear in *Microforms Review* as well as other government publications reviewing media.

Local Publications

All libraries should collect publications from their local area. Local publications are probably the most heavily used, on a per capita basis, of the various levels of government. If the area served is a large metropolitan city, it is easiest to acquire just the publications of that city and the county.

22. To locate appropriate institutions, consult the *Directory of Government Documents Collections and Librarians*, 3rd ed. (Washington D. C.: Congressional Information Service for the Government Documents Round Table, American Library Assn., 1981).

A library surrounded by many small cities has a more difficult problem. Acquiring the publications of more than fifteen to twenty cities is nearly impossible. This number may be too high in many instances depending upon distances, publishing patterns, and subjects emphasized.

Of all the levels of government, the selection and acquisition of local publications is the most challenging and rewarding. Ideally the collection should be as comprehensive as possible; at a minimum it should include the budgets, evaluative reports, proceedings, and minutes of the City Council or Board of Supervisors, annual reports, and statistical reports.

Bibliographic control is almost nonexistent. The problems in building a local collection will not be in deciding what to select, but in finding out what has been issued and acquiring it. Get an organizational directory from each of the constituencies from which you plan to acquire materials. Do not forget major special districts, such as school and water districts. Become familiar with the organization of each political entity through these directories. Request copies of the agendas for the Board of Supervisors and the City Council(s). Review the agendas for items that contain reports. Since these reports are frequently in short supply, contact the appropriate agency immediately. In order to receive these agendas regularly, it is advisable to provide the person responsible for their distribution with self-addressed, stamped envelopes.

Depending upon local conditions, it may be useful to visit the county or city offices the day following each meeting of the City Council or Board of Supervisors. Copies of reports distributed to council and board members may be returned to the file following the meeting and will be available from the city or county clerk. It is also important to read the newspaper for local events, especially small local weeklies that frequently contain more news of local government activities.

Personal contacts are extremely important in acquiring local publications. An educational process is frequently involved. Some administrators and staff must be constantly reminded of your existence and continuing needs. At first you may have problems locating the appropriate individuals and you may also be appalled by their low regard for the importance of the local information. However, persistence will pay off, and you frequently must be very persistent given the high turnover rate in some local governments. Eventually your contacts will begin to call you or send you new publications as they are issued.

Index to Urban Documents, published by Greenwood, is the only major index devoted entirely to local publications, but is limited to cities of over 100,000 population. This compilation is useful in developing a collection of local publications on specific subjects. Publications indexed are available on microfiche from the publisher. Microfiche subscriptions are also available by geographic or subject areas.

The literature contains a surprising number of books and articles on the topic of selecting and acquiring local government publications. A particularly useful article is Michael Shannon's "Collection Development and Local Documents: History and Present Use in the United States."[23]

Conclusion

The goal in selecting government publications in any library should be to develop a "relationship between the documents collection and other library collections . . . [which is] that of a single resource in meeting user needs."[24] This integration is achieved by a well-written collection development policy for government publications and the adherence to such a policy in the selection process.

Libraries can no longer support comprehensive collections in all levels of government. The development of functional collections and interinstitutional cooperation demand a dynamic decision making role in the selection and acquisition of government publications. Reductions in the budgets of both libraries and governments, the growing tendency of governments to publish in microformats, publishing by commercial publishers, and interinstitutional cooperation are all important factors that influence selection decisions. Resource sharing is an area that has an untapped potential, especially among depository libraries.[25] Quality service is not provided by having all publications but by consciously and systematically developing a collection to meet the needs of the user.

Selection Sources

Administrative Notes. v.1– . 1980– . Washington, D.C.: Supt. of Documents. Irregular.
American Statistics Index. v.1– . 1973– . Bethesda, Md: Congressional Information Service. Monthly.
Bishop, Olga B. *Canadian Official Publications.* Guides to Official Publications. Oxford: Pergamon, 1981.
Cherns, J. J. *Official Publishing: An Overview.* Oxford: Pergamon, 1979.
Coxon, Howard F. *Australian Official Publications.* Guides to Official Publications. Oxford: Pergamon, 1980.

23. Michael Shannon, "Collection Development and Local Documents: History and Present Use in the United States," *Government Publications Review* 8A:59–87 (1981). See also Peter Hernon, ed., *Municipal Government Reference Sources, Publications and Collections* (New York: Bowker, 1978); Yuri Nakata, Susan Smith, and William Ernst, Jr., *Organizing a Local Documents Collection* (Chicago: American Library Assn., 1979), pp. 3–12.
24. Bernard M. Fry, "Government Publications and the Library," *Government Publications Review* 4:115 (1977).
25. Hernon and Purcell, *Developing Collections of U. S. Government Publications*, p. 57.

Directory of Government Documents Collections and Librarians. 3rd ed. Washington, D. C.: Congressional Information Service for the Government Documents Round Table, American Library Assn., 1981.

Documents to the People. v.1- . 1972- . Chicago: American Library Assn. Bimonthly.

FAO Documentation: Current Bibliography. v.1- . 1967- . Rome: Food and Agricultural Organization of the United Nations. Bimonthly.

Fry, Bernard M., and Peter Hernon, eds. *Government Publications: Key Papers.* Guides to Official Publications. Oxford: Pergamon, 1981.

Government Publications Review. v.1- . 1974- . Elmsford, N.Y.: Pergamon. Bimonthly.

Government Reports and Announcements. v.74- . 1974- . Springfield, Va.: U.S. National Technical Information Service. Biweekly.

Hajnal, Peter. "Collection Development: United Nations Material." *Government Publications Review* 8A:89–109 (1981).

_____. *Guide to United Nations Organization, Documentation, and Publishing.* Dobbs Ferry, N. Y.: Oceana, 1978.

_____. "IGO Documents and Publications: Volume, Distribution, Recent Developments and Sources of Information." *Government Publications Review* 9:121–30 (1982).

_____. "UNESCO Documents and Publications as Research Material: A Preliminary Report." In *Collection Development and Public Access of Government Documents.* Proceedings of the First Annual Library Government Documents and Information Conference, Boston, 1981, pp. 103–13. Ed. by Peter Hernon. Westport, Conn.: Meckler, 1982.

Herman, Ed. "Directory of Government Document Dealers and Jobbers, 1981." *Documents to the People* 9:229–34 (1981).

Hernon, Peter, ed. *Municipal Government Reference Sources, Publications and Collections.* New York: Bowker, 1978.

_____. "State Reference Sources." *Government Publications Review* 7A:47–83 (1980).

_____and Gary R. Purcell. *Developing Collections of U. S. Government Publications.* Greenwich, Conn.: JAI Press, 1982.

Index to Current Urban Documents. v.1- . 1972- . Westport, Conn.: Greenwood. Quarterly.

International Bibliography: Publications of Intergovernmental Organizations. v.1- . 1973- . New York: UNIPUB. Quarterly.

Lane, Margaret. "Distribution of State Government Publications and Information." *Government Publications Review* 10:159–72 (1983).

_____. "Scattered Notes for State Documents Librarians." Column in *Documents to the People,* 1981 +.

Malthby, Arthur, and Brian McKenna. *Irish Official Publications.* Guides to Official Publications. Oxford: Pergamon, 1980.

Marulli, Luciana. *Documentation of the United Nations System.* Metuchen, N. J.: Scarecrow, 1979.

Marulli-Koenig, Luciana. "Collection Development for United Nations Documents and Publications." In *Collection Development and Public Access of Government Documents.* Proceedings of the First Annual Library Government Documents and Information Conference, Boston, 1981, pp. 85–102. Ed. by Peter Hernon. Westport, Conn.: Meckler, 1982.

_____. "International Documents Roundup." Column in *Documents to the People,* 1980 +.

Monthly Checklist of State Publications. v.1- . 1910- . Washington, D.C.: Library of Congress. Monthly.

Samore, Theodore, ed. *Acquisitions of Foreign Materials for U. S. Libraries.* 2nd ed. Metuchen, N. J.: Scarecrow, 1982.

Smith, Barbara. "British Official Publications: Publications and Distribution." *Government Publications Review* 5:1-12 (1978).

UNDOC: Current Index. v.1- . 1950- . New York: United Nations Publications. 10/year.

UNESCO. Director General. UNESCO 1979-1980. Paris: UNESCO, 1983.

UNESCO List of Documents and Publications. v.1- . 1973- . Paris: UNESCO. Quarterly.

Weech, Terry L. "Collection Development and State Publications." *Government Publications Review* 8A:47-58 (1981).

Westfall, Gloria. "Access to French Publications." *Government Publications Review* 8A:161-73 (1981).

————. *French Official Publications.* Guides to Official Publications. Oxford: Pergamon, 1980.

Yearbook of International Organizations. 19th ed. Brussels: Union of International Assns.; Paris: International Chamber of Commerce, 1981.

Further Readings

Boisard, Genevieve. "Public Access to Government Information: The Position of France." *Government Publications Review* 9:203-19 (1982).

Dimitrov, T. D., ed. *International Documents for the 80's: Their Role and Use.* Proceedings of the Second World Symposium on International Documentation, Brussels, 1980. Pleasantville, N. Y.: UNIFO, 1982.

Fry, Bernard M. "Government Publications and the Library." *Government Publications Review* 4:111-17 (1977).

Gaines, Robert F. "Recent Developments in Depository Systems for State Government Documents." *Documents to the People* 6:229-30 (1978).

Marulli-Koenig, Luciana. "Collection Development for United Nations Documents." *Government Publications Review* 8A:85-102 (1981).

McClure, Charles R. "An Integrated Approach to Government Publications Collection Development." *Government Publications Review* 8A: 5-15 (1981).

Morton, Bruce, and J. Randolph Cox. "Cooperative Collection Development between Selective U. S. Depository Libraries." *Government Publications Review* 9:221-29 (1982).

Nakata, Yuri, Susan Smith, and William Ernst, Jr. *Organizing a Local Documents Collection.* Chicago: American Library Assn., 1979.

Parish, David. "Into the 1980's: The Ideal State Documents Reference Collection." *Government Publications Review* 10:213-19 (1983).

————. *State Government Reference Publications: An Annotated Bibliography.* Littleton, Colo.: Libraries Unlimited, 1981.

Rose, Frances. "Publishing and Information Policies of the Government of Canada: Some Recent Developments." *Government Publications Review* 5:391-97 (1978).

Shannon, Michael. "Collection Development and Local Documents: History and Present Use in the United States." *Government Publications Review* 8A:59-87 (1981).

SMALL PRESSES

Eric J. Carpenter

In our Lord's House of Literature, there had better be room enough for the whole multifarious show, including some of its sideshows. The one thing we did not wish to do was deprive literature or ourselves of the genuine, whatever shape it might happen to take.[1]

The selection and acquisition of small press materials is one of the most challenging, important, and enjoyable types of collection development activity for any librarian. Many of the books that have helped define the spirit of our age, such as the *Communist Manifesto* and James Joyce's *Ulysses,* were originally published by small press publishers, men and women more interested in creative self-expression and dissemination of ideas than in profit. In a free society the librarian has an obligation to acquire and preserve materials that articulate ideas and express artistic visions outside the mainstream of political, social, and cultural thought. In this era of increasing control of major publishing houses by corporate conglomerates, it is the small alternative press publisher, not primarily concerned with profit, who is free to publish materials expressing controversial ideas challenging the opinions and standards of the establishment. As Christopher Lasch has said:

> The publishing business, formerly one of the last strongholds of the independent entrepreneur, is rapidly being swallowed up by corporate capitalism.. . . In the last 20 years, more than 300 mergers have taken place in the publishing industry. . . . New authors find it more and more difficult to get published at all. Even established authors find most commercial publishers increasingly indifferent to a book that promises only a modest sale. . . . Today, the censorship of ideas has entered American life through the back door. The economics of centralization and standardization threaten to achieve what

The author wishes to thank Cristine Rom for valuable suggestions.

1. Theodore Weiss in *The Little Magazine in America: A Modern Documentary History,* ed. by Elliot Anderson and Mary Kinzie (Yonkers, N. Y.: Pushcart Pr., 1978), pp. 68–69.

could not be achieved, in a country officially committed to liberal principles, by government repression: uniformity of thought.[2]

Librarians should resist this subtle censorship by acquiring items published by small alternative presses.

In a free society it is important, particularly for academic and public librarians, to develop a balanced library collection, one that includes books spanning the political spectrum, avant-garde art, literature, music, titles for minority groups, and materials for readers interested in alternative lifestyles. Small alternative press publications add vitality, diversity, and balance to the collection. Books and periodicals from the large, establishment trade and academic houses may be easier to acquire, but they are not the daring, antiestablishment works published by small alternative presses. These publications are issued by small press publishers with motives and methods radically different from large commercial publishers. To successfully build a small press collection, a librarian must understand these differences and adopt appropriate methods of collection development.

Defining the small press movement is difficult. James Danky, in his excellent chapter "The Acquisition of Alternative Materials in Libraries" in *Alternative Materials in Libraries*, defines such materials as those produced by "non-standard, non-establishment groups or individuals."[3] Though Danky's chapter—and the entire book—are highly recommended for further study, his definition of small press publishers seems to depend more on ideology than size. It is the size of the small press, however, that is the cause of problems for librarians in identifying and acquiring their publications. These problems are our primary concern here. In this chapter, therefore, the small press publisher is defined as small, independent, and noncommercial, an alternative to the large profit-motivated houses. The sixth edition of *Alternatives in Print* provides information on 2600 publishers. They issue titles on an astonishingly diverse range of subjects from alternative lifestyles and technology to children, ecology, education, health, homosexuality, literature, politics, racial and ethnic minorities, religion, senior citizens, and, of course, the women's movement.

These subjects are of interest and importance particularly to patrons of public and academic libraries. Librarians developing collections for such patrons should therefore familiarize themselves with the small press world and begin acquiring the chapbooks, little magazines, alternative newspapers, pamphlets, and other fascinating and important materials issued by

2. Christopher Lasch in the *New York Times*, reprinted in *Editor's Choice: Literature & Graphics from the U. S. Small Press, 1965–1977*, ed. by Morty Sklar and Jim Mulac (Iowa City: The Spirit That Moves Us Press, 1980), p. 1.
3. James Danky, "The Acquisition of Alternative Materials in Libraries," in *Alternative Materials in Libraries*, ed. by James P. Danky and Elliot Shore (Metuchen, N. J.: Scarecrow, 1982), p. 13.

small presses. The purpose of this chapter is to describe some of the principles, sources, and techniques needed to identify, select, and acquire these materials.

Identification

The inadequate bibliographic control of small press publications sometimes makes identification difficult. Unlike large commercial publishers, small ones lack large budgets for marketing and distribution and often do not list their titles in *Books in Print*. Cataloging small press publications deposited for copyright at the Library of Congress has never been a priority for LC, and many small presses do not participate in the Cataloging in Publication Program. Rapid cataloging by libraries that acquire small press titles has helped alleviate this problem in recent years, and it is now easier to find citations for small press titles in the major bibliographic databases: OCLC, RLIN, etc. It is still sometimes difficult, however, for librarians to obtain adequate bibliographic data needed to select and order small press books, little magazines, newspapers, and other materials.

This poor bibliographic control presents a challenge to the librarian that can be met with dedication, proper use of existing small press bibliographic tools, and ingenuity. It takes extra effort to build a collection of small press materials, but the work is both stimulating and rewarding. One discovers the intellectual ferment of the small press world. The reward is seeing important small press books, little magazines, and newspapers added to the library collection and circulated.

The first important bibliographic tool is *Alternatives in Print*, in its sixth edition in 1980. This book, compiled by a Task Force of the American Library Association's (ALA) Social Responsibilities Round Table (SRRT), serves as an international publisher's trade list for "nearly 2600 presses, many of which cannot be located through standard bibliographic tools." A complete publications list for each publisher categorizes works by format and includes prices for each title. There are indexes by author and title for all books and pamphlets and separate title indexes for periodicals and audiovisual materials. This work is indispensable for selecting and acquiring small press titles, though catalogs from social science publishers tend to predominate. Because small presses tend to have short lives, change addresses frequently, and print relatively few copies of each title, it is crucial for librarians to maintain current information on important publishers. Bibliographic tools for small presses tend to become dated quickly and are not revised regularly. Despite the importance of *Alternatives in Print*, publication of future editions is doubtful at this time. ALA/SRRT has, however, issued in 1984 a *Field Guide to Alternative Media: A Di-*

Alternatives in Print. 1st ed.– . 1971– . New York: Neal Schuman.
Irregularly.
List of publications available from nearly 2600 small press publishers.
Coverage emphasizes United States, but extends worldwide.
English-language publications predominate.
Includes book, pamphlets, periodicals, and audiovisual materials.
Publication after the sixth edition is doubtful.
The principal arrangement of the book is by publisher. Complete addresses are given for each, and a complete publications list for each publisher is arranged by format. Authors, titles, and prices of each publication are listed. There are separate indexes by author and title for all books and pamphlets. Magazines and audiovisual materials are also indexed separately by title. All subjects are covered, but the emphasis is on the social sciences.

---

rectory to Reference and Selection Tools Useful in Accessing Small and Alternative Press Publications and Independently Produced Media, edited by Patricia J. Case.[4] Maintaining supplemental files and contact with other knowledgeable people in the small press world is important as a means of supplementing and updating the information found in *Alternatives in Print* and other similar sources.

The second indispensable bibliographical tool for identifying small press publishers and their publications is *Small Press Record of Books in Print,* in its twelfth edition in 1983. It is published by Dustbooks, the small press equivalent to the Bowker/Xerox conglomerate. Though it covers fewer publishers (1800) than *Alternatives in Print,* it appears annually and covers more literary and small presses. There are four indexes to *Small Press Record of Books in Print*: author, title, publisher, and subject. The author entries contain complete information on each publication: the price, ISBN, pagination, physical dimensions, and binding (often useful for making cataloging, binding, and storage decisions). Many entries also contain a short description of the contents of the book. A valuable subject index lists the complete name of the author as well as the title, in contrast with *Alternatives in Print,* which has only a subject index to publishers.

COSMEP (formerly the Committee on Small Magaazine Editors and Publishers, now known as COSMEP, the International Association of Independent Publishers) issues an important *Catalogue of Independent Press Publications* as a set of ten microfiche. This is a small publisher's trade list arranged first with individual publishers' catalogs, followed by a publishers' index and then separate subject, author, and title indexes for each publication. It is a very useful tool and can be purchased from COSMEP. The *COSMEP Catalogue,* a valuable listing of representative pub-

4. Patricia J. Case, *Field Guide to Alternative Media: A Directory to Reference and Selection Tools Useful in Accessing Small and Alternative Press Publications and Independently Produced Media* (Chicago: American Library Assn., 1984), 44p.

Small Press Record of Books in Print. 1st ed.- . 1966–68- . Paradise, Calif.:
Dustbooks. Annually.
List of publications available for over 1800 small press publishers.
Some 16,000 entries in latest edition.
Coverage emphasizes United States and Commonwealth but extends
worldwide.
English-language publications predominate.
Includes books, pamphlets, broadsides, posters, and poem cards, but
excludes periodicals.
The author entries of this book provide full information needed for purchase:
title, publisher, date, dimensions, pagination, binding, price, ISBN, and a brief
description of its contents. The title and subject indexes refer back to the author
entries. A publisher/author index provides complete addresses for publishers.
This title covers all subjects, but literary titles are more frequent.

---

lications by COSMEP members, also appears every few years. Four editions
have been issued since COSMEP's founding in 1968. The latest edition
(1984) contains descriptions and ordering information for over 500 titles
from 150 small independent publishers.

Dustbooks publishes the small press equivalent to the Ulrich's directories for serials, the *International Directory of Little Magazines and
Small Presses* in its nineteenth edition in 1984. For librarians developing
collections of modern English-language literature, this is the single most
important source. There are lengthy entries for both individual periodicals
and presses designed to assist authors submitting materials for publication,
publishers communicating with each other, and also librarians and booksellers acquiring titles. The information provided is current, usually reliable, and updated monthly in the "New Listings" column in *Small Press
Review*, also published by Dustbooks.

Having discovered these three basic sources for identifying small press
materials, one must use them creatively to develop a good small press
collection. Compile lists of important small press publishers in the area(s)
of interest to your library, describing the types of patrons you serve and
the types of materials you wish to acquire. Ask to be included on their
mailing lists if they are maintained (many small presses find such lists too
costly), or at least to receive a set of brochures and catalogs. You may be
surprised at the responses. Small press publishers sometimes send personal
letters, free copies of books and little magazines, and other materials. The
attention of libraries and librarians is very important to many of these
publishers, who want to see their works distributed and read. Follow up
on the responses you receive. Purchase books for yourself and your library.
Such an expression of interest and support (however limited) can mean
much to the small struggling publisher who may believe that few librarians
know or care about his or her work. These investments often yield rich

International Directory of Little Magazines and Small Presses. 1st ed–.
   1965–. Paradise, Calif.: Dustbooks. Annually.
   Directory of currently available little magazines.
   Coverage emphasizes United States and Commonwealth, but extends
      worldwide.
   English-language magazines and presses predominate.
   Nineteenth edition has 3535 entries.
   Includes list of 200 distributors, book jobbers, and magazine agents.
   Entries for magazines and publishers are here interfiled alphabetically. The mag-
   azine entries include: name of magazine, press and editor, address and phone
   number, description of types of materials used and the editorial policy, fre-
   quency, price, pagination, circulation, discounts, back issue availability, and prices.
   Press entries include name of the press and editors, comments of editors on
   editorial policy and recent contributors, prices, type of binding, number of titles
   published in the most recent year, etc. Added subject and regional indexes list
   titles and names only and refer readers to the full entries under magazine/press.
   Early editions were largely limited to literary titles, but later editions cover many
   subject areas.

---

returns in information and personal contacts; the small press world is a
highly personal one where such contacts are very important and highly
valued. Personal contacts can also be developed at small press gatherings
and at small press bookfairs. For example, the New York Small Press
Bookfair has exhibits by many small press publishers where a librarian
can contact small press people, sample their wares, and sign up for mailing
lists.

Selection

The primary principle that should guide the librarian in selecting small
press titles is that few of them are ever reviewed, and then usually in other
press publications. The *New York Times*, the *Times* (London), and other
major newspapers seldom pay any attention to the small press world.
Unfortunately this is also true of *Choice* and the other standard library
reviewing journals (with one notable exception, *Library Journal*, which
is discussed below). Consequently, the librarian must discover and read
regularly the reviewing sources that do exist. Moreover, the selector of
small press materials must develop his or her powers of discrimination
and make informed selections without relying on reviews. This means
relying more on information about particular authors and publishers and
by acquiring titles that seem intrinsically important even if they are not
currently in demand.

While risks are necessary in selecting small press titles, the selector
should try to avoid acquiring vanity press publications. Bill Henderson, a
noted author, publisher, and spokesman for small presses, observes that:

Self-publishing and small-press publishing should never be confused with "vanity" publishing. The vanity press is deservedly held in disrepute by both commercial and small presses, for it publishes anything for which an author will pay, usually at a loss for an author and a nice profit for the publisher. The vanity publisher entices the author with promises of advertisements and reviews, but reviews are rarely obtained—because reviewers shun vanity press books—and advertisements are crammed together in blocks. After so-called publication, vanity press books usually remain in publisher's warehouse until they are pulped. The author never receives any money in return.[5]

Vanity presses can be difficult for the novice to identify, but they almost never appear in the Dustbooks directories. They seldom issue any catalogs, and they are shunned by reviewers. If a selector is in doubt about a particular press, he or she can contact a small press distributor or librarian colleague to verify the reputation of the press in question.

Reviews for small press publications tend to appear most frequently in other little magazines and alternative sources. It is therefore extremely important that librarians collecting small press titles subscribe to and read these small press reviewing journals. Jim Danky's discussion of these sources in *Alternative Materials in Libraries* is excellent.[6] An appendix to this book, "Sources," has entries for many major sources of reviews for small press books, and therefore only the most important titles are mentioned in this chapter.[7] These include the monthly *Small Press Review* from Dustbooks, which contains useful, though not often analytical, reviews of both small press books and little magazines. The "Dustbooks Small Press Book Club Selection List" is a useful feature with reviews of one or two paragraphs and a backlist section for titles still available. A special library issue appears each June with excellent library-oriented articles on collection development topics such as a status report on small press collections. These articles and the advertisements for many small presses make this issue indispensable reading for librarians interested in small presses.

While *Small Press Review* is most useful for reviews of literary publications, *Sipapu* is an important source for reviews of nonliterary materials. It is a self-described "newsletter for librarians interested in third world studies, the counter-culture, peace & alternative and independent presses." The editor of *Sipapu*, Noel Peattie, is himself a librarian and therefore emphasizes selection and collection development for alternative press materials.

Peattie is also the editor of the section "Little Magazines" in the fourth and latest edition of *Magazines for Libraries*.[8] This is another standard

5. Bill Henderson, "The Small Book Press: A Cultural Essential," *Library Quarterly* 54: 62 (Jan. 1984).
6. Danky, pp. 18–22.
7. Ibid., pp. 183–206.
8. Noel Peattie, "Little Magazines" Section in *Magazines for Libraries*, 4th ed., ed. by Bill Katz and Linda Sternberg Katz (New York: Bowker, 1982).

source for good reviews of small press periodicals written by well-qualified librarians. The alternatives, fiction, lesbian and gay, literary reviews, and women sections of this title should also be consulted. Each section contains lists of abstracts, indexes, and basic periodicals followed by a list of general titles. Each entry provides the information needed for ordering, indicates where the magazine is indexed, and has a short critical review.

Library Journal (LJ) includes Bill Katz's valuable "Magazines" column in each issue and contains reviews and newsnotes on new and important small press periodicals, both literary and nonliterary. Katz gives basic price and address information together with witty commentary and good advice for making selection decisions. This column should be scanned regularly.

LJ also publishes its annual "Small Press Roundup: Best Titles of 19--" in the December 15 issue. Susan Shafarzek now contributes this article, formerly written by Bill Katz. Both books and periodicals issued by small presses during the year are reviewed briefly, and price and address information are included. Each article opens with a valuable selection on reviews and sources, and is followed by a review of titles from individual presses that is organized by region. A complete list of addresses for all publishers cited concludes the article. The emphasis is on literary titles, but other subjects are included.

Little magazines are also covered regularly in *Serials Review*, a quarterly devoted to all aspects of serials librarianship. Cristine Rom edits an excellent column containing several pages of reviews and commentary on little magazines in each issue. Feature articles on important small press periodicals and interviews with their publishers also appear regularly. The Small Press Billboard includes advertisements and additional information. Regular scanning of *Serials Review* provides information on new and important small press periodical titles.

A new journal, *Small Press: The Magazine of Independent Book Publishing*, began publication in late 1983.[9] It is self-described as a "how to" magazine aimed directly at current and would-be publishers, intending to assist in the process of publishing. Though the first two issues contained no book reviews, the publisher says reviews might appear in future issues. The articles on publishing, production, marketing, and distribution are, however, filled with useful information on many aspects of the small press world.

The relative paucity of review sources for small press publications forces librarians selecting these materials to develop other sources of information. One useful technique is compiling and exchanging lists of important authors and publishers for various subjects collected. Many of the major libraries use this method in building collections of modern literature. Scan-

9. *Small Press: The Magazine of Independent Book Publishing*, v.1- . 1983- . (New York: Bowker).

ning publishers' catalogs and regularly examining small press books and periodicals themselves as they come into the library helps identify important authors and publishers. Exchanging lists with other librarians is also useful. This can be done in conjunction with a visit to a library containing a small press collection; such visits can be extremely important for both the novice and veteran. Chapter IX in *Alternative Materials in Libraries* contains a directory of libraries with collections of alternative materials. Planning such a visit carefully is, of course, important to assure a cordial reception, but most librarians working with small press collections are glad to welcome visiting colleagues and trade information on important authors and publishers, selection techniques, and vendors. The highly personal world of the small press includes small press publishers and librarians alike.

Acquisition

Once the small press title has been selected, the next challenge is to obtain a copy. To meet this challenge a librarian should keep several principles in mind. The first is that the channels of distribution for small presses are quite different from those of large commercial publishers. The print runs of small presses are much smaller than those of large trade houses. Alternative publishers are often one-person enterprises struggling to handle all aspects of book publishing, from editorial work to actual production and distribution. These publishers do not have time or money to handle the torrent of orders, claims, and vouchers generated by the computers of book jobbers and libraries. As a result librarians often become irritated with small presses and reluctant to acquire their publications.

This need not happen. A little understanding, patience, and creativity can make dealing with small presses a pleasant experience. The best way to acquire titles from a particular publisher is often to order direct, even if it means filing a few more orders slips and handling a few more invoices. A librarian should remember that the patron won't care how the book was acquired as long as it is on the shelf in the library when he or she wants it. Also, try to understand the financial position of the typical small press publisher and work with it. Most cannot afford to wait two or three months or longer for payment. Don't hesitate to prepay for important titles. Often only a small amount is involved, and if a librarian is concerned about the reliability of a publisher, the publisher's existence and reliability can be verified with a phone call.

A variety of small press jobbers and distribution services exist. Get acquainted with these dealers and sources and send orders to them rather than to book jobbers, who prefer to deal with large trade publishers.

James Danky's chapter has an excellent list of these small press distributors, and there is a more lengthy list at the back of the *International Directory of Little Magazines and Small Presses*. This larger list, however, also includes trade book jobbers and distributors to bookstores, so it must be used with care.

The first type of small press jobber offers a wide range of plans and services to libraries similar to those of trade book vendors. Small Press Distribution offers a firm order service as well as standing orders and approval plans.[10] Another such multipurpose jobber is Bertram Rota Ltd.[11] Rota specializes in small press literary publications from the United Kingdom and also offers standing orders and a limited approval plan. Specialist vendors also exist in some fields. Printed Matter, Inc., opened in 1976 to distribute contemporary artists' books, the book serving here as a medium for artistic expression.[12] Printed Matter sells books created and published by artists from around the world to libraries and is considered a major dealer in this field.

Specialist bookstores also act as book jobbers for libraries. Gotham Book Mart is one of the best literary bookstores in the United States.[13] It also acts as a jobber for literary small press publications. Membership in the Small Press Book Club is still another method of acquiring important titles. A subscription to *Small Press Review* includes membership in the club, and ten titles (five books and five little magazine issues) are listed each month in the magazine centerfold. Selections are made from "the small press worldwide, and chosen for the book club for quality, variety and uniqueness." Any number of titles may be selected, and orders sent to Dustbooks. The selections are judicious, and buying from the book club is a good method for small libraries to acquire a few preselected titles from various small presses. The club also has half-price sales that offer important titles at low prices.

The librarian working with a small press jobber should rely on personal correspondence. Most of these dealers have specialists on their staffs who work regularly and sometimes exclusively with small presses. These people are valuable contacts and sources of elusive information on the small press world.

Alternative/literary bookstores can be found in many cities, especially large ones (Grolier Book Shop, a poetry bookstore in Cambridge, Massachusetts, is a delightful example), and some of these stores also sell through the mail and send catalogs to libraries.[14] Regular visits to book-

10. Small Press Distribution, 1784 Shattuck Ave., Berkeley, CA 94709.
11. Bertram Rota Ltd., 30–31 Long Acre, London WC2E 9LT England.
12. Printed Matter, Inc., 7–9 Lispenard St., New York, NY 10013.
13. Gotham Book Mart, 41 West 47th St., New York, NY 10036.
14. For the Grolier Book Shop contact Louisa Solano, Grolier Book Shop, 6 Plympton Street, Cambridge, MA 02138.

stores are an important means of maintaining contact with the small press world. Browsing among alternative books and magazines is a wonderful way to spend an afternoon. Len Fulton's *American Odyssey, a Bookselling Travelogue* is a record of a journey he and Ellen Ferber made across the United States selling his novel *The Grassman* and other Dustbooks titles.[15] It is a fascinating documentary and testimony to the importance of personal contact in the small press world. An annotated list of 250 bookstores in twenty-four states they visited is a useful, though now somewhat dated, appendix to *American Odyssey.*

Other proven methods of working with small presses include establishing standing orders for series or even blanket orders with important publishers. This is not as costly as it sounds. Many small presses issue only a few inexpensive titles each year. It is the libraries with standing orders that are most likely to get the few printed copies, particularly if it is first printings the library seeks, before they become available only on the out-of-print market.

Small Press Periodicals

The complexities of collecting small press periodicals require special consideration. The editorial diversity, vitality, and bibliographical anarchy so characteristic of the small press world are particularly evident in its periodicals. These include, for example, newsletters of alternative lifestyle groups, political newspapers, and literary little magazines. These periodicals are important contemporary information sources. Librarians have an obligation to provide alternative sources of information for citizens in a democracy. As Sanford Berman points out:

> People in a democratic pluralistic society, in order to make wise decisions and to satisfy legitimate personal or group needs, require access to a greater variety and higher quality of information and ideas than what the conglomerate Media furnish.[16]

Small press periodicals are also primary research materials for students of contemporary culture. The history of contemporary artistic, literary, political, and social movements is recorded in such publications. Such important modern writers as James Joyce, Marianne Moore, and William Carlos Williams found their first audiences through little magazines.

Selecting small press periodicals requires careful consideration, but any library can add at least a few important titles at minimal cost. Many of these periodicals cost only a few dollars each; some titles are even free

15. Len Fulton, *American Odyssey, a Bookselling Travelogue* (Paradise, Calif.: Dustbooks, 1975).
16. Sanford Berman, "The Local Library and the Small Press," *Small Press Review* 13: 37 (June 1981).

from publishers delighted to have their periodicals on library shelves. Small academic or public libraries can build collections of local and regional little magazines, alternative newspapers, etc., at modest expense. Subscribing to these serials *does not* require the same kind of long term, annually escalating financial commitment involved in acquiring more expensive journals with longer life expectancies. Adequacy of indexing is also an important factor for some librarians in selecting periodicals. Indexing of small press periodicals was very inadequate until the early 1970s when *Alternative Press Index, American Humanities Index,* and Marion Sader's *Comprehensive Index to English Language Little Magazines, 1890–1970* began publication.[17] A number of small press periodicals do their own indexing. Charles W. Brownson's "Access to Little Magazines" provides a summary of the state of little magazine indexing in 1983.[18]

Once the decision to subscribe is made, the order should be placed promptly. Little magazine editors change addresses frequently and can be hard to locate. They also print relatively few copies of each issue. Acquiring backfiles therefore can be difficult. Specialist dealers such as the Phoenix Book Shop in New York can often supply issues if the publisher's supply is exhausted.[19] Reprint or microform publishers can also supply back files. Kraus Periodicals, for example, has published reprints of the titles in Marion Sader's *Comprehensive Index,* also published by Kraus.[20]

The maintenance of small press periodicals subscriptions is often a challenge that can test the mettle of even the experienced serials librarian. Little magazines change constantly. They change titles, publication schedules, and even physical formats. Claiming and billing policies of libraries often bedevil little magazine editors and vice versa. Tomo Montag, an experienced small pressman, describes these and related problems in his enjoyable article, "Stalking the Little Magazine," which appeared in *The Serials Librarian.*[21] Montag also suggests solutions for some of these problems and provides a useful annotated bibliography of reference sources on little magazines. In addition he gives a Recommended Reading List and his "Idiosyncratic List of Essential Little Magazines." One of Montag's observations on the little magazine is an excellent comment on the importance and challenge of collecting all types of small press periodicals:

> The serials librarian expecting the little magazine to behave as other "serials" behave will be disappointed; the magazine as art-object will not easily be

17. *Alternative Press Index*, v.1– . (Baltimore: Alternative Press Center, 1969–); *American Humanities Index*, v.1– . (Troy, N. Y.: Whitson, 1975–); Marion Sader, *Comprehensive Index to English Language Little Magazines, 1890–1970*, ser. 1, 8v. (Millwood, N. Y.: Kraus-Thomson, 1976).

18. Charles W. Brownson, "Access to Little Magazines," *RQ* 22: 375–87 (Summer 1983).

19. Phoenix Book Shop, 22 Jones St., New York, NY 10014.

20. Kraus Periodicals, Route 100, Millwood, NY 10546.

21. Tom Montag, "Stalking the Little Magazine," *The Serials Librarian* 1: 281–303 (Spring 1977).

molded to fit the librarian's necessarily practical requirements and normal library procedures. Whatever the difficulties of tracking down, ordering, and processing—collecting—little magazines, the challenge is one every responsible serials librarian ought to consider. Little magazines are essential to contemporary literature; the librarian who ignores them betrays that literature.[22]

Cataloging and Preservation

A few concluding observations about the cataloging and preservation of small press materials are appropriate. Cataloging small press materials requires dedication and ingenuity. As Sanford Berman explains, standard Library of Congress cataloging practices do not make small press materials adequately accessible to patrons.[23] LC does not assign sufficient numbers of unbiased and easily comprehensible subject headings and other added entries for small press titles to allow patrons to find them easily in card catalogs. Storing small press materials can also create problems. Many small press titles are published as paperbacks; binding these permit many to survive the rigors of life in the stacks, but some require special handling. Some fragile or outsized books, little magazines, and newspapers (those not available on microfilm) may need to be placed in acid-free envelopes and stored in filing cabinets (or in special acid-free periodical boxes). Such methods of preservation are used in special collections, but they can be adapted for use in general circulating collections as well. Whether or not to integrate small press publications into the general circulating collection or restrict them to special collections where they are less accessible but more secure and better preserved, is a decision that must be based on local conditions and needs. Cristine Rom discusses this problem and other aspects of collecting little magazines in her valuable article, "Little Magazines in Special Collections and Rare Book Departments."[24] Collecting small press materials is truly stimulating and important work for a collection development librarian. Selecting the books published today that may be destined to have the impact on the next century that the *Communist Manifesto* and *Ulysses* have had on our own is a challenge indeed. If the history of publishing contains any lesson for the book selector, it is that such landmark works are more likely to be issued by small alternative publishers than by the publishing establishment.

22. Ibid., p. 282.
23. Sanford Berman, "Access to Alternatives: New Approaches to Cataloging," in *Alternative Materials in Libraries*, pp. 31–66.
24. Cristine Rom, "Little Magazines in Special Collections and Rare Book Departments," *Credences: A Journal of Twentieth Century Poetry and Poetics*. n. s. 1:100–19. (Fall/Winter 1981/82).

Selection Sources

Alternatives in Print: An International Catalog of Books, Pamphlets and Audiovisual Materials. 6th ed. Comp. by the ALA/SRRT Task Force on Alternatives in Print. New York: Neal-Schuman, 1980.

COSMEP Catalogue of Independent Press Publications. San Francisco: COSMEP, 1982. (10 Microfiche.)

Field Guide to Alternative Media: A Directory to Reference and Selection Tools Useful in Accessing Small and Alternative Press Publications and Independently Produced Media. Ed. by Patricia J. Case. Chicago: American Library Assn., 1984.

International Directory of Little Magazines and Small Presses. Ed. by Len Fulton and Ellen Ferber. 19th ed., 1983–84. Paradise, Calif.: Dustbooks, 1983. Annually.

Sipapu. Winters, Calif.: Konocti Books, 1970– . Semiannually. (Available from Noel Peattie, Route 1, Box 216, Winters, CA 95694).

Small Press Record of Books in Print. Ed. by Len Fulton and Ellen Ferber. 12th ed. Paradise, Calif.: Dustbooks, 1983. Annually.

Small Press Review. Paradise, Calif.: Dustbooks, 1968– . Monthly.

Further Reading

Anderson, Elliott, and Mary Kinzie, eds. *The Little Magazine in America: A Modern Documentary History.* Yonkers, N. Y.: Pushcart Press, 1978.
  Essays and memoirs by prominent small press authors and editors with an excellent annotated bibliography of little magazines. A basic work.

Danky, James P., and Elliott Shore, eds. *Alternative Materials in Libraries.* Metuchen, N. J.: Scarecrow, 1982.
  The first book-length guide, indispensable.

Glessing, Robert J. *The Underground Press in America.* Bloomington: Indiana Univ. Pr., 1970.
  Coverage through the 1960s with a directory of underground newspapers. Now out-of-print but available through the University Microfilms Books on Demand Program.

Kostelanetz, Richard. *The End of Intelligent Writing: Literary Politics in America.* New York: Sheed & Ward, 1973. (Available from R. K. Editions, P. O. Box 73, New York, NY 10013.)
  A penetrating analysis of the interest groups and dynamics of the modern literary establishment by an avant-garde writer. See especially chapters thirteen and fourteen on New Literary Periodicals and Alternative Publishers for lists of important authors and presses.

Peattie, Noel. *The Living Z: A Guide to the Literature of the Counterculture, the Alternative Press, and Little Magazines.* Milwaukee: Margins, 1975. (Order from Midwestern Writers Publishing House, P. O. Box 8, Fairwater, WI 53931.)

Shore, Elliott. "Collecting the Alternative Press." In *Collection Management*, Library Journal Special Report #11. New York: Bowker, 1979.

West, Celeste, and Valerie Wheat. *The Passionate Perils of Publishing.* San Francisco: Booklegger Press, 1978.
  A combination how-to book and guide to alternative publishing. Lists reference sources particularly for feminist publishers. Exuberant and useful.

MICROFORMS

Sara Eichhorn

Libraries increasingly view microform as a means of strengthening their research holdings without requiring an expansion of physical facilities. Its compact form is ideal for massive sets of valuable material, whether a collection of United States census data, a complete run of the *New York Times*, or the ERIC collection of documents. Microform editions may be the only format in which a library can purchase needed rare or out-of-print material. Libraries consequently have been devoting larger portions of their acquisition budgets to microform, and the micropublishing industry has eagerly responded to this rapidly growing market.

Microform librarianship is still in its infancy. The microform industry, although older, is also still developing. Along with the standard concerns associated with the acquisition of printed materials, additional problems must be considered when selecting microform. Additional funds must be available for hardware, such as readers, reader printers, and storage cabinets, and staffing must be adequate to service the microform acquired. Librarians need to develop strategies for microform selection and to identify and master the selection tools available to assist them.

That the selection of microform materials is fraught with costly pitfalls is well recognized within the library profession and even by some in the industry. Carol Cooper, of Clearwater Publishing Company, comments:

> There is so much material in the marketplace, and libraries clearly need some guidance in the acquisition of such large and expensive collections. Many are not aware of the technical concerns they [should] have, particularly with German and French films—many of which are diazo. Others may not be qualified to assess the value of titles to their libraries' holdings and the needs of their patrons. Some collections duplicate others. Many have no bibliographic access. Some promise guides which have yet to be produced. The list of concerns is a long one and published information is scarce.[1]

1. Letter from Carol D. Cooper, vice president, Clearwater Publishing Company, Inc., February 8, 1981.

Clearwater and other micropublishers have decided to publish newsletters to help fill the information void. But not all have the librarian in mind. The industry, after all, is profit-oriented and some firms consist of little more than an owner with a camera. According to one microform expert: "Some just have P. O. boxes and steal prints from public domain stuff." Providing indexes, guides, and cataloging records requires a higher level of skill and entails an additional expense that some micropublishing firms are unable or unwilling to undertake. Fortunately, librarians and leaders in the industry now recognize the problems. They have helped establish publication standards and are attempting to enforce them.

Despite the problems inherent in microform, its advantages are so overwhelming that libraries are compelled to accept the challenges.

Developing a Microform Collection

What follows are some suggested strategies and sources for selecting and developing a microform collection. Unlike acquisition practices for printed materials, which are more or less standardized and accepted throughout the profession, those for microform are still in a formative stage and subject to improvement.

ESTABLISH A POLICY FOR MICROFORM MANAGEMENT

The selection of microform clearly differs from that of materials in paper format. Articulating rules for the selection of microform should be part of a library's collection development policy. *Yale University Library's Guidelines for the Handling of Microforms* addresses the kinds of microform to be purchased and even specifies "standard preferred formats."[2]

Though a discussion of hardware is outside the scope of this paper, one can say that the type of equipment owned or planned for acquisition will limit the selection policy. Some titles, for example, are available only for specific types of equipment.

An inventory of microform equipment already owned by the library is a useful first step in formulating a policy for microform selection. This inventory may point out deficiencies in the equipment or indicate that some pieces should be discarded. The inventory or equipment manual should list the specifications of each piece of equipment, such as the number of lenses and their magnification ratios. One should include in this manual reviews from *Library Technology Reports* and *Micrographics Equipment Review* for each type of equipment in the library's possession.[3]

2. "Guidelines for the Handling of Microforms in the Yale University Library," *Microform Review* 9:11–20 (Winter 1980). Quarterly.
3. *Library Technology Reports* (Chicago: American Library Assn., 1965–). Bimonthly; *Micrographics Equipment Review* (Westport, Conn.: Meckler, 1976–). Annually.

After the inventory, the level of investment to be made in microform should be established. Many factors beyond the obvious one of financial resources must be considered. The materials selected must be consistent with the library's overall purpose and goals. A large research library might invest heavily in a wide range of hardware to permit it to take advantage of many valuable research collections available in various forms. A government publications department, on the other hand, may want to limit its investment and equipment to the single form common to its most heavily used materials—microfiche—and in the process simplify its microform selection policy. In both cases, the amount of hardware acquired should bear some relationship to anticipated or planned use. This in turn may limit or increase the investment in microform. It makes little sense for a library to invest heavily in microform if it has an inadequate number of reader printers or poorly maintained, and therefore unusable, equipment. Accordingly, a policy for microform selection must be consistent with the library's present or planned hardware, the library's financial resources, its overall collection development goals, and the current or potential role of microform within the context of those goals.

DEVELOP FORMAT SELECTION CRITERIA

Format policies should spell out types of microform and hardware. Newspapers, for example, are most conveniently stored on *microfilm*, long strips of film rolled on reels with multiple microimages in a linear sequence. Other materials ranging from college catalogs and annual reports to government documents are commonly stored on *microfiche*, flat rectangular sheets of transparent film with microimages arranged in a grid sequence. *Microcard* and *microprint* are *microopaques*, meaning they are viewed by reflection rather than by projection. Most libraries choose materials on microfilm or microfiche rather than microopaques because the photocopying equipment is simpler and more readily available. Clearly, the greater variety of microform types collected has repercussions on the level of investment in the microform materials themselves, the hardware needed to read them, storage cabinets, furniture, and physical space.

Once the criteria address the physical types of microform to be acquired, the kinds of microform to be purchased should be clearly specified, such as silver halide, diazo, or vesicular. *Silver halide* film is made to standards set by the American National Standards Institute and should be selected when archival quality is desired. *Diazo* and *vesicular* films are becoming increasingly popular in libraries because they are less expensive.

Other technical criteria to be spelled out include the appropriate or desired polarity and reduction ratio. *Negative polarity* film (light letters on a dark background) is equally as popular as *positive polarity* film (dark letters on a light background). Polarity may be an important consideration if the library lacks a bimodal reader printer capable of producing positive copies from negative and positive microform. Specifying that the reduction ratio be in the range of 18x to 48x is necessary to ensure that the image is readable on the library's hardware.

The critieria should reflect careful consideration of the advantages and disadvantages of selecting materials on microform instead of in their original formats. Serials should be purchased on microform when the original is on poor quality paper, when popular magazines are heavily used or vandalized, when bulky items, such as newspapers, would be difficult to store in their original form, or where hardcopy was *never* acquired. On the other hand, equipment and storage costs must be considered along with the delays in micropublication. Journals and foreign newspapers sometimes are not available in microform until a year or two after their original publication. It may be determined that large monographic collections should be purchased only when a bibliography, index, or reel guide is available to provide bibliographic access to the set. This, in turn, may require investigative research beyond simply calling or writing the micropublisher. Certain G. K. Hall subject catalogs can be helpful in providing access to large microform collections. A library should acquire reel guides for microform collections in its areas of interest where these are owned within its library system or geographic region. Reel guides may be used as selection sources as well as to assist with interlibrary loan requests.

INVESTIGATE BACKGROUND LITERATURE

Some excellent books and articles are available to provide useful background information on microform selection. Allen B. Veaner's *The Evaluation of Micropublications: A Handbook for Librarians* is designed for librarians responsible for the acquisition and evaluation of micropublications; it is also helpful in developing a microform selection policy.[4] Alice Harrison Bahr's *Microforms: The Librarian's View*, now in its third edition, has an excellent chapter on microform selection and acquisition.[5] In 1977 the Bookdealer Library Relations Committee of the Technical Services Division of the American Library Association published a pamphlet, *Guidelines for Handling Library Orders for Microforms*, which provides information on placing microform orders.[6] Ralph Folcarelli, Arthur Tan-

4. Allen B. Veaner, *The Evaluation of Micropublications: A Handbook for Librarians*, LTP Publication no. 17 (Chicago: Library Technology Program, American Library Assn., 1971).

5. Alice Harrison Bahr, *Microforms: The Librarian's View*. 3rd rev. ed. (White Plains, N. Y.: Knowledge Industry Publications, Inc., 1980).

6. *Guidelines for Handling Library Orders for Microforms*, Acquisitions Guidelines, no. 3 (Chicago: American Library Assn., Resources and Technical Services Div., Bookdealer Library Relations Committee, 1977).

nenbaum, and Ralph Ferragamo's *Microform Connection: A Basic Guide for Libraries* has a chapter on selecting and acquiring microform.[7] It discusses selection criteria, selection tools, general and specialized guides, reviews and announcements, acquisition guidelines, and procedures for checking in microform.

In the serial literature, Robert C. Sullivan and Albert J. Diaz have published excellent articles on the acquisition of microform. Sullivan offers guidance on the reference sources and procedures used in the acquisition of microform for libraries and sets forth guidelines for selecting and ordering microform.[8] He also discusses the literature for evaluating microform and reports on the evaluative techniques used at the Library of Congress. Diaz lists and describes articles, books, and services that provide information about publications available on microform.[9] The rapidly developing field of microform librarianship is thus acquiring a growing shelf of valuable background literature.

General Selection Tools

Guide to Microforms in Print is a comprehensive annual list (by author and title) of books, journals, newspapers, government publications, archival material, and collections currently available from micropublishers throughout the world. Titles are listed only if they are offered for sale on a regular and current basis. The listings provide essential order information, such as number of volumes, date, price, publisher, and type of microform. A companion volume, *Subject Guide to Microforms in Print*, lists the same titles under 135 subject headings derived from the Library of Congress. Coverage for this guide has been international since 1978 when the guides absorbed *International Microforms in Print*. Another title no longer being published is *Microlist*, which was issued in 1977 and 1978 as a supplement to *Guide to Microforms in Print*. *Microlist* has been replaced by the annual *Guide to Microforms in Print Supplement*.

The *National Register of Microform Masters* should be used by large research libraries to avoid expensive rephotographing of materials. This source lists master microform holdings of about 3000 United States and foreign libraries and micropublishers. Types of materials listed include foreign and domestic monographs, pamphlets, serials, and foreign doctoral dissertations. Excluded are technical reports, typescript translations, ar-

7. Ralph J. Folcarelli, Arthur C. Tannenbaum, and Ralph C. Ferragamo, *The Microform Connection: A Basic Guide for Libraries* (New York and London: Bowker, 1982).

8. Robert C. Sullivan, "The Acquisition of Library Microforms. Part I," *Microform Review* 6: 136–44 (May 1977); "The Acquisition of Library Microforms. Part II," *Microform Review* 6: 205–11 (July 1977).

9. Albert J. Diaz, "Microform Information Sources: Publications and Hardware," *Microform Review* 4: 250–61 (Oct. 1975).

Guide to Microforms in Print. Author, Title. Westport, Conn.: Meckler,
1961– . Annually.
Cumulative annual microforms in print list.
Contains microform for sale from micropublishers throughout the world in
  alphabetic sequence by author and title.
Includes books, journals, newspapers, government publications, archival
  materials, collections, and other projects on microform.
Provides author, title, volume, date, price, publisher, and type of
  microform.
Microforms entered by author and title.
Books are entered under author in this guide. The date given is that of the
publication in its original form. If an author is not named, an editor or compiler
is treated as an author. If none of these are listed, the publication is listed under
title. Journals are entered directly by title, provided that they are not issued by
a government agency or sponsoring society. Newspapers are entered directly by
title. A supplement provides both author/title and subject listings.

Subject Guide to Microforms in Print. Westport, Conn.: Meckler, 1962/63– .
Annually.
Cumulative annual microforms in print list.
Contains microform for sale from micropublishers throughout the world in
  alphabetic sequence by subject.
Includes books, journals, newspapers, government publications, archival
  material, collections, and other projects under appropriate subject
  classifications.
Provides author, title, volume, date, price, publisher, and type of
  microform.
Microforms entered by subject.
Micropublications are entered here under the appropriate subject divisions derived from the Library of Congress. Titles can be listed under more than one
subject heading. A supplement provides both author/title and subject listings.

---

chival manuscript collections, newspapers, U. S. masters theses and doctoral dissertations. The *Register*, issued annually, has been cumulated for
the period 1965 to 1975. At present it lists both master microforms, which
are used to make commercial copies, and master preservation microforms,
which are solely for preservation purposes and not used to make copies.
Libraries should be encouraged to notify the *Register* each time they pho-
tograph materials so that there will be a national record of what has been
filmed and is still in-print.

According to a *Library of Congress Information Bulletin*, the annual
compilation of the *Register* has been automated.[10] This may allow it to
be expanded to include not only masters but service copies. The Library
of Congress is looking at ways of linking information in the 007 field of
the MARC record with location information. This fixed field describes

10. *Library of Congress Information Bulletin* 41: 82–84 (Mar. 12, 1982).

Micropublishers' Trade List Annual. Westport, Conn.: Meckler, 1975– .
Annually.
Annual collection of micropublisher catalogs on microfiche.
Catalogs from U. S. and foreign micropublishers; brochures included when
there is no master catalog.
Printed list of micropublishers provides a corresponding microfiche number
for each publisher's catalog.
Internal indexes are utilized when a micropublisher is represented by
several catalogs.
Supplemental catalogs and a replacement index of *MTLA* are distributed each
December.

---

polarity, dimensions, reduction ratio, color, emulsion on the film, generation, and base of the film.

Sometimes additional information about micropublishers is needed. *Microform Market Place* is a directory of micropublishers in the United
States. It lists key personnel and provides a subject and geographic index
of micropublishers. *Resource Center Index*, formerly *International Micrographics Source Book*, lists micropublishers and includes educational
and professional organizations that offer their publications on microform.

An underutilized selection source is *Micropublishers' Trade List Annual*
(MTLA). The most recent edition of this source includes the annual catalogs available on microfiche from 289 foreign and domestic micropublishers. Even though a library subscribes to and uses *MTLA*, it is advantageous to be on the mailing list for major micropublishers in order to
be constantly aware of new microform collections. New collections are
announced through brochures, flyers, and annual catalogs issued by micropublishers.

Critical Reviews

The general selection sources cited above provide information about micropublications but offer no critical evaluations. *Microform Review* is the
only periodical providing quality evaluations of micropublications for libraries. Published quarterly, each issue contains reviews in which critical
evaluation is provided in addition to full information on selected micropublications. The microformat is described in detail, such as 35mm roll
microfilm, position IIA or 105mm × 148mm microfiche, 84 image format.
Quantity of microform, or size of the set, is indicated. For example, a set
may contain thirty reels. Film type is specified—silver halide, vesicular, or
diazo. Also listed is reduction ratio, the relationship between the dimensions of the original or master and the corresponding dimensions of the

Microform Review. v.1- . 1972- . Westport, Conn.: Meckler. Quarterly.
   Quarterly journal of microform librarianship.
   Includes articles on microform and reviews of microform collections on all
      subjects.
   10 or more reviews each issue. Time lag varies from a few months to more
      than a year between micropublication and the review.
   Announcements in "Comments and News" section.
   Book reviews in "Book Reviews/Inter Alia" section.
   Micropublishers advertisements.
   Signed reviews by librarians and scholars provide critical evaluations and full
   information about micropublications, including microformat, quantity, film type,
   reduction ratio, film polarity, resolution, and external and internal finding aids.

---

microimage; e. g., reduction ratio is expressed as 1:24. Film polarity is
listed in all reviews, specifying whether the film is positive or negative.
Reviews indicate whether safety film has been used and whether the film
contains a resolution test chart. (Resolution is the number ratio that describes the quality of the image and is described as the number of lines
per millimeter.) External finding aids (reel guides, indexes, and bibliographies) and internal finding aids (eye-legible headers and other aids on
the film) are indicated in each review. The sequence of the filming is
described. Project editors are named. Experienced microform librarians
learn to recognize the thoroughness of some project editors. Other important considerations covered in each review are whether hard copy is
available, whether selected parts are available, what the replacement policy
is, whether time payments are permitted, whether the microform is reg-
istered in the *National Register of Microform Masters*, and any additional
remarks the reviewer may wish to make.

   Major micropublishers of materials for libraries share a concern about
the need for more critical reviews of *Microform Review*'s caliber to provide a higher standard of critical guidance. Some had their materials reviewed by journals that normally review works published in paper format
only. Linda Hamilton of Research Publications states that her firm has
been successful in submitting hardcopy indexes of microform collections
for review as indexes.[11] And Jack Carey of the Congressional Information
Service finds that CIS microfiche collections have been reviewed, or at
least commented on, in *Serials Review*, *Government Publications Review*,
Law Library Journal, *RQ*, and the *International Journal of Law Libraries*.[12] He notes, however, that reviews in these publications have focused principally on the hardcopy indexes. One micropublisher reports he

   [11]. Letter from Linda K. Hamilton, vice president, Academic Publishing, Research Publications, Inc., Feb. 21, 1983.
   [12]. Letter from Jack H. Carey, Communications Department, Congressional Information
Service, Inc., Mar. 4, 1983.

becomes concerned whenever he receives a request for a review copy by a scholarly or professional journal that does not customarily include microform in its review coverage.[13] Publications that normally review printed material often lack the expertise to evaluate publications in microform. This underscores the importance of having available to the library expertise to evaluate both the subject matter and the format when considering the purchase of microform material.

Union Lists and Guides

Union lists and guides to microform collections may serve as valuable selection tools. A union list of microform records the holdings of a number of libraries, while a guide describes the contents of one or more microform collections. Suzanne Dodson's *Microform Research Collections: A Guide 1984* describes the contents and associated indexes and bibliographies of hundreds of collections available from micropublishers throughout the world. For each, the Dodson guide provides information on individual collections, including title, publisher, format, price, citations to reviews, arrangement and bibliographical control, bibliographies and indexes on which the collection is based, and scope content. Reichmann and Tharpe's *Bibliographic Control of Microforms*, although published in 1972, is still useful. It describes catalogs and lists issued by commercial publishers, libraries, associations, societies, and government agencies. Microform sets and manuscript and archival collections are discussed. If a set or collection is based on a published bibliography, that source rather than the title of the set is cited as the entry. Union lists may also be used as selection tools if they are well done. With the assistance of librarians at other University of California campuses, this author has prepared for publication a *Guide to Research Collections on Microform in the University of California Libraries*. It provides information on over 850 microform sets held by the University of California libraries. It records each set by title and micropublisher, provides descriptive information about content, format, and number of pieces, records citations to reviews, identifies bibliographies and indexes on which a set is based as well as guides issued by micropublishers, and indicates call numbers assigned by each campus to sets in its holdings.

Specialized Selection Sources

Serials. A number of selection sources that limit their scope to serials on microform are available. *Serials in Microform* is the sales catalog for

13. Letter from P. Anton Kobasa, sales manager, Greenwood Press, Feb. 22, 1983.

University Microfilms International; it is, however, a valuable selection source for serials, newspapers, and documents dating from 1669 to the present. *Microforms Annual: An International Guide to Microforms* is a combined record of serial titles issued by several micropublishers, though all its listings can be purchased through Microforms International Marketing Corporation. *Ulrich's Periodicals Directory* and *Irregular Serials & Annuals* are also helpful because they provide information on the availability of a serial in microform. In both works, an abbreviation for the micropublisher follows a notation on microform availability. Unfortunately, however, not all micropublishers submit information to Ulrich's.

Newspapers. The most valuable selection tool for newspapers on microform is *Newspapers in Microform*. This source records United States and foreign newspapers held by libraries as reported to the Library of Congress. Both the cumulated volumes for 1948 to 1972 and 1973 to 1977 and the annual supplements are divided into foreign and domestic sections. Arranged alphabetically by state and nation, city and title, this source lists microform masters as well as service microforms. Some micropublishers' holdings are also included in this work. Another useful source is *National Preservation Report*, which lists current newspaper microfilming projects of both foreign and domestic institutions. Users of this source should be forewarned that a reported intent to microfilm a project is not always carried out.

Dissertations and Theses. The basic sources for doctoral dissertations and masters theses on microfilm are *Dissertation Abstracts International* and *Masters Abstracts*. They list dissertations and theses, respectively, completed at North American, British, and European institutions that are available from University Microfilms International (UMI). Dissertations and theses not available from UMI can sometimes be obtained in microform from institutions to which the dissertations or theses were submitted.

CONCLUSION

It should be clear that selection procedures for microform are different from those for the printed format. Ease of entry into the micropublishing field and the lack of common standards within the industry requires that librarians ordering materials in microformat editions proceed with great caution and only after thorough evaluation according to the locally established criteria. With the founding of *Microform Review*, critical reviews of micropublications have become available. And other leaders in the micropublishing industry also are increasing their efforts to provide improved selection tools for libraries.

Selection Sources

Dissertation Abstracts International. Ann Arbor, Mich.: University Microfilms International, 1938– . Monthly.

Dodson, Suzanne Cates. *Microform Research Collections: A Guide 1984.* Westport, Conn.: Meckler, 1984.

Eichhorn, Sara. *Guide to Research Collections on Microform in the University of California Libraries.* Irvine, Calif.: n. p., 1984. Prepared for publication.

Guide to Microforms in Print. Author, Title. Westport, Conn.: Meckler, 1961– . Annually.

———. *Supplement.* Westport, Conn.: Meckler, 1979– .

International Microforms in Print; A Guide to Microforms of Non-United States Micropublishers. Weston, Conn.: Microform Review Inc., 1974/75.

Irregular Serials & Annuals; An International Directory. New York: Bowker, 1967– . Annually.

Masters Abstracts. Ann Arbor, Mich.: University Microfilms International, 1962– . Quarterly.

Microform Market Place; An International Directory of Micropublishing. Westport, Conn.: Meckler, 1972– . Annually.

Microform Review. Westport, Conn.: Meckler, 1972– . Quarterly.

Microforms Annual: An International Guide to Microforms. Elmsford, N. Y.: Microforms International Marketing Corp., 1971– .

Micropublishers' Trade List Annual. Westport, Conn.: Meckler, 1975– .

National Preservation Report. v.1– . 1979– . Washington, D. C.: Library of Congress.3/year.

National Register of Microform Masters. Washington, D. C.: Catalog Publication Div., Library of Congress, 1965– . Annually.

Newspapers in Microform. Washington, D. C.: Library of Congress, 1948– . Annually.

Reichmann, Felix, and Josephine M. Tharpe. *Bibliographic Control of Microforms.* Westport, Conn.: Greenwood, 1972.

Resource Center Index. New Rochelle, N. Y.: Microfilm Publishing Inc., 1972– . Semiannually.

NONPRINT MEDIA

Allan C. Rough

To paraphrase Gertrude Stein, in the concept of the generic book, a book is a book is a book. . . . Indeed, the format created by Gutenberg's press in the fifteenth century had been preceded by many other book formats: clay tablets, parchment and papyrus manuscripts, and so forth. The generic book does not recognize the artificial boundary between print and AV.[1]

Many nonprint or audiovisual librarians describe themselves as librarians first, nonprint librarians second. The acquisition, selection, and reference tools of the media specialist are quite similar in nature and in use to those of the print librarian. There are, however, significant exceptions that must be recognized and learned if nonprint materials are to be selected by subject specialists who may or may not be media specialists as well.

Films, videocassettes, slides, phonorecords, and all other formats of audiovisual materials have been most commonly used in the classroom by teachers to complement textbooks. Critics charge that all too often media use has been abused by lazy teachers who substituted a film instead of preparing a lecture. College and university libraries have used this argument to avoid the purchase of nonprint media. Nonprint materials also have been judged lacking in intellectual content and hence excluded from collection management policies. Modern teaching methods employ nonprint materials to great advantage, however. History, political studies, and journalism scholars can learn much from examining the recorded events of modern history. In another vein, no text can capture the incredible beauty and diversity of nature as well as a program such as *Life on Earth*, a series that has merit in the classroom and in the library's permanent collection.

The author gratefully acknowledges the assistance of Angie LeClerq, head of the Undergraduate Library, University of Tennessee.

1. Louis Shores, *Audiovisual Librarianship; The Crusade for Media Unity (1946–1969)* (Littleton, Colo.: Libraries Unlimited, 1973), pp. 15–16.

In recent decades librarians have recognized the value of adding nonprint materials for their research potential as well as for their curricular support. For example, the Vanderbilt Television News Archive in Nashville, Tennessee, has been videotaping and indexing the evening news broadcasts on ABC, CBS, and NBC since August 5, 1968. Bibliographic access to the collection, through the *Television News Index and Abstracts*, allows researchers to borrow entire broadcasts or compilation tapes on specific topics for a fee. An additional research collection in the area of television is the Academy of Television Arts and Sciences-UCLA Television Archives, which houses a large collection of entertainment television programs as well as news and documentary tapes. *Television Network News: Issues in Content Research*, by Adams and Schreibman, documents many research opportunities for the use of these and other collections.

Print Reference Materials

One book that should be a part of the print reference collection of any nonprint media department is Mary Robinson Sive's *Selecting Instructional Media: A Guide to Audiovisual and Other Instructional Media Lists*. The preface to the book describes it accurately, perhaps immodestly, as "one of the leading, if not the leading, reference guide to audiovisual selection tools."[2] The entries in this volume are arranged by subject and by media type. It aims more at the school library than the academic library, and therefore omits some important college-level sources. Nonetheless, it provides information that would be prohibitively time-consuming to construct from other sources. Sive also includes a well-written chapter entitled "An Introduction to Media Selection," which is both thoughtful and informative, citing dozens of references in the areas of selection criteria, policies, and procedures. The references listed at the end of her essay are quite comprehensive and will not be duplicated here unless they should be included in all libraries.

Another book that should be included is Pierce S. Grove's *Nonprint Media in Academic Libraries*. This volume was the product of the Audiovisual Committee of the Association of College and Research Libraries in 1975. It remains one of the best sources for information, strategies, and procedures on the selection, classification, and cataloging of nonprint materials.

There are five annual guides to the film and video industry that should be considered for purchase. The *Audiovisual Market Place: A Multimedia Guide* lists hardware and software sources, services, and dealers. It is

2. Mary Robinson Sive, *Selecting Instructional Media: A Guide to Audiovisual and Other Instructional Media Lists*, 3rd ed. (Littleton, Colo.: Libraries Unlimited, 1983), p. 5.

Sive, Mary Robinson. *Selecting Instructional Media: A Guide to Audiovisual and Other Instructional Media Lists.* 3rd ed. Littleton, Colo.: Libraries Unlimited, 1983.

> Comprehensive, annotated bibliography of references and resources for audiovisual libraries and media centers. Designed to assist in the selection and purchase of instructional media, curriculum development, classroom instruction, and school media center operation materials.
>
> Features excellent bibliographic essay on media selection procedure.
>
> Reference tool arranged in 24 subject areas and 17 media specific listings. Complete index to authors, titles, subjects, and formats.
>
> Annotations include classification and identifying number, main entry, purpose of list, criteria for selection and inclusion of titles, grade level, arrangement, subject, number of entries included, types of indexes provided, period covered, revision and updating policy, formats available, and producers represented.

This work is extremely valuable for narrowing down the possible sources for subject specific instructional media in all formats.

---

particularly useful for determining current addresses of vendors, and also provides information on festivals, awards, and grants. A better source for locating award-winning programs can be found in the *Educational Media Yearbook*, edited by James Brown and Shirley Brown. It duplicates some of the material in the first book, but also provides an excellent annual review of educational media developments, organizations, and trends. Richard Gertner edits both the *Motion Picture Almanac* and the *Television Almanac*. Although they overlap each other to some extent, they provide ready reference to a "Who's Who" in motion pictures and television, important awards, production companies, theater distribution circuits, associations, and services not easily found in other publications. *The International Film Guide*, edited by Peter Cowie, does for the whole world what the *Motion Picture Almanac* does primarily for the West.

RETROSPECTIVE SELECTION SOURCES

Educational Film Locator is the single most important tool for the retrospective selection of film or video materials. This union catalog of the holdings of the fifty-member Consortium of University Film Centers provides excellent annotations and inexpensive alternatives to the rental of films from producers or distributors. Good subject headings and suggested grade levels make it possible to quickly identify appropriate materials. If a particular film is held by a large number of the participating institutions, it is a fairly safe bet that it is an important, useful title that should be examined for possible acquisition. On the other hand, any title held by only one institution should not automatically be considered inferior to other titles. In many cases, certain films are available exclusively from that

Educational Film Locator. 2nd ed. New York: Bowker, 1980.
> A union catalog of titles held by 50 member libraries of the Consortium of University Film Centers.
> Lists approximately 40,000 titles.
> Provides a map of the geographical locations of the film libraries and a chart specifying their lending policies.
> Has a structured thesarus of subject terms with cross-references.
> Entries arranged alphabetically by title indicate the following: black and white or color, running time, sound, medium, synopsis, series statement, producer/distributor code, ISBN number, date, subject class, audience level, and holding library code.
> This was the first basic bibliographic tool for locating rental educational films and, although it is now dated, it remains an essential source of information on important, popular titles.

institution. This is especially true with out-of-print titles unavailable from the original producer. Since it was last updated in 1980, the gaps should be filled from the individual catalogs of participating film centers published since then. Complete information on rental conditions and catalog availability is listed at the front of the volume.

The National Information Center for Educational Media (NICEM) produces a series of single media and multimedia, content-area indexes that are essential additions to all collections. Access Innovations, Inc., acquired the NICEM database and publications from the University of Southern California in 1984. They plan to continue the publication of most, if not all, of the existing indexes, and expect to issue new titles as well. These indexes are not useful for evaluation purposes, but are important as location and identification tools. The single media series includes: *Index to 16mm Educational Films, Index to 35mm Educational Filmstrips, Index to Overhead Transparencies, Index to Educational Video Tapes, Index to Educational Audio Tapes, Index to 8mm Motion Cartridges, Index to Educational Records, Index to Educational Slides,* and the *Index to Producers and Distributors.* The multimedia indexes include: Psychology, Health and Safety Education, Vocational and Technical Education, Environmental Studies, and Special Education Materials. These volumes have adequate subject indexes with brief, but useful, annotations. They also may be searched online in DIALOG under the database name "AV-ON-LINE." The boolean search capability permits subject searches that are media, date, and/or audience-level specific.

Film File is another tool that has proven to be useful in a nonprint media reference collection. It is an index to films and videocassettes that are currently available from participating distributors. The subject area index and topic cross-references are detailed and quite useful. The index provides titles without descriptions, but does include grade level, release

Film File. 4th ed. Minneapolis, Minn.: Media Referral Service, 1984.
> Provides information on the availability of over 23,000 titles in film and video formats from more than 140 U. S. and Canadian distributors.
> Entries arranged alphabetically by title within 16 major curriculum headings. Alphabetical index also provided.
> Includes excellent subject index with extensive cross-references.
> Does not give program descriptions or contents notes.
> Data provided includes format, grade level, running time, release date, distributor, codes for animated or captioned titles, foreign-language versions, and series.

This work is updated more frequently than any other similar reference tool and is most useful for locating new titles. It also provides valuable information on changes in the film and video industry, including failures, mergers, company take-overs, and address changes.

---

date, length, coded availability information, and distributor's addresses. The publisher's intention is to make the *Film File* the largest and most current listing of educational films and videocassettes available. It also provides a convenient listing of changes in the film and video industry, including address changes, and it lists companies that have been acquired by other companies and those that have gone out of business.

Feature films are best located through either James L. Limbacher's *Feature Films on 8mm, 16mm, and Videotape,* or through the *Film Programmer's Guide to 16mm Rentals,* by Kathleen Weaver. Both volumes give sources for the rental or purchase of feature films. The *Film Programmer's Guide*'s pricing information is now out-of-date, but still useful for comparison purposes. Two similar works that concentrate on video are *Consumer's Handbook of Video Software,* edited by Charles Bensinger, and *The Video Source Book.* The *Consumer's Handbook* is particularly useful for locating hard to find feature films on videotape. *The Video Source Book* has improved with each update and provides excellent subject access to both theatrical and nontheatrical productions on film and videotape.

An expensive, but convenient, resource that supports all of the above references is *Educational Media Catalogs on Microfiche* (EMCOM). This is a comprehensive collection of audiovisual software distributor's catalogs on more than 100 microfiche. It is an attractive and compact alternative to collecting and maintaining the individual catalogs of the included distributors. It is updated every six months and each new index lists the fiche that should be purged as new, current catalogs are released.

An alternative to *EMCOM* is a free membership in Cine Information's *Film User's Network* (Filmnet). This is a computerized information system designed to make connections between filmmakers and film users. Filmmakers and distributors can obtain subject-coded mailing lists of interested

Video Source Book. 6th ed. Syosset, N. Y.: National Video Clearinghouse, 1984.

Provides bibliographic and descriptive information on more than 40,000 titles available in one or more video formats from more than 850 distributors.

All titles are assigned to a main category and to a narrower subject category.

Descriptions are brief but useful.

Does not provide information on film availability, only video.

Provides release date, running time, color or black and white, captioning information for the hearing impaired, format, availability or foreign broadcast standard copies (PAL, PAL-M, SECAM), use restrictions (including open and closed circuit rights), series information, program description, major awards, availability of ancillary materials, audience rating, grade level, language, sound, silent, dubbed or subtitles, producer, and distributors.

This is an excellent tool for identifying locations of desired video materials.

film users. Film purchasers who are members will receive catalogs and information on new releases as they become available. This is an excellent, efficient way to collect distributors' catalogs.

CURRENT REVIEW SOURCES

Since the previewing process is expensive in terms of time and money, it is always desirable to select award-winning or otherwise recommended titles for preview. Media reviews tend to be a little less critical than is desirable but they help to narrow down the number of choices in a given area. *Media Digest* is the most important tool to use in locating reviews of programs in all formats of media. It also provides information on film festivals, awards, and prizes for entertainment and educational films. *Choice* and *Booklist* are the two best journals that provide reviews of multimedia suitable for college-level audiences. The reviews in *Choice* are especially good since they are written by subject specialists who have good media awareness, rather than by media specialists who may not be experts in that field. These reviews tend to be more critical, and are therefore more useful, than those found in most other journals. *Media and Methods* is another interesting multimedia journal that should be in most collections, but the brief reviews vary tremendously in both quality and usefulness.

There are far more journals that deal primarily with film and video than with other media. Two of the best are published by the Educational Film Library Association (EFLA): these are *Sightlines* and *EFLA Evaluations*. EFLA sponsors the American Film Festival and also publishes a number of media-related publications available at a discount to members. The reviews in *EFLA Evaluations* are of the films shown at the American Film

Festival, which are selected by panels of media specialists and film users. The reviews are generally useful, informative, and reliable guides to superior productions. *Sightlines* is one of the better journals devoted to nontheatrical films and an essential guide to the entire industry. Membership in EFLA is highly recommended for institutions that seek to be kept informed of the educational film market.

Landers Film Reviews; The Information Guide to 16mm Films and Multi-Media Materials is a third critical tool. The most important difference about this journal is that producers pay to have their materials reviewed in it. Anything submitted will be reviewed, but reviewed carefully, honestly, and completely. A fourth acquisition that should be made is for *Film Library Quarterly*, which provides reviews that are generally more detailed, lengthy, and scholarly than the other publications. A fifth selection should be *AAAS Science Books & Films* published by the American Association for the Advancement of Science. This journal is well known to most science book selectors, and it reviews films with the same care that is given to reviewing books.

American Film, Film Comment, and *Film Quarterly* are three journals that are particularly good candidates for institutions with film study programs. Between them they review both theatrical and nontheatrical films, video, and television. They also review books dealing with the film industry and are therefore quite important in selecting reference books, as well as media, for your collection. *Channels* and *Dial* also have proven to be useful in keeping current on commercial and noncommercial television, respectively. Both preview forthcoming programs that should be noted and reported to interested faculty and others for timely viewing. *Afterimage* and *Jump Cut* are two journals that provide insight into the independent film and video production world.

WHICH FORMATS TO COLLECT?

Any and all nonprint formats available, past and present, are potential options for acquisition. Among the various audio formats are audiocassettes, eight-track cartridges, open-reel tapes, phonodiscs, and compact digital discs (CDs). The vast majority of educational audio materials are available on only two of these formats: audiocassettes and phonodiscs.

Visual formats include slides, filmstrips, overhead transparencies, 8mm, Super 8mm, and 16mm films, several types of videotapes, and videodiscs. It simply isn't practical for most libraries to collect all, or even most, of these formats. It is much wiser and more economical to limit the variety of formats in order to minimize equipment proliferation and compatibility problems. Slides can do the work of both overhead transparencies and filmstrips, with more flexibility than either of the others. Videotapes are able to show the same programs as all three types of film mentioned above. It is obviously cost efficient to limit all purchases to the smallest number of formats that can satisfy collection development goals. These could, or should, include at least audiocassettes, slides, and one of the videocassette formats. Laser videodiscs, 16mm films, and compact digital audiodiscs would be good options to consider adding as well. By limiting your purchases to these formats, your equipment dollar will go much farther, and your users will not have to learn how to operate too many different types of equipment.

Film vs. Video. When audiovisual librarians and other media-related professionals compare the respective merits of film and videotape, the discussion almost invariably centers on the perceptual impact and effectiveness of the two. There is no question that the visual and psychological impact of film and video is different. Film is still the best and least expensive medium for showing exclusively to large audiences. The resolution of the film image is much sharper than is now possible with current video technologies. Video is more flexible, however, and can be shown equally well to individuals or to small or large groups in properly equipped rooms. It should be noted, however, that high resolution, large-screen video systems are now in development that will rival the quality of film in a few years. Video is often the more adaptable, economical choice.

Some critics have compared video and film to Cain and Abel, film being "Abel," the pure medium, while video represents "Cain," the unworthy brother and mortal enemy of film. This is unfortunate since it obscures the real nature of the problems facing all librarians in a cost-conscious society. Film prices have risen steadily over the last decade. In contrast, videocassette prices have been decreasing just as steadily in that time, making the medium more attractive. Eight to ten years ago, most film and video distributors charged the same price for both formats. From about 1977 on, progressively larger price cuts by some of the biggest distributors in the nation have ranged from twenty to more than sixty percent off of the 16mm price. If the added costs of inflation are factored in, the actual savings are even more impressive. These two formats can, and should, coexist in many collections when conditions warrant.

Which Video Format(s) to Collect? Uncertainty about the future of video technology, as well as cost, has delayed the development of research and curriculum-based video collections. Many institutions have been frightened by the incompatability of different formats, and the possibility of getting locked into a system that would be obsolete within a few years. It appears that 3/4-inch videocassettes have become the preferred format for both educational and industrial users. Those institutions that purchase in this format probably have little to fear in terms of obsolescence. It is also likely that both Beta and VHS 1/2-inch videocassette formats will survive at least through the end of the century.

Concerning hardware, comparable industrial quality Beta and VHS players are generally fifty percent less expensive than their 3/4-inch counterparts. The tradeoff is that their picture quality is not quite as good as the larger format, but it is good enough to be considered, given the price savings for hardware and often software as well. The recurring question is whether Beta is better than VHS or vice versa. There is little technical reason to prefer one over the other. The most important consideration is to determine which format is more common at an institution. Compatability with existing equipment should be the primary consideration.

The laser videodisc will finally find a home in academic libraries after more than fifteen years of "it's just around the corner" predictions. Its superior image quality and durability make it a natural for the near and distant future of nonprint media in libraries. It also provides efficient random access searching of specific frames or chapters with an ease that is unequaled by any other format. This feature is greatly enhanced when a videodisc player is connected to a microcomputer providing the kind of interactive learning capability that educators have dreamed of for years. The long-awaited software is starting to become available from many of the producers of films and videocassettes.

Environmental Factors. The longevity of film and videotape is greatly affected by environmental storage conditions that have a negligible effect on videodiscs. *A Handbook for Film Archives*, edited by Eileen Bowser and John Kuiper, is perhaps the best overall source of information on the proper storage and handling conditions for film, audio- and videotape. In an article, "How Long Will Videotape Really Last?", James B. Meigs pointed out a number of conditions that can either prolong the life expectancy of tape, or spell its doom.[3] Temperature and humidity fluctuations are particularly damaging to magnetic tape and should be avoided, but properly maintained tapes could last for 100 years or more. Laser videodiscs are currently the most permanent form of motion picture storage; under normal conditions, a disc will not deteriorate for hundreds of years, if ever.

Basic Collection Development Strategies

DEALING WITH VENDORS

Librarians used to dealing with book jobbers may find it disturbing that there are few comprehensive jobbers in the area of nonprint media. Each

3. James B. Meigs, "How Long Will Videotape Really Last?" *Video Review* 5:24–26 (July 1984).

vendor will have to be contacted individually. There are, however, at least two advantages to this system that can be exploited by the knowledgeable selector. Since sales representatives generally keep excellent files on the purchases of their clients, they can suggest new, unreviewed titles in areas in which you have already purchased, as well as in areas identified as being in your collection development goals. Of course, the ability of a sales representative to assist you in this area varies widely from individual to individual. The most helpful ones are invaluable, while others can be gently discouraged.

A second advantage that comes from developing good working relationships with sales representatives is that they are often able to give extensions on previews and may negotiate prices lower than advertised. Not all vendors advertise discounts or bonuses for quantity purchases, but many give them. This is one reason to batch as many orders as possible to a single vendor once a year. The more money spent with a vendor, the more likely he or she will be to offer either a discount or free equipment. The negotiation process can be similar to the process one uses to purchase an automobile; one doesn't always have to pay list price. Some vendors have firm prices and are unwilling to negotiate, but it never costs more to ask.

GENERAL PURCHASING STRATEGIES

Build on Strengths. In a smaller, developing collection of nonprint media, it is important to build on a few strengths, rather than to develop a broad but shallow collection. Selectors should work closely with individual departments to acquire several of the best titles in any given subject area, rather than just one or two. If a selector purchases only one or two titles for each department, no one department's needs would be truly satisfied. On the other hand, if one is able to develop a small but viable collection of ten to twenty titles in cultural anthropology, for example, where none existed before, at least the basic needs of this department could be addressed.

Maximize Discounts. Since most vendors have subject strengths, it is often easy to identify those who should receive your special attention. While it is important to examine the offerings of as many vendors as possible, particularly the smaller, independent houses, it is also important to maximize your purchasing power with each of them. If, as part of your selection process, you are able to identify a group of vendors whose products suit your current needs, request an adequate supply of catalogs for distribution to faculty and attempt to negotiate a volume discount while still in the previewing stage. In some cases, vendors will be able to send most, if not all, of the titles they have in a particular subject area for thorough examination. In this way, study and acquisition of the best products a particular vendor has is possible, while still serving the needs of a larger group of faculty.

Plan Purchases Early. Previewing, as a process, should go on all year, but purchasing should be done in large blocks whenever possible. Attempt to spend at least fifty percent of the media budget within the first quarter of each new fiscal year by ordering the titles that have been recommended for purchase from the companies who are willing or able to give volume discounts. Plan to spend an additional twenty to twenty-five percent near the end of the second quarter, and attempt to totally encumber funds by the end of the third quarter. A significant number of nonprint media vendors are likely to have special sales offers twice a year, most often in late spring and after Thanksgiving. Ordering titles in late fall will usually allow you enough time to have them delivered by the spring semester. The late spring sale provides an opportunity to encumber any unspent funds or to spend new funds from unexpected sources. If orders have already been prepared for the beginning of a July fiscal year, they can be sent on short notice if unexpected funds materialize. Some nonprint media vendors can ship their products with an invoice in less than one week's time if they understand the need for instant delivery. Try to identify and cultivate those that can, just in case year-end money is allocated. At least the orders will be ready for the next fiscal year.

FILM AND VIDEO CONSIDERATIONS

When to Rent, When to Buy? Although films can last longer than seven years, a purchased film should be expected to pay for itself in rental cost savings in that time. As a general rule of thumb, commercial vendors most often charge at least ten percent of the purchase price of a film or video-cassette as a rental charge. If a program is likely to be used more than ten times in a five-year period, it should be a strong candidate for purchase. Many institutions rent films from other college or university audiovisual centers such as Pennsylvania State University, the University of Illinois, or any of the other members of the Consortium of University Film Centers listed in the *Educational Film Locator.* These services often have rental rates that are half as much as those of the commercial vendors. If the clerical, bookkeeping, postage, and handling costs of renting films are examined, it is usually still less expensive to purchase a title that is used at least ten times in five years. Another important factor to remember is that rented films don't always arrive on time through the mail. A film that is owned will give users a greater sense of security.

"Life of Program" Leases. One further note about media purchases, particularly film and video, is in order; these materials are rarely, if ever,

sold to an institution in the same way that a book or a desk is. Most "purchases" are in fact "life of program" leases, or "permits" to use materials until they wear out. Producers retain program "ownership" rights, and generally an institution is prohibited from reselling, loaning, or giving a program to another institution. If an institution contemplates sharing media with other affiliated institutions, it is wise to spell that out in the purchase order. Other conditions and restrictions may apply and they vary widely from distributor to distributor.

Some vendors require that a purchasing institution sign a separate, formal agreement identifying the rights of the institution and the rights of the producer before any materials will be shipped. Do not sign any such agreement until its implications are understood and found to be acceptable. Any objectionable clauses should be negotiated with the producer to avoid any possibility of copyright abuse. Cable distribution rights, local or regional, are rarely included in the standard price, but are often available for an additional fee. If more than one copy of a program is required, consider attempting to acquire duplication rights to it. When these rights are available, it is often possible to save a great deal of money over the purchase of individual copies.

What to Buy First? Obviously, the first films or videocassettes to be considered for purchase by a library should be those titles currently being rented on a regular basis by the faculty. Unfortunately, many campuses do not have a central film rental or booking service to coordinate these rentals. It is not uncommon under such conditions for two or more departments to be renting the same film at the same time. This is compounded when departments independently build up their own media collections. It is particularly frustrating to find out that two departments regularly rent a title owned by a third department. When a campus-wide rental service is available, it is quite easy to determine the frequency of rental of a particular title and to determine if it should be purchased as a cost-saving measure.

There are two methods that can be used to obtain this information when centralized booking is not available. The first is to contact each department and ask for a list of the audiovisual titles they own, the titles they rent, and the frequency of rental. It is most important to explain the reason for the request and to offer a "carrot," which is your intention to purchase heavily rented titles. Many departments will happily share this information if they believe that they could eliminate a portion of their film rental costs from their budgets.

The second method is to get this information directly from the film vendors. Most vendors gladly provide film rental and preview services as a way to advertise and promote their offerings. Whenever a producer/distributor sends a free preview film or videocassette to an individual faculty member for purchase consideration, it is with the knowledge that it is possible, even likely, that this individual does not have a budget for materials purchase. Librarians who have cultivated good working relationships with sales representatives often find them quite receptive to a suggestion that all previewing be coordinated through the library, which does have a purchase budget and can identify other individuals on campus who may be interested in previewing the program as well. It is obviously in their best interest to reduce the number of individual contacts with a given institution. Additionally, most sales representatives have preview or rental information arranged in their files by institution and can provide that information, along with the names of the departments or individuals who requested the titles. There is one caveat to be considered at this point: some faculty members may see this as an invasion of privacy. Strict observance of the client confidentiality that our profession demands will prevent problems.

Off-air Licensing. An alternative method of acquiring video materials inexpensively is to purchase licenses to videotape programs off-air. The Television Licensing Center (TLC) in Wilmette, Illinois, acts as an information source for off-air licensing information and as a broker for obtaining the rights to many of the programs identified in its newsletter. There is an ever-increasing number of important programs broadcast on commercial and public television stations that are available in this manner. Time-Life Video, PBS Video, and TLC in particular offer a significant number of programs that can be added to a collection immediately through licensing. If an institution's broadcast signal and recorder are good enough, a copy made in this way could be virtually as good as one purchased directly. The only real difference is in the delivery system; one uses a traditional mail delivery system, while the other uses an electronic distribution system.

Conclusion

Most recorded human history is still to be found on the printed page in books and journals. Computer technology and other nonprint information storage methods may one day render the book obsolete, but that day is far in the future. Yet books simply can't present some information as well as other media can. While great authors may achieve a measure of immortality through their books, the authors as individuals are given a more tangible form of immortality if their voices, mannerisms, and physical presence are preserved on film, videotape, or audiotape to complement their writings. Today's college freshmen were born after John F. Kennedy was assassinated; yet he can still live for them in the classroom or library apply to MRDF, along with a host of difficulties peculiar to the machine-readable format. Unlike most material acquired by libraries, MRDF are not intelligible to the human eye and their use requires equipment and technical expertise far more complex than that needed for the use of microforms or other nonprint formats. Machine-readable data is rarely available from the well-established commercial sources typically used by libraries; rather, it is procured from data archives, academic research institutes, government agencies, individual researchers, and even banks or marketing firms. Bibliographic control of machine-readable data has been abysmal.

The development of machine-readable information is, by definition, a recent phenomenon. Space does not allow a comprehensive historical review of MRDF, but there are a number of articles and books that provide a valuable overview that will enable the novice to gain some basic understanding of the use and importance of MRDF. The January 1977 issue of *Drexel Library Quarterly*, "Machine-Readable Social Science Data," provides an introduction to MRDF and touches on acquisition processes, cataloging issues, and reference work. "Data Libraries for the Social Sciences," the winter 1982 issue of *Library Trends*, also contains a number of well-written and useful articles. A recent collection of articles in *Numeric Databases* provides both an overview and some topical treatments of data.[2] Another informative work, albeit with a British emphasis, is Catherine Hakim's *Secondary Analysis in Social Research: A Guide to Data Sources and Methods with Examples*. A dated but still useful work is the *Reader in Machine-Readable Social Data*, edited by Howard D. White.[3] *Reanalyzing Program Evaluations* contains an excellent discussion of secondary analysis for applied social research as well as an interesting section on access to government-sponsored data. Finally, *Data Bases in the Humanities and Social Sciences* presents an excellent collection of papers on subjects ranging from individual archives, such as the Roper Center, to specific data files and databases. Both Sue Dodd, of the Institute for Research in Social Science at the University of North Carolina, and Judith Rowe, of the Princeton University Computer Center, are experts in the field of MRDF and anything either one has written is likely to be of interest to a selector.

While the bibliographic control of machine-readable data is deplorable, dramatic progress has actually occurred in the last five years. Recent advances include the development of a MARC format and inclusion of MRDF in *Anglo-American Cataloguing Rules*, second edition (AACR2), and a format for bibliographic citation. As the standardized formats are

2. *Numeric Databases* (Norwood, N. J.: Ablex, 1984).
3. Howard D. White, ed., *Reader in Machine-Readable Social Data* (Englewood, Colo.: Information Handling Services, 1977).

on film or videotape. The performances of great actors or dancers can be preserved for future generations to study and to enjoy. Virtually every facet of research can be supported by audiovisual materials in one form or another. Subject specialists should accept the responsibility for selecting the best nonprint, as well as print materials to support the teaching, reference, and research mission of the modern university and its libraries.

Selection Sources

Adams, William, and Fay Schreibman, eds. *Television Network News: Issues in Content Research*. Washington, D. C.: Center for Telecommunication Studies, George Washington Univ., 1978.
Audiovisual Market Place 1983: A Multimedia Guide. New York: Bowker Co., 1983. Annually.
Bensinger, Charles, ed. *Consumer's Handbook of Video Software*. New York: Van Nostrand Reinhold, 1981.
Bowser, Eileen, and John Kuiper, eds. *A Handbook for Film Archives*. Brussels, Belgium: Fédération Internationale des Archives du Film, 1980.
Brown, James W., and Shirley N. Brown. *Educational Media Yearbook, 1983*. Littleton, Colo.: Libraries Unlimited, 1983. Annually.
Cowie, Peter. *International Film Guide 1984*. New York: Zoetrope, 1984. Annually.
Educational Film Locator. 2nd ed. New York: Bowker, 1980.
Educational Media Catalogs on Microfiche. Hoboken, N. J.: Olympic Media Information, 1984. Annually with semiannual updates.
Film File. 3rd ed. Minneapolis, Minn.: Media Referral Service, 1983. Annually.
Gertner, Richard. *Motion Picture Almanac*. 55th ed. New York: Quigley, 1984. Annually.
————. *Television Almanac*. 29th ed. New York: Quigley, 1984. Annually.
Grove, Pierce S. *Nonprint Media in Academic Libraries*. Chicago: American Library Assn., 1975.
Limbacher, James L., ed. *Feature Films on 8mm, 16mm, and Videotape*. 7th ed. New York: Bowker, 1982. Irregularly.
Sive, Mary Robinson. *Selecting Instructional Media: A Guide to Audiovisual and Other Instructional Media Lists*. 3rd ed. Littleton, Colo.: Libraries Unlimited, 1983.
Video Source Book. 5th ed. Syosset, N. Y.: National Video Clearinghouse, 1983.
Weaver, Kathleen, ed. *Film Programmer's Guide to 16mm Rentals*. Albany, Calif.: Reel Research, 1980.

Journals

AAAS Science Books and Films. v.1– . 1965– . Washington, D. C.: American Assn. for the Advancement of Science. 5/year.
Afterimage. v.1– . 1972– . Rochester, N. Y.: Visual Studies Workshop. 10/year. (Address: 31 Prince St., Rochester, NY 14607.)
American Film Magazine (Washington); A Journal of the Film and Television Arts. v.1– . 1975– . Washington, D. C.: American Film Institute. Monthly.

Booklist. v.1– . 1905– . Chicago: American Library Assn. 22/year.

Channels (Channels of Communication). v.1– . 1981– . Mahopac, N. Y.: Media Commentary Council. Bimonthly. (Address: Box 2001, Mahopac, NY 10541.)

Choice. v.1– . 1964– . Middletown, Conn.: Assn. of College and Research Libraries, American Library Assn. Monthly.

Dial. (11 regional editions.) v.1– . 1980– . New York: Public Broadcasting Communications. Monthly. (Address: 304 W. 58th St., New York, NY 10019.)

EFLA Evaluations. v.1– . 1946– . New York: Educational Film Library Assn. 5/ year. (Address: 45 John St., Suite 301, New York, NY 10038.)

Film Comment. v.1– . 1962– . New York: Film Society of Lincoln Center. Bimonthly. (Address: 140 W. 65th St., New York, NY 10023.)

Film Library Quarterly. v.1– . 1967– . New York: Film Library Information Council. Bimonthly. (Address: Box 348, Radio City Station, New York, NY 10101.) Quarterly.

Film Quarterly. v.1– . 1945– . Berkeley: Univ. of California Pr. Quarterly.

Jump Cut; A Review of Contemporary Cinema. v.1– . 1974– . Berkeley, Calif.: Jump Cut Associates. Biennially. (Address: Box 865, Berkeley, CA 94701.)

Landers Film Reviews; The Information Guide to 16mm Film and Multi-Media Materials. v.1– . 1956– . Escondido, Calif.: Landers Associates. 5/year. (Address: P. O. Box 27309, Escondido, CA 92027.)

Media and Methods; Exploration in Education. v.1– . 1965– . Philadelphia: American Society of Educators. (Address: 1511 Walnut St., Philadelphia, PA 19102.)

Media Digest: A Bi-Monthly Media Resource for Education. v.1– . 1971– . Finksburg, Md.: National Film and Video Center. Semimonthly. (Address: 4321 Sykesville Rd., Finksburg, MD 21048.)

Sightlines. v.1– . 1967– . New York: Educational Film Library Assn. Quarterly. (Address: 45 John St., Suite 301, New York, NY 10038.)

Television News Index and Abstracts: A Guide to the Videotape Collection of the Network Evening News Programs in the Vanderbilt University Archive. v.1– . 1968– . Nashville, Tenn.: Vanderbilt Television News Archive, Vanderbilt Univ. Library. Monthly.

Directory of Selected Associations, Distributors, and Organizations

Cline Information Services (Film User's Network), 419 Park Avenue South, New York, NY 10016. 212-686-9897.

Educational Film Library Assn., 45 John St., Suite 301, New York, NY 10038. 212-246-4533.

National Information Center for Educational Media (NICEM), Access Innovations, Inc., P. O. Box 40130, Albuquerque, NM 87196. 800-421-8711.

PBS Video, 475 L'Enfant Plaza, S. W., Washington, D. C. 20024. 800-424-7963.

Television Licensing Center (TLC), 733 Green Bay Road, Wilmette, IL 60091. 800-323-4222.

MACHINE-READABLE DATA FILES

Karin Wittenborg

An early indication of the ambiguity surrounding machine-readable data files (MRDF) is that there appears to be little agreement on a precise definition of the files themselves. A simple and satisfactory statement is that "to social scientists, a 'data file' or 'data set' will most often refer to a set of numeric values which can be manipulated by a predesigned statistical routine."[1] Indeed, most MRDF are numeric; but there are non-bibliographic textual data files as well. In addition, while MRDF seem to be most prevalent and most heavily used in the social sciences, they are becoming increasingly common in the humanities and the sciences.

In the past, many libraries have been reluctant to acquire MRDF, as they presented a number of obstacles. To some, they seemed prohibitively expensive; to others, they fell outside the library's purview since they did not appear in bibliographies, abstracting and indexing services, or even databases. In addition, they require a computer and a degree of technical expertise to use; and they simply are not easily accommodated into established library systems for cataloging and circulating. In many institutions, the academic departments assumed responsibility for acquiring data and fulfilled this function adequately, although they typically failed to publicize the availability of the data or to make it accessible to a wide spectrum of potential users. Today, libraries are becoming increasingly aware that it is their role to provide information regardless of the format. Libraries are already organized to provide access to information, and they may simply need to make a few changes to accommodate MRDF.

Machine-readable data files present a myriad of collection development challenges. All the problems typically associated with any format or subject

The author gratefully acknowledges comments and suggestions from David Langenberg, Judith Rowe, Sue Dodd, Ilona Einowski, Libbie Stephenson, and Joyce MacDonald.

1. Sue Dodd, "Toward Integration of Catalog Records on Social Science Machine-Readable Data Files into Existing Bibliographic Utilities: A Commentary," *Library Trends* 30:3. (Winter 1982).

adopted, MRDF will begin to appear with more regularity in bibliographic utilities, in reference sources, and as citations in books and articles. In essence, they will become legitimized and enter the bibliographic mainstream. *Population Index* began providing coverage of MRDF in 1980 and *Social Forces* now mentions MRDF in its instructions to authors. These developments are encouraging to those who have struggled for years without access to adequate information necessary to identify and to acquire MRDF. The future promises increased efforts to establish bibliographic control and a more systematic dissemination of information concerning data files. Nevertheless, we are caught in the present with inadequate documentation and few selection tools. Judith Rowe writes that "there is, at this point, no single printed or computer-readable reference tool which can serve as a comprehensive finding aid for MRDF. . . . Many useful files remain elusive."[4]

Selection Tools

Nevertheless, there are a number of methods the selector can use in an effort to keep informed. Membership in the International Association for Social Science Information Service and Technology (IASSIST) is invaluable. IASSIST is an organization whose members are primarily interested in the acquisition, organization, and use of machine-readable data. The *IASSIST Quarterly* and conference proceedings are worthwhile, but perhaps most important are the personal contacts. In a realm where so much of the material is fugitive or ephemeral, it is often the case that printed sources are of little help, but a well-placed telephone call may produce just the needed information or assistance. The local chapter of IASSIST in California has been extremely active.

Other associations that may be useful are the Association of Public Data Users (APDU), the International Federation of Data Organizations for the Social Sciences, and the European Association of Scientific Information Services. There are also a number of newsletters that contain useful information on data and data archives. Unfortunately, many are as fugitive as the material they cover and may cease just as one comes to rely on them. One of the well-established newsletters, *Survey Research*, is a free publication issued quarterly by the Survey Research Laboratory at the University of Illinois. It contains helpful information on current research, publications, and data sets. The bimonthly *APDU Newsletter* contains a wealth of timely information that reflects the association's interest in facilitating the use of public data. This publication is a productive source

4. Judith Rowe, "Expanding Social Science Reference to Meet the Needs of Patrons More Adequately," *Library Trends* 30:332 (Winter 1982).

IASSIST Quarterly. v.1– . 1976– . Princeton, N. J.: International Assn. for
　Social Science Information Service and Technology. Quarterly.
　Journal of the professional association that concentrates on issues relating
　　to the collection, preservation, and distribution of machine-readable
　　data.
　Signed articles dealing with technical and theoretical issues.
　Announcements of conferences, classes, and workshops.
　Includes information on the availability of data catalogs and new books
　　that may be of particular interest.
The *IASSIST Quarterly* (formerly *IASSIST Newsletter*) is a very useful publication for anyone dealing with the acquisition and distribution of machine-
readable data. The signed articles may cover a range of issues from methodology
of collecting survey data to technical issues in cataloging the data. The announcements of new publications and conferences are particularly useful.

---

for information on data catalogs, new releases of data, and the names and
telephone numbers of contacts in government agencies. The *ESRC Newsletter* of the Economic and Social Research Council (formerly the Social
Science Research Center, London) provides a wealth of information concerning British research and includes brief notes on data acquisitions. Of
greater specific value is the *Data Archive Bulletin*, which contains information on new acquisitions, brief articles of interest, book reviews, and
frequently provides the names and addresses of data archives in other
countries. The *European Political Data Newsletter*, a joint, quarterly publication of the European Consortium for Political Research and the Nor-
wegian Social Science Data Service, covers a wide range of issues ranging
from sources of data to development of software. The Bureau of the
Census issues a monthly newsletter, *Data User News*, which covers such
topics as new data files, methodologies, products and services, and announcements of conferences and workshops. Periodically, the bureau also
issues "Telephone Contacts for Data Users," a detailed subject breakdown
of available data accompanied by the name and telephone number of the
individual responsible for each area.

　Much of the machine-readable data likely to be of interest to academic
researchers can be obtained from established archives or from government
agencies. One of the largest and best known archives is the Inter-University
Consortium for Political and Social Research (ICPSR) at the University of
Michigan. Founded in 1962, the consortium was a partnership of Michigan's Survey Research Center and some twenty universities, and its primary
concern was with political data. Its present membership approaches 300
and its scope and coverage have broadened considerably. Its two major
functions are: (1) to collect and disseminate machine-readable social science data and (2) to train social scientists in quantitative analysis. Membership fees in the ICPSR are based on the size, program, and location

APDU Newsletter. v.1– . 1976/77– . Princeton, N. J.: Assn. of Public Data Users. Bimonthly.

Membership newsletter of the association.

Announces availability of new files and software.

Announces significant personnel changes in federal agencies, new publications of interest to data users, conferences, and meetings.

Provides information on data catalogs and reference books.

Profiles member organizations.

This is an invaluable source for information about public data. It provides useful selection information about files and also reports on developments in federal agencies that may affect data users.

Data User News. v.10– . 1975– . Washington, D. C.: Government Printing Office. Monthly.

Newsletter issued by the Bureau of the Census. Continues *Small Area Data Notes.*

Articles of interest to data users with particular emphasis on census products.

Includes information on relevant publications of other federal agencies.

Lists training courses, workshops, and meetings relating to use of census material.

Summarizes recent important bureau reports.

Data User News is an essential publication for anyone dealing with census data. It is a timely and concise publication. The articles are brief and clear. There is a good coverage of new publications and names, addresses, and phone numbers of contact people.

of the institution. Additional fees for the data itself or for extra copies of codebooks are nominal.

ICPSR publishes an annual *Guide to Resources and Services*, a classified catalog of its extensive holdings. "The content of the Archive extends across economic, sociological, historical, social, psychological, as well as political concerns. Surveys are available from over a score of countries and the geographical breadth is increasing regularly. Topical expansion is taking place to include urban studies, education, electoral behavior, so-cializations, foreign policy, community studies, judicial behavior, legislators (national, state, and local), race relations, and organizational behavior."[5] Each entry for a MRDF includes such information as principal investigator, title, ICPSR number, former titles, data class, and related publications. The data class is an indication of the amount of processing done by ICPSR and it may be significant to the user. Class IV indicates, for instance, that the data is in exactly the same condition as received. It may be completely satisfactory or it may require a good deal of work. At the other end of the spectrum is CLASS I data, which has been checked,

5. ICPSR, *Guide to Resources and Services 1982-83* (Ann Arbor, Mich.: ICPSR, 1982), p. 2.

> *Guide to Resources and Services.* v.1– . 1970– . Ann Arbor, Mich.: Inter-University Consortium for Political and Social Research. Annually.
> Classified catalog of the data holdings of the ICPSR. Updated by the *ICPSR Bulletin.*
> Contains full bibliographic information and abstracts for each data file available from the consortium.
> Separate indexes by ICPSR study number, by title, by principal investigator, and by subject.
> The *Guide to Resources and Services* is distributed to members and is an essential reference and selection document. It also includes useful general information on membership, training programs, and computing assistance.

revised as necessary, and meets ICPSR specifications. The *Guide* is updated by the *ICPSR Bulletin*, which announces new acquisitions, revisions, conferences, or other items of likely interest to its members. In addition, the ICPSR staff is responsive to inquiries concerning the availability of data not included in the *Guide* or *Bulletin*. Two excellent reference volumes that also serve as a guide to data sources are the *American National Election Studies Sourcebook: 1952–1978* and the *American Social Attitudes Data Sourcebook: 1947–1978.*

The Roper Center, established in 1946, offers access to an extensive collection of polls from the Gallup Organization; Yankelovich, Skelly, and White, Inc.; CBS News/*New York Times*; the National Opinion Research Center; the *Los Angeles Times*; the Commission of the European Communities (Eurobarometer surveys); and other sources. Educational institutions have the option of membership or may use the resources at higher rates on an ad hoc basis. In addition to providing data and documentation, the Roper Center undertakes searches for data on a given subject and also performs data analysis.

There is no comprehensive catalog of the Roper holdings, but the center does issue descriptions of its major American collections and it publishes *Data Set News*, which announces the availability of new files. The Roper Center has recently made an effort to improve access to information about its holdings. It issued a 1982 data acquisitions list that provides basic bibliographic information and enough descriptive matter to guide a selector. Presumably, this list will be an annual publication. Also published in 1982, *A Guide to Roper Center Resources for the Study of American Race Relations* covers question-level data from the 1930s to the present. If similar aids continue to be produced, access to the Roper collection should be much improved.

While ICPSR and Roper are two of the largest and best-known archives in the United States, there are a number of other collections that should not be overlooked. For instance, the Louis Harris Data Center at the

University of North Carolina (Chapel Hill) archives the Harris Surveys. A useful reference tool for that material is the Institute for Research in Social Science (IRSS) Technical Papers #6, *Source Book of Harris National Survey: Repeated Questions 1963-1976*. The Data and Program Library at the University of Wisconsin has a sizable collection of machine-readable data and its 1984 catalog is available in hardcopy, microfiche, or on tape. The Center for Human Resources at Ohio State University has disseminated the data from the *National Longitudinal Survey (NLS) of Labor Market Experience*.

Depending on the scope of the data collection program, one would want to acquire the catalogs, as available, from certain archives and data libraries. A selector should also be on the publication mailing lists for organizations that produce materials of likely interest for the programs and research of one's institution. One of the complications in data acquisition is that there appears to be a good deal of duplication. For instance, the NLS data are available directly from Ohio State and also from ICPSR: it is therefore important to evaluate the source of the data. Certain considerations to keep in mind are cost, timeliness, and format. Since ICPSR collects data from other archives and researchers and disseminates data to its membership, it may be more cost effective to wait until ICPSR has acquired and released the data; on the other hand, an urgent research need may prompt the decision to pay a higher price in order to acquire the material as soon as possible. In order to make such a decision, the selector would have to weigh each factor in light of the institutional context.

Government agencies are prolific producers of machine-readable data and, in the past, access to that data has been extremely difficult. An early attempt to consolidate information about government-produced data resulted in the 1977 *Catalog of Machine-Readable Data in the National Archives of the United States*. That publication is slated for revision and is currently updated by the *National Archives Computer Data Bulletin*. The National Technical Information Service issued its *Directory of Computerized Data Files and Related Software Available from Federal Agencies* in 1974 and it has been continued by a 1982 *Directory of Computerized Data Files*. Typically, however, it was necessary to contact each individual agency to determine what machine-readable data were available. Finally, in 1981, the first significant effort to centralize such information resulted in *A Directory of Federal Statistical Data Files*. While far from comprehensive, the directory is a major advance in the process of making such data available to researchers. It is hoped that the intention to enlarge and continue the directory will be fulfilled.

A significant portion of the 1980 Census was made available in machine-readable form and it is likely that the demand for census MRDFs will increase. The State Data Centers, established in most states, act as distributors for census data as well as other governmental data and can provide useful assistance in identifying and acquiring needed MRDF. Addresses and telephone numbers for the State Data Centers are listed in the March and April 1981 issues of *Data User News*, accompanied by a brief overview of the program organization and activities. In addition, a number of nongovernmental organizations acquire census data and offer their versions for sale. Many of these companies are listed in the "Directory of Data Firms" included in each February issue of *American Demographics*. One's choice of a source for the data will depend largely on local research requirements and cost or time constraints.

Demand for international data has also increased recently, and Linda Hoffman's timely article on "Statistical Data in Machine-Readable Form from International, Intergovernmental Organizations" covers a number of major sources. Once again, ICPSR offers a good deal of data from the same organizations, and if the institution is a member it may be advisable to acquire through the consortium rather than directly from the source when possible.

Selection of data for foreign countries, as may be expected, is often more difficult than for the United States. Fortunately, both ICPSR and Roper do have a great deal of data on other countries, so those sources may be the best place to start. Depending on the research interest in an institution and the scope of the work, it might also be reasonable to collect catalogs of data archives in other countries. For example, the Steinmetz Archives in Amsterdam has just published the fifth edition of its catalog and guide. However, it is important to remember that such catalogs may be hard to locate and are soon outdated, so most selectors should be extremely conservative in pursuing items with limited yield. Certain organizations publish helpful catalogs, such as the Centro Latinoamericano de Demografía's *Boletin del Banco de Datos* (Data Bank Bulletin), published in 1982. The bilingual catalog documents data from censuses and from demographic and fertility surveys.

Collection Development Issues

Apart from the actual selection decision, there are a number of other issues that the bibliographer must consider. First, each data supplier needs to be informed of the local tape specifications in order to fill an order. In essence, the specifications ensure that the tape format will be compatible with the computing system at the user's institution. The selector need not understand all the technical details as long as the person completing the tape information is knowledgeable about the local computing configuration.

Another consideration is the cost and convenience of maintaining the data. Libraries make different arrangements according to their institutional requirements and their relations with the campus computing centers. At a number of institutions, it has been effective to house the tapes at the computing center and to shelve the codebooks in the library. Once good working relationships are established, the computer center can be considered much the same as any shelving location. However, it is absolutely critical that adequate bibliographic links are established between the data itself and the codebooks so that the user can easily locate both.

The codebooks may appear in a variety of formats: handwritten, mimeographed, published hardcopy, microform, or machine-readable form. Generally, a user consults the codebook initially to see if the data are appropriate and an occasional user may use the codebook alone. For those users, it is inconvenient to have a machine-readable copy only; it may be advisable to print or produce a computer-output microfiche codebook. Either alternative is easily done, but the microfiche may be favored in terms of saving space and eliminating binding costs.

MRDF, once acquired, may be superseded by a new version. For instance, CLASS IV data acquired from ICPSR may ultimately be upgraded to CLASS I. In that case, should the CLASS IV data be discarded and be replaced by the more useable CLASS I data? Presumably, the user will prefer to use CLASS I data but it is also possible, indeed likely, that the researcher may want to perform reanalysis on the earlier version of the data and the upgraded version is of no use. It is possible to keep all versions, although it can be quite costly to maintain large bodies of data. It may be wise to discard the earlier version if one can verify that it will be archived and accessible from another location. Similar problems are encountered with cumulative versions of data. For instance, should annual versions of the *General Social Survey* be discarded when a cumulative version becomes available? What is the impact on the users and what is the cost to the library? These considerations must be weighed within the context of each institutional environment.

The selector of MRDF shares the traditional dilemma of judging which material is essential to the collection and which is marginal. The dilemma, however, intensifies as one weighs the cost of MRDF both in purchase price and in maintenance costs. The purchase price may rarely be the decisive factor, but in most cases the storage and maintenance costs will be significant. Regardless of whether the library or the computing center assumes storage costs, it is an expensive proposition to house machine-readable data in an environmentally secure and user-accessible area. It makes sense, therefore, to acquire MRDF as selectively as possible and to rely on obtaining copies of data from the appropriate archives when needed. The existence of data archives is one positive note in an otherwise difficult acquisition area. In general, we do not have to concern ourselves that something may become unavailable if not purchased at the start. Selectivity does not mean that one should restrict acquisitions exclusively to patron requests. That practice makes no more sense for MRDF than it does for print materials. In any institution one can anticipate the demand for certain material with some degree of certainty. One may know, for example, that there will always be an interest in the biennial *American National Election Study* or the *General Social Survey*, and one does not wait for the request to prompt the acquisition. At the present time, there is no formal interlibrary loan for MRDF.

Since the identification and acquisition of MRDF is often problematic, the selector frequently is in closer contact with the user than would be the case for more traditional materials. The contact with faculty and students provides ample opportunity to learn more about their research interests and needs. In addition, the acquisition of MRDF may have a significant public relations benefit for the library. Many individuals who may have been categorized as nonusers suddenly take an interest when they discover that the library will acquire data. They feel that their needs are met as well as the needs of more traditional scholars. Also, the library is seen as adapting to new technologies rather than clinging to an old role.

There are few formal opportunities to learn about the selection, acquisition, and management of machine-readable data files, although a few library schools are beginning to include some mention of them. In the past, most selectors have learned from the available literature, by talking with other librarians or archivists, or simply by trial and error. Recently, however, ICPSR has offered a week-long summer workshop on "Data Management Library Control, and Use of Computer Readable Information." Certainly ICPSR is a reliable source of information and the course should be an excellent opportunity for a newcomer in the area of data files.

The field of machine-readable data seems to be in almost constant flux. New information and new tools appear with astonishing frequency and the knowledge and tactics one has taken pains to acquire become outdated with alarming speed. However, the overall picture is one of progress. Bibliographic control is improving and there are more formal organizations and associations prepared to provide assistance. The selector must simply make a great effort to keep in touch with the current published sources and to make the best possible use of personal contacts.

Selected Bibliography

GENERAL SOURCES AND BACKGROUND READING

Boruch, Paul F.; P. M. Wortman; D. S. Cordray; and associates. *Reanalyzing Program Evaluations*. San Francisco: Jossey-Bass, 1981.

Chen, Ching–chih, and Peter Herron. *Numeric Databases*. Norwood, N. J.: Ablex, 1984.

Conger, Lucinda D. "Data Reference Work with Machine-Readable Data Files in the Social Sciences." *Journal of Academic Librarianship* 2:60–65 (May 1976).

Dodd, Sue. "Toward Integration of Catalog Records on Social Science Machine-Readable Data Files into Existing Bibliographic Utilities." *Library Trends* 30: 335–61 (Winter 1982).

Hakim, Catherine. *Secondary Analysis in Social Research: A Guide to Data Sources and Methods with Examples*. Contemporary Social Research Series no. 5. London: Allen & Unwin, 1982.

Heim, Kathleen M. "Social Science Data Archives: A User Study." Ph.D. diss., University of Wisconsin, 1980.

Hoffman, Linda M. "Statistical Data in Machine-Readable Form from International, Intergovernmental Organizations." *Government Publications Review* 9: 167–74 (May/June 1982).

Isaacson, Kathy. "Machine-Readable Information in the Library." *RQ* 22:164–70 (Winter 1982).

McGee, Jacqueline M., and Donald P. Trees. "Major Available Social Science Machine-Readable Databases." *Drexel Library Quarterly* 18:107–34 (Summer/Fall 1982).

Raben, Joseph, and Gregory Marks, eds. *Databases in the Humanities and Social Sciences*. Proceedings of the IFIP Working Conference on Databases in the Humanities and Social Sciences, Dartmouth College, 1979. New York: North-Holland, 1980.

Rowe, Judith. "Expanding Social Science Reference to Meet the Needs of Patrons More Adequately." *Library Trends* 30:327–34 (Winter 1982).

SELECTED JOURNALS AND NEWSLETTERS

American Demographics. v.1– . 1979– . Ithaca, N. Y.: American Demographics Inc. Monthly. (Address: P. O. Box 68, Ithaca, NY 14950.)

APDU Newsletter. v.1– . 1977– . Princeton, N. J.: Assn. of Public Data Users, Princeton Univ. Computer Center. Semimonthly.

Data Archive Bulletin. v.1– . n. d. Colchester, England: ESRC Data Archive, Univ. of Essex. 3/year.

Data User News. v.1– . 1965– . Washington, D. C.: Government Printing Office. Monthly.

ESRC Newsletter. v.1– . 1967– . London: Economic and Social Research Council. 3/year. (Address: 1 Temple Ave., London EC4Y OBD England.) (Former title: *SSRC Newsletter*)

European Political Data Newsletter. v.1– . 1971– . European Consortium for Political Research. Quarterly. (Address: Hans Holmboesgt 22, 5014 Bergen, Norway.)

IASSIST Quarterly. v.1– . 1976– . Santa Monica, Calif.: International Assn. for Social Science Information Service and Technology. Quarterly. (Received on membership.)

ICPSR Bulletin. v.1– . 1981– . Ann Arbor, Mich.: Inter-University Consortium for Political and Social Research. Irregular.
Population Index. v.1– . 1934– . Princeton, N. J.: Office of Population Research, Princeton Univ. Quarterly.
Social Forces. v.1– . 1922– . Chapel Hill: Univ. of North Carolina Pr. Quarterly.
Survey Research. v.1– . 1969– . Urbana: Survey Research Laboratory, Univ. of Illinois. Quarterly.

DIRECTORY OF SELECTED ASSOCIATIONS, ARCHIVES, AND ORGANIZATIONS

Association of Public Data Users
Princeton University Computer Center
87 Prospect Avenue
Princeton, New Jersey 08544

Center for Human Resources Research
Ohio State University
5701 N. High Street
Worthington, Ohio 43085

Data and Program Library Service
3133 Social Science Building
1180 Observatory Drive
University of Wisconsin—Madison
Madison, Wisconsin 53706

European Association of Scientific Information Services (*see Yearbook of International Organizations*)

International Association for Social Science Information Service and Technology (IASSIST)
Membership: $35.00/institutional; $20.00/individual
Address: Ms. Jackie McGee, IASSIST Treasurer
The Rand Corp.
1700 Main Street
Santa Monica, California 90406

International Federation of Data Organizations for the Social Sciences (*see Yearbook of International Organizations*)

Inter-University Consortium for Political and Social Research
Institute for Social Research
P. O. Box 1248
Ann Arbor, Michigan 48106

The Roper Center
The University of Connecticut
Box U–164
Storrs, Connecticut 06268

Social Science Data Library
Institute for Research in Social Science
Manning Hall, 026A
University of North Carolina at Chapel Hill
Chapel Hill, North Carolina 27514

Survey Research Laboratory
University of Illinois
1005 W. Nevada Street
Urbana, Illinois 61801

SELECTED CATALOGS AND OTHER SOURCES OF DATA

Centro Latinoamericano de Demografia (CELADE). *Boletin del Banco de Datos.* Santiago, Chile: CELADE, 1982.

Converse, Philip E.; Jean D. Dotson; Wendy J. Hoag; and William H. McGee III. *American Social Attitudes Data Sourcebook, 1947–1978.* Cambridge: Harvard Univ. Pr., 1980.

Inter-University Consortium for Political and Social Research (ICPSR). *Guide to Resources and Services.* Ann Arbor, Mich.: ICPSR, 1976/77– . Annually.

Martin, Elizabeth; Diana McDuffee; and Stanley Presser. *Sourcebook of Harris National Surveys: Repeated Questions 1963–1976.* IRSS Technical Papers no. 6. Chapel Hill: Univ. of North Carolina Pr., 1981.

Miller, Warren E.; Arthur H. Miller; and Edward J. Schneider. *American National Election Studies Sourcebook: 1952–1978.* Cambridge, Mass.: Harvard Univ. Pr., 1980.

Roper Center. *Data Acquisitions: 1982.* Storrs, Conn.: The Roper Center, 1982.

Steinmetzarchief. *Steinmetz Archives: Catalogue & Guide: Dutch Social Science Data.* 5th ed. Rev. and enl. Amsterdam: Swidoc, 1983.

U. S. Department of Commerce. Bureau of the Census. *Directory of Data Files.* Washington, D. C.: Government Printing Office, 1979.

_____. National Technical Information Service. *A Directory of Computerized Data Files.* Washington, D. C.: Government Printing Office, 1982.

_____. Office of Federal Statistical Policy and Standards and the National Technical Information Service. *A Directory of Federal Statistical Data Files.* Washington, D. C.: Government Printing Office, 1981.

U. S. National Archives and Records Service. *Catalog of Machine-Readable Records in the National Archives of the United States.* Washington, D. C.: Government Printing Office, 1977.

Editors and Contributors

ERIC J. CARPENTER, Collection Development Librarian at Oberlin College since 1981, previously served for eight years as Subject Librarian for English and American Literature, Acting Curator of the Poetry/Rare Books Collection, and Head of Collection Development in Lockwood Library at SUNY Buffalo. His publications include reviews of little magazines in *Serials Review* and articles in *Literary Research Newsletter* and *New Horizons for Academic Libraries*; he has also lectured on small presses and collection development.

NANCY C. CRIDLAND, History Subject Specialist at Indiana University Library, has published numerous book reviews in *Library Journal* and has edited the second edition of *Books in American History: A Basic List for High Schools and Junior Colleges*, published in 1981 by the Indiana University Press.

SARA EICHHORN has been the Microform Librarian at the University of California, Irvine, since 1978. She is coauthor of an article entitled "A Survey of Current Microform Practices in California Libraries" (*Microform Review*), and she presented a paper entitled "Standards for Public Service in Microform Collection" at the Ninth Annual Microforms Conference in Arlington, Virginia, in 1983 (also published in *Microform Review*).

RUSSELL FULMER is Assistant Director for Technical Services at the Arthur Lakes Library, Colorado School of Mines in Golden, Colorado. He formerly worked as a cataloger at the University of Alabama and as Coordinator of Technical Services in the Jackson, Mississippi, Metropolitan Library System.

ROBERT GOEHLERT, Subject Specialist for Economics, Political Science, and Forensic Studies at Indiana University Library, has written about librarianship in numerous journals including *Government Publications Review*, *Information Processing and Management*, *Journal of Academic Librarianship*, *Special Libraries*, *Library Acquisitions: Practice and Theory*, and *RQ*. He is author of *Congress and Lawmaking: Researching the Legislative Process* (ABC-Clio Press, 1979) and coauthor of several bibliographies including *The United States Congress: A Bibliography* (Free Press, 1982), *The Parliament of Great Britain: A Bibliography* (Lexington Books, 1983), and *Policy Analysis and Management: A Bibliography* (ABC-Clio Press, 1984).

WILLIAM HEPFER is Head of the Serials Department at the State University of New York at Buffalo. He is the coeditor of *Serials Review* and has worked in the Pennsylvania State University Libraries and the Texas A&M University Library.

STANLEY P. HODGE is Chief Bibliographer of Ball State University Libraries and was formerly Head of Resource Development at Texas A&M University Library. He is the author of articles in *College & Research Libraries*, *Library Acquisitions: Practice and Theory*, and *Texas Libraries*, and has presented papers on collection development at regional and national conferences.

JUDY HORN is Head of the Government Publications Department, University of California, Irvine. She was formerly Foreign and International Government Publications Librarian as well as the Political Science and Law Subject Specialist at the University of California, Santa Barbara.

MICHAEL A. KELLER, Music Librarian at the University of California, Berkeley, has written about music librarianship in numerous articles including "Music Serials in Microform and Reprint Editions" (*Notes*, 1973), "Music Literature Indexes in Review" (*Notes*, 1980), and "An Analysis of the LC Shelflist for Music" (*Cum Notis Variorum*, 1983).

STEPHEN MacLEOD is the Social Sciences Bibliographer for the Stanford University Libraries. He serves on the ACRL Anthropology and Sociology Section's Bibliography Committee and the Education and Behavioral Science Section's Psychology/Psychiatry Committee.

DONALD J. MARION is the Physics Librarian in the Institute of Technology Libraries at the University of Minnesota–Minneapolis. He also serves as the Astronomy Bibliographer and teaches a course on Information Sources for Science and Technology. Marion is the author of "Microform Conversion in an Academic Physics Library," published in *Special Libraries*.

PATRICIA A. McCLUNG's professional career has taken her to Harvard's Widener Library, the University of Virginia Library—where she was North American Bibliographer for six years, and to the University of California, Los Angeles, where she began working on this project while a Council on Library Resources Management Intern with Russell Shank. Now Associate Director of Program Coordination at The Research Libraries Group, she has published in *Wilson Library Bulletin*, *Collection Management*, and *Proceedings of the American Antiquarian Society*.

RAYMOND G. McINNIS, Social Sciences Librarian at Western Washington University, is author of *New Perspectives for Reference Services in Academic Libraries* (1978) and *Research Guide for Psychology* (1982), as well as general editor of the series "Reference Sources in the Social Sciences and the Humanities" (Greenwood Press).

MARCIA PANKAKE, Bibliographer for English and American Literature at the University of Minnesota, has published jointly with Paul Mosher "A Guide to Coordinated and Cooperative Collection Development" (*Library Resources & Technical Services*, 1983).

JOHN PINZELIK is the Chemistry Librarian at the M. G. Mellon Library of Chemistry at Purdue University. He is Professor of Library Science with B. S. and M. S. degrees in chemistry, and coauthor of *Index and Bibliography of Mass Spectrometry, 1963-65*, published by Wiley in 1967.

BILL ROBNETT is the Director of the Division of Reader Services in the Fondren Library of Rice University. He was formerly an instructor in Biology at the University of Agriculture of Malaysia, and Science Librarian at Oberlin College. Robnett has written several biological sciences papers in scholarly journals.

ALLAN C. ROUGH is Head of Nonprint Media Services at the University of Maryland, College Park. While employed as Head of Nonprint Media at Adelphi University in Garden City, New York, he was elected Chairman of the Long Island Media Consortium, which has been recognized as a model of multitype library cooperation, and he has lectured on copyright and nonprint media.

WILLIAM Z. SCHENCK, Collection Development Librarian at the University of Oregon, has been active in the American Library Association's Resources Section of RTSD both as a member of the Executive Committee, 1980-83, and Chair of the Bookdealer Library Relations Committee, 1981-83. He has published widely, primarily on topics related to acquisitions.

ANDREW D. SCRIMGEOUR, recently Librarian at the Iliff School of Theology and now Librarian of Regis College, has published in association with Ronald F. Deering, Alber Hurd, and Donald D. Thompson the results of a collection overlap and preservation study: "Collection Analysis Project: Final Report" (American Theological Library Association *Proceedings*, 1981, pp. 162–206).

BETH J. SHAPIRO, Associate Director for Readers' Services at the Michigan State University Libraries, has presented papers on social science collection development at a number of institutes and conferences, was the editor of *A Directory of Ethnic Publishers and Resource Organizations* (1976), and has written about both librarianship and sociology in journals such as the *Journal of Academic Librarianship, Insurgent Sociologist, Journal of Sport History*, and the *Sociology of Sport Journal*.

SUSAN J. STEINBERG is American and Commonwealth Studies Bibliographer at Sterling Library, Yale University, and authored with several colleagues "Guidelines for the Handling of Microforms in the Yale University Library, Parts I and II" and "Parts III and IV" published in *Microform Review* 9:72–85 (Spring 1980).

CHRISTIE D. STEPHENSON is Collection Development and Technical Services Librarian of the Fiske Kimball Fine Arts Library at the University of Virginia.

MARCIA TUTTLE, Head of Serials Department at the University of North Carolina Libraries, and author of *An Introduction to Serials Management* (JAI Press, 1983), was a speaker on Serials Selection at the George Washington Collection Management and Development Institute. President of the Resources and Technical Services Division of ALA (1984/85), she has served on the Acquisitions Committee of the Resources Section, and chaired the Serials Section of RTSD, 1979–81.

JACK WEIGEL is Head, Branch Libraries of the University of Michigan Libraries and is also Librarian in Charge of the Physics and Mathematics Libraries. Weigel has degrees in mathematics and physics, has reviewed over 100 books, and has served on the science jury of the American Book Awards.

JOHN WHALEY, Associate Director for Collection Management at Virginia Commonwealth University, was a bibliographer at both SUNY-Binghamton and the University of North Carolina—Charlotte, before becoming Head of Reference at the University of California, Irvine, in 1980. He has published in *Library Resources and Technical Services*, and worked on the planning and implementation of the RTSD Collection Management and Development Institutes.

KARIN WITTENBORG, Assistant University Librarian for Collection Development at UCLA, formerly held the positions of Chief of the General Reference Department and Curator for the Social Sciences at Stanford University. She has presented papers on machine-readable data at the ALA/RTSD Collection Management and Development Institutes at both MIT (1982) and UC Irvine (1984), has served as member of the RLG task force on machine-readable data files (1983–84), and was awarded a Council on Library Resources Management Internship in 1981–82.

Index

Pamela Hori

Numbers in boldface indicate pages on which full descriptions appear.